INSIDE INDEPENDENT NIGERIA

Inside Independent Nigeria

Diaries of Wolfgang Stolper, 1960–1962

Edited by

CLIVE S. GRAY

ASHGATE

Published by
Ashgate Publishing Limited
Gower House
Croft Road
Aldershot
Hampshire GU11 3HR
England

Ashgate Publishing Company
Suite 420
101 Cherry Street
Burlington, VT 05401-4405
USA

Ashgate website: http://www.ashgate.com

British Library Cataloguing in Publication Data
Stolper, Wolfgang F.
  Inside independent Nigeria : diaries of Wolfgang Stolper,
  1960-1962
  1.Stolper, Wolfgang F. - Diaries 2.Government economists -
  Nigeria - Diaries 3.Americans - Nigeria - Diaries 4.Nigeria
  - Politics and government - 1960-1975 5.Nigeria - Economic
  conditions - 1960- 6.Nigeria - Economic policy
  I.Title II.Gray, Clive S.
  966.9'051'092

Library of Congress Cataloging-in-Publication Data
Stolper, Wolfgang F.
  Inside independent Nigeria : diaries of Wolfgang Stolper, 1960-1962 / edited by Clive
  S. Gray and Wolfgang F. Stolper.
      p. cm.
  Includes bibliographical references and indexes.
  ISBN 0-7546-0995-2
      1. Nigeria--Economic conditions--1960- 2. Economic assistance, American--Nigeria. 3.
  Nigeria--Social conditions--1960- I. Gray, Clive S. II. Title.

  HC1055 .S755 2003
  330.9669'051--dc21   2002026183

ISBN 0 7546 0995 2

Typeset by Martingraphix
Printed and bound in Great Britain by MPG Books Ltd., Bodmin, Cornwall.

Contents

List of Photographs

Editor's Introduction

In 1960, Wolfgang Stolper, then 48, was an economics professor at the University of Michigan, best known in the profession for (i) his co-authorship of the Stolper-Samuelson theorem on protection and real wages,[1] and (ii) as the American academic most knowledgeable about the economy of then communist East Germany.[2] A Harvard PhD, Stolper first studied law at the University of Berlin, then law and economics at Bonn University, where he was a student of Joseph Schumpeter.

Hitler took power before Stolper could finish his degree at Bonn. His father, Gustav Stolper, was a prominent opponent of the Nazis and emigrated to the United States in 1933. The next year Wolfgang followed his father and stepmother, soon reconnecting with Schumpeter at Harvard.[3]

Stolper's involvement with developing country issues started already in 1946, when in the course of a summer job with the International Labor Office, then headquartered in Montreal, he was assigned joint responsibility for a report on 'Economic Development in Asia'. The report served as background for committee sessions of a 1947 ILO conference in New Delhi.

Over a decade later, in 1958-59, Stolper took leave from Michigan to write a book on the East German economy at MIT's Center for International Studies (CIS).[4] During this stay he became curious about the economic fortunes of Europe's African colonies then on the verge of independence, and suggested to colleagues that the new nations could usefully apply lessons from communist countries such as East Germany – more precisely, lessons on how not to run an economy.

Following Stolper's East German project, CIS director Max Millikan invited him back to MIT to join the Center's Africa project. The CIS supported a European tour on which Stolper gathered African data and talked with officials responsible for colonial affairs and academic Africanists. The trip left him eager for a first-hand experience in Africa.

Meanwhile, Nigeria's Federal Ministry of Economic Development (MED) asked the local Ford Foundation office to provide a team of western economists to help prepare a five-year development plan for the country that was scheduled to become independent from Britain on October 1. Among the people through whom the Foundation's New York headquarters put out feelers was David Bell, then a lecturer in the Harvard economics department who had helped organize and provide Harvard advisory assistance, funded by Ford, to the planning commission in Pakistan. Bell learned of Stolper's interest and enlisted him to head the Nigeria team.[5]

Stolper reached Nigeria for the first time on July 18, 1960, spending eight weeks before returning to Michigan for the fall semester. On February 15, 1961, he arrived in the then federal capital, Lagos,[6] for a resident tour that lasted close to 16 months.

During both stays he maintained a diary in the form of hand-written letters to his wife, Martha Vögeli, who remained at the family home in Ann Arbor, Michigan, until meeting Stolper in Dakar, Senegal, in early June 1962. Vögi, as she was best known, transcribed the letters by typewriter more or less as she received them.

In May 1998 Stolper invited the undersigned to edit the diary for publication. The invitation arose from a personal and professional association dating from August 1961, when I started a two-year tour in Lagos as assistant economist in the Nigeria mission of the US International Cooperation Administration (ICA), reorganized by the Kennedy administration in 1962 as the US Agency for International Development (USAID). By chance my wife and I were assigned an apartment directly across the street from Stolper's house, facilitating an interaction that became increasingly close as the Five-Year Development Plan neared completion. Stolper's role in influencing economic policy from within the host government, and his work in directing the Plan's preparation, interested me keenly, and led to my choosing such a role for my own career, rather than accepting USAID's invitation to continue with the agency.[7]

Moreover I played a minor role in the debate at the time about the macroeconomic framework underlying the Five-Year Plan. In entries for April–May 1962, Stolper refers to my critique of his analysis of inflation scenarios during the Plan period (1962–68), published under his name in a document accompanying the Plan, entitled 'Prospects for the Nigerian Economy.'[8]

In June–July 1998 Stolper's manuscript was transcribed onto a personal computer by Irita Grierson of the University of Michigan economics department. The editing got underway in August 1998, and was largely completed by February 1999. At that time Stolper wrote a postscript comprising pages 299–302 of the present volume. He also reviewed the edited version, forwarding corrections and supplying missing data, especially by way of identifying personalities mentioned in the diary. Over two years later, as negotiations with our publisher (Ashgate) were reaching fruition, Stolper wrote a two-page addendum to the postscript.

Wolfgang Stolper died on a hospital operating table in Ann Arbor on April 1, 2002, six weeks short of his 90th birthday. Into his last days he followed closely my e-mail consultations with Ashgate. In late March he and I fixed an appointment to meet on April 11 in Ann Arbor to make a final selection of photographs for the volume. I regret deeply that the meeting could not take place, and that Wolfgang could not live to see his diary in print.

The procedures followed in the process of editing, notably the criteria by which about one quarter of the original material was excised, are described at the end of this introduction.

Readers should find the diary of interest at four levels:

- A candid account of a Western academic's impressions of Nigeria's economy, politics, society and culture in the early 1960s on his first exposure to Africa;
- A perspective on the making and implementation of economic policy in newly independent Nigeria, in a context of growing corruption;
- An early episode in the performance and perceptions of western economists as advisers in ex-colonial developing countries in Africa and the less-developed world as a whole; and

• An intensely personal account of Stolper's feuds and friendships, while heading a Nigerian government office, with his fellow American team members, with Nigerian politicians and officials, and with other (mainly British) expatriates – advisers, officials, diplomats, businessmen and short-term visitors.

Impressions of Nigeria. Stolper was intensely curious about the country whose economic development he had come to assist. The diary describes a dozen or so separate trips that he undertook in one or more of the three regions – East, West and North – into which Nigeria was then divided administratively, as well as a number of one-day forays into the Western Region hinterland of Lagos. A small sample of his observations:

July 24, 1960 – settlements, large and small, ranging from red mud huts to cement villas with Mercedes and Opel vehicles in front, along the road through Lagos' hinterland...much of the farmland lying fallow...an impressive number of well-kept schools, surrounded by forests of cocoa trees...everyone speaking recognizable, if pidgin, English...

August 1, 1960 – the "fantastic" city of Ibadan, largely a jumbled assortment of mud huts with tin roofs, spread over many hills "like Rome"...the "cradle of Christianity of Yorubaland"...amidst a jumble of petty traders, the Temple of Shango, the God of Thunder...dirty, raising Stolper's respect for missionaries...the juju market featuring dried bats' wings and other things "simultaneously revolting and picturesque"...

August 9, 1960 – the northern city of Kano's crumbling mud walls...ubiquitous vultures on top of the roofs...groundnut pyramids of 9,000 tons each...the huge local market featuring foodstuffs and household implements crafted from second-hand iron and steel...

August 29, 1960 and *April 4, 1961* – the "hellhole" of Benin, "one of the unhealthiest places in Nigeria," dirty and "not yet recovered from the massacres of the last degenerate days of the Empire of Benin"...the brassworkers' guild with beautiful figures modeled on the museum pieces of the 15th–16th century...an interview with the Oba in his "palace," a huge compound built out of mud...visiting two pagan shrines...

May 27, 1961 – visiting Ilorin, a Yoruba province in the Northern Region, and seeing "the real Africa for the first time"...being poled up the Niger River to Tada, a "romantic-looking," traditional African village of thatched mud huts, where the village head allowed Stolper's party to photograph Nupe bronzes...

September 3, 1961 – the market in the northern city of Maiduguri, "much more colorful than the southern markets" – blacksmiths, leatherworkers, hatmakers, hordes of tailors working their Singer sewing machines under trees...

September 4 & 5, 1961 – enroute to, at and on Lake Chad, a plethora of bird life: crown birds, cattle egrets, Marabou and Abdin storks, geese, ducks and bush fowl...camel trains carrying dried fish..."unbelievably primitive fishing methods" using traditional reed boats, only 100 fishermen having learned to use nets...fish rising in the lake in between floating islands of papyrus...

May 2 & 5, 1962 – modern and artisanal tin mines on the Jos plateau...a Ministry of Mines and Power official explaining to digruntled artisanal miners why the Federal Loans Board won't give cash to individual miners with no evidence of the potential of their sites...Nok, where the archaeologist from the Jos museum pays miners for stone-age tools and shards of figurines...

May 8, 1962 – Oguala village, home of Stolper's Ibo steward-cook, Felix...greeted like a king by Felix's parents, his mother being one of nine wives...more children than Stolper had ever seen "in one spot outside a kindergarten"...

Economic policy in Nigeria. Stolper arrives in July 1960, fresh from lunch with a senior Colonial Office official at the Oxford and Cambridge Club in London. The man is "enthusiastic about the Nigerians," says Stolper will love them as he does, regards the place as "a great country with a great future," describes the finance minister, Chief Festus Okotie-Eboh, as "*very* good."

As this is written, almost 40 years later, what images does Nigeria convey to us? In 1967, before the end of the six-year plan Stolper helped write, the nation erupted into a $2^1/_2$-year civil war pitting the former Eastern Region (renaming itself Biafra) against the other regions. A few months earlier, Chief Festus, by then the epitome of macro corruption, was abducted and assassinated by rebel soldiers, as was the first prime minister, Sir Abubakar Tafawa Balewa, depicted positively by Stolper throughout the diary.

Thirty of its 39 years since independence have seen Nigeria under military rule. In 1998 the country tied for 4th place in Transparency International's corruption index.[9] The dictator during 1993–98, General Sani Abacha, rivaled only by Congo/Zaire's Joseph Mobutu as a looter of his country's patrimony, got Nigeria suspended from the Commonwealth for hanging nine human rights activists in 1995.

The extent of Nigeria's petroleum reserves was not widely known as Stolper completed his tour. Today, at roughly 2.3 million barrels per day, Nigeria is the world's tenth largest oil producer. Notwithstanding the discovery and exploitation of this resource – a case can be made for saying *because of* it – Nigeria's per capita GDP in 1997, estimated by the Economist Intelligence Unit at $356,[10] was substantially below its real level in 1960 when he started his work.[11] The national currency, the naira, at par with 10 UK shillings (= $^1/_2$ pound sterling) up to 1971 when it exchanged for US$1.40, is now worth 1.2¢ on the free market, following cumulative inflation during 1960–97 of 44,000%, or a mean of almost 18% per annum.[12]

The government's overvaluation of the naira, in some years in the 1980s exceeding 300%, has severely depressed returns to nonoil exporters. In 1961, agricultural exports, notably groundnuts and groundnut cake, cocoa, and palm kernels and palm oil, were valued at $390 million, accounting for 80% of total exports. In 1997 agricultural exports totaled $530 million, or 3% of the total.[13] During 1987–93 they had averaged $266 million per year. What do these figures imply as regards income-earning opportunities for the rural population?

First, we convert the 1961 dollar figure to 1997 prices, multiplying it by intervening consumer price inflation in the industrial countries as a whole. According to the IMF's *IFS* database, these prices rose 5.5 times, giving a multiplier of 6.5. Thus, 1961 agricultural exports were $2.5 billion in 1997 prices, or about five times their 1997 level. Meanwhile the rural population had grown by about 50%.[14] The resulting diminution of income-earning opportunities for that population is clear.

Press accounts abound of fuel shortages and queues, as state-run refineries have been allowed to deteriorate in order to generate rents for persons licensed to import refined products.

Only the dictator's fortuitous death in June 1998 has opened up prospects for reversing Nigeria's political and economic decline, marked by presidential elections in March 1999 and the return of an ex-general known as the only military leader before this year to hand over power to a civilian administration.

In this 20–20 hindsight, it is interesting to scan Stolper's diary for events and insights hinting at the potential for the 1962–68 Development Plan to be derailed and for Nigeria's polity and economy to follow a checkered, even downward course for nearly a half century.

To begin with, the concept of *corruption* that has become virtually synonymous with Nigerian governance was not unknown in Stolper's day. Three weeks into his second (resident) stay he refers to finance minister Festus as "reputedly one of the most corrupt" of the ministers, but adds that he "serves Nigeria well anyway." A year later (2.10.62) he cites his own minister (Waziri Ibrahim) as saying that costs of all government construction are inflated by corruption, and can never be reduced. Two weeks later (2.24.62) he refers again to Festus' "greed and corruption," finding it not incompatible with his being a "darn good finance minister."

The reader will not find a coherent statement of what can happen in the long run to a society whose state disposes of substantial wealth but whose institutions are too weak to check the diversion of state power and resources into personal gain. Stolper's most concrete information about corruption pertains to operations of the three regional development corporations, all of which he describes (8.5.61) as "hopelessly corrupt and impossible to reform." From his Ford-supported colleague in Enugu, Frank Moore, he gets first-hand detail about the Eastern Region corporation (ERDC),[15] its industrial section run by a black American named Daniels whom Stolper describes (6.23.61) as a "mad empire builder."

With hindsight about Nigeria's subsequent course, the reader will find on the naïve side Stolper's solution to this problem: to replace the regional bodies with a single national development corporation whose main purpose would be "to pump money into the private sector" (8.5.61). On the other hand Stolper must be credited with early insights into the damper that commercial enterprises created, owned and operated by the state would place on economic growth. Long before the literature on state-owned enterprises in mixed as well as 'socialist' economies had demonstrated this with facts and figures, making privatization one of the principal conditionalities of "structural adjustment programs" managed by the IMF and World Bank, Stolper was opposing the establishment of such units. He argues consistently that the state should reserve its scarce resources for physical infrastructure and human capital, at most acting as a conduit for foreign credit to privately owned industrial, agricultural and other commercial ventures.

A related early insight into state-imposed hindrances to economic growth is Stolper's insistent complaint about the culpability of western machinery suppliers in encouraging the regional development corporations to purchase and operate state farms and factories on the basis of fraudulent 'feasibility' studies that grossly understate costs of production. German and Israeli suppliers come in for particularly harsh criticism, but their British and American counterparts do not escape mention.

Arising in part from his German heritage, Stolper becomes friendly with the German ambassador. During their periodic social exchanges he complains repeatedly about German companies selling unprofitable factories to the ERDC. On

12.7.61 a representative of Cuttino Karo – labeled "German crooks" on 3.6.62 – which has sold ERDC a brewery along with bottle and flat glass factories, appears in Stolper's office "in alarm, sent by the German ambassador." The man heatedly asserts the feasibility of their factories.

Four months later (4.9.62) Stolper accosts another representative of the company at a German luncheon. This man says a company geologist has found sand suitable for glass-making at several places in Eastern Nigeria. The fact that the sand will have to be trucked from scattered locations, noted scathingly by Stolper, is excused on the ground that this will create transport jobs.

Israel comes in for criticism regarding a number of operations in the Western and Eastern regions. Israeli firms – some of them, Stolper notes ironically, controlled by trade unions – are accused (5.11.62) of displaying their appreciation for Nigerian nationalist aspirations by accepting a 49% share in local companies, but then milking these dry through control of supplier firms from which they buy at exaggerated prices. The Isarelis are also accused (4.28.62) of "invent(ing) the farm settlements, which are idiotic, almost criminally expensive."

From his one-time Michigan student Mordecai Kreinin, subsequently a professor at Michigan State, Stolper learns (2.2.62) that Moore's criticism of Israeli operations in the East has aroused anger in Israel. Stolper notes, "Apparently anyone who is critical of Israeli aid is suspected of anti-semitism or at least political motives." Stolper notes ironically that Moore comes from a Jewish background.

Performance and perceptions of Western economists. Within two weeks of first arriving in Nigeria (7.27.61), Stolper summarizes his mission in these words: "I have the most enviable assignment a man can have: developing an integrated plan for the most important African economy with the biggest and most hopeful future of any African nation."

The task of preparing independent Nigeria's first Five-Year Plan is in the background throughout the diary. The Plan outline is adopted by the House of Representatives on April 4, 1962, two months before Stolper's departure. Drafting the final segments of the published volume takes several weeks longer, and up to the last minute (6.4.62) Stolper is correcting galley proofs as "the highest paid proof reader in the world."

Stolper is anxious to distinguish his status in Nigeria from that of the typical foreign adviser in a developing country. The day after arriving (7.18.62) he describes himself to the British Permanent Secretary (PS) in his ministry, Economic Development, as "a Nigerian civil servant with a specified job to do in a specified time, taking general directions from my superiors, rather than an academic who would do a research job as he pleased in his own good time," and as "an executive officer who would *do* things rather than advise on how they should be done." As time passes (6.12.61) he talks about having to assert himself as the "boss" of the Economic Planning Unit *vis-à-vis* his Ford colleague Hansen.

Stolper sees the plan expansively, as a statement of economic policy just as much as, if not more than, a list of investment projects to be carried out during the five years. This is one of the issues he sees between himself and the man who becomes his principal nemesis during the 16-month resident tour, Narayan Prasad, an Indian seconded from the World Bank to serve as the Prime Minister's economic adviser.

Consistent with his view of the Plan, Stolper takes an interest in all major economic issues that arise during its preparation, writing memos to his minister, PS, and officials in the Ministry of Finance not only about investment magnitudes but also about fiscal and monetary policy and, in particular, the importance of avoiding unsustainable balance of payments deficits leading to imposition of exchange controls. He insists repeatedly on the connection between investment magnitudes and macroeconomic policy arising from the fact that excessive expenditure spills over into imports and increased foreign exchange deficits.

The diary's underlying theme is that, by designing a Five-Year Plan framework based on a realistic assessment of the executive capacity of Nigeria's public administration, which meant curbing the proclaimed spending targets of politicians as well as some leading bureaucrats, Stolper was adding significantly to the chance that the country's population would benefit from healthy economic growth for some years to come.

The plan framework would achieve this in three principal ways:

1 Wasteful public expenditure would be curbed, leaving more resources for investments that would promote rather than hinder growth. Early in his resident stay (3.1.61) Stolper remarks that "we find ourselves spending more time shooting down proposals – not too successfully – than developing them." The single issue on which he fights hardest as the Plan takes shape, and which causes the greatest heat between him and Prasad, is the overall magnitude of the investment program. Stolper wants a realistic program tailored to Nigeria's executive capacity and a level that can be supported without resort to inflationary finance. To Prasad he attributes the view that what the Plan says doesn't matter – the planners can yield to political pressures for higher investment targets in the knowledge that lack of executive capacity will lead to substantial underspending.

2 Given realistic investment targets, Nigeria would avoid inflation, balance of payments deficits and consequent exchange control, with deleterious consequences for growth. Stolper accuses Prasad (10.18.61) of "tak(ing) the line that only a fiscal catastrophe will teach a country a lesson," against his own view "that it was worth every effort to prevent such a catastrophe."

3 Thirdly, foreign donors, particularly the United States, would view the framework as creating sufficient probability of fruitful use of large infusions of aid to provide Nigeria with substantially greater investment resources than would otherwise be available. It was partly a US Government source that led Stolper to take this position. His erstwhile colleague at the Massachusetts Institute of Technology, Arnold Rivkin, led two official missions to Nigeria to review the economy and its budding five-year plan as a basis for the USG to make a multi-year commitment. At a meeting on 9.28.61, Prasad as chairman asked Rivkin to indicate how much aid the US might give Nigeria. According to Stolper, "Rivkin said that depended on the plan, no project could be evaluated except in the context of the plan." Two months later, having received no more than preliminary memoranda on the Five-Year Plan, the USG announced a commitment of $225 million over the five years 1962–67.

At various points Stolper indicates satisfaction that his work on the Plan framework served these objectives, making his mission successful. To be sure, this feeling alternates with low points, such as when (8.8.61) he lapses into cynicism about the planning exercise, saying, "one can't help thinking from time to time that all this is futile, and the real decisions will all be different, made by people one doesn't even know."

For some two decades following Stolper's Nigeria assignment, governments of developing countries, their sources of aid and the fraternity of development economists continued to proclaim the usefulness of multi-year development plans, and donor agencies funded foreign advisers to help write them. There was general agreement with Paul Clark's thesis:[16]

> ...(A) major advance towards comprehensiveness (in planning) may be at least a necessary condition for more rapid economic development...(T)he most important improvement immediately attainable is to introduce more inclusive and coherent aggregative plan frameworks.

Gradually, however, evidence accumulated that, particularly in Africa, the plans were not having much effect. Most of them served as smokescreens behind which corrupt politicians conducted business as usual. Ministries of planning had little influence in formulating the policies that determined whether and how plans were implemented, and the ministers made little effort to keep public spending in line with investment programs set forth in the plan documents.

Meanwhile economic growth slowed in many countries. This was partly under the brunt of external shocks such as the two oil price hikes of the 1970s, but more importantly a result of two major factors:

1 Misguided policies that prevented the labor, capital and foreign exchange markets from transmitting adequate incentives for investment, employment creation and exports; and
2 Wasteful public expenditure, motivated by corruption and political expediency, on badly designed infrastructure, uncompetitive state enterprises and bloated civil service payrolls.

Starting around 1980 an increasing share of aid to Africa took the form of fast-disbursing, nonproject credits in support of programs of 'structural adjustment' involving policy conditionalities. The governing documents, drafted by IMF and World Bank staff and approved by client governments after negotiation with missions from Washington, were given the titles 'Policy Framework Paper' and 'Letter of Development Policy.'

Far more concise than the multi-year plans they effectively supplanted, these documents committed their signatories to pursue market-oriented policies and reorient public expenditure to productive uses. Donors continued to provide foreign economic advisers, but less and less of this assistance was devoted to helping planning ministries prepare multi-year development plans. Instead, the advisers worked with finance ministries to improve budgeting, expenditure control and tax performance, they helped central banks implement prudent monetary policy, they helped directorates of personnel management reform the civil service, they worked with line ministries to improve sectoral policy formulation, investment planning and execution.

In a nutshell, one can say that events have overtaken the type of intervention that Stolper's Ford team conducted in Nigeria (and from which the present editor and many of his Harvard colleagues fashioned their early careers). Nevertheless, the diary's author has to be credited with never losing sight of the importance of sound policy as opposed to a coherent multi-year plan. Nearing the end of his tour (4.3.62), Stolper repeats his "insist(ence) that the only control methods that really work are indirect ones using incentives and the market."

Feuds and friendships. The diary is frank about Stolper's opinions of colleagues and counterparts, Nigerian and expatriate. Nigerians range from Chief Adebo, Western Region secretary and later ambassador to the US, "a truly great man, honorable and incorruptible, certainly the greatest Nigerian I have known," to greedy, corrupt and stupid – e.g. finance minister Festus when he serves an eviction notice on a USAID-rented apartment building after the mission rejects a rent increase part way through a long-term contract (2.10.62).[17] British civil servants, holdovers from colonialism, range from the "only really able and nice Englishmen (*sic*) I have met" (5.7.62) – Stolper enumerates seven individuals – to a deputy PS who is not only "a stupid man, but also nasty and vicious" (10.16.61).

However, the mother of all feuds described in the diary is that between Stolper and the Prime Minister's Indian adviser, Prasad, whose name is mentioned 460 times in the present (edited) version.

The potential for conflict over overlapping responsibility was recognized early on by the Ford Foundation representative in Nigeria, Donald Kingsley. When he learned that the World Bank had agreed to second Prasad to the Prime Minister, Kingsley visited the Bank to ask if Prasad would take responsibility for economic planning. The Bank respondents demurred, saying that Prasad would have no staff and would not carry out line duties.

Subsequently, following Stolper's first visit and before Prasad's arrival in Nigeria, the planning ministry wrote to Prasad asking him to receive Stolper in his Bank office. Stolper explained his responsibility, as he understood it, to guide the Five-Year Plan's preparation. According to a personal communication from Stolper, the discussion was cordial and Prasad indicated he had no desire to intervene in Plan preparation. The diary refers in passing (4.6.61) to "our agreement in Washington not to have public differences until we had ironed them out in private."

Prasad arrived in Nigeria in late 1960, while Stolper was teaching at Michigan following his eight-week summer visit. The diary first mentions Prasad in its entry for February 20, 1961, five days after the start of Stolper's resident tour. The subject is Prasad's proposal for a statistics subcommittee under the Joint Planning Committee (JPC) – 'joint' between regional and federal government officials responsible for planning – which one of Prasad's duties is to chair.

The next mention, a week later (2.27.61), gives the first hint of conflict: "...real differences between Prasad and us appeared [in a discussion of planning targets]. He wants us to make a sort of bargaining plan, which we don't want...Prasad is also trying to make himself responsible for the plan, which he isn't, and we have to assert ourselves. I fear we will get into some difficulties with him, in spite of the fact that on a practical working level his and our approaches come to pretty much the same thing."

In March (3.10.61), PS/Finance Clarke complains to Stolper about Prasad writing frequent memos to the Prime Minister with little factual basis. Stolper later (3.16.61) reflects: "We are a little leery of being pushed in the middle between Prasad and the Ministry of Finance; our good relations with Finance are among our strongest assets." That day Stolper and Hansen meet with Prasad to try to clear the air. They find him "looking tired and somewhat beaten. I like him and think he is good, but he does free-wheel too much...We agreed to consult mutually and work out strategy."

However, this does not happen. Statements by Prasad in Stolper's first JPC meeting (4.6.61) strike him as "nasty" and leave him "upset and mad." The main substantive disagreement is over whether the Five-Year Plan should be essentially a list of investment projects – the position Stolper ascribes to Prasad – *versus* the need to establish a macroeconomic framework within which the effective demand for investment, and the supply of domestic and foreign finance, can be estimated.

By mid-April (4.14.61), two months after returning to Nigeria and with over a year to go, Stolper is accusing Prasad of a "flagrant lie," saying he has no trust in him and that Prasad "gives the whole business of economic advising a bad name" (4.16.61). At Stolper's initiative the two men are no longer on a first-name basis.

Yet within another month (5.14.61) Stolper says they have composed their differences. "The blowup apparently served a useful purpose, and sweetness and reason prevail." Six weeks later (6.25.61) everything is still "milk and honey." Stolper accepts that "Prasad *is* Advisor to the Federal Government, we are only advisors to the Ministry of Economic Development. He has access to the Prime Minister, we do not."

Referring (7.2.61) to a discussion with a visiting World Bank mission, Stolper says, "I defended Prasad, and what's more I meant it. I have not only got to like him, but while I think I am much the better economist, he is superb as a negotiator, and much better than I can ever hope to be as a political and policy center."

Differences of opinion persist, but as of late August (8.25.61), Stolper is "happy to say that all debates are now good-humored and lack the acrimony of the first attacks...I am quite reconciled to being Prasad's staff, and even to have him produce a project plan for bargaining purposes instead of a straightforward feasible plan. But the exchange control debate is more serious. And I also fear [Prasad's] anti-British, anti-colonial bias will play into the hands of more irresponsible Nigerians."

Shortly thereafter (8.28.61) Stolper sees "trouble brewing" with Prasad over exchange control. Prasad answers a Stolper memo on the subject by "pull(ing) his experience, and also some nationalism." As regards plan investment targets, in early October (10.9.61) Stolper sees "Prasad's chickens coming home to roost. He told the Easterners to think big, never mind finances, they can be found. Now they did it! It is a mess."

By mid-October the differences have once more become personalized: (10.17.61) "He does not keep me informed, and I now have evidence that he does not want to...he does not play square with me, though I have with him." A month later (11.20.61): "Despite my exasperation, which is genuine enough, I continue to find the job fascinating. I only wish I could take it easier and personalize less. I still like Prasad. I also admire his political *savoir faire*. But as an economist I am becoming quite conceited. My predictions were correct and he still cannot visualize the effects of his suggestions. By now I am not impressed when he pulls his experience on me."

As Stolper is about to take off for a six-week Christmas break, Clarke tells him (12.12.61) that his troubles with Prasad are over, as World Bank President Black had talked to Prasad. Clarke adds: "Prasad doesn't know it, but [Central Bank Governor] Fenton and I had something to do with it. And you did a brilliant job." Stolper tells the diary: "The 'you' referred obviously also to Lyle [Hansen]. In general, I have won my fight."

Notwithstanding, the differences with Prasad simmer on, peaking abruptly within a month of Stolper's final departure in June 1962, when an editorial committee consisting of the advisers and PSs of Finance and Economic Development is finalizing the Five-Year Plan document. In late May Stolper discovers that macroeconomic projections he had made before the Christmas break were altered by Prasad some time during December-February.

Specifically, new (and lower) revenue projections that materialized during Stolper's absence showed that maintaining Plan investment targets would require a reduction in either consumption per head or government recurrent expenditure. Stolper's junior colleague, Peter Clark, took this information to Prasad, who increased the estimate of public investment underspending in the national income accounts without adjusting the financial accounts accordingly, creating an inconsistency. Stolper also resented Prasad's raising the investment expenditure shortfall after encouraging the regional governments to present high spending targets on the assumption that this would stimulate more foreign aid.

Stolper writes (5.30.61), "I am stinking mad and told Prasad yesterday that he has double-crossed me for the last time...He is a charming host, a smooth operator, a poor economist, a catastrophic adviser, and an untrustworthy colleague. Fortunately the PM doesn't take his advice most of the time." Stolper continues: "I decided this time to fight in the open. So I told [MED PS] Lardner what had happened, that Prasad had altered assumptions without authority of JPC or NEC [the National Economic Council, the Ministerial counterpart of the JPC], which neither he nor I were empowered to do. I wrote a memo asking to be put on record, to protect myself. A copy went to Prasad and another to Stanley Wey [Secretary to the Prime Minister and thus Nigeria's top civil servant]. So I am going to the PM after all."[18]

The story ends with a lengthy interview between Stolper and Wey (5.31.62). Stolper complains about Prasad, and Wey makes supportive noises to the effect that they "had no idea that he would run everything." He regrets that, "because the British had deliberately excluded Africans when real decisions were being made,...they had not really learned their job and needed assistance. Moreover, they felt, or had felt, that they wanted it from an Indian, and you have to be careful with Indians."

Editing guidelines

The editor followed two guiding principles: (i) to condense the manuscript from its original by more than 500 pages, and (ii) to eliminate or trim references to housekeeping details and social functions that readers might find repetitive. He also took the liberty of rearranging Teutonic constructions and removing pieces of redundant verbiage in the substantive material.

During 1998–99 Professor Stolper, then going on 87, read, corrected and approved the manuscript, and supplied new material to expand many of the explanatory footnotes, only a handful of which are original.

Clive Gray
Greensboro, Vermont
June, 2002

Notes

1 Wolfgang F. Stolper and Paul A. Samuelson, 'Protection and Real Wages', *Review of Economic Studies*, 1941. Briefly, the theorem states that, while without offsetting domestic policy measures, free trade may reduce the real remuneration of an economy's relatively scarce factor of production – in the United States, labor – it will increase the remuneration of the relatively abundant factor – in the US, capital – sufficiently to enable the scarce factor to be subsidized, leaving all factors better off through free trade.
2 In 1960 Stolper published *The Structure of the East German Economy* with Harvard University Press.
3 Schumpeter himself emigrated to the US in 1932 and was a professor in the Harvard economics department at his death in 1950. At various points in the diary Stolper refers to Schumpeter's Bonn seminar and classmates in it, several of whom he connected with during his stay in Africa. In 1994 Stolper published a biography of Schumpeter (Stolper, 1994).
4 *The Structure of the East German Economy.*
5 The other two were Lyle Hansen, a former Harvard adviser in Pakistan, and Peter Clark, for whom the Nigeria assignment was a first job upon completing his economics PhD at Massachusetts Institute of Technology. Stolper describes at length interactions with both fellow team members at various points in the diary.
6 In 1983 the more centrally located town of Abuja was designated as the federal capital.
7 My next job, after completing the USAID/Nigeria tour in 1963, was as member of a Ford-funded advisory team in Kenya's Ministry of Economic Planning and Development.
8 I expanded and published my critique in the *Nigerian Journal of Economic and Social Studies* (Gray, 1963, pp. 320–27). Professor Stolper responded to it in Stolper (1966).
9 Transparency International (1998).
10 EIU (1999), p. 18.
11 According to the World Bank's celebrated 1980 report, *Accelerated Development in Sub-Saharan Africa*, prepared under the direction of Stolper's University of Michigan colleague Elliot Berg, Nigeria's per capita GDP in 1979 was $670, having grown by 3.7% per annum compounded from 1960. Working back to 1960 at that rate, we obtain a base figure of $336. Taking account of 100% inflation in the industrial countries between 1980 and 1997, the proper comparison is between 1960's $336 and half of $356, or $178 for 1997.
12 Calculated from indices in the IMF's *International Financial Statistics* CDRom database.
13 Figures from FAOSTAT data base.
14 Rural population growth is estimated by comparing 1996 and 1960 estimates, obtained by subtracting urban population from total population figures in World Bank (1998) – figure for 1996 – and *IFS* CDRom database – figure for 1960. Urban population calculated in turn by applying 13% coefficient for 1960 according to World Bank (1980), and 40.4% coefficient for 1996 according to World Bank (1998). Estimates are offered with the caveat that Nigerian population data are subject to an even higher margin of uncertainty than pertains to most African countries.
15 At some points Stolper uses the initials ENDC, for Eastern Nigeria Development Corporation.

16 Clark (1965), pp. 56–57.
17 This is the same Festus whom Stolper also describes (see above) as a "darn good finance minister" who "serves Nigeria well."
18 Stolper means through the PM's secretary. He never met Prime Minister Balewa.

References

Clark, Paul G. 1965. *Development Planning in East Africa*. Nairobi: East African Publishing House.
Economist Intelligence Unit. 1999. *Country Profile – Nigeria – 1999–2000*. London: EIU.
Food and Agriculture Organization of the United Nations. 1999. *FAOSTAT data base*. Rome: FAO.
Gray, Clive S. 1963. 'Credit Creation for Nigeria's Economic Development – A Polak Model of Money, Income, and the Balance of Payments in Nigeria'. *The Nigerian Journal of Economic and Social Studies*, November, pp. 247–353.
International Monetary Fund. 1999. *International Financial Statistics – CDRom Database*.
Stolper, Wolfgang F. 1960. *The Structure of the East German Economy*. Cambridge: Harvard University Press.
_____. 1966. *Planning Without Facts*. Cambridge: Harvard University Press.
_____. 1994. *Joseph Alois Schumpeter – The Public Life of a Private Man*. Princeton: Princeton University Press.
_____ and Paul A. Samuelson. 1941. 'Protection and Real Wages'. *The Review of Economic Studies*, pp. 58–73.
Transparency International. 1998. 'The Corruption Perceptions Index – 1998'. Press release, Berlin, September 22.
World Bank. 1980. *Accelerated Development in Sub-Saharan Africa*. Washington: The World Bank.
_____. 1998. *African Development Indicators*. Washington: The World Bank.

Cast of Characters[1]

Abacha, General Sani – Nigeria's dictator during 1993–98.

Aboyade, Ojetunji – Economist at University College Ibadan (UCI). Served as WS' successor as adviser to the Federal Government for the Second Five-Year Plan.

Ackley, Gardner – Chairman of University of Michigan Economics Department.

Adams, Sherman – Assistant to US President Eisenhower, forced to resign for accepting gifts from lobbyists.

Adebo, Chief S.O.– Chief Secretary, Western Region government.

Adebola, ... – president of Nigerian Trade Union Congress.

Adetokimbo, Sir – Chief Justice of Nigeria.

Adewolo, ... – Official in Federal Ministry of Economic Development Economic Planning Unit (FMED/EPU).

Ajumogobia, ... – Permanent Secretary, Federal Ministry of Education.

Akande, Sam – Senior Assistant Secretary (Technical Assistance), FMED/EPU. Tutored WS in Yoruba.

Akilu, Alhaji Ali – Permanent Secretary (Economic Development), Northern Region (successor to Peter Gibbs).

Akintola, S.I. – Western Region premier.

Akintomede, Michael – Director of Western Region farm settlements and institutes.

Aluko, Sam – Economist at UCI, prominent critic of Federal Government policies.

Archer, ... – Prepared report costing implications of Ashby Commission Report on Nigerian education.

Ardsvik, ... – Norwegian, agricultural specialist on World Bank mission.

Ashby, Sir Eric – British educationist, led 1960 commission that wrote report on Nigerian education.

Atta, ... – Deputy Permanent Secretary, FMED, later Permanent Secretary, Federal Ministry of Defence.

Awolowo, Chief Obafemi – Head of Action Group political party and leader of Opposition in Federal Parliament.

Ayida, Alison – Senior Assistant Secretary (Foreign Aid), Federal Ministry of Finance.

Azikiwe, Nnamdi – Governor-General, subsequently President of Nigeria.

Baldwin, Kenneth – Economic Advisor, Northern Region government.

Balewa, Sir Abubakar Tafawa – Nigeria's Prime Minister from before independence in 1960 until his assassination in January 1966 coup that touched off the Biafran secession.

Balogh, "Tommy" (later Lord Balogh) – Economics Professor at Oxford University.

Barback, Professor ... – Head of UCI Economics Department and Nigerian Institute of Social and Economic Research (NISER).

Barton, Philip – Permanent Secretary (Finance), Eastern Region, succeeding O. Williams.

Bauer, P.T. – Professor at London School of Economics, noted critic of state intervention in markets.

Beier, Uli (wife: Susanne Wenger) – Beier was a professor at UCI, Susanne later became a priestess in a Yoruba cult.

Bell, David – Economics Lecturer at Harvard University during 1958–61, later President John Kennedy's Budget Director, President Lyndon Johnson's Director of US Agency for International Development (USAID), and Head of International Affairs at Ford Foundation. Helped arrange WS' assignment to Nigeria.

Berg, Elliot – Economics Professor and WS' colleague at University of Michigan, later his successor as director of UM's Center for Research on Economic Development.

Bernstein, Joel (wife: Merle) – Director of ICA (International Cooperation Administration) – renamed USAID in 1961 mission in Nigeria, 1960–64.

Berry, Sara – Economist and historian (now Professor at Johns Hopkins University) whose PhD thesis on cocoa was published by Oxford University Press.

Bevan, William – Vice-principal, UCI.

Bhatia, ... – Participant in International Monetary Fund mission.

Black, Eugene – World Bank President, 1949–62.

Bloomfield, ... – Official of Nigeria Produce Marketing Company.

Bronk, ... – Manager, Eastern Region Development Corporation.

Brown, Charles – American economist on UCI faculty.

Brown, ... Dr. – Professor of Medicine, UCI.

Brown, ... – Permanent Secretary (Economic Planning), Eastern Region.

Bull, Lt. Col. (ret.) "Tom" – businessman, co-passenger on WS' first trip to Nigeria.

Callaway, Arch – Economics graduate student at Massachusetts Institute of Technology (MIT), conducting field research from Ibadan.

Chukujekwe, Steven – Principal Assistant Secretary (Economic Planning), Western Region government, subsequently Permanent Secretary in the new Midwest State.

Clark, Paul – Professor of Development Economics at Williams College.

Clark, Peter (wife: Gretel) – Junior member of WS' Ford-sponsored team in FMED/ EPU.

Clarke, Reginald – Permanent Secretary, Federal Ministry of Finance.

Coatswith, ... – Permanent Secretary (Agriculture), Eastern Region.

Coleman, James – Political Science Professor/Africa specialist at University of California at Los Angeles.

Cross, Ray – Fisheries Officer, Baga Research Station, Northern Region.

Dagash, Mallam Musa – Permanent Secretary (Mines and Power), Eastern Region.

Daniels, ... – Head of Industrial Division, Eastern Region Development Corporation (ERDC).

Daramola, J.B. – Permanent Secretary, Federal Ministry of Commerce and Industry.

Deko, Chief Akin – Western Region Minister of Agriculture.

Dike, K.O. – Nigerian anthropologist, UCI rector.

Dina, Chief Isaac – Permanent Secretary (Finance), Western Region.

Dinour, ... – Israeli Economist based in Ghana.

Dolgin, George – Economic Officer at US Embassy, Lagos, 1961–63.

Dorros, ... – US Vice-consul in Lagos.

Drew, Peter – Head of wheat irrigation experiment, Yo, Northern Region.

Duncan, Peter – Official in Western Region Ministry of Economic Planning.
Edwards, ... – Assigned by Michigan State University to head Economics Program at University of Nigeria (Nsukka).
Eggertson, Professor ... – Dean of UCI Medical School.
Elias, T. – Nigeria's Attorney General.
Elkeston, ... – Deputy Permanent Secretary, Federal Ministry of Commerce and Industry.
Elliot, Hugh – Official working on farm settlements in Eastern Region.
Emmerson, ... – US Consul-general in Lagos.
Engler, Dr. ... – Head of Kreditanstalt für Wiederaufbau (German Bank for Reconstruction).
Ezera, Kaly – Parliamentary Spokesman on Five-Year Plan for Eastern Region NCNC party.
Faaland, Just – Norwegian Economist, Director of Christian Michaelsen Institute, Bergen.
Fagg, Bernard – Director of Antiquities.
Farmington, ... – General Manager, ATMN tin mining company and appointed member of Northern Region House of Representatives.
Fenn, ... – Northern Region Marketing Board secretary.
Fenton, Roy – Governor of the Central Bank of Nigeria.
Fleming, Robert – Representative in Nigeria of Rockefeller Brothers Fund.
Fluth, Dr. ... – Physician at Baptist mission leper colony in Eastern Region.
Fogg, David – MIT Fellow in Eastern Region planning unit.
Fullbrook, Lt. Col. ... – Nigerian Army's Quartermaster General.
Gaitskell, Arthur – Founder of Sudan's Gezira scheme, consulting on Eastern Region agricultural policy.
Galbraith, John Kenneth – Harvard Economics Professor, later John Kennedy's ambassador to India.
Galsworthy ... – UK Colonial Office staff member met by WS en route to Nigeria.
Garba, ... – Deputy Permanent Secretary, Federal Ministry of Finance (1962).
Gaskill, Peter – Chief Mining Engineer, Eastern Region.
Gibbs, Peter – Deputy Permanent Secretary (Finance), Northern Region, in charge of planning.
Glass, John – Participant in MIT African Fellows program, assigned to Northern Region government.
Gordon, Lincoln – Harvard Business School professor and friend of WS.
Goss, John – Principal Agricultural Officer, Bornu Province, Northern Region.
Gould, Burton – Program Economist, USAID/Nigeria, 1961–65.
Gray, Clive (wife: Ethné) – Senior Fellow in Development, John F. Kennedy School of Government, Harvard University, 2000–01. Economist, USAID/Nigeria, 1961–63. Edited the present diary.
Greatbatch, Bruce – Private Secretary to the Sardauna of Sokoto, Northern Region.
Grierson, Irita – Secretary in University of Michigan Economics Department, transcribed WS' diary electronically in 1999.
Haberler, Gottfried – Noted international trade economist and Harvard professor.
Hamilton, ... – Industrial specialist on World Bank mission.

Hansen, Lyle (wife: Ann) – Second member of WS' Ford-sponsored team in FMED/EPU.

Harkort, Guenther – State Secretary for Economic Affairs in Germany's Ministry of Foreign Affairs, friend of WS from 1930s at Bonn University.

Hartley, ... – Director, West African Institute for Oilpalm Research (WAIFOR).

Hartmans, ... – Official of Food and Agricultural Organization (FAO), Rome.

Helander, Sven – Swedish economist, visiting lecturer at UCI.

Hill, ... – Head of Nigerian Timber Association.

Hill-Humphries, Polly – British expert on Ghanaian cocoa farmers.

Hutchinson, Edmond – USAID Assistant Administrator for Africa.

Ibrahim, Waziri – Third Federal Minister of Economic Development, 1961–62.

Igwagwu, Ebenezer – Economist with FMED/EPU.

Inneh, Chief ... – Hereditary chief of the Benin Brassworkers' Guild.

Jackson, E.F. ("Teddy") – Economics Professor at Oxford, co-author with Pius Okigbo of book on Nigeria's national accounts.

Jackson, Sir Robert (also "Commander") – British official whom WS describes as the driving force behind Ghana's Volta Dam. Husband of Barbara Ward (also known as Lady Jackson).

Jansen, Cornelis L. – Dutch economist charged with establishing planning unit in Liberia.

Jensen, "Bernie" – Ford Foundation-sponsored economic adviser to Nigeria's Northern Region government.

Johnson, Ken – Official in Federal Ministry of Commerce and Industry.

Kaldor, Lord Nicolas – Noted British Keynesian and tax economist.

Keep, Graham – Official of Central Bank of Nigeria.

Kennedy, John F. – President of USA, 1961–63.

Kenyatta, Jomo – First Prime Minister/President of Kenya, 1963–78.

King, ... – Permanent Secretary, Federal Ministry of Lagos Affairs.

Kingsley, Donald – Ford Foundation representative in Nigeria.

Knapp, J. Burke – World Bank Vice-president.

Koenigsberger, Otto – Head of Development Planning Unit, University College, London, wrote report on construction costs in Nigeria under United Nations technical assistance.

Kontos, William – Deputy Director of US ICA/USAID mission.

Kreinin, Mordecai – Native-born Israeli, WS' student at Michigan, later Professor of Economics at Michigan State University.

Kyle, Peter – Staff member in USAID/Eastern Region office.

Lardner, Godfrey – First Nigerian Permanent Secretary, FMED (1961–62).

Latham, Richard – Tax adviser in Northern Region Finance Ministry.

Lawan, ... – Permanent Secretary (Agriculture), Northern Region.

Lawson, ... – from Colorado, wrote report on Northern Region livestock.

Lawson, ... – Permanent Secretary, Federal Ministry of Health.

Lewis, "Ben" – Economics Professor at Oberlin College.

Lewis, "Toby" (wife: Jean) – Second Permanent Secretary at FMED during WS' tenure.

Leyton, ... – Official in Northern Region finance ministry.

Lilienthal, David – Founded Tennessee Valley Authority in US.

Longe, ... – Permanent Secretary (Agriculture), Western Region.

Lugard, Lord – British Governor of Nigeria in early 20th century.

Lumumba, Patrice – First Prime Minister of independent Congo (1960), assassinated 1961.

Mandrides, ... – Owner of Nigerian Oil Mills, Maiduguri.

Mason, Edward S. – Harvard Economics Professor, founder of Harvard Development Advisory Service, arranged for WS' stay at Harvard during 1962–63 to write *Planning without Facts*.

Massaglia, ... – Political Officer, US Embassy in Nigeria.

Mbamara, Stephen – Assistant Secretary, FMED/EPU.

McKay, Ian – director, Nigerian Broadcasting Corporation (appointed 1962).

Michelmore, Margery – US Peace Corps Volunteer sent home after UCI students found and publicized an indiscreet postcard she had written about impressions of Nigeria.

Millikan, Max – Director of MIT's Center for International Studies, where WS was a visiting scholar during 1958–60.

Mladek, ... – Acting Head of International Monetary Fund Africa division, headed IMF mission to Nigeria.

Moore, Frank – Ford Foundation-sponsored economic adviser to Nigeria's Eastern Region government.

Morrison, Neil – Deputy Permanent Secretary, FMED.

Murray, John – Deputy Permanent Secretary, Federal Ministry of Finance.

Nicolescu, ... – Economics Professor at Vanderbilt University.

Nixon, ... – Political scientist on MIT research team in Western Region.

Nkrumah, Kwame – First President of independent Ghana.

North, W. Haven – Program Officer, USAID/Nigeria, 1960–64.

Nwanze, ... – Chief Oil Palm Research engineer, Eastern Region.

Nyerere, Julius – First Prime Minister/President of Tanganyika/Tanzania, 1960–85.

Obineche, Cheido – Economist with FMED/EPU.

Odutola, Chief – Western Region businessman, owner of several tire retreading plants.

Oguala, Felix – WS' Ibo steward-cook.

Ogunsheye, Ayo – Economist, Director of Extra-mural Studies at UCI.

Okeke, P.N. – Eastern Region Minister of Agriculture.

Okigbo, Pius – Head of Eastern Region Economic Planning Unit, with E.F. Jackson co-authored book on Nigeria's national accounts which was eventually published under Okigbo's sole authorship.

Okotie-Eboh, Chief Festus Sam – Nigeria's Finance Minister 1960–66, assassinated in 1966 coup.

Okpara, Dr. Michael – Premier, Eastern Region government.

Oluwasami, ... – UCI Agricultural Economist.

Omanai, Henry – Deputy Permanent Secretary, Federal Ministry of Finance.

Onitiri, Bola – Economist at UCI, specializing in international trade.

Padgett, ... – Deputy Permanent Secretary (Finance), Eastern Region.

Palmer, Joseph – US ambassador to Nigeria.

Pardo, ... – UNESCO representative in Nigeria, a Maltese who sought to recruit WS for his country.

Phelps, ... – Official at Federal Ministry of Finance.

Pite, Christopher – Acting Chief Statistician, Federal Statistics Office.

Posadowski-Wehner, Count – German Ambassador to Nigeria.

Prasad, Narayan – Indian economist seconded from World Bank as adviser to Nigerian Prime Minister during early 1960s.

Price, Wally – Agricultural supervisor, Bornu Province.

Pye, Lucien – MIT Political Science Professor.

Reynolds, Kathy (and husband) – Ford Foundation-sponsored advisors on organization and management, Eastern Region.

Rice, Emmett – USAID-sponsored Research Adviser to Central Bank of Nigeria.

Richardson, ... – Canadian High Commissioner in Nigeria.

Rivkin, Arnold – MIT Professor and head of two missions sent by USAID to evaluate Nigeria's development prospects and aid requirements.

Rossiji, Chief ... – Action Group secretary and Parliamentary Spokesman on Five-Year Plan.

Rowane, Chief ... – Head of Western Region Development Corporation.

Sadler, ... – UK Trade Commissioner in Nigeria.

Samuelson, Paul – MIT Professor of Economics, 1970 Nobel prizewinner, authored influential joint article with WS in 1941.

Saunders, ... – Deputy Permanent Secretary (Finance), later Undersecretary (Planning), Northern Region.

Schatz, Sayre – US economist teaching at UCI.

Schmidt, Wilson – Economics Professor at George Washington University, subsequently at Virginia Polytechnic Institute, and member of Rivkin missions.

Schumpeter, Joseph – Noted Austro-American economist. Professor of Economics at the University of Bonn, 1925–32, and Harvard University, 1932–50, in both of which schools WS was his student.

Sen, Sudhir – WS' fellow student in Schumpeter seminar at Bonn University, adviser to Nkrumah administration in Ghana during WS' stay in Nigeria.

Shaddock, Ken – Deputy Permanent Secretary, FMED, from October 1961.

Shagari, Alhaji Shegu – Federal Minister of Economic Development during WS' first visit to Nigeria (President of Nigeria 1979–83).

Singer, Hans W. (later Sir Hans) – WS' fellow student in Schumpeter's Bonn seminar, later economist with United Nations and Professor at Sussex University.

Sokoto, Sardauna of (Sir Ahmadu Bello) – Head of Northern People's Congress and Northern Region premier.

Stewart, Jan – Agricultural Economist identified by WS as being from Edinburgh, did study of Nigerian agricultural statistics in 1960.

Stolper, Martha Vögeli ("Vögi") – WS' first wife, transcribed her husband's letters from Nigeria.

Stolper, Wolfgang – Professor of Economics (*Emeritus*), University of Michigan. Author of the present diary, which he wrote during 1960–62 as head of a Ford Foundation-financed team of economic advisors in Nigeria's Federal Ministry of Economic Development, charged with helping write the country's First Five-Year Plan.

Stonebridge, Patricia – Secretary to WS' team at FMED/EPU.

Sule, ... – Federal Minister of Mines and Power.

Talib, ... – Permanent Secretary (Finance), Northern Region (successor to John Taylor).

Tansley, Sir Eric – Head of Nigeria Produce Marketing Board, London.

Taylor, John – Permanent Secretary, Northern Region Ministry of Economic Development.

Thompson, Charles – Permanent Secretary during WS' initial tour at FMED.

Tibbets, ... – General Manager, Central Bank of Nigeria.

Tsakkos, ... – Manager of private Northern Region groundnut oil mill.

Vincent, ... – Senior Assistant Secretary, Ministry of Finance, later transferred to Central Bank of Nigeria.

Wachuku, Jaja – Second Federal Minister of Economic Development during WS' tenure.

Ward, Barbara – (also known as Lady Jackson – wife of Sir Robert Jackson) British economist and writer.

Ward, Peter – UCI researcher studying quelea birds in Northern Region.

Waterston, ... – Director of Federal Agricultural Research.

Weast, ... – Economic Officer at US Embassy, Lagos, 1959–61.

Wells, Jerry – WS' student at Michigan, later professor at Pittsburgh University, researched his doctoral thesis from Ibadan.

Wey, Stanley – Permanent Secretary to Nigeria's Prime Minister.

Whalley, ... – Senior Assistant Secretary (Economics), FMED.

Willi, Hans – UTC General Manager.

Williams, Caroline – Trainer of Home Economics Teachers at Ileysha Farm Settlement, wife of farm supervisor, Taio Williams.

Williams, Fataye – Manager of Manor House, Iseyin, Western Region.

Williams, G. Mennon ("Soapy") – Ex-governor of Michigan, Assistant Secretary of State for Africa during J.F. Kennedy's presidency.

Williams, Nancy – Wife of G. Mennon.

Williams, Owen – Permanent Secretary (Finance), Eastern Region.

Williams, Taio – Supervisor of Ileysha Farm Settlement, Western Region.

Wilson, Andrew – Permanent Secretary (Economic Planning), Western Region.

Note

1   "..." signifies that diary does not indicate person's first/Christian name. "WS" stands for Wolfgang Stolper, author of the present diary. This list omits many persons whom WS met once and does not mention subsequently. The title "Professor" follows American rather than British usage.

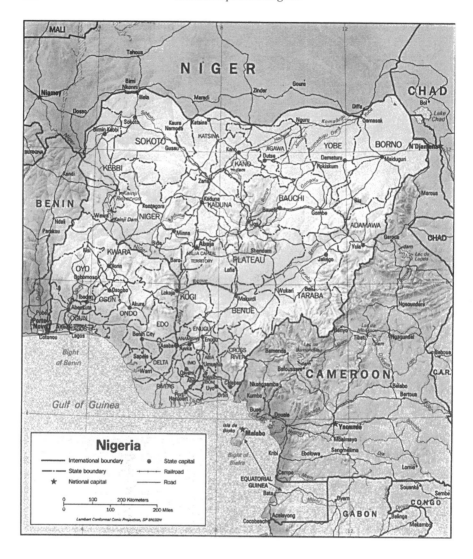

Chapter 1
July 17–30, 1960
Arrival in Nigeria: First Impressions, First Tour in the Countryside

July 15, 1960 (London)

...I telephoned Galsworthy...and took off to the Colonial Office. He is 44, very nice, knowledgeable. He gave me a number of names: Fenton, the Governor of the new Central Bank of Nigeria (CBN), a young (40) Englishman who resigned from the Bank of England to accept the job. The resignation came at the request of the BoE, fearing an eventual conflict of interest. Galsworthy said the Minister of Finance, Chief Festus O...something or other – I have to look it up[1], was a personal friend of his – they were on a first name basis – was *very* good, and easy to get along with, which is important since I will work with him.

I raised the question of communist trade missions and was told not to worry. The Nigerians are quite up to the communists. In fact Chief Festus was in Prague and handled the situation marvelously. The Nigerians do not want bilateral deals or anything that would cost them freedom of action. They did not object to trade but would not tolerate trade missions in their country. They have seen what happens elsewhere and don't like it.

Galsworthy was enthusiastic about the Nigerians. He repeated again and again that he loved them, and so would I. It was a great country with a great future. They were intelligent and hard working, and had a sufficient resource base. We talked about Fenton's effort to establish a capital market by developing Treasury bills of different maturities. And there are attempts to establish a stock market. A tremendous amount of African private capital formation is going on in construction. The road from the airport, formerly through the bush, now has African housing along it. They build, buy and sell and know its value.

Galsworthy like everyone else disagrees with Bauer on marketing boards, thinks they did a good job. He took me for lunch at the Oxford and Cambridge Club...

July 18, 1960 (Ikoyi-Lagos, Nigeria)

So this is Nigeria. I am somewhat tired despite sleeping most of the day after arriving...

July 16 (London). In the morning I talked to E.F. Jackson. So far no particular help in finding a replacement or anything else. But at least I know who worked with Jackson on the national accounts, a man by the name of Okigbo.

...Took off finally at about 7:00 PM...I sat beside a retired Lt. Col. Bull, British Army, who had built bridges all over the world and was doing it now in Nigeria. After a few cracks about Americans coming in when money was to be made, after the British had opened up the country by giving their lives – cracks which were not malicious – we got on fine. He talked interestingly and enthusiastically about Nigeria's future, offered to introduce me in the Club.

The Britishers here have no racial prejudices whatsoever. Clubs, residential areas, everything is desegregated. I noticed again and again that every one who has been here fell in love with the place and the people...It was light when we landed at Kano, and the airport [see Photo No. 1] looked like any other – except for the vultures sitting on the roofs, waiting for God knows what. There were also quite a few American Army transport planes, probably bringing troops in into the Congo, but I don't know. I am quite sure that we don't have bases in Nigeria and that the transports were not permanently stationed here.

July 17. Kano is high, and it was quite cool. I was and am still wearing the suit with which I left America...Then we were off to Lagos, but we had another hour's delay while we were circling over Lagos to wait for the fog to dispel – this being the rainy season. You could see the coast line and the heavy surf.

Lagos airport is smaller than Kano's. Much to my surprise it not only didn't rain, but it was really very pleasant – cooler than in New York. I was told that it was both cooler and dryer than usual, that they had had very little rain this year and hoped it would stay that cool. I was met by Oduba, a Ministry of Information official who took charge of my immigration and luggage – though I noticed everyone was treated equally courteously and quickly. The officers were all Nigerian. I am told that few British officers are left, even in the army. Oduba also gave me a welcoming letter from Thompson, inviting me for a drink this evening (July 18). But I was too tired after the trip and went to bed. There are now a few minutes time to continue before I get fetched for the office.

The airport-Lagos drive is about 11–12 miles, paved highway, lots of cars, trucks, bicycles and people. Every car seems to be of a different make or year. The road is lined with new African housing, some shanty towns, but as there is no overcrowding it isn't depressing. There are palms and a few other trees and a lot of bush or brush, rather undistinguished. The soil is red, probably low iron content. You see no naked grown-ups but lots of naked children. Women carry heavy loads on their heads and as a result walk beautifully erect.

The parts of Lagos I have seen – which do not include the slums – are not unattractive. You enter Lagos over a long bridge. There are lots of shanty buildings but the new Government buildings are attractive. Almost all new building is cement bloc, painted with a kind of cement plaster, mostly colored.

We then entered Ikoyi, a residential suburb that is apparently the best part of town and contains mostly villas or large apartment blocs. It is not European, but mixed. I am put up in a Government house, and have a most attractive apartment, consisting of a living-dining room, study, dressing room, bedroom, bath and kitchen. The bedroom and study are air-conditioned. I have two servants, a cook and washerman...

As I said, it is reasonably cool. The windows in the non-air-conditioned rooms are open day and night and there are no screens, but there seem to be few flies or mosquitoes. Lots of big lizards outside, some in color which behave pretty much as our squirrels do...I slept until 6:00 PM. At 7:00 PM Thompson drove me around Ikoyi, to the lagoon – too dirty to swim in – but very attractive. Little mangrove swamp left on the island. All being rapidly developed for housing, all concrete.

Then to his house. He is a Permanent Secretary (PS), top of the top civil servants. It was not unpleasant, though warm. All his windows and doors were open, and there were lizards running up and down his wall which turned out to be geckos and which are supposed to eat bugs. Otherwise, nothing tropical about it.

Thompson has been in Nigeria for 27 years, first in the bush, now at headquarters. We talked a little of my job. He felt, as I hoped he would, that I should spend the first month talking with as many people in the Federal and Regional Governments and in private industry about their development plans and ideas. After a week or ten days in Lagos I should go to the Regions. After a month he hoped I could meet with the Joint Economic Committee and give them a proposal as to what I felt should be done and how I wanted to proceed. On the whole this is precisely how I wanted to proceed, except that I hoped to have all summer.

July 18. At 9:00 AM the car came and brought me to Thompson, who called in some assistants...I'll get a car of my own in a few days and also a Nigerian driver's license on the basis of my American license and an assurance that we have driver's exams. Actually I am not too eager to drive myself, the traffic is quite heavy and the driving rather bad...From the Ministry I went to the US Consulate, a modern building quite close to the center of town. Emmerson, the Consul General and a friend of Ed Mason's and Dave Bell's,[2] was in the Southern Cameroons, but the Consul, Dorros, a youngish man from North Western University, was in and we had a pleasant chat. From there I went to Weast, the Economic Officer, from California, who has been here over a year and knows his way around. Then I finally met [Don] Kingsley at the Ford Foundation, about 50–55, pleasant, and now I am home...

July 19, 1960

It continues to be cool, but everyone tells me (a) that this is the cool season anyway, and (b) that it is unusually cool and dry. It hasn't rained since I have arrived, and I am told that we have the usual dry spell of August a month early. After September it begins to build up and in February it is really unbearable. It will be impossible to write without having a blotting paper underneath the arm, and clothes get moldy in non-air-conditioned rooms.

July 18. Coming out of Thompson's office I had a nice encounter. As I was looking for my car, I noticed two Nigerians eyeing me. After a short while they came up to me and wanted to know where I got my suit – the blue dacron-cotton one – and how much it cost and where they could get it. I told them, giving the Harvard Coop address. The one introduced himself as a crown counsel which corresponds roughly to an assistant solicitor general, and he invited me to his wedding next Saturday. I may go if I can.

At 5:00 PM, Thompson in shorts and sneakers fetched me for a drive and a walk. I got into my shorts too, and off we went. The beach is protected by huge granite boulders to keep it from eroding. The breakers are about as on Fire Island on a mildly stormy day, real breakers not simply waves. The danger is a very strong undertow and tricky currents which frequently make diving through breakers dangerous. Thompson said that he himself took the danger seriously only after two narrow calls. There were people on the beach, but no one swam. Also there is of course no rescuing facility.

About 100 yds out was a stick, or so it looked, which is where the beach used to be 5 years ago. It was all that could be seen of a Belgian freighter that ran ashore in a fog. The beach is in part being built up by sand being pumped in. People go swimming in a bay protected by moles on both sides. On the beach the usual urchins offered to watch your car "good," but they have not yet taken to damage it when you tell them firmly "no thanks."

From the beach, and after a brief walk, I was taken through Lagos to the harbor, all of it artificially built up. Everything is completely flat and is reclaimed land from the swamps. There is very little mangrove swamp left anywhere in Lagos and so far I have noticed remarkably few mosquitoes – but I am told this is Lagos and not Nigeria, and it is the cool season. The reclaiming is done by pumping sand from the bay or the ocean into the swamp. There is a remarkable amount of building going on. Houses, apartment houses, offices everywhere, with gardens which gradually are being built up on the sand. The foundations of all these houses require special treatment: they are either piles or rafts. The power station with at present 25 MV (and 60 MV being installed now) is a huge building whose foundation is a raft in the sand used to fill in the swamp. Thompson said he shuddered to think what would happen if there were a tidal wave here as violent as the Chilean one.

I saw something of the slums, part of which are being cleared. But here as elsewhere slum clearance runs against sharply rising real estate prices and the long run prospects are not good. There are tin huts, and run down cement buildings, open air shops, and crowds of people on foot, on bicycles and in cars. But it seems an orderly and quiet crowd, and there is remarkably little noise I am told that in Lagos there is the usual urban unemployment as people stream in from the country but thus far I have seen no evidence of it.

Thompson and I talked about the Congo and American politics...On the Congo he thought the Belgians were beneath contempt in the way in which they had panicked. They should have hung on instead of giving the Congo its independence, arrest trouble makers and set about systematically preparing the country for independence by training people and giving them administrative independence gradually as fast as possible to make them learn their job. I couldn't agree more. About my question how all this affected Nigeria he thought that was extremely difficult to say. The Nigerians were a little smug about it because it couldn't happen here, on the other hand, being a Federation they could not move as fast as Ghana to send troops, and they were probably too much intrigued by their own national politics to be much interested in what happened outside their borders. (This could mean that after independence Nigeria may be less of a stabilizing factor in African affairs than we hoped.)

I am getting along fine with Thompson who is probably also relieved at what he got in me. Unfortunately, he is retiring in December of this year and I will have to get used to a new PS in the Ministry of Economic Development (MED) and quite a few other ministries. To anticipate a brief discussion we had this morning, he mentioned to me that the Prime Minister would get an economic advisor from the [World] Bank – which I knew – and he wanted to make quite clear to the Prime

Minister that the MED did not wish to build up a rival economic advisor; that I was part of the executive, actually working rather than advising, and not only working out a new development program but also building up a planning staff.

I assured him that I understood I was a Nigerian civil servant who with a specified job to do in a specified time, taking general directions from my superiors, rather than an academic who would do a research job as he pleased in his own good time. He said – I believe with more relief in his voice than he meant to show – that he was not worried about me but about the Prime Minister. I come back to this conversation later.

About 7:30 PM Whalley (pronounced Wally), the Senior Assistant Secretary (Economics) fetched me to his home...There I met his charming young wife, active in the choir – you have to be active here because you depend on the entertainment you provide yourself – daughter of a musician. Both are around thirty, he perhaps over, she below. After dinner with wine served by Africans whom she had trained – this is again a major activity of wives here, to teach the Nigerians how to do things in the European manner, from hygiene to sewing – I was taken to the Ikoyi Club where an evening of Scots dancing was on the program. The house in which the Whalleys live seemed spacious; all windows and doors were open to the breeze and there were the geckos on the wall...

The Ikoyi Club reminded me a little of a small edition of the hotel in Yellowstone Park, but there are nicer wings, a bar, and I am told, very pleasant air-conditioned rooms with private bath. I met a few people, with one of whom, a Scott named Simpson, I will have professional contact. He is a statistician in the Ministry of Health. He told me that Lagos was growing at the rate of 4% per year – which means a lot – that the country was growing as a whole at 2% as far as anyone knew.

It seems that the dearth of statistics is a handicap and a barrier into which all planning and everything else runs quickly, and one of my tasks will be to set up some improved organization together with the Department of Statistics. Simpson also said death rates in age groups below five years were appallingly high – 20%-50% – the chief causes being pneumonia, diarrhea and a third disease I can't remember. He also wanted to know whether I had had polio shots and was relieved that I said yes. He believes that out here they are more important than yellow fever, but added he couldn't convince many people of it. After a few jabs at me as an American, without real spite and which I parried with sufficient humor, I think, we parted amiably...

July 19. This morning my first stop was the CMS Bookshop, CMS standing for Church Missionary Society, to buy Sir Alan Burns, History of Nigeria. Then off to the Ministry where I got some more documents. I worked in the Minister's office (he was absent) and at 11:00 AM Thompson took me to see Fenton, the CBN Governor. Like all central banks the Bank was plush, trying by the very stone in which they are built to give the feeling of Sound Money. The offices are air-conditioned, and the Governor's office was also sound-proofed. The visit was short since I had little to ask at this stage. Thompson led off by explaining that I was going to see people in Lagos and then in the regional capitals; he expected me to report and to come up with a first plan of procedure by the end of August at the meetings of the National Economic Council, which Fenton suggested should meet in Kaduna, the Northern capital, where it had not yet met.

Then Fenton gave me a real shock by suggesting that I might have a rough plan worked out by March 1961! I pointed out that this was physically not possible, that I just had got here; that I had to be back by September to teach, that I wouldn't be back in Lagos until February, and that March 1961 was simply out of the question; moreover Thompson's letter had specified March 1962. Thompson fortunately came to my aid and told me later that Fenton had given him a jolt also. Apparently Fenton had in mind that the first budget of an independent Nigeria should already reflect the new program, but this simply will have to await the second budget. Fenton stressed that while things like monetary policy could be done, they had to be done simply since the country was primitive – Lagos was not Nigeria – the statistics were poor, as I would find in my work. He warned me, as if I needed the warning, not to do too sophisticated a plan.

We talked briefly about the capital market which he had started to create, by selling short-term Treasury bills. A real stock market was still a long way off, but he hoped to have a dozen or so good stocks on the market which people could buy with reasonable security, and thus gradually get into the habit of investing. Most purchasers would, of course, be institutions rather than individuals, but they would include not only expatriate firms or banks with some loose cash, but also financial intermediaries in which the small man (whose annual cash income might be £25 a year and who could therefore hardly be counted upon to invest in stock) actually saved…

Thompson is writing letters to all the other PSs, and on Monday I will start calling for appointments. He then spoke of his recruitment woes, which fall into two classes. First, expatriates or technical assistance costs a lot more. Even if the money is found outside the budget, as in my case, it raises problems except with the top echelon, because the locals don't like the idea that someone doing the same work they do gets paid twice to three times as much.

If you raise their salaries this then gets reflated down the line to the lowest point, because the salary scheme of the British civil service is a lot more rigid than ours. The UN is trying to build up an international civil service, but this does not avoid the problem altogether. Its salaries are higher and recruitment problems are made difficult if a man can join the UN's OPEX and be sent to, say, Nigeria, at a higher salary than if he worked for the Nigerian Government directly.

The second problem is that while a country gets flooded with offers of technical aid, almost none of the offers include actual work but always advisors. While Thompson is happy to get increased know-how, frequently his problem is to put into use the know-how he's got already. He was therefore relieved that I felt myself not so much as an advisor, but as an executive officer who would do things rather than advise on how they should be done.

Both Fenton and Thompson pointed out that, with Independence, things were bound to change more than the Nigerians had yet realized. They have their own money now, for example, and it is up to them to make their own monetary and fiscal policy. But it was just as well not to trumpet that fact over the rooftops because the country had to get used to it gradually.

Thompson finally said he didn't want me to misunderstand things. He was always open to suggestions and criticism, and I should feel free to come any time I felt like it – he undoubtedly meant it – but for the time being he would prefer if I made such comments orally rather than in writing. There would, however, be occasions when my comments as a professional economist would be looked for and expected.

I raised two issues which worry me: the prospective steel industry and the prospective River Niger dam project. The latter seems to be more or less decided upon; in fact in the budget speech for 1960–61, Chief Festus Sam Okotie-Eboh, who seems to be everybody's friend and a really efficient Minister of Finance, described the Niger Dam project as the keystone for 1962–67. If so, this may swallow practically all capital resources, thus prejudging the plan I am to come up with. Moreover, the budget speech made no mention of recent discoveries of sizable natural gas deposits which could generate electricity at less cost than the prospective dam. On the other hand, the dam project is conceived as an integrated river basin development of electricity, navigation and irrigation.

Thompson said that the prospective electricity rates would subsidize navigation and irrigation rather than the other way round; that the dam would be located in the heart of Nigeria, equidistant from South and (backward) North, thus offering the prospect of equalizing their economic prospects. Moreover investigations showed the project to be feasible and economic. Anyway, I fetched today the 1,000 page report of Nedeco (Netherlands Engineering Consultants) and two shorter volumes of feasibility reports which I have to glance at at least by this weekend. With air-conditioning and not too many other distractions, that ought to be possible.

As regards steel, there also seem to be feasible solutions. Thompson thought one should have started with a re-rolling mill using scrap, but that wasn't grand enough. I'll get the basic studies for that sooner or later. But poor as the country was, its standard was rising rapidly and it was felt that the domestic market would support such an industry.

Still, while there is a really impressive list of manufacturing plants, total manufacturing employment, at perhaps 30,000, is infinitesimal and is bound to remain so for any foreseeable future...

July 21, 1960

July 20. Buffet supper at Kingsley's. Among the guests: Parsons, a former NY Herald Tribune correspondent now writing training manuals in Nigeria...; Dan Nylon, whom I knew from the bombing survey and who is here as part of a management training program; Haynes, an American Negro, public administration expert formerly with the UN in Geneva; Professor Smith from Aberdeen, who is to do an economic survey of the Eastern Region. Most except Smith were old Nigeria hands (at least compared to me). The talk was good, mostly general. Why do we want to develop Nigeria? Aren't they happier without us? Can you get development without causing social and personal tension, and so on. Typical intellectual talk, with Kingsley enjoying baiting his guests, and us giving back as well as we could.

I enjoyed it most when Kingsley brought out some sculptures, some old, some new, and when he and Nylon talked about the open country: the incredible variety of customs and languages from village to village; the inability of neighboring villages to understand each other's language; the fact that one village put in a cement water tank to improve its water supply without turning a hair while the neighboring village will resist it, and continue to drink contaminated water from the ground because its gods have forbidden it to use a cement tank which would make the water supply dry up; the existence of villages which have sculptures and bronze casters in one region making as fine pieces as the old ones; the fact that before long Hausa traders would come around and try to sell me masks and sculptures, and one generally pays a fourth to a third of what they ask; the burying habits with old people being buried in the compound, sometimes in the wall (at least the men, while women are buried outside), while dead children of less than three months of age are thrown to the dogs to eat, apparently because they were not really ever alive but were really ghosts which played a trick on the parents; that the society of some of the Yoruba tribes (with the accent on Yoruba) is very tightly knit and authoritarian, hell for young people but secure and friendly for old ones; and much of the kind which I was unable to keep in mind. Interesting though it was, there was no point of reference as yet, no personal experience to which I could relate it.

I was also told of the high degree of corruption and enrichment by local robber barons. Europeans are not allowed to own land. Land in Lagos, as I wrote, is to a large extent man-made by dredging the lagoon, hence Government property. Access to the land is therefore a matter of political influence. You then start drawing building plans, and houses which in the US would cost perhaps £20,000, cost here £60,000 what with graft, inefficiency of labor and fabulous profits. Once plans are ready, the house is rented before it is built, for five years' advance rent. The Ford Foundation pays £10,000 cash down, which is immediately used to buy more land and continue the process. With rapid economic expansion in Lagos no one's fingers have been burned yet. In fact the richest contractors are now Sir something or other, and in retrospect a considerable capital accumulation is taking place. Unfortunately much of the profits is deposited in Switzerland, and one of the problems will be to get Nigerians to invest their money at home.

July 21. This morning visited Joel Bernstein, head of the local ICA[3] mission, who invited me Friday evening to meet the Minister of Education and Dean Taggart from Michigan State. I had a lengthy talk with him about my problem and he described several ICA programs, but also their restrictions: they can invest only in technical aid, i.e., in people, and have trouble getting money for "bricks and mortar." The Michigan State people are here to help establish a new university in the Eastern Region. The problem with University College Ibadan (UCI) is that, while it is first-rate and has University of London standards, it out-oxfords Oxford.

Economics is a rather new subject and, in the allocation of funds, very low on the totem pole. More technical fields are even lower. Emphasis is on educating the whole man, liberal arts, all of which is fine and needs to be continued. On the other hand Ibadan has not admitted any day students, every one had to be resident, every one had a room of his own and servants exactly as in Oxford and Cambridge, and until Dike[4] came they taught English and European history but frowned on research in African history. Dike actually left in disgust, taught at Northwestern for a while and now has come back to be the new principal.

Everyone agrees that the English-type training is good for the top people, even though perhaps two people could share a room, but there is also room for lower-level and particularly more technical education, and Ibadan certainly should use day students; and less elegant housing might lead to less alienation of students from their environment.

Bernstein mentioned his dream of a research institute located in Nigeria – Lagos or Ibadan – which would serve all of West Africa. I brought up Michigan's new Center for Development Research and our interest in establishing contact with such an institute, with students and junior faculty going both ways and vigorous social research, particularly in economics. Bernstein thought he would be interested in a proposal from the University of Michigan, but it may be too early to do something about it. Certainly I can't do anything right now, being too busy with other things.

...I then went home to meet my guest, Williams, permanent secretary of finance, Eastern Region (ER). He is in his forties, I should guess, was in Pakistan where he knew the Mason group;[5] he also knew Philip Chantler. Having common friends and acquaintances helps a good deal, I find. Williams told me the ER has yet to work out a systematic regional plan. Okigbo, who worked with Jackson on the national accounts, will run the planning section in the new development ministry. In the past, they simply added up individual projects which had historically grown, and call this their program. He understands my assignment to work out feasible planning targets, ensure consistency and show their implications.

Financing problems will be marginal as far as I am concerned, and such policy questions as how to stimulate the growth of private investment and how to mobilize more savings will probably be outside my frame of reference. Actually I have to check back with Thompson on this, because I don't see how I can keep things quite so separate. But it is clear that basic policy questions are not within my frame of reference, though Williams told me that, before I left, everyone would be picking my brains.

He also warned me to be prepared for constant frustrations. Data simply do not exist; people won't always do what you ask them and certainly not on time; and worst of all is not so much that any advice you may give will be ignored, but that you will be accused of giving bad advice, or of being deliberately misleading. He thought, though, that I would not have to suffer much from this last problem, which afflicted more the permanent civil service...

July 21, 1960

July 20. At 8:00 Col. "Tom" Bull...came to fetch me to dinner in a dinner club, with a view of Lagos...The hours here are quite late. No one has supper before 8:15 PM and the customary hour seems to be 9:30 PM. Yet people are in their offices by 8:00 or 8:30 AM. I am already exhausted by this life, and I am glad that tonight I will neither entertain nor be entertained.

Talk was mostly small, though there were some local tidbits. Even in Lagos there is still apparently a great deal of superstition, and though witchdoctors are driven out, many people prefer to go to the Juju man rather than a doctor. There is no more crime here than in any other urban aggregation, but there are assaults on white women and even young girls because the Juju men believe this to be the only safe method of curing syphilis. Bull said that he and his wife (who is still in England) never leave their young daughter with their stewards, but either stay at home, or get baby sitters or a nanny. In spite of such things and some obvious inefficiencies, everyone is quite enthusiastic about the country.

July 21. Spent first a few minutes with Thompson, who had written the various PSs except Defense, although the latter would also want his slice of development funds. We talked about my terms of reference, and I asked about the detail to which I was expected to go. Suppose I found that the rate of savings should be stepped up to 15% of GNP, was it or was it not incumbent on me to say how I thought this could be done? Or would this be considered a policy question outside my frame of reference? He thought this was precisely the kind of question which ought to be raised with the Joint Economic Committee and he hoped I would have a document which could be circulated for discussion at the August meeting. He would be ready to discuss it with me informally beforehand. All of which suits me fine except that everything is a great deal faster than I thought it would be.

...There is trouble with housing for Lyle Hansen[6] if and when he comes. It is just impossible to get a house before Independence. We talked with Kingsley, who thought the Foundation could do something about a car, but housing for a non-governmental agency was simply too difficult. There are 3–bedroom apartments available in a new apartment bloc, with an annual rent of £800, which for Lagos is apparently reasonable, but one would have to pay five years' rent in advance, which neither the Government nor Ford were prepared to do!

We also discussed medical services, which used to be adequate to good, but have been steadily deteriorating with Nigerianization. Not that Nigerian doctors and nurses aren't good, but the place is overcrowded. All Government officials are entitled to free services for their families. But while Europeans are content with one wife and three children, the African is apt to have ten wives and 60 children.

The Ford Foundation hasn't yet gotten itself listed in the phone book and Kingsley, who is lucky to have a private phone, can't get it listed under his name, instead it is listed under the name of the contractor who built the place, gets the bills, pays them, and sends another bill to Kingsley, who pays him and writes a letter to the phone company hopefully waiting for action. These are apparently the minor frustrations of living in Lagos.

After Kingsley, Sellwood [the Foundation's chief administrative officer] took me to the Lagos Town Council, where I got my Nigerian driver's license for 10/-. It was all friendly and relatively quick, and done on the basis of my Michigan license, after assuring the examining officer, Forbes, that the State of Michigan not only required a test, but even imposed driver education. Forbes said a proper driving school would make a mint, Nigerian drivers are fierce because the people running the driving schools never learned it themselves, etc. I must say, driving is fierce here, making Brussels quite harmless by comparison.

And now to work for the afternoon and evening. My desk is piled high.

July 22, 1960

July 21. After I had worked for about an hour,...Jan Stewart from Edinburgh and another young man, an assistant of Eli Devon in Manchester, came over for a drink...Their visit was quite important to me. The two are surveying the domestic market for foodstuffs, financed by the US Department of Agriculture. Virtually nothing is known about this, as I also found out today at the Department of

Statistics. They are trying to work out sample surveys. Both are off to the Northern Region today after spending some time in Ibadan...

I began to discuss one idea I had about increasing the saving and capital market habit of cocoa farmers and also making the price received by them closer to the world price without actually reducing the amount of money withheld by the Marketing Board. I thought that the marketing board might pay, as before, say 50% of the world price in cash but then pay each farmer over and above the cash a certain amount in 10-year debentures at the going interest rate. These debentures could be held to maturity or sold on the market, but not discounted at banks. Thus if farmers wanted to consume and/or invest more, they could sell to private persons who would thereby have to restrict their consumption.

In order to prevent increased imports the big traders would probably not be allowed to use these debentures as collateral for loans nor would they be allowed to buy them. They would therefore be something like series E bonds. The immediate effect, until they became due, would be to leave as much cash with the Marketing Board as before, but the Board would, of course, allow for a contingent reserve. One might decide to permit rediscounting at variable rates. One advantage I can see is that world and domestic prices would converge, and thus cocoa production might be more influenced by world prices – if this is desirable. It would give increased choice to the cocoa farmers, also desirable. Stewart thought it made sense, and couldn't see any drawbacks. I will now try it out on Thompson when we go for our walk.

I am also trying to learn about federal finances. Although the Federation collects export taxes, the proceeds revert to the Regions of origin. This means the Federal Government has only a mild interest in world cocoa price movements. It has borrowed some of the marketing boards' reserves, but Thompson said the Regions want increasingly to retain these for local investment. All of this is important for me in that it relates to projections of Federal income for 1962–67. Only that part is relevant which the Federal Government retains or can borrow at home or abroad. A commission has reported on the problem, and its suggestions have been substantially adopted. I have to study the constitution.

Stewart also spoke of a struggle between the Departments of Agriculture and Forestry about forest reserves. The Forestry people want to keep large reserves despite ignorance of the demand for forest products. I am told that the Sapele plywood mill is a growing and profitable concern, but the consumption of firewood is likely to fall with increasing use of oil. (In Lagos we cook with electricity; some people have bottled gas on the grounds that during the hot season, the electricity goes off at least once a week.) Apparently the struggle between Forestry and Agriculture proceeds largely without reference to economic factors.

July 22. Spent the first two hours at the Statistical Department with its acting head, Adebayo. My main interest was estimates of capital formation and other production statistics. Data on domestically consumed agricultural produce – e.g. oil palm kernels – are virtually non-existent. Even with the major export crops, only marketing board purchases are known. As regards domestic trade, movements by truck or by canoe on inland waterways are known to be substantial, but no estimates of volume exist. Canoes are licensed but it is not known what they carry, where to, or how much. Some sampling initiatives are in progress. A new population census is being prepared, and the first Statistical Yearbook will appear in about two weeks, containing about 140 tables. I picked up documents for the University [of Michigan] that will also be useful here.

There is universal free primary education in the Western and Eastern Regions, but it is not yet compulsory. It is estimated that about 70% of the children now go to school in these two regions, but much less in the North which, while the largest region, is also the most backward.

From there I went to Thompson's office. I am happy to say that he and I get along very well indeed, and I hope this will also be true for his successor when I return. We made up a schedule for the rest of my stay, and it will be rough. Tentatively, I will be in Lagos next week, seeing all the PSs, who should put me in touch with their economic and planning officers to learn about their forward planning. As there are 14 ministries, including important ones like Commerce and Industry, Mining, Transportation, Labor, etc., it will be a hectic week.

Around Aug. 1 I will drive to Ibadan for a week, probably staying at the University. Then over the weekend by train to Kaduna, capital of the Northern Region, for about three days. Then by train to Enugu, the Eastern Region capital, also for three days. Then back to Lagos by air. This will give me a week to work up a report for the Joint Economic Committee, which is to meet with me for final direction around August 31. After that I may or may not sit with the National Planning Committee, which meets Sept. 6 in Kaduna, a date which has been postponed by two weeks because of the forthcoming Western Region election. (The elections fill all the papers here. The Action Group, which runs the Western Region, is in opposition, the Federal Government being run by an alliance of the Northern and Eastern Regions.) God knows when I will be able to do all the reading I must do.

While discussing the trip and individual ministries' responsibilities, Thompson took me aside to explain the politics as well as economics of the river development. The major purpose of the river Niger dams is navigation – the dams on the Benue are still in the distant future. The navigation is essentially internal. No ocean steamers will be able to go up the rivers in the foreseeable future, and Port Harcourt will remain a rail head. The Northern Region (NR) has however always felt shut off from the sea, and the dams to improve year-round navigation of the Niger are important to increase their contact with the South.

The Benue is completely within the NR, but the Niger is in part a border river so it is not within the Western Region – regional jealousies are strong, and the Northerners fear somehow that the Westerners might shut them out from trade in the South. Since freedom of navigation is guaranteed by international treaty, this is reassuring to the Northerners. The river project thus assumes a crucial political significance in holding the Federation together, and seems to be seen in this light by the Prime Minister, who is a Northerner.

The second problem is that the Niger Delta is silting up, and at present the only feasible entrance is the Escravos bar, where the River Benin enters the Bight of Benin. This also is rapidly silting up and a contract is now let to build a huge mole to keep the bar open and dredge the entrance. At present, no fully loaded ships can enter. Actually the hinterland (Sapele, Warri on the map) is probably the most densely settled area in Africa south of the Sahara and it would get an enormous boost. Old ports which have silted up would be revived, and trade is expected to increase rapidly. The port of Port Harcourt has doubled its capacity already, and

Lagos also appears a reasonably busy port with three or four big steamers going and coming all the time – there is a big German freighter in port right now.

July 23, 1960

July 22 (continued). The walk on the beach was lovely. The beach is and is not like Fire Island. The surf is about the same. Where you drive to the beach over a road which is all filled-in mangrove swamp, there are lots of huts, which have mostly to do with revival meetings of a sect called The Seraphim and Cherubim, for whom meeting at the sea shore seems to be important. There were people lying on the sand in the sun, both black and white. We walked without hats, barefoot in the sand. The differences are also many. First, there are the palms, mostly coconuts; then there are huge cacti one has to watch out for; most startling is perhaps the almost complete absence of shells. Tropical waters around West Africa don't seem to have much life of this kind.

We walked about half an hour along the beach to a fishing village which consisted mostly of Ghanaians. Thompson said that while there were quite a few Nigerians in Ghana, the reverse was rather rare, Nigerians being on the whole very much more enterprising. Along the beach there were fishing canoes, all made of hollowed out trunks. They are actually good-sized, can hold about 6 or 7 men I would say and seem to be quite heavy. Many of them were decorated with stylized carvings and painted on top.

There was also a new fence against erosion of the beach which partly seems to have been made by bulldozers, but partly by the people themselves with coconut stems and some leaves. I took some pictures of the fishing village. I tried to get a picture of some very peculiarly looking pigs, but they got scared. The nets were spread out and the men were fixing them. No women were in sight, but they were preparing meals.

We also watched a boat come in and I wished I had the movie camera, because it was fascinating to see how they rode the heavy breakers, paddling like mad in step to stay on top, not quite making it on the first wave, but getting up on the second, and then jumping out and pivoting the boat around before the heavy undertow would suck it back. They get the heavy boat up on the beach by 2 men sitting on one end and the others turning the boat up; then alternating with the turners sitting and the sitters turning. [See Photo No. 2.]

I took pictures, which required paying a shilling in lieu of cigarettes to a head man who appeared from the village. At least I think he was someone special. He was older and colorfully dressed. Also he didn't seem to want to have his picture taken. The others posed, but I finally induced them to continue with their work. The catch were sole (which is supposed to be good), some variety of catfish and some shark. There were also some fish I did not recognize. One woman appeared to buy some of the fish.

A little further up was a coconut grove, and the lagoon came quite close to the ocean. The distance in the narrowest spot was perhaps 150 yards. Thompson said that the engineers were afraid that the sea might break through there which would alter the already dangerous currents in the harbor. I watched a fisherman work with his square net, which is first carefully folded, and then thrown out spreading over a surprisingly big area, then almost immediately withdrawn. The fisherman seems to look first where there is some fish. He wades in quite a bit. Then he strings up the fish he has caught, and folds the net again for the next operation.

Nobody swam, of course. Too dangerous.

Thompson has a wife and two children in the UK. This is quite the pattern here. The main reason is not health, which by now is quite under control with injections and generally increased knowledge of living in the tropics, but schooling after the age 11 or 12 is still too difficult here. The pattern is that families come here during UK school vacation.

At Bernstein's in the evening were the Education Advisor to the Federal Government, a Britisher named Bunting, with his wife; Enuna (?) and wife, President of the Nigerian teachers union, a heavy-set man around 50 or so; Koteen of ICA, who supervises African and European ICA projects, and Mr. and Mrs. Adams of the ICA staff...

Koteen urged that Michigan apply for an ICA contract to work with Ibadan and the Nigerian Institute of Social and Economic Research (NISER), and I didn't need much pushing, because I thought of this myself. However, I pointed out it was a matter for the Department to decide, I was sure our new Center for Development Research would be interested but I wanted to wait until after my visit to Ibadan in two weeks. I found the talk interesting and fruitful, particularly as both Bernstein and Koteen really wanted the kind of thing that we in Michigan would want to do: some honest-to-goodness operational research into economic development...

Monday at 10:00 AM I'll meet my ministers. We talked mainly of the need to pool questions with the Stanford people who are about to arrive for the transport survey. After all, the various ministries would have a right to be annoyed if they got asked the same questions over and over again...

I get along very well with Thompson whom I like a great deal. He also raises pretty much the same questions I have in mind which at this stage are admittedly rather simple. Thus he wondered whether I thought that in the course of my work the Economic Survey couldn't be brought up to date, which I had also thought of; and whether it could not be set up on an annual basis much like the Ghanaian Annual Report, a thought that had also occurred to me.

July 23. Today is the first day I didn't go out in the evening. I got quite a bit of reading done, mainly about the proposed Niger-Kaduna River dam project, which seems more feasible and less costly than I imagined it would be. I walked over to the Ikoyi Hotel, which is about 10 minutes away, to get the air edition of yesterday's London Times, so I am not quite out of touch with the world. The Nigerian papers, which I will send you, are almost completely engrossed with their own affairs, specifically the forthcoming elections in the Western Region.

I also bought from a Hausa trader a boat with 5 bronze sculptures. Not particularly good, but rather fun, and a good present for someone. I traded as advised to do. He started with £5, I offered £1, he came down to £4, I offered £1:10/-, and we settled on £2. It now stands before me and is rather enjoyable. He then wanted to sell me a little bronze elephant for 10/- and came down to 10/- for the elephant plus two ducks, but I resisted and since even the £2 was more than he hoped for, he left me alone, after assuring me that he, Youssouf, was a pure Hausa man, and his word was good. Incidentally he also had a kind of mobile, which I am sure is not exactly traditional. The sculpture comes from Kano, he said.

When I leave here in '62 I am sure Lagos will look quite different again. And it is fascinating.

July 25, 1960

July 24. I had my first impression of the countryside. The Government let me have the car and driver for the day. I just paid the gas, and gave the driver a generous tip which has made him quite devoted to me. The destination was a swimming pool in a town called Ijebu-Ode (pronounced Djebuode) about 71 miles from Lagos. If it is on the map you follow the road from Lagos to Ibadan to Shagamu, then turn East to Ikene and Ijebu-Ode. The swimming pool was actually 6 miles south from there. The pool was a dammed brook, the only one in the South safe for swimming. I was told it was icy, but actually it is warm as Silver Lake late in July. It was a lovely spot, with banana trees, coconut trees, hibiscus, and other odd tropical plants around it. In the sun it was very hot, but in the shade pleasant. These days one notices the tropics. As long as you drive or don't have much exercise it is reasonably cool – abnormally so this year. Once you walk or do any exercise it gets to be hot and clammy.

On the way I stopped a lot to take pictures. None are likely to be particularly picturesque. The landscape just isn't. First you go through the rain forest, but actually there are only few patches of it left. Most of it has been cleared. The patches are about 20 miles north of Lagos, where the new road to Ibadan has been built through the swamp. I was told that they had considerable trouble with the road. When they had thought they had filled in the swamp, it turned out that the road rested on floating vegetable matter, and one day a whole section simply turned over and disappeared in the swamp, blacktop, road equipment and all. Now this problem seems licked. At least the road has remained there for some time. Driving though is hazardous. About 40 miles N. of Lagos essentially only the center of the road which winds quite a bit through slightly rolling country is paved, and every time you meet a car both have to get off the pavement. In the dry season this is OK, but in rainy seasons which have more rain than this year, it is apt to mean a very soft shoulder. Incidentally rainfall varies between 70 and 110 inches, and is this year at the lower limit.

The villages are nothing spectacular. Mud huts, all red, most with corrugated iron roofs, fairly far apart so that you don't get a feeling of crowding or slums. Cooking and living is done outside the house. Cooking on little wood fires, although I saw people carrying gasoline camp stoves like ours on their heads. Shady places with sticks and palm leaves are set up outside and people were sitting there. It being Sunday, there was little work. There were many individual huts and small settlements in the forest or fields, in some clearings. In the larger towns there were substantial villas of cement, virtually all of them belonging to Africans. An astonishing number of Mercedes and Opel Rekords were driven by Nigerians, or stood in front of mud huts and villas. And in Ijebu-Ode which recently got electricity there were even air-conditioners on the villas. On some of the rivers, which I think really are part of the River Ogun delta, there were a few romantic looking villages. And in Shagamu, a town of 25–30,000 I should think, I ran into the political campaign. A caravan of cars came, and in no time at all, there were hundreds of people greeting it, discussing, all rather friendly. (It isn't always, I am told.) They grinned when I took pictures and for a change didn't want a shilling for being taken.

We stopped at one very small settlement which I wanted to photograph. I bought cigarettes for the driver at the cost of 2/3, which is 30 cents, rather expensive for even the driver who makes £7 a month. No wonder in the country cigarettes are traded by the piece, and the little trader must have had quite some capital invested. It took a visit through a lot of people before the change to 3/- could be produced, and another shilling could be changed into pence, so that I would have money for kids as "dash" for being photographed.

What was striking was the meticulous orderliness of the stand. You will see it on the picture, which I sent off today to be developed and which will be sent home directly. There were small plates with nails, cigarettes, everything, an astonishing variety of things all in unbelievably small quantities. Actually this seemed to be a rather well-to-do retailer. I have seen in almost every settlement a table like this, frequently less than a fourth the size.

Agriculture. It certainly looks different from what we are used to. You won't see a field by Western standards, though you quickly learn to see that in fact it is all cultivated or fallow land. Actually the biggest need here is for agricultural research, and even more at this stage for some centralization of the hard-won knowledge of what to do with the soil. As it is, it can be used for two years and must then lie fallow for five. A workable crop rotation which would allow the soil to be used for many years in succession is apparently as yet unknown. But commercial fertilizers are known to work. Because cattle can't be kept as long as the tsetse fly is not controlled, there is insufficient manure. There were quite a few goats, which are immune to sleeping sickness, very few chickens which everywhere are susceptible to disease, and here even more so. And I saw a single solitary duck. No pig was in sight, though I saw two at the Ghanaian fishing village.

The fallow fields make the place look like a wilderness. But even the cultivated part looks different. This is essentially cocoa country. All cocoa trees are planted, but they must have shade when they are young, so other trees are left or planted. In between are bananas, particularly around settlements, and coconut trees. Bananas and coconuts have no particular season but ripen all year long. There are oil palms, and wine palms, and kolanut trees. The basket which my driver holds in the picture of the little stand had kola nuts in it. I resisted buying one, though. In between are timber trees, rain trees which give shade, and others which the driver didn't know. The vegetables were mostly yams, but there were quite a few beans, corn, and some tomatoes, all usually grown intermixed.

I sat beside the driver – which I don't do during the week when I am driving in style – and asked him to explain everything to me. Afterwards I gave him 5/- which moved him to deep thanks, and he was very friendly and open. Today he asked whether I could get him a book on economics, particularly economic development. He was interested. I will try to think of one suitable for an intelligent but essentially untrained man. He is Catholic, has four children, 2, 4, 6 and 8 years, has been driving for 17 years and is a mechanic. He is an Ibo.

After the picnic and before returning home, I went to the town of Epe, south of Ijebu-Ode, a sleepy lagoon port, which 100 years ago was as big as Lagos! This was the first reasonably picturesque spot I have seen here. There are native boat yards, an old-fashioned government steamer, huts and houses built against the hillside...

All of this is in the Western Region, comparatively rich – witness the many cars – with cocoa as the main crop, very profitable. I was impressed by the great number of schools – mission, local authority, primary, secondary, boys, girls, coeducational – all well kept and well designed, most of them a series of one story buildings built around a football field, surrounded by what looks like wilderness but is in fact cocoa, and occasionally rubber trees. The Western Region is the only one that has kept free and fairly universal primary education. Everyone spoke recognizable English, though one has to watch out to understand it, and it sometimes approaches pidgin English. This is true even for small kids. A very impressive achievement.

In the Eastern Region, free education had to be abandoned when it turned out there were a lot more kids than anyone thought possible. The annual tuition is even now only £1–2, I am told. Even so, when the ER, which is much poorer, and which has to rely on oil palms rather than cocoa, abolished free primary schools, there were serious riots and bloodshed by irate mothers. The story is that when the British police commissioner came back from one tour, he was held up in one town by lots of women with big hatchets – a kind of straight instrument used to clear the bush, stuck his head out of the car and inquired, "Were you waiting for me?" and got the cheerful answer, "Oh no, sir, we are waiting for the minister!"

In the evening I entertained Thompson for dinner...We discussed the fact which has just hit me with brutal force, that it will be extremely difficult to find money for the [Federal Government's] second Economic Program, hence development of an integrated program for the Federation and the Regions is essential. The reason is quite simple. When the Federation was set up, a lot of money was accumulated from the profits of cocoa and palmoil, and the budget produced annual surpluses simply because it took time before the development program could get going. Gradually it gained momentum, was extended from 1960 to 1962, and raised from £90 million to £175 million.

With the establishment of the Federation, however, export taxes go to the regions and are no longer available to the Federal Government. In the future the regions demand that they rather than the Federal Government should be able to borrow from their marketing boards. This leaves the Federal Government with a small internal capital market, which has just been started with a few Treasury bills, and external borrowing. A lot of external borrowing has already been done, the biggest being a [World Bank] loan of £10 million for the construction of the so-called Bornu extension of the Nigerian railroad. (On the map in the NE part of the country, from about Jos in the Center to Maiduguri near Lake Chad.)

Thus in the past the problem with the investment program was essentially the simple one – Thompson used the word 'simple' – of finding out what everyone planned to do, cutting it back a little, and summing it. My task will be to establish hard priorities, because it will be impossible to do even a fraction of what people want to do.

If you think I have been busy, this has been nothing yet. The tempo is increasing, and I am slightly worried...My itinerary: Aug. 1–5 Ibadan; leave Ibadan by train on Sat., Aug. 6 at 5:45 PM for Kaduna, arrive Kaduna 12:15 PM Aug. 7, presumably hot and dirty plus experience of Nigerian railroads. Leave Kaduna on Aug. 9 for Kano.

Leave Kano by air on Aug. 11 for Enugu, return to Lagos by air on Aug. 16. Every day filled with interviews and reading.

This week I am trying to see as many Permanent Secretaries as possible, and then read, read. Today I was royally received in the Ministry of Transportation and Aviation, leading to further appointments with the Ports Authority and the Railway Corporation tomorrow and Thursday afternoon. Inland Waterways have to wait until I can get to Lokoja (on the confluence of the Niger and the Benue) – if I can squeeze it in...

July 25. To the Consulate at 3:00 PM to meet Emmerson, who invited me to a black-tie dinner Wednesday evening to meet Senator Hartke from Indiana. Emmerson was very nice, particularly since he had had a letter from Dave Bell about me, but I think he would have been nice anyway, since he thinks what I am doing is very important from the American standpoint. He like everyone else is enthusiastic about the Nigerians, their future and their importance in Africa and the world...

I am beginning to like my Northern boat with its figures a lot. It is primitive, particularly the hands and faces, but it is really a nice piece. Thompson said it is a good typical example of Northern work. He also said that the mobiles – or rather things that look like the Swedish clockspiel – were also traditional and antedate Western influence...

July 27, 1960

I forgot to write last time that I was introduced to my minister, Alhaji Shegu Shagari, Shegu being a word for Sheik. He is a young Northerner with Arab rather than Negro features, intelligent, a former school teacher, as are many others in responsible positions. The visit was rather formal and stiff, but friendly and consisted mostly of an official welcome and thanks for my willingness to help the Nigerian people. I made appropriate comments, being for the first time not quite at ease, mainly because I didn't know what questions to ask.

Thompson later told me, as I had suspected, that the Ministry of [Economic] Development does not carry too much weight. Thompson himself was originally stationed in the Prime Minister's Office, where the work really belongs. He opposed the setting-up of a special ministry. It was set up mainly for political reasons. The government is a coalition of the NCNC and the NPC. In the allocation of ministries [among] the coalition partners, there were not enough ministries to divide, and so the Ministry of Economic Development was created.

Now the World Bank will appoint a top man as economic advisor to the Prime Minister. He will undoubtedly wish to have a staff, and eventually the planning will really be done in his office. However, what with research and technical aid, there is enough to do also for the Ministry of Economic Development...

July 27. Today started at 8:15 AM at the Ministry of Pensions, which has no capital expenditures, but is in charge of Nigerianization. The visit was extremely pleasant – the PS, a Scotsman, had studied in Kiel and told me about it (he didn't like it, too many Nazis already in 1935) – but there wasn't much there for me. At 10:00 AM I was in the Ministry of Commerce and Industry, meeting with the four top civil servants, whom I had to convince that I knew what I was doing by pointing out that I knew nothing about Nigeria. This seemed to reassure them considerably. If I had worked on Nigeria before, they argued, I would have lots of preconceived ideas, all of them wrong. Well, this is one way of putting one's ignorance to constructive use. Actually the talks were less productive than I had anticipated, but I am going back on August 18.

At 12:30 PM I met in Thompson's office with Turton-Hart from the Chamber of Commerce, to decide on the best way of approaching private business. The United Africa Company (Lever Brothers), Holt Company, and Shell Oil are easily approached, being the big fellows, but the smaller fellows are more difficult to talk to.

At 2:30 PM I had a very interesting interview with Pavell of the Investment Company of Nigeria. He used to be a manufacturer, is now a development banker. The ICN is a new venture, with some Government and mostly private, some Nigerian and mostly expatriate capital, designed to foster new industries. But the man made an excellent as well as a pleasant impression, and the work they are doing is also impressive. Actually Nigeria seems rife for a burst of activity by private business, and they seem to know it. I am curious how far I will modify my impression gained in Lagos, which is a bustling city quite beautifully situated, with lots of building going on. We will see next week in Ibadan.

I can't repeat too often that my reception has been very cordial. Actually Kingsley, whom I see off and on, told me there was some stickiness before I came. Some people didn't want the project, others wanted Britishers. Some wanted to approach ICA, others the UN, others Ford. Kingsley told me I had completely overcome the hesitations – of which I had not been aware or else I would have been more self-conscious. Anyway I am off on a good start, from both the Nigerian and Ford Foundation standpoints.

I have the most enviable assignment a man can have: developing an integrated plan for the most important African economy with the biggest and most hopeful future of any African nation. Moreover, there are political aspects to the work which are also fascinating and important. The plan must be designed so that the Regions, which are much more autonomous than I had realized, and the Federal Government, which not only has less power but also retains less revenue than I realized, will pull together and not against each other. There are strong autonomous, almost (but not quite) separatist tendencies in Nigeria, and I have a chance to help weld the territory into a nation. Even hardships are worth this opportunity. It is like peaceful army service. As long as I have an air-conditioned apartment, which will be essential in the humid season, I will get enough sleep.

Kingsley, as others, warned me, however, that the tropics are debilitating, even if I don't notice it yet, and that in the long run one simply cannot work as long and as fast and efficiently as at home. I certainly intend to take it easier when the pressure of this summer lets up.

July 28, 1960

It is now 10:00 PM...The party at the Consul General's was extremely nice. Senator Hartke wasn't there, but four members of his party were, including Ficher of the Senate Committee on Foreign Commerce, who knew all the answers to Nigeria's troubles after 24 hours in Lagos, and was amazed that I had 18 months to prepare a plan, when a Senate Committee had only three months for such a job – he didn't say with how many staff. Even though he had some sensible things to say, when he told me on parting that I'd better produce a good plan or else I would hear from him, I couldn't resist pointing out that I was a Nigerian, not American, civil servant.

Two prominent African businessmen were also present with their wives, but the American party, not unreasonably, monopolized them. Also present were Dorros, the Vice-consul, the Canadian representative, and some junior members of the Consular staff, one of whom happened to be from Flint and was also a University of Michigan graduate, Christensen by name...

This morning, 8:15 AM at the Ministry of Health, 9:30 AM at the Marketing Board, and 11:45 AM back again at Health to talk with the only medical statistician in Africa, except for his successor, the only African medical statistician. This visit was unusually pleasant – he is from the Campbell clan also.[7] Actually, almost every top civil servant seems to be a Scotsman.

He pointed out that in Nigeria you could find everything from the most sophisticated Westernized African, such as his successor, to cannibals on the Cameroon border, where census takers take the risk of being eaten, and officials are allowed in only with armed guards to prevent them from being killed with poisoned arrows. He also had the theory that cannibalism around here had its origin in a protein shortage, which could not be otherwise made good. I wonder whether he made this up, or whether it is a generally accepted theory. The protein deficiency actually is fierce here, and he showed me grim pictures, along with grim figures.

Tomorrow...I'll go to Col. Bull, whom I call Tom, who will show me the proposals for a £200,000 re-rolling mill they hope to erect in Lagos, based on scrap steel and electric furnaces from Italy. Apparently the Italians, who also lack coal, have developed the best electric furnaces at this stage, better than the Germans, and probably than the Americans...

Today the weather was more as I supposed the tropics to be. Not very hot, but it rained and was humid. You sweat climbing stairs, and I notice sometimes that I get a heartbeat if I try to walk too fast upstairs. Maybe I am just overfed...

July 31, 1960

July 29. To the Ministry of Works, where I got something of a shock when I was told that they wanted an £80 million road program. What with the dam of £53 million there isn't much money left, and yet they may be right...

Dinner party at Thompson's. Unfortunately all these parties start at 8:15 PM; one eats at 9:00 PM and it goes on until 1:00 AM. Present were Fenton, the Governor of the Central Bank, the permanent Secretary of Transport, the director of the railway, the two people from Stanford making a transportation survey, and myself. The evening was partly business – particularly for the Stanford people – partly social.

We talked about Nigeria's prospects, which depended largely on political stability and the inflow of capital and technicians. Afterwards the talk got on to the experiences of Thompson and others in the bush, the juju men in Afra and elsewhere, who had a sweet little racket. These people fomented trouble wherever they were, and when quarrels became nasty they would suggest that the juju could settle it. When the parties agreed, they would be led to a place in a gorge with a small river, which was curtained off and had to be approached through a tunnel to the other side of the curtain. The winning party would come back and the losing party would disappear. The river would become red, suggesting that the loser had been killed by the powerful juju.

Actually the losing party would be seized and sold into slavery. Some of this still goes on, although there is now considerable skepticism *vis-à-vis* jujus. Still, if you read the papers, you will see a column about jujus, with some people expressing strong belief in it. This particular juju was apparently very highly organized, with spies everywhere. When someone got sick they would sell a very expensive juju against someone else who had bought a juju to make the person sick; and because of the spy system, they probably could prove who had bought the juju; they had probably even sold it.

The question arose also whether there had been organized states before. Actually very little is known, but it seems now certain that Benin state was highly organized and well run before the Portuguese came. When the British conquered it around 1900, it was completely degenerate, with bloodthirsty tyranny, cannibalism, human sacrifices on an enormous scale. But Thompson attributed this degeneracy to the enormous profits to be made by slave raiding and exports to Brazil and America. This seems plausible. Early Portuguese accounts do not apparently mention the human sacrifices and complete arbitrariness of the government.

July 30 (Saturday). Accompanied Thompson to a soccer championship game, Police versus Electricity Corporation (ECN). The stadium was packed. The Governor General, Sir J. Robertson, sat behind me. We were introduced and exchanged pleasantries. More important and equally pleasant was to meet Professor Njohu, the ECN Chairman, a Professor of Botany at Ibadan. Formerly a minister, he got fed up with politics and returned to the University. But he is apparently an unusually able man, and was persuaded to return at least partly to public life. Under him the ECN has turned a deficit into a surplus.

In the evening after the game, Thompson came to my place...He is resigning, partly because he feels new blood is needed, partly because he wants some family life, having seen his wife and children only during the children's vacations since they were 12 years old...

July 31. Had a talk with the Stanford people, who think the country is ripe for a big steel mill. Apparently one has discovered how to coke the coal, and there is iron ore, and fabulous amounts of natural gas...

Notes

1 The Minister's correct name was Festus Okotie-Eboh. He was abducted and shot to death by rogue military personnel in 1966.
2 Edward S. Mason and David Bell, Professor and Lecturer, respectively, in the Harvard Economics Department.
3 International Cooperation Administration, the then name of the US Government foreign aid agency. Under the Kennedy Administration it was renamed the US Agency for International Development, a title that remains to the present day.
4 K.O. Dike, a noted scholar of African history.

5 A team of economic advisers to the central and regional governments of Pakistan, organized by Edward Mason.
6 The second member of Stolper's Ford Foundation-financed team.
7 I wrote 'also' because my brother-in-law is a Campbell.

Chapter 2

August 2–17, 1960
First Tour of the Three Regions

August 2, 1960 (Ibadan)

The new impressions begin to pour in on me...

August 1. The day didn't start out too well because the driver was an hour late. This hadn't happened to me yet, but I am told it is reasonably normal. What happened was that there was no one around to sign the card for the petrol (or to put it into American, the voucher for the gas). Hence we not only had to chase to Ibadan, but were about half an hour late for my appointment with Chief Dina in the Ministry of Finance.

Ibadan is really a fantastic place: 500,000 people, the largest African town, living essentially in mud huts with tin roofs. [See Photo No. 3.] Shanty town does not describe it. Potentially, the location is beautiful. Ibadan is built on many hills, like Rome. There are wide streets for the through traffic, but the rest are just disorderly huts. The potential is shown by the Government quarters, which are modern, attractive and spacious. There is also modern housing built of cement, which has water and electricity. (You can't drink the water, however, without boiling it, though a few people do.) There is water piped all over town, and there are taps where people get it.

No sewerage of course. There are also a few modern buildings, a television tower, a cooperative skyscraper, but the rest is just an accumulation of huts. Everyone seems to be engaged in petty trading. There are little stalls in front of almost every hut, selling tiny heaps of peanuts, or a few cola nuts at a time, or a cigarette at a time. Still, no one is hungry, although there are serious deficiency diseases. I'll get a tour of historic Ibadan on Thursday.

Chief Dina was one of the persons recommended by Ed Mason. He is an impressive man. He sat temporarily in the Ministry of Finance while the regular PS was away. His chieftaincy is recent I believe: it is a title conferred here very much like knighthood in England. There is a natural aristocracy in the West, unlike in the East, where they are trying to create chiefs, though there is no tradition of them.

Dina greeted me, and after a short discussion handed me over to a young New Zealander, Peter Duncan, who is acting PS in the Ministry of Economic Planning. The Western Region is not only the richest – having cocoa which is a profitable export crop – but also the most advanced. They have universal free education (but not compulsory) and 90% of the children now go to school for four years. The real problem is, of course, secondary and technical, including commercial, education...

I am put up at one of the University apartments, very comfortable but less fancy than Lagos, where I am a VIP. No air-conditioning, but Ibadan is about 748 ft.

according to the folder I got, so you don't really need it during the rainy season. On the other hand, I have to sleep under a mosquito net, and I had to ask first how to get into the bed, never having slept under netting before. This year mosquitoes and other vermin are unusually few, probably because it is cooler and dryer than normal...

After a nap I had a longish talk with Professor Barback, 40, head of the economics department and of NISER. First we talked about cooperation with me in the planning work. Thompson had specifically asked me to seek a closer relationship, which suited me, of course, very well. We discussed a number of projects: putting the national accounts on a current basis; starting an industrial census, possibly on a sample basis, to learn about industrial structure, use of domestic materials, costs, etc.; and a market study, based on import data, along the lines of W.A. Lewis study for Ghana. Cooperation was promised, evidently in good faith and with sincerity. It remains to be put into reality.

I also raised the problem of interchange and cooperation with Michigan. It looks as if something could be worked out that both Ibadan and Michigan would want, financed by ICA or a private foundation. The trouble is that at this moment, Ibadan is producing its first graduates, and won't have good ones who might profit from study in the US or elsewhere until a year from now; but this doesn't really matter, because it will take time to work things out. Also, while Barback would welcome our staff here, he would find it difficult to send anyone now, since he is not only understaffed, but is just getting the department going...

August 3, 1960 (Ibadan)

August 1 (continued). In the evening I hoped to get to bed early, but three fellow Americans who thought I was lonely invited me out, and I accepted...We went first to a Lebanese restaurant, but the lady from USIS couldn't take the dirty table napkin put on our table with aplomb as a special service, nor could she get used to the rest of the atmosphere. So we went to another restaurant run by an English lady which was spotless but rather less interesting.

I am getting a bad sleep deficiency. The place is comfortable enough but very noisy. When I go to bed at midnight it is just hopeless to try to sleep before 2:00 or 3:00 AM. and I have to get up at 7:15 AM at the latest. This is OK for one or two nights, but then begins to be wearing.

August 2. I started in the Ministry of Economic Planning, with Duncan as its acting PS in the absence of Chief Dina, who held the desk in Finance. Present were three excellent young Nigerians, including Bambgebose, whose name I also had from Ed. Mason. The WR is much better off than either the other regions or the Federal Government in having trained manpower available, although they too complain about being understaffed. Bambgebose is starting interesting economic studies, their chief statistician, Igun, and his assistant, Ernina, are starting to build up industrial and construction statistics by samples, and the Region actually has produced a Five-Year Regional Development Plan for 1960–65 which has some projections I can use.

The Trade and Industry PS, Chemmie (?), whom I saw next, outlined their organization and what they are doing, and sent me along to the Chairman of the

Western Region Marketing Board, an impressive Nigerian, who gave me statements on their price policy, the impossibility of forecasting cocoa prices for more than a year – cocoa prices are just crazy – then told me I was lucky to find him in his office, because of an election coming up on August 8, and he was a district chairman, though not running for office himself.

In the afternoon I was taken to Waterston, director of Federal Agricultural Research, who then drove me around the experimental fields. They are working on citrus fruits, yams, rice, and an experimental cattle herd, kept in unscreened stalls, healthy in spite of the tsetse fly, through good feeding and medical treatment.

I saw for the first time a small plot of oil palms, and they certainly look different from the wild ones. They are smaller, for one thing, which makes harvesting easier. There are also new strains of cocoa, not only more pest-resistant but also bearing fruit after four years instead of 7–9, though they don't yet know for how many years this new Amazon variety will bear.

Incidentally, rice is a good food, if unpolished. When boiled properly the vitamins do not go into the water but sink into the rice. More rice cultivation in the delta swamps would solve a lot of the nutrition problem, and experiments are going on to produce rice in salt water and in brackish swamps. The major difficulty, though, is social: farmers just won't grow rice properly except in one town, Abakaliki, where rice has been successful. Whether this resistance has to do with yam cults and other religious customs, is uncertain.

In the evening a delightful party at Duncan's, to which he invited Arch Callaway (of MIT) and Rose, the Secretary of Agriculture, with their wives…The gist of the discussion was that £1 million spent on agriculture would create a lot more employment and wealth than £1 million spent on industry. Also, an unemployment problem is building up rapidly, involving school leavers who feel they are too good for farming. The idea of spreading literacy fast in order to improve productivity on farms is not working. Yet when you reflect, it is rather funny that Nigerians should think of themselves as qualified with six years of schooling, which in Switzerland or the States is considered less than the minimum even for unskilled employment. There are obviously lots of problems to be solved.

August 3, 1960 (Ibadan)

I have just come from lunch, which here is both less fancy and less plentiful than in Lagos. The difference is of course that between a university and a government.

First I was in the Ministry of Health, talking with the (Nigerian) Chief Medical Officer and his (English) junior colleague, both extremely able MDs. I got some notion of the hospital building program and the whole health picture. And I was again warned against taking vital statistics seriously. But both agree that the population may well be 40 million already, and that it is almost certainly growing at a rate faster than the 2% officially assumed. The evidence is that the expected school population was vastly exceeded, much to the embarrassment of the education planners and the Ministry of Finance, which had to shell out extra money. Also some censuses in individual towns indicated sizes 40% greater or so than originally thought.

I raised the question of social obstacles to birth control. And got the answer that this was at present out of the question. A woman without children is inferior, can be divorced and sent back to her parents. Children give women a sense of security, apparently not only for old age, but also *vis-à-vis* the husband. On the contrary, Dr. Franklin, the chief medical officer said that a birth control clinic would remain empty, but if tomorrow he could open a fertility clinic with 5,000 beds, he would have to turn women away.

After that I was back at UCI with Barback, and got another glimpse of the University. It is beautifully modern, with a lot of building going on. Certainly the economists are better off than we are, they have a nice theatre, a beautiful modern Protestant church, a less interesting Catholic one, meeting rooms, a theatre and elegant dormitories, much better than in the States. And there is an increasing amount of air-conditioning. Barback's office is, and they are getting a new building which will also have air-conditioned offices...The more I see of here, and of the work done here, the more I think a collaboration with Michigan desirable.

Otherwise I am now quite out of touch with things, no mail, no paper, nor any radio.

August 4, 1960 (Ibadan)

August 3 (continued). The party at Barback's was very nice...I talked mostly with Chief Dina, who appeared in beautiful African chief's robes, and who wore all the time the kind of cap or turban customary here. I am quite tempted to get myself one of these elegant gowns, but though the tailoring and the cut is Nigerian, the cloth is definitely Manchester.

Dina wanted to know a lot about American politics, whether Kennedy would win, why there was a Catholic issue, etc...I tried to learn something about Nigerian politics, which in part go along tribal lines, but not completely. The Government parties are the NPC which represent the northern Moslems and the NCNC which is primarily of the Ibos in the East. The AG represents mainly the Yorubas of the West. Calabar voted AG, and Ibadan, which is Yoruba, voted NCNC.

The reason appears historic. Ibadan is essentially a cosmopolitan city, and has really no *city* background as such. Rather it was an armed camp of refugees from the civil, or as we rather impolitely refer to them, intertribal wars which seem to have lasted 200 years and led to the English being asked in. In Ibadan the English are popular and were asked in by the people as protection against the Jebbus, also a Yoruba group, which had oppressed the other groups, had prevented them from profitable trading with Lagos and the British, and had raided them for slaves. As they had gunpowder and the poor fellows in Ibadan had not, the Jebbus usually won, but they couldn't stand up to English armaments. Anyway, the Jebbus are now AG, but Ibadan is a stronghold of NCNC.

This explains also the quite fantastic look of Ibadan which is like nothing I ever saw. I tried to describe it before. Today I got a brief tour of it. I was first taken by Oshinowo of the Ministry of Economic Planning to the highest point where the people of Ibadan erected a tower as a monument to Col. Bowers, who was resident here and ended the war with the Fulanis of the North. Apparently he and a Welshman named Taffy Jones, who is said to have learned to speak Yoruba before

English, built the major thoroughfares and Mopo Hall (the City Hall), were immensely popular with the Ibadan people, and one got a tower, the other got the major thoroughfare named after him. I took pictures, but the view was unfortunately hazy. From there we went to the City Hall, where I met the senior officials, the city manager, who is British, and his deputy who is a Nigerian. I was shown the view and the various offices, and it was explained what went on – all transactions being in Yoruba. The busiest office was the one dealing with land transfers which with this complicated system of land tenure seems to cause endless trouble.

From the city hall, I went to the Mosque, but couldn't get in because you have to take off your shoes, they don't have slippers for you, and it was too filthy to walk barefoot. But it cost me 6d for "dash" for the attendant anyway. Oshinowo, being a Christian, insisted then on showing me the "cradle of Christianity in Yorubaland," to use his words, and the visit was well worthwhile. There is a new undistinguished grey stone Gothic church there. But there is also the old mission house of the 1850s or so, and in an enclosed garden there were open schoolrooms for 700 children, who had a well-behaved lesson. The principal, an impressive, shy, and somewhat saintly looking Nigerian led us in. He was young. Suddenly there was a peaceful, quiet atmosphere. It was Nigerian as the rest, but trees were planted, there was a garden, there was a cistern, now unused, with water supply. And it was amazing what a little order and love could do to the supposedly difficult African soil.

The contrast became even stronger when I was led to the Temple of Shango, the God of Thunder. In the first place, without a guide you would never find it, although it is right on the main road. It is a hut with an open door, right beside and in the middle of petty trading stores. It smells musty and of smoke inside and there is a small room, perhaps as big as our dining room, which is divided $1/3$ through with a wall covered with figures of various religious significance. The priest, an old man, came out, and after agreeing that I would pay "dash" – it cost me 10/- after some negotiation in Yoruba – he told me in Yoruba that this statue was a warrior, and that a monkey, etc. The statues were rather ugly, and the whole atmosphere oppressive. Behind the statues was something like an altar. Also a place where the old priest had lain down. There was a big kind of pot with what to me looked like stones of odd shape, but naturally so which were symbols of the God of Thunder, Shango, and the usual twin figures. Those are symbols to keep the spirits of dead twins away. I was glad I saw it, and glad I got out. There was something dirty about it, and my respect for missionaries went up. Unfortunately I can't find out anything about the cult, what the God does, how one worships him etc. O. is a Christian and doesn't know.

The impression was strengthened by driving through the part of the market given to medicines, to use the polite term for this, or the juju market as it is usually called, where traditional medicines and charms are on sale. I hope my pictures will turn out well. [See Photo No. 4.] I didn't see any dried monkey heads, but there were dried bats' wings, dried skins of various sorts, and miscellaneous things which were simultaneously revolting and picturesque. With all this, a visit to the 10th floor of the Coop Building, the only skyscraper, and to the Liberty Stadium, to seat 35,000 by Oct. 1, the morning tour approached the end, and I had to got o the appointment with the Ministry of Agriculture and National Resources.

To my surprise, there were 9 people there, from the PS to all the department chiefs who all briefed me. I will write this up when I get back to Lagos. The major impression is that of a hardworking, understaffed, group of devoted civil servants, who actually have got considerable results. The impression one got in the States from reading that no one knew what kind of agriculture to use, is not quite correct any more: one knows about seed improvements, about timing of plantings, about next problems for research. They also painted a picture of peasants being quite money conscious. They said that the application of fertilizer to cassava and yam production worked, but yields increased little, and there was no point, at present fertilizer prices to apply it. But if fertilizer prices came down farmers would try it. They also said that food production could easily be increased. They even start cattle farms, trying to breed tsetse fly resistant strains. It seems also that good food alone made anything, animal or vegetable, quite resistant to diseases.

At 1:00 PM I chased to Duncan's to take a bite, and then we were off to Apoje, about 50 miles SE of Ibadan, to see the government plantation. It rained all the time, and there was some campaigning going on. Also two bridges were being repaired, so the 50 miles took two hours. But the plantation was fascinating. The acting manager, a Scot named Lamont, took us around in his Landrover. The plantation has oil palms, citrus fruits and cocoa trees, and it was beautiful. Cocoa trees need shade and are thus planted under shade trees, of which quite a few are bananas with their broad leaves. This gives the whole cocoa part of the plantation a strange appearance, but quite unlike the messy appearance of the individual farms I tried to describe in my last letter (so much happens, that I can't quite remember what I did describe and what I forgot).

The lemons were the biggest I have ever seen, like big oranges, but apparently they have no market. Oranges can be sold but not abroad, because the varieties here, though they taste good, stay greenish. For similar reasons there is also trouble with grapefruit selling. On the other hand cocoa and palm oil are big money makers. Palm kernels are harvested over the whole plantation once a week. They must be harvested on time, or else they will ferment on the tree and get ruined. I was shown the Pioneer mills, which automatically extract the nuts, squeeze the oil out of the skin, crack the nut, sort the nut kernel from the shell (by a mud bath and a flotation process), dry them and then, after a hand sorting where women pick out any shells which have got stuck with the beans, pack them. About a dozen people were employed in a relatively small-scale operation, highly efficient, taking up the floor space of our big barn in Vermont.

Lever Brothers has just built a bigger modern mill. Unlike the pioneer mill which works by steam and is fired by the nutshells, the new mill has lots of electric equipment. Lamont was quite pessimistic on its success, said it was on too large a scale, couldn't work continuously since the plantation, big though it was, could not supply it fully. Also electrical equipment was sensitive to the climate and required expert maintenance and supervision which was not and would not be available. Lamont was sure it would fail.

Cocoa trees are grown from seedlings distributed and grown by the Extension services. It is a rather nice tree, but the blossom is tiny and comes right out of the stem. I was shown the fermentation process, and the drying, and chewed a cocoa bean, which has a rather pleasant taste. Oil palms on the other hand are started from the seed, which germinates in ovens at 95 degrees, then put out into seed beds, transplanted into larger fields, and finally put on the plantation in rows. They start yielding after about six years. The new cocoa varieties yield after 3–4 years though it takes still seven years to get sizable amounts…

We drove home in streaming rain, which has only now stopped, and with occasional lightning, and I got back about 8:00 PM…

August 7, 1960 (Kaduna)

August 5. I was again on my feet continuously. 9:00 AM at the Ministry of Lands and Labour. The most important thing here was the discussion of the industrial estates. The system of land tenure is very complicated, making land acquisition extremely difficult and therefore costly. Also, no non-Nigerians can alienate land. This has always been British policy in West Africa. In order to aid industrialization, the Government acquires land and develops it for industrial estates, or industrial parks, to use the American phrase. Once developed, i.e., once the land has been acquired and graded, and streets, electricity and water put in, it is then leased to private firms for 99 years. This transfers all headaches of land disputes to the government, which however can legally proceed with the development while a case is in court, since only the compensation can be disputed. I got some idea of the amounts of money involved and the policy was discussed. The one hour allotted to this ministry went rather quickly.

At 10:00 AM to the Ministry of Works and Transport. The Nigerian PS, Akinjeni, called in his road engineers, who welcomed me with open arms. They said WR roads were better than Federal roads and their building program was held up by the fact that the Federal program built to lower specifications than the regions. E.g. they couldn't take heavier bulldozers over Federally-built bridges. The WR is also developing a road inventory and system of priority rating.

The chief engineer referred to the Niger Dam as a fine idea, but said a program was urgently needed for the other major rivers, otherwise in 20–25 years they would all silt up. I asked why this didn't happen a long time ago. Apparently the intensity of cultivation has increased sufficiently for run-off to bring in a lot more soil. According to the engineer, the fairly simple remedy is to forbid shifting cultivation within a certain distance of the rivers. Standard international legislation to protect river banks is available and could be enacted quickly. In any case there should be closer cooperation of hydrologists with the other regions and the Federal Government, and they would be obliged if I could do something about it.

Two other problems came out. One related to road planning. As soon as a new bituminous road was built, villagers got together and by communal effort built a road big enough for a truck and passable to the main road except in heavy rain. Once finished, that road stayed within village control and budgets until something went wrong, e.g. a bridge built by the villagers collapsed. They would then ask the regional government to take over the bridge and the road, a request which could not easily be denied. As a result, however, the roads were poorly laid out, throwing off the government's road building program. Later Chief Dina told me this situation required the roads to be re-mapped, which was actually a good sign.

The other point related to the population of Ibadan. Both the chief engineer and the chief hydrologist were quite sure that Ibadan had closer to 1 million inhabitants than the 5–600,000 normally stated. There was a smallpox scare a few years back and all trucks coming into Ibadan were stopped, people were asked their addresses and vaccinated. Based on this experience, a figure of half a million was way too small. The difficulty is that the Yorubas are traditionally urban-minded even if they have farms. They will live in towns, but go into the bush and build a mud hut to use during the harvest. While urbanization makes electrification and provision of water much easier, it makes a population census much harder.

At 11:00 AM to the Ministry of Education. Met the PS, Twiso, just returned from studying German education, and the chief educational planning officer, a Scot, whose job is to provide schoolrooms and teachers. There is universal, free but not compulsory, primary education, telescoped from the six years in England to five. Despite some dropout, perhaps 75–80% of eligible children actually finish school. 10% are supposed to go on to secondary grammar schools, preparing for college, and 50% to secondary modern, teaching commercial and technical subjects. Many of these are preparing for the new farm settlement schemes.

At 12:30 PM to the Odutola Tire Co., a tire retreading firm. (The dot underneath the o means it is pronounced open and quick like in "spot.") This is an example of outstanding success of Nigerian enterprise. Chief Odutola, is a very impressive man, taller and broader than I, wearing Nigerian dress of superior material and subdued design. I told him I wanted to meet businessmen, learn about obstacles to development, and ask their advice or at least their willingness to talk later. The Chief – a nonhereditary title, given somewhat like a knighthood – had been a gold miner. He started in a small way with his own and some family money.

Then he was named a director of the Western Region Development Corporation. To give an example to others he took a loan of £10,000 to enlarge his factory. This was so successful that it was repaid in a year or so, as was a new loan of £20,000. He would not tell me his total sales – the company is a closely held family affair – but he said they were sizable. I would guess the factory was easily worth £150,000.

Odutola now has three tire retreading plants, and is contemplating the construction of a tire factory. The machinery I saw was German and English. The rubber used is all Nigerian, mostly produced within the plant from sheets purchased from farmers and carbon black. As it was lunch hour, I did not actually see the factory in operation, but it looked very efficient. Incidentally all workers were Nigerian. Most greeted the boss in the ordinary manner, but a few, mostly youngsters prostrated themselves before him. I was told later that Yoruba society is very polite, and that children or relatives are expected to show extreme deference to their parents or elders.

Odutola employs about 200 workers in his three factories. The biggest, in Ibadan, he runs himself, assisted by three expatriate managers. He used to have four, but replaced one with a Nigerian. The other two factories are run by expatriates. Getting managers and capital on reasonable terms are the major problems of industrial expansion, according to Odutola. There is money around, but it does not get channeled into what we would consider productive uses.

(When I saw Dina on my final visit yesterday, he made the point that traditionally the Yoruba farmer would spend additional money to get additional wives, but that the pattern was changing to fancy clothing, radios and housing. While these were steps in the right direction, a lot more changes had to occur before savings would flow into a capital market.)

In the afternoon, and after a hectic bite to eat, I went to the Nigerian Tobacco Company, an offshoot of the British American Tobacco Company. Run by an Englishman, named Rowett, it made a very efficient impression. Rowett explained the layout and technology, and then we went to his office to talk economics over what passed as coffee. Naturally I had to smoke local cigarettes, made mainly from local tobacco, which incidentally I find quite good. Most Europeans smoke the better local brands called Bicycle and, not inappropriately, Guinea Gold.

I asked, first, how far the machine dictated how many people were employed and at what speed they worked, or whether the manager had some choice in his capital-labor ratios, and second, about the quality of the labor and of Nigerian management.

The answer to the first question was quite illuminating. The process of cigarette making is highly mechanized, but some hand operations remain. On the whole, the number of machine operators is about the same in Nigeria and the UK. Efficiency is slightly lower because of wastage. The machine that actually makes the cigarette – most of the machines are devoted to preparing the tobacco – consists of a huge roll of cigarette paper that is continuously filled with tobacco, then twisted and glued and finally cut into cigarette-length pieces. To ensure the glue sticks and everything works, a little piece of light metal the size of a cigarette presses down lightly on the cigarette. This piece eventually gets worn, whereupon it tears the paper. Rowett said every so often he has to discard a whole day's output because the machine operator won't notice it, whereas in the UK the machine would be stopped almost immediately and the piece replaced. Still, this sort of wastage is only about 5% so that output per machine operator is roughly comparable to that in Britain.

It is entirely different with supervisory personnel. Because they have no previous experience with machines, the machine supervisors find it difficult to imagine what goes on inside one. In Britain a supervisor would handle two or three types of machines, but in Nigeria he handles only one, which he has to keep in running order. This immediately raises the labor input compared to the UK, thus lowering wages.

On the managerial side, Rowett said he has one submanager who will come along, but he will never be able to manage anything as big as the NTC. His chief failing is that, if anything unforeseen happens, he tends to get excited and lose his head. At this stage it is extremely difficult for Nigerians to learn to manage large-scale operations.

Another major cost item in an underdeveloped country factory is the need to keep a fabulous amount of inventory. Rowett said he had to keep 18-month supplies of all spare parts, and to reorder one had to plan nine months in advance. This too must lower wages. I don't know what is customary in America, but it is probably less than a year's inventory, and one reorders from the nearest warehouse.

At 7:45 PM, after an hour's rest, Callaway from MIT fetched me for dinner. All guests were Nigerians: they included Ayo Ogunsheye, Director of Extra-mural Studies at UCI and his wife, he in Nigerian, she in European dress. O. (pronounced Ogunche) is an economist and one of my bosses on the Joint Planning Committee. Also Dr. Bessier of the Chemistry Department, and Ahimie, an industrial relations economist in the Extra-mural section…

The Nigerians were obviously out to bait me in a friendly manner, mainly to find out what kind of a man I was. I think I did pretty well. There was a latent intellectual anti-Americanism, but less than one might expect. It came out in such questions as: Are you a capitalist? Do you think we should have a free market economy or planning? I parried the first easily enough: Yes, I was, but then what is capitalism now would hardly have been recognized as such only a generation ago. (Senator Goldwater thinks it is socialism anyway.) We had licked the problems of mass unemployment, mass poverty and degrading income differences, the latter really only in the last 15 or 20 years, and I thought we did rather better than the Soviets on those accounts. My East German studies interested them, and they came in useful, because of the meaningfulness of comparing a free and a communist regime.

On Nigeria I pleaded that I was here less than three weeks – today only is it three weeks though it seems longer – that I believed that Nigeria was ready for a burst of private investment from abroad and at home, that I was pragmatic and favored anything that worked as long as it safeguarded the freedom of the individual.

Who would win the US election? Did I think that science was western? I didn't get the meaning of this last question until later. The proper answer was: science is universal. I thought they were referring to the origin of science, and there I stuck to my guns and pointed out that, Babylonians and Egyptians, and alchemists not withstanding, what we understand by it today and what has had success did come from the Greeks.

Somehow the talk got on archaeology, and my statement, learned from Mendenhall,[1] that no civilization older than the Near Eastern ones had been found, was misunderstood as denying Africa's cultural heritage. I had intended nothing of the kind and wouldn't have said so even had I believed it. So this was straightened out, not without some heat, however. I asked what happened in Shango cult worship, and was told one didn't know unless one belonged. How did one belong? One was called, but it was all secret. There were lots of secret cults around and one belonged if one was called. Then it turned out that Uli Beier, a German and his Austrian wife, both belong. Beier is a UCI faculty member, interested professionally in Yoruba culture.[2]

Mrs. Callaway said she doubted the sophisticated Beier could actually believe that stuff. However Mrs. Beier might, she was a neurotic artist. This led to heated words about why it was so impossible to believe in Shango, when it was possible to believe in Christ. Didn't we really have a closed mind and look down on Yoruba culture? Mrs. Ogunsheye was a believing Anglican, but it was not clear whether the others were believing or only nominal Christians.

Dr. Bessier, the chemist, appeared to be an agnostic with considerable knowledge and sophistication. In any case I got him to agree that it was our cultural pattern which had brought about economic development, and not theirs, and that it was all very well to be proud of one's inheritance but no one had yet figured out how to change and how not to change at the same time. These people were lively and sophisticated and obviously westernized without having lost contact with their own cultural background…The evening was good fun and instructive since Dr. Ogunsheye is apparently one of Nigeria's outstanding applied economists. But it was again 2:00 AM before I turned the light out. It was a full day.

August 6 (Saturday). Not much less hectic a day. I started with Frank Ward, General Manager of Mobil Oil and president of the Ibadan Chamber of Commerce. An open, informed, intelligent, and interesting man. He thought Nigeria had a good chance. The next two years would be crucial – 1961 would be a boom year in the glory of independence, but 1962 would bring second thoughts. There would be growing inflationary pressure, both from unions to raise minimum wages, and from government, directly through budget deficits and use of the Central Bank, and indirectly through unaffordable social security charges. He specifically mentioned the National Provident Fund as raising costs substantially.

He said political stability was essential for the future, but that chances of getting it were excellent, and that the crux of future development lay in the cooperation of the Federal Government and the Regions. At present the WR goes ahead and does what it wants. He was enthusiastically in favor of the Jebba dam. Mobil would use the river for transport when this was possible. And whole new areas would be opened up for modern agricultural settlement. If the next two years are safely passed, he felt the chances for continuous growth were good. He has seven Nigerian sub-managers, all internally trained, and he thought rather good.

Next stop was Arthur Day, General Manager of Barclays Bank. On Nigerians as managers, he thought there were too few who could take the long view. If sent to London for advanced training, few came back to get ahead in Barclays. Instead they started out on their own, usually without success since they overestimated their training. But there were exceptions. Saving in banks was set back a few years ago when most native banks failed, mainly due to incompetence. The two which survived are not efficiently run, and make political loans or refuse them on political grounds. (This he thought should be confidential.)

Interest rates are now tied to the UK bank rate, but will eventually be tied to the CBN rate. Actually they are about what they are in the States. During the cocoa buying season they have to ship £80,000 a day into the country in £1 notes. He knows several illiterate farmers who are good and make at least £4,500, he actually hands them the notes. Some of the money comes back as deposits, some goes into construction and flows back through the builders. Also they like to buy good textiles. He showed me two shares in a local company which he is trying to sell for one of his illiterate Yoruba women traders, who are apparently shrewd businesswomen and good risks. He has to write the Bank manager in Lagos for help in finding a buyer. The opening of the Lagos stock exchange in October or November will be a help.

At Treasury I saw Ejuitchie, the undersecretary, who gave me material I will take back to University of Michigan. Then I went for a final visit to Dina. We talked about the WR income tax, a political hot potato. In discussing it earlier with Ogunsheye I had taken the line that income taxes in a country like Nigeria were administratively not feasible, hence I would abolish them and substitute property taxes and high import duties on luxuries. Without being aware of it, I had touched a sensitive nerve. The WR Government party, the Action Group, is for income taxes, and what I proposed happened to coincide with the NCNC program. My argument was that you could not define income clearly in this kind of economy, nor assess it in the absence of bookkeeping by businesses. Property ownership was probably a better guide to income and duties on luxuries would provide the desired progressivity. Also I had heard hair-raising stories about people owning four cars and not paying taxes, and corruption in tax assessment.

Assessment apparently works by the tax man seeing how a fellow dresses, how he lives, how he makes a living. How much a carpenter makes is known roughly, and if he dresses well he gets assessed somewhat more. Ogunsheye, Ejuitchie and Dina all admitted the force of my argument, but refused to give in. They thought the tax collection apparatus could be improved. Dina thought sooner or later income tax would have to come, and should be introduced early to accustom people even if collection was spotty, inefficient and unjust. Once abolished it would be difficult to reintroduce, and increasingly the growth of the economy and of business habits would ease enforcement and make collection more just.

From Dina I went to Duncan's place where he had brought four of his assistants, all Nigerians, two of whom had been at Harvard. They were a bright and good bunch, eager and pleasant, and any of them would be good to have assigned to me. The trouble is that they are also badly needed in Ibadan, which nevertheless seems to have more good Nigerians than any of the other regional governments...

At 3:00 PM Callaway appeared at the flat to tell me of his MIT project and establish my connection. I told him I was still with the Center in spirit but not in flesh, I still expected to do something for them, but did not know what or when, and was more or less committed to Ed Mason to write a book on government and the economy in Nigeria. However I felt quite certain that after two years I would want to write more than one book.

My impression is that the project is not going well, that it has no direction or center, and that Arnold Rivkin is not quite the man to run as big an affair. Callaway is a nice fellow and a good economist – Haberler[3] thought so and recommended him strongly – but he gets too involved in cultural and related matters without being clear how they relate to the problem of economic change, which is our problem after all.

Apparently Callaway and Nixon, the political scientist on the project, do not get along, and Callaway has little contact with NISER. I got this first from Barback, who told me everyone disliked Nixon – he was just an operator picking other people's brains without contributing anything – that he liked Callaway but feared he (C.) thought he was unpopular. I offered to say something to Callaway but was told better not to do so. It all started when Callaway appeared with wife and four children after being told in writing to come alone at first because of lack of housing. Anyway, it is quite clear that Callaway does not like Barback, but I didn't say anything.

C. brought me to the train an hour early...The carriage was modern, not airconditioned, but good. I had the upper berth, the drawback being that the linen could not be tucked in. The communal shower had cassava stored in it and was unusable. There was however a private toilet and wash basin. You get your berth automatically with your ticket, but you have to rent the bedding separately. Dinner was served in the compartment, and bottled water was served with the compliments of the railway. My roommate was a Hindu who didn't eat beef, and was on his way to Kano to set up an importing business.

The train came from Lagos. It takes two hours by car from Lagos to Ibadan, but five hours by a train pulled by a steam engine burning the infernal Nigerian coal, hence it is impossible to have a window open. From Ibadan on, there was a diesel locomotive, and we had the windows open all the time, with only moderate dirt.

Unfortunately the train started only at 5:45 PM, and we were at the Jebba bridge across the Niger only at 2:00 AM, so I saw nothing. The crossing is supposed to be interesting. But I'll see the Niger next week at the Onitsha ferry crossing. The landscape is rather pretty though undistinguished. There are the usual mud huts and villages. The train moves for a long time NE, so it takes longer to get into savanna area, which really starts about 50 miles or so N of Ibadan. In fact I saw savanna only this morning, it looks like a park landscape, with trees spaced at some distance. Palms seem to exist only where it is very wet, in swampy ground or near rivers. There were quasi-hills, apparently mainly granite extrusions from the normal and ever-present red soil. The villages look poorer. The huts are still made of mud, tend to be circular rather than square and have thatched rather than galvanized iron roofs. The people also look different, like black Arabs. Everyone is friendly, waves at the train.

August 7. Arriving in Kaduna at 12:15 PM it was hot. I missed my Ministry of Finance greeter. So I had to fight through a crowd tearing away at my suitcase to earn a shilling, and three taxi drivers almost came to blows over who was to take me. Fortunately Turner arrived in time and brought me to the Catering Rest House. It has a central hall with bar, sitting room, terrace and dining room, and the sleeping accommodations are in chalets, really double motels. I have again a large room and bathroom, a bed with mosquito netting, and so far have killed a few cockroaches which are big, ugly and harmless. No scorpions yet...Everything is clean, efficient and friendly. People wear fezzes. I hear the North is characterized by "dirt and dignity," but Kaduna is a nondescript town that served as Lord Lugard's administrative center, Kano being the old center. But I'm told there isn't much to see in Kaduna outside of the government buildings which I will see tomorrow, and the textile mill which I asked to see...

August 11, 1960 (Enugu)

August 8. Kaduna is a pleasant little town, rather nondescript, with a reasonably good climate. Outside the Moslem element is much in evidence, though I didn't see a mosque. (There probably is one.) Historically, Kaduna never amounted to anything until Lord Lugard, early in the century, shifted his capital there because the climate was better than in Kano.

In general, the Northern Region is much poorer and this shows in understaffing in the ministries, relative absence of Nigerians below Ministerial level, and the dearth of information and forward planning. There isn't even an attempt at general primary education. Many emirs don't send their own children to school, though education is recognized as necessary. As a result, there are few educated people to go around, and industries don't get them at all. At the same time, the Northern Region isn't content with Nigerianization but insists on Northernization, which makes sense in government, schools and medical services, but not in industry. Yet it is difficult for industries to find good workers, even unskilled ones, and Ibos from the East or Yorubas from the West are frequently dismissed.

To complicate my day, the Government people work yet on another schedule. They start at 7:30 AM, work till 9:00 AM. Then everyone goes home for breakfast, and returns at 10:30 AM to work till 2:30 PM. Thus, lunch is closer to 3:00 PM. Since I also worked in the afternoon, this schedule left something to be desired. Anyway, I started at 8:00 AM with Agriculture to find that there was a separate ministry on Animal Health and Forestry, a most unusual distinction not found elsewhere and not really sensible. I find that while no one has any notion of how many acres of groundnuts are planted and how much is consumed domestically, people have better ideas of the scientific possibilities of improving agriculture.

There is a problem of overgrazing by the nomadic Fulani, who have yet to learn that a fat cow is better than a scrawny one, and who breed animals for meat and not for milk. There is a reforestation problem, which is common to Africa and requires basic research. 'Forest' has to be understood loosely, as with us in Arizona or New Mexico: a tree every so often. It seems that trees left to themselves remain stunted; but if the soil around them is mechanically disturbed, they will grow normally. No one knows why, and the forest officer pleaded with me to get Ford money for five years to do systematic scientific studies, of value to all of Africa.

At Trade and Industry there was little information on forward planning, but I found here as elsewhere jealousy, particularly against Ibos and the Eastern Region. The NR has good iron ore, stretching across the border, and the coal seam mined near Enugu also goes into the North. The Eastern Region is planning an integrated steel mill, which the North resents because they want it, and since they are poorer, feel they ought to get it.

The next stop was Nigeria Development, Ltd., a development corporation trying to launch private businesses and handicapped by an absence of entrepreneurs. They have a million pounds which they can't give away: there just aren't any Northern businessmen. Murphy, the director, a peppery Irishman, probably somewhat younger than myself, felt that one should loosen up on immigration, that the undoubted discrimination against Levantines, particularly Lebanese and Syrians but also Greeks, should go; that workers would be more productive if they got paid better, and to anticipate a discussion we had in the evening, that there was just too much interference from second-rate British civil servants who didn't like business. Not that they were socialist, far from it, they just were stuffy and little petty tyrants. This was the first (but not the last) time in which I heard one Englishman talk scathingly of another.

The low level of education also kept people down, in addition to the burden of the extended family, and the general backwardness and poverty of the rather vast area. Locally the region is run by Native Authorities which in practice means by emirs who keep everything quiet, but unfortunately thus far stagnant. But things are beginning to change…

Things quieted down with my visits to the Ministries of Health and Education, but there, too, I found no forward planning beyond 1962, and a worry where the money was coming from.

After lunch, to Kaduna Textile Mills. The mill is completely modern, employing 1,400 people plus 57 expatriates. Not one Nigerian manager, and only three foremen. The factory was set up by a Lancashire firm which furnishes the technical and management staff. It is a textile man's dream, manufacturing a single type of yarn from local cotton, and a single type of cloth, the lowest grade at that. The daily wage is 4/7 for an unskilled worker and, though African labor is the lowest paid, it is also the most expensive in the world.

Why? In England a worker watches 48 looms, in Kaduna 12. A few go up to 24. Many quit; the work is strenuous, many live miles away. There are a few who walk (not bicycle) ten miles each day, then work eight hours, and walk ten miles home, all for 4/7. No wonder they are tired. Those who make more because they are efficient find their whole family descending on them. So they quit to get rid of their families. Many just get tired of the new job. The turnover means high training costs. The tiredness and low educational level mean carelessness and higher operating costs. Machines are maintained less efficiently. The plant is doing well, and doubling its capacity from profits. But it pays no taxes for five years, and gets 90% tariff protection. It could not compete on world markets. The low level of education means that only six people so far were suitable for foreman training. Three failed, two were so-so, and one was superb…

August 12, 1960 (Enugu)

I seem to be unable to get started today because of traders coming to offer me their wares. I got rid of them, by buying a few presents.

August 8 (continued). In the afternoon the driver took me to the airport. The idea was to get my ticket to Kano reconfirmed. But there were a few interesting pictures to be taken, though nothing spectacular. Markets, the soldiers' quarters, which must be unique, because each soldier has his individual hut, round, some with thatched roofs, others with tin roofs. Between them are the cooking facilities…The horse stables are distinguishable from the huts only by being somewhat bigger. There are the ubiquitous vultures on top of the roofs, which I suppose as scavengers are quite useful for disposal of leftovers, repulsive animals though they are.

August 9. 7:30 AM in the Ministry of Lands. The North has a completely different land tenure system, with no individual ownership whatsoever. All land is either crown land, or held communally by the emirs. In some respects it is simpler than in the South, but just as much of a handicap to development.

At 8:00 AM to the Ministry of Works – they had no idea what they wanted to do after 1962, and little idea of what to use for money until then.

Then to the Ministry of Local Government, which in the North is also different. There are 68 or so Native Authorities (NAs), usually under emirs, which together raise about £12 million compared with the Regional Government's £18 million budget. The NAs are responsible for local roads and schools, and are desperately poor and running out of money. Astoundingly, while each NA produces budget estimates for the coming year (which form two fat printed volumes every year), no accounts of actual expenditures are printed. A British researcher, Deece, getting his degree at Oxford with Ursula Hicks and writing a thesis on local finance, told me he has to travel hundreds of miles to collect material, because the accounts of actual spending are available only in typewritten form with rarely even carbon copies made.

I requested estimates for the last ten years for the University of Michigan Library, and was promised them if possible. It is not certain that a continuous set exists even for ten years. There is only one complete set back to 1911, though it may be possible to assemble another one by writing to the various NAs for their copies. Even this is not certain.

At 11:30 AM the Finance PS, Gibbs, told me that Northern Nigeria has only six trained economists, and he didn't see how he could let me have one, though he would try. One of their men just got a scholarship to Oxford University, Miami, Ohio, and I promised to invite him once to Michigan.

All in all, the visit in Kaduna was pleasant, hard work, worthwhile, but remarkably short of positive results. This contrasted very sharply with the Western Region, with its many good, well-trained Yorubas. Moslem religion, emirates, and

British non-interference to the point of preventing missionary activity except on a small scale, so as to avoid trouble, have kept the education level low. Most people seem to agree that Islam has produced great cultures and activity only in periods when "heresy" was rampant. I don't know whether this is so, and would like to check with our scholars in Ann Arbor. But here opinion points to stagnation under orthodox Islam.

At 2:30 PM my plane, a trustworthy DC-3, left for Kano. (No substitute for the magnificent DC-3 has yet been developed. They are economical, need little take-off and landing space, are reasonably fast and easy to maintain.) The flight was less than one hour. I was met by Fenn, a youngish Englishman with a London degree, who took me to the Central Hotel, placed a car at my disposal and later joined me for dinner.

Kano is quite a place. [See Photos Nos. 5, 6 and 7.] An enormous walled city, it was conquered shortly before World War I. Its wall then was 40 feet high, now it is perhaps 12–15 feet high, since it was built of mud and is not kept in repair. No Europeans live inside the walls, nor are Southerners – Yorubas or Ibos – permitted to live within the wall. Only Hausas and Fulani, Tuaregs and in general Moslems are permitted to live inside. Inside the walls are huge areas not built up, evidently intended to provide pasture and food in case of siege. All houses are of mud, except for a few modern ones made of cement brick. Every three years, the houses have to be thoroughly fixed. This is about as long as mud lasts, since it is made without straw. (Adobe lasts a lot longer.)

There are lots of pools of stagnant water used to make the bricks, and for the animals, but inside each compound I am told water is piped to a communal pump. The water comes from about 20 miles outside the city, is pumped to a reservoir on top of a mountain, and distributed from there. I couldn't get into one of the houses. There are a few wide streets. You enter the city through gates, the doors of which are now removed. (The British still had to storm them.)

Women, however, may still enter only through one of the gates. There are lots of little streets. The town is very much as one expects a Saharan city to be. Kano is at the Southern end of the trans-Saharan trade-route, though the Sahara proper really does not start until about 200 miles north. Now in the rainy season – it actually rained a little – everything is green, and the fields around the city are filled with groundnuts, millet, corn, guinea corn, and a few cassavas. But in the dry season it gets to be pretty parched. Inside the city there are a few mountains, and I climbed one to get a good view and take pictures.

In the evening Fenn came for a drink...He drove me around the city, and we talked of whom I wanted to see. The main impression is flat country full of groundnuts, trees planted near houses, a piggery which stank to high heaven with hundreds of unpleasant vultures eating some horribly stinking stuff, I don't know what.

At dinner we were joined by Jan Stewart and Ogley and his wife, on their tour of the North. The discussion focused on problems of getting information. No one had the faintest idea of groundnut acreage, domestic consumption, production or anything. The only thing known is marketing board purchases for export. If there is a bad crop, one knows people reduce their sales, but whether and by how much they reduce their own consumption is anybody's guess. Stewart showed me his results so far, indicating that food crop production may have increased by as little as 10% since 1951, when he and Prest[4] made the first national income estimate. This would mean that it has not kept up even with presumed population growth, about 50%. These are the limits, with no indication of a reasonable estimate.

August 10. Visited the oil mills. Neither mill was crushing, both shut down for maintenance. This was fine, because I saw what unskilled labor can do to machinery. Crusher drums of hard steel had huge chunks chipped out, because despite all care metal pieces had got in with the nuts. Machinery does not last as long here as in Europe or America, and pieces break which never break in Europe. Hence a need for large inventories – about 1 year's worth.

Labor productivity is low, again mainly due to lack of education and for social reasons. Casual labor actually earns more to start with, since it is paid by the piece, and men rolling and loading drums, or feeding machines with groundnuts, all done manually, can make as much as £1 a day, while regular production workers start at 4/6 or 4/7 a day. But the casual works for only 3–4 months, the others all year round. The casual labor is organized by the manager hiring a boss and agreeing on a certain amount of work for a certain amount of money. It is then up to the boss to decide how many people to hire. The work requires physical strength and stamina, and this depends on nutrition, so wages go up in proportion to how well you are fed. There are no Nigerian supervisors, managers, or owners.

The real complaint, however, is reserved for marketing board policy. I first talked with Tsakkos, a Greek Cypriot, who managed the firm of Manitsides, another Greek Cypriot. Tsakkos was rather circumspect. But he complained bitterly that marketing board (MB) policy was discriminatory and tried to curtail domestic oil processing. The domestic oil crushers must pay the same price as the foreigner, i.e., the world market price less freight cost, but including the export tax. This actually makes sense if you don't want to subsidize local groundnut crushing.

The complaint is that the crushers cannot buy as many groundnuts at world market prices as they want. They are guaranteed 80,000 tons as a minimum, or one quarter of the crop, with a maximum of 150,000 tons, no matter how large the crop. The policy is not transparent and completely the reverse from that pursued in other countries, where domestic fabrication of local product is encouraged even by subsidies. Actually only 10% of the groundnut oil is used domestically, the rest is exported. But Tsakkos said the market was increasing slowly since groundnut oil was superior to palmoil for eating and cooking, and "the African generally wants the best," a statement which obviously must be taken with lots of salt.

If Tsakkos was restrained because he was Greek, Baldwin was not. He is a peppery Englishman who runs the Nigerian Oil Mills for a Lebanese...Where Tsakkos complained that they had used up their quota of nuts and had to shut down for three months with all the added cost this implied, Baldwin stated bluntly that the damned second-rate expatriate Britishers hated the Lebanese, that the quota was low because they didn't like private industry to interfere with their MB, that they liked even less to see private industry run by Lebanese who were willing to live hard like Africans; the MB was telling them they were not viable, but that was a damned impertinence. If private industry wanted to lose money that was its own business and none of the business of a civil servant.

He even suggested the United Africa Company (Lever Brothers) might be operating a racket; it preferred handling groundnuts rather than compete with oil producers, and there was personal spite on the side of the British, who fortunately had left. Even now, however, it was hard to track down a decision in order to appeal against it. The MB would refer to the PS, who would refer to his minister, who denied ever making such a decision.

I talked several times with Fenn about the MB policy, pointing out that it didn't seem to make any sense to an economist. He privately agreed, but gave the official board explanation, which doesn't stand up. The argument in brief is that the board has a good and steady market abroad. If it diverted exports to meet local demand, the customer – read Unilever for all practical purposes – would develop alternative supplies. If in the next year the oil crushers couldn't use the nuts because they were not profitable, the MB would not be able to sell. Hence the MB must remain in the export market with sufficient supplies.

I pointed out that the argument would not stand up. To stay in the foreign market, the MB would need no more than 300,000 tons. Groundnuts competed with plenty of other oil seeds and American lard. All fats and oils had become increasingly substitutable for each other, hence the elasticity of demand for the product of an individual country ought to be high after one season. In a given season, if the MB found the crushers wouldn't buy as much as in the past, they might be stuck with 100,000 tons or so, but the next year they would be right back in the market. Besides, the groundnut crushers had developed a market, and did also sell abroad.

All this was privately admitted but officially denied. Fenn said he thought MB policy should be changed, and agreed the firms should be allowed to lose their money. But he also pointed out, what Baldwin had not, that Baldwin's mill had in fact not used all its quota, and that the shouting about the upper limit was in his – though not in Tsakkos' – case somewhat beside the point.

Tsakkos, incidentally, showed me a piece of American machinery which made my American heart jump with pride. To lift the oilcake as it exits the crusher, the mill has several baggerlifts costing £800 each and taking up a lot of space. They will be scrapped and their place taken by a single gadget, costing £45, which does the lifting work even faster. It is a tube with the diameter of a rain spout. Inside is a sort of drill, and on top a small electric motor which works the drill, which lifts the stuff. He now uses one, and can afford to keep two in inventory.

In the afternoon I was treated to an exhibition of pest control put on for the producer representatives of the MB. The MB had its annual meeting; an assorted group of local sheiks, some looking like noble Romans, others somewhat less noble, some in spectacular dress, others less so, was shown what was done with the money they voted for pest control. A tent was set up from which we watched groundnut pyramids of 9,000 tons in bags being sprayed, dusted, and gassed, until nothing was alive inside, all with an explanatory lecture. [See Photo No. 8.] Only five pyramids for local crushers remained, and even this was an impressive sight – about 45,000 tons. It must be truly spectacular to see all 600,000 tons before they are evacuated by train.

We were then taken to the research institute and the experiments were explained in simple language for sheiks and economists. So all in all it was a satisfactory afternoon, followed in Fenn's office with an inspection of documents explaining the setting of the season's price. The document was secret so I couldn't get a copy, but I got what I needed.

Then we returned to the city for more sightseeing. First the mosque, built ten years ago by the Public Works Department. We were allowed on top of the minaret, specially built for unbelievers!...We couldn't enter the mosque because prayer was underway. Also, I was not allowed to take pictures of the faces of houses which had designs on them, though I suspect that Baba, the driver, probably was too careful. He claimed to be an Arab, but actually was from the Sudan, and being both a Northerner and Moslem, was permitted to live inside the wall.

He took us next to the huge local market. There were no art products of any kind, lots of cassava flour, onions, dried mushrooms, salt in open bowls. Hordes of children followed us shouting "dash, dash" which means a tip; there were mats, shoe polish boxes cleaned and made into cassava graters. Except for the salt you saw few imported things. Salt comes from across the Sahara on camels and I actually saw one camel...

There were lots of second hand bottles and cans for sale, but most of the stuff seemed to be food and a few household implements made from second hand iron and steel. In one place was a small car graveyard with people taking cars apart and hammering the metal back into sheets and strips...I was taken aback when a pimp, a tall Northerner, offered me, in the midst of a crowd, a girl who was reasonably good-looking and painted. She smiled at me, and seemed slightly insulted at my lack of interest after an obvious show of surprise which I couldn't repress. I wouldn't be surprised to learn that she had been offered to me for sale!...

August 11. Morning flight to Enugu. On the plane I met Bronk,...who runs the Eastern Region Development Corporation (ERDC), has a brother who is a historian in Cambridge, and knew about Ann Arbor, because his brother has lectured there. So part of the trip was spent on business, but partly I slept. I find that gradually I get to the limit of my absorptive capacity, and I'm glad this intensive trip is coming to an end soon. It is high time not only to write up my notes of this trip in detail, but also that I have time to read and think, before writing my memo to the Joint Planning Committee.

We arrived in Enugu at 2:00 PM, and met Faaland[5] and Brown, PS of Economic Planning. At the Rest House, where Faaland is also staying, we exchanged experiences and decided on my program. The discussion with Faaland was the first occasion forcing me to work out my ideas about what to do in the future and how to go about my job in detail.

Unfortunately, I won't be able to see Abakaliki this time. I wanted to because of the successful rice scheme, but it turns out to be the place where girls won't dress, because it is against custom to wear cloth, Independence or not, and wearing cloth will supposedly make them sterile! Also, last year six people were eaten there. All this just 50 miles east of here.

August 12. Faaland showed me his terms of reference, very similar to mine. He also showed me his first memorandum, dealing essentially with organizational matters, some but not all of which are applicable to my situation.

Next I went to the Ministry of Education. School construction is done almost completely by the local people. Ibos are avid for education, and will do anything to get it. The government pays the teachers, but the people get together to build the schools. High school equipment is funded partly by grants, but the buildings are locally supplied. The University is Zik's[6] baby, who has kept it outside the Ministry of Education. Universal free education was introduced against the advice of Ministry staff, who pointed out there wasn't any money. Only nine months of salaries were voted, in the hope something would happen. When nothing did, they had to introduce fees, which led to large-scale rioting, mainly by women, who are traditionally responsible for educating their children. Bloodshed and deaths ensued, and a debate in the House, with cries of "throw the black man out, get the white man back," etc. I asked for the proceedings. They must be something!

At present the first four years are again tuition-free, the next four years cost fees which increase with the grade, and currently it is not intended to free them. The real increase in cost will come as trained teachers are substituted for the cheaper untrained ones. At present there is one trained teacher for 2.8 untrained ones. The aim is to get to a ratio of 1:1.

Next came Williams in Finance. He is a British Treasury civil servant who is sent as a sort of troubleshooter to various parts of the Commonwealth. I had already met him in Lagos. Forward planning in the Ministry does not extend beyond one year. I'll get all the documents they have. And tomorrow Williams will fetch me and Faaland for a drive in the country and for dinner at his house.

Town Planning was next. They are also responsible for questions of land tenure which seems to be similar to the Western Region. What startled me most was that the cost of developing an acre of industrial estate in Port Harcourt was only £400 against £3,000 in Ikeja. There is something funny somewhere. An Israeli is doing most of the actual physical planning.

Health was next; the only Ministry with a Nigerian PS. I got the hospital building plans, and a confirmation by the chief medical officer that population was increasing at more than 2% per year. At 11:30 AM I went to Major Riggs of Community Development. This was actually a very important visit. This Ministry helps people help themselves. It has only £190,000 for four years, yet seems to have accomplished near miracles. It furnishes villages wishing to build a school, road or bridge with the few technical means they need to do an efficient job. He repeated that there was no trouble at all in getting people to do things, they were eager. If the village will furnish free labor and local material, the Ministry will send it a bulldozer and carpenters, fitters or other skilled people. The whole question of priorities is settled semi-automatically, since a village will decide on the order of things it wants. It usually won't be in a position to build at the same time a school, a water tank, a road and a bridge.

At 1:00 PM Faaland and I went to the Ministry of Works, to hear their story. Most of their work deals with roads and bridges, but they also do some electricity installation...Only water supply now has forward planning...

To the ERDC at 3:45 PM. Businessmen with workable ideas are in short supply, though coming along. Bronk took over two years ago when the ERDC was in a mess from which it has not yet fully recovered. The previous chairman's experience was limited to running a small drugstore and pharmacy. Some of their doings are surprising, such as investment of £1 million in a real estate company buying properties mainly in Lagos. Which hardly seems the thing for a development corporation to do. But cement is a good thing, and glass may come in soon...

August 14, 1960 (Port Harcourt)

Sunday afternoon in a gloomy rain. The accommodation has air conditioning which works – so one doesn't have to sleep under mosquito net – but I will have to share the room with Col. Bull who is expected this evening, and there is nothing whatsoever to hang one's clothes or coat on. The food is miserable and the service poor, but the place is clean and, I hope, hygienic. Nowhere on the trip have I had the fancy accommodations of Lagos, but it has nowhere been bad. Maybe the weather gets the locals down, too. In any case they seem to be noticeably less cheerful in this Rest House.

August 13 (continued). Today saw the PS Agriculture, whose Department is a mess and which he is now reorganizing. Didn't learn much...

At 4:30 the Williams' appeared to take us into the country. Only 5–6 miles outside Enugu we saw a really primitive village. [See Photo No. 9.] Mrs. Williams, who uses her time to discover the countryside, had been there before, and wanted to buy pottery for her garden. This gave us an entrée. Normally people don't like it much if you walk in. The village was surrounded by a mud wall with one entrance. In it, romantically but quite unhygienically, were the huts, mostly round, but one had mud pillars and was reasonably substantial. The English they understood was more or less limited to "pot," "one shilling," "five shilling," "dash." They even let me take some pictures without all running away, but they may not turn out because the sky was overcast, and the village itself was shaded by trees and shrubs, both leafy and palms, including bananas.

The women brought Mrs. Williams green peppers as "dash" and everyone was happy when 3 shillings changed hands against three pots. Pottery incidentally is an old art, and is made without a wheel. The village was crowded, though there can't have been more than 20 huts. Goats and chickens were running around, but the main smell was of burnt wood. The men wore pants but no shirt, the small girls and old women wore nothing above the waist, but some of the middle-aged women wore blouses. There were hordes of children, mostly naked. You could see that this region is thickly populated. The fields were orderly, but strangely enough, there was a lot of cocoyams, the poorest of all foodstuffs. Agricultural experts say the land is fertile and could be made to yield plenty.

Near the village was a small juju-shrine. (The country is about 90% Christian, but that doesn't seem to prevent them from going to the juju shrine.) Actually there wasn't much to see. Certainly there was nothing artistic about it: four sticks a yard high, with a tin roof. A sheep skull nailed to one stick, and cloth, probably for wiping blood. Under the roof small earthenware bottles, what it was about I don't know for sure, but it has to do with pacifying ghosts.

Further on we came on an enormous market, where the road, which makes our Vermont road look like a four-lane highway, came to an end. It was a lovely sight. A new market building was being built cooperatively with cement, but trading took place on the ground. It is always the same things, except this time we saw some dried fish. On one side was an ancient drum the size of a man, with a women's head stuck on to it. I was not allowed to photograph the market. There was a shrine beside it, and that was probably the reason. The market itself was in a lovely grove of huge tropical trees, all with flying buttresses and root systems spreading over a large area. I think the people feel it to be a holy place.

Next, Williams took us to a juju shrine in the form of a railway train. There was a building which, so an inscription said, cost £150, 7 shillings, 4¹/₂d. In it was a carving of a train, primitive but with all detail, people, equipment and so on. I got off on the wrong foot because I offered "dash" but by mistake produced a 3d piece instead of a shilling. The two look very much alike. So no picture. Fortunately, an unemployed miner came along who knew a little English and explained that the masks – he said max – for dancing were kept there. The juju man had his 'office' in a room behind it and no one was allowed there.

August 14. This morning I was driven down to Port Harcourt...It rained most of the time. Even so the drive was beautiful, particularly the first third south of Enugu. It is hilly country, the roads wind, there are hairpin turns. Mostly the road follows the ridge. The distant view might be Vermont but the foreground is huts, palms, cassava and cocoyams and other non-Vermont-like vegetation. The road was excellent, and since it was Sunday trucks were few. But every so often I saw villages teeming with people, and women and men with baskets on their heads streaming to the markets.

Gradually the vegetation changed, with oil palms becoming dominant, but always food crops in between. The drive down took five hours for 180 miles, the train would take nine hours, which gives you an idea of the number of stops it makes and the density of the population.

PH is a new town, built since 1912. I went first to the docks, which are being expanded to accommodate an oil refinery. There are minor industries such as furniture, cigarettes, aluminum sheet, and steel window and door frames. The big thing will be the refinery, and perhaps a steel re-rolling mill, based on local scrap. Otherwise it is a completely uninteresting town...

Today it is exactly four weeks since I arrived in Lagos. It is just impossible to continue absorbing new things at the rate I have been doing the past month.

August 17, 1960 (Lagos)

August 15. Port Harcourt turned out to be a miserable nest. The Rest House was clean enough, had airconditioning which even worked, but there was not even a hook to hang one's cloth on, and the hot water worked only sporadically. Also I had to share the room with Col. Bull, which turned out to be just a minor inconvenience. Enugu had forgotten to introduce me in PH so I had to do this myself. But everything worked reasonably well.

I started off with the Provincial Secretary, Smith, who didn't know who I was but was helpful anyway and made various appointments. First I went to see the Chairman of the Marketing Board, where the story was the same as elsewhere, except that the product was palmoil and palmkernels, mostly for export.

My next stop was Pennycuick (pronounce Pennycook), a Scotsman with an upset stomach but a courteous manner, who is the managing director of the bulk oil plant in PH. At this plant the palm oil delivered by Pioneer Oil Mills or individual farmers is cleaned and refined, stored in tanks which look like gasoline tanks, and then shipped abroad to margarine or soap factories. The process is rather simple. Nevertheless, where abroad two people service 20 boilers, here it takes 20 men to do the same job. Carelessness, inability to adapt. The same story here as elsewhere: African labor is the worst paid and most expensive in the world.

Col. Bull had got me an invitation with Brian Shaw, head of Shell Oil's air operations. Bull is Nigerian representative of Bailey Bridges and British Aircraft and sells quite a few to Shell. It was a pleasant, strictly non-business lunch, cold corned beef and salad with Danish crisp brod, and a welcome change from the always identical fare in the rest houses.

An afternoon visit with the Shell Oil manager finished my day. The discussion was less '*ergiebig*' [fruitful] than I hoped because decisions about the future are made in Lagos. In the evening another meal in the local club which was both better and cheaper than in the hotel.

August 16. Started at 6:00 AM for Benin. I drove the Mini-Minor (a little Morris) about ten miles out of PH. While it was a zippy car, it felt funny, until in Aba we discovered a flat tire! We found a new tire and had another example of inefficiency: it took $1^1/_2$ hours to get the new tire mounted – no charge, however. A second new tire for the spare which also went bad was changed in another garage in five minutes.

This didn't end the adventure. We drove to Onitsha to catch the ferry across the Niger. It got hot and muggy. Onitsha is North of PH, it is a big town whose main pride is a new market; it was rather fantastic with all the stands inside in the shade. It was almost impossible to pass, what with bicycles parked, food sellers who sit in the alley cooking rice and African dishes and selling them to the sellers. A unique thing is that prices are fixed! It is also astounding what there is for sale: canned goods from England, creams from Holland, paperbacks from the US and England, millions of watches, mostly from France I am told.

The first ferry was full...Then we caught a small one. There was a tremendous ado until everyone was aboard, although there were only three cars (a Pontiac station wagon with ducks running around in back, a Volkswagen and us) and six trucks; I can't even guess how many people with packs. Finally everything was set, and we started across. The Niger runs fast and dirty, but a breeze made it not entirely unbearable. It took just one hour to cross. The landing was fantastic. The captain, who must make this trip about 5–6 times a day, just couldn't point the ferry in right, and we had drive onto the ramp through water. We saw few native boats on the river, but some motor boats were carrying only passengers.

From then on it was plain driving. By 6:00 PM we were in Benin, where we had to share a room again. This time no airconditioning, hence sleep underneath mosquito nets, but it was cool and there was a hot bath, which even worked. It poured all evening and most of the night, and the electricity went off as it does here when it rains too hard, I am told. But we were tired, and went to bed at 9:30 PM. For the first time rain was as in the books, drumming on the tin roofs.

In the Rest House, Benin bronzes were for sale, but I wasn't sure whether they were genuine, and didn't really like any of them, so I didn't buy.

August 17. We got off at 6:00 AM in pouring rain, alternately driving an hour each. By now I was used to left hand drives, where the shift is not as in the mirror, and hence requires thought. We breakfasted on rye crisp and paté, then drove on to Ife, where they have the really marvelous bronzes dating back 600–1000 years, whose origin is a mystery. The museum is a small modern building in a typical disorderly African town. We were the only visitors...

Lunching in the car again – this time on bristling sardines – we drove through pouring rain to Lagos, arriving at 4:30 PM...I am really glad to be back in Lagos. I don't think I can absorb much more – two more days of interviews here, then I must sit down and think, read and write.

Notes

1 George Mendenhall, *Emeritus* Professor of Ancient Near Eastern and Biblical Studies at the University of Michigan, whose course I audited (it was my custom to audit a course that interested me, as far as possible every semester at Michigan.)
2 The Beiers were later divorced. Beier left Nigeria but Mrs. Beier became a priestess of the Shango Cult and the fourth wife of a Yoruba drummer, drummers being an elite group among the Yoruba.
3 Gottfried Haberler, then Professor of International Economics at Harvard.
4 Alan R. Prest and Ian G. Stewart collaborated in the first systematic attempt to estimate Nigeria's national accounts: *The National Income of Nigeria, 1950–51, Colonial Office Research Studies* No. 11 (London: HMSO, 1953).
5 Just Faaland, an economist with the Christian Michaelsen Institute in Bergen, Norway.
6 Nnamdi Azikiwe, head of the Eastern Region's dominant NCNC party and first Governor-General of independent Nigeria.

Chapter 3

August 18–September 11, 1960
Visit to Benin, Completion of First Tour
in Nigeria

August 20, 1960

August 18. Just to be settled and in familiar surroundings again makes a difference. I started with an appointment at the Ministry of Works, but the Chief Engineer was out, so the talk stayed in generalities. Next I stopped at the Port Authority, run by two very efficient Port of London Authority fellows, one of the truly efficient and money making operations in Nigeria. I got what I wanted, which was expansion plans, cost and means of financing, and also an invitation to accompany two Development Loan Fund people from Washington, who were to inspect a shed constructed by an American loan.

In the afternoon we were whisked by motor boat across the lagoon to Apapa. Since it is between seasons with little cocoa, groundnuts or palm oil left to ship – the new season starts in September – the sheds were relatively empty. [See Photo No. 10.] Still, the enormous number of bags stacked scientifically in huge square mountains was impressive; and the method of taking them down rather dangerous: they pull out a bag about 5 rows up, and then the 20 or so rows come tumbling down, to be carted away to the shop or railroad.

The Apapa docks are constructed on shifting sand, and sand constantly leaks into the sea, causing holes and bumps and requiring sand and concrete to be constantly pumped through holes into the foundations. There were quite a few ships in, including passenger steamers from England and Ghana, and three boats were waiting in the lagoon.

The visit was short, but I will return Tuesday for the whole morning, to see more, including the complicated management operations which ought to give an idea of the traffic scheduling and also of the statistical raw material available to work up.

The rest of the afternoon and the evening were spent writing, first a brief memo addressed among others to Gardner, Ford, and ICA, about two ideas; (i) exchange between Michigan and Ibadan; and (ii) training of future civil servants. The rest took a lot more time: it was a first draft of what I want to submit to the Joint Planning Committee (JPC), with which I am to meet on September 2. This causes a good deal of worry. I have a lot of ideas as to what ought to be done next and what I want to do, but I won't have time to polish the document, since it must be distributed to the members by Monday. So I have just this weekend to do it.

Today I had my first major taste of local inefficiency. Before my trip, I handed over some interview notes to be typed; two were done, the rest are lost, and I'll have to do them over again. This, I am told, is quite normal here. The African who was supposed to do the work, was supposed to be a typist-stenographer, but I am afraid he isn't much good.

While shopping in Kingsway, the local department store run by United Africa Company, I had my first taste of racism; a minor one at that. A middle-aged English woman yelled at a uniformed African doorman, "Don't you touch me, you touched me," and when he tried to point out that he hadn't deliberately, she just yelled "Shut up." It was a scene, and I felt embarrassed. It's the only time I have run across this. There are a few intermarriages, the barriers are social rather than racial. It is quite common in government and a few businesses for white men to take orders from Africans – after all, all ministers are Nigerians – so this was unusual. I wanted to say, "Madam, remember this country is going to be independent in six weeks," but thought better of it. Maybe he *did* pinch her, though I doubt it.

My Ministry of Commerce interview didn't work out, because the senior assistant secretary, Clayton, with whom I had an appointment, had to see the Minister. Another official came after a while and helped. What I wanted to know was what information on industries, particularly planned ones, is available. There is an updated list of all intended new industries in Nigeria, but as it depends on the cooperation of the Regions, there is no guarantee that it is complete. Moreover, it omits information such as proposed investment value, number of workers, capacity, etc. But the ministry intends to start finding all this out...

10:30 AM – met with the newly organized Chamber of Commerce, with four British and two Nigerian businessmen present. My objective was to make contact, explain who I was, and enlist the Chamber's future cooperation. I particularly want investment plans and cooperation with an industrial census that I think should be undertaken. The problem is never the big fellows, such as Shell, who talk quite openly but the little ones, who are afraid to divulge anything for fear of competition. Nevertheless, the two Africans (one of whom ran a printing plant) thought that, with enough advance publicity, the small fellows would cooperate.

The Africans were interesting in another respect. They expressed fear of foreign investors, give the foreigners' stronger capital position. They wanted protection from being driven out by large foreign firms. As an example one of them said he wanted to start a flour mill with £10,000 but was turned down, because a foreign mill with £1 million investment is coming in, and how can you compete with that. Well, it is dubious, but it is questionable whether even a £1 million flour mill will be economical.

The talk got briefly onto productivity, and everyone agreed the major problem was supervision. Once trained, African labor is reasonably efficient, if properly supervised. But the printing manager said they did not dare modernize their plant, because it would take too long to train the labor for new machinery. The story is always the same: lack of supervision, lack of flexibility, which can be traced back to education. Also the climate, which one tends to forget in an airconditioned office, and the bad diet of carbohydrates, which does not make for strength.

After lunch I was off to see Elder of the Produce Marketing Board. The main problem I raised was the policy towards further processing of domestic materials. I got a slightly different picture from the one in Kano. The anti-Lebanese, anti-Syrian aspect of the matter was clear. But Elder pointed out that groundnut crushers did not pay export taxes as I had supposed, and that one major reason for the decision to limit groundnut crushing was that oil and nuts competed with each other in the world market; that the Board was the world's major seller of groundnuts and as such in a strong position, and it didn't like to be undercut by the crushers. I have to do quite a bit of reading on this – I got some policy papers – and think about the proper policy, but things are slightly different from what they appeared to be in Kano. Strangely enough, the PMB officials did not really give me the proper argument for their side, whether from ignorance, sympathy with the crushers, or for what other reason I can't figure out.

The PMB people were also most helpful in promising introductions to their people in London and I shall certainly have my hands full in the four days there.

Dinner with Thompson. We discussed my memo, which I must redo today. He wanted one point omitted, and some rephrasing. I also want to reorganize it and add another point. Altogether he liked it and thought it was just what was needed – which reassured me. He warned me, however, that some of my proposals, particularly on data collection, constituted a long-term proposition and might not be useful for my exercise, which is true.

Later we were joined by Dr. Pius Okigbo (the 'g' is hardly pronounced), who worked with Jackson on the National Accounts, was a lecturer at Northwestern, where he got his PhD, and is taking over the Planning Section in Enugu. He is supposed to finish the national accounts in two weeks (I hope he does). I had to argue quite a bit to convince him that I need the worksheets and not merely the finished product. But I think I won my point.

Okigbo is an obviously intelligent and lively person. He is also somewhat conceited. Everyone is mad at him right now, as he is playing hard-to-get. In Enugu they were furious because he didn't bother to answer letters from the Ministry. I tried hard to convince him that he had to get to Enugu and prepare his targets for me. Since I believed it I think I was successful...

August 22, 1960

August 21. Worked hard to rewrite my JPC report. Thompson is off to London on business tomorrow morning, and my report should be mimeoed today to be distributed in ample time for discussion. For the rest of the day I read secret files which I can't take along, files having to do with foreign borrowing plans, the reactions of potential foreign investors, etc...

On the whole, however, the pressure is likely to let up during the next two weeks, though I must write up my memos on the trip discussions and prepare things for Lyle Hansen, who arrives Sept. 1 and will stay until the end of January. We may also get a Dutchman from the Dutch Colonial Service.

Thompson came for supper, and we went through my report, polishing it here and there, and particularly eliminating unintentional political hot potatoes. For example, I referred to the Jebba dam, but should have referred to the Niger dam. Jebba is actually 80 miles south of the projected site. But the real reason is that it is close to Ilorin, which is disputed territory, claimed by the South.[1] It is ruled by a (Northern) Fulani emir, but the population is Yoruba, and to complicate things further, it is Moslem. I have to learn all these things gradually, and only hope that when Thompson is gone there will be someone who can help me with these matters.

Lagos *is* a hardship post, even if my letters don't indicate it. The main reason is the sameness of everything, the lack of recreation. The radio is abominable, there is no music, not even a decent movie.

August 25, 1960 (Lagos)

August 22....Scott, in charge of technical assistance for the ministry, showed me the file on UN schemes. My main concern is a UN/ICA team for the Northern Region. Then spent time in Commerce and Industry, going through a file giving details on the individual industries which are being considered...

August 23....A fascinating 3-hour tour of the Port, with a nice Anglo-French traffic manager, Thompson. Saw the various warehouses and their organization, in some respects the center of activity. The object is to clear goods as fast as possible. Noted the different methods of storing and sorting. Thompson showed me neatly stacked conveyances to move heavy loads, then pointed out that it took eight years to get the Nigerians to stack them properly so one could find what one wanted and nothing was in the way. Heavy sacks of groundnuts and cocoa are still head-carried. Labor productivity is now high, but it took eight years of very hard work to get there, and constant supervision is still required. There are quite a few Nigerian foremen and managers, but Nigerianization is proceeding too fast at the top, the next two years will see too much turnover and efficiency will deteriorate before it can be improved again.

The authority handles its own railway, has up-to-date workshops and is now trying to increase dock space. On the way back the motorboat took me around the harbor, past the floating dry dock, to the navy yard, and back to the car.

In the afternoon, two fascinating hours with Peter McGlashlan, Shell/BP's manager, with whom Thompson made an appointment, and who had heard about me through the Chamber of Commerce. He will send me nonconfidential data on future operations. The main thing I learned is that the amount of oil is huge, and should make Nigeria a major world oil producer. Production costs are relatively high because of swamps, inaccessibility, depth of wells, etc. But to Europe there is an enormous freight advantage compared to the Near East, which offsets the higher cost except for Kuwait. Nothing is as cheap as Kuwait...

Nigeria can never use all its oil and will always be an exporter of crude oil. The refinery will serve the domestic market, but not export except perhaps to Ghana or Togo. Exports of crude oil depend mainly on construction of pipelines and of a port. Also because of the ocean currents, the river mouth silts up and must be dredged, and experimental dredging is now underway. Nigerians are very impatient to sell oil, but won't see that you can't increase sales suddenly, particularly with the current glut on the market. Some have no notion of the technical difficulties of laying pipelines through the swamps. Furthermore, Shell must get a better idea just how much oil there is before pipeline size can be determined. Still, Nigeria is already exporting considerable amounts, about 500,000 tons per year.

The gas oil is the real *embarras de richesse*. Some will be sold to the ECN for heating fuel. But industrial uses are not in sight. A petrochemical industry is out of the question for Nigeria. Even in England, a single plant normally suffices for domestic and export sales of most plastics and petrochemicals. Production of phosphate fertilizer is being considered, based on imported phosphate from Togo, and exports to the US of the finished product. Domestic use of phosphate fertilizer is likely to be diminutive. The only industry conceivable is nitrogen fertilizer.

There is some thought of liquefying methane at -300°F, but this is a new process, likely to be done in Algeria rather than Nigeria. Some gas will be bottled for domestic use. But there are fabulous amounts here. It can be used for steel making but this raises political questions because it competes with the coal, also found in the Eastern Region. The Coal Corporation recently had to lay off workers.

So far Shell has spent over £60 million in exploration. It will take until 1972 before past investments are recovered. No dividends will be paid for years to come, all earnings will be ploughed back into expansion...

August 29, 1960

I was this weekend again in Benin, and the trip, which started out rather badly, was nevertheless a success.

August 26....Arch Callaway came from Ibadan, and joined the Kingsleys for dinner...Kingsley worked for the ILO, for UN, for Ford, and has been around. For me it was valuable to hear more about the specifically Nigerian problems of inefficiency, which after a while begin to go on one's nerves. When I leave this VIP apartment I will have to face it all the time...In my permanent quarters I'll have to supervise and train 2–3 Nigerians who should be willing, but will have to be taught virtually everything. The gap between the top people in government and business, who are second to none, and the less educated, is fantastic. And I am more and more convinced that filling this gap is the major problem of economic development, and a slow-moving, time-consuming one.

August 27. We left Lagos at 5:30 AM, taking $3^1/_2$ hours to get to Ibadan. One reason it took so long...was that I had to change some traveler's checks. Using a bank in an underdeveloped country is not only very expensive – the cost of changing money is fantastic – but very slow. The transaction, which in the US or Europe would take just three minutes, took half an hour, and was so fast only because we showed impatience. The calculations are slow, the paperwork is slow and there is much of it. The manager has to check everything. And then the person who does all this can't give you the money, but sends you to another place where you again stand in line.

...We finally reached Benin at 4:45 PM. Nothing had worked. There was no accommodation in the catering rest house. Callaway's friend was out of town, and we had to wait to find out where we would stay. But after a while things began to click. We went first to the police station and got a constable to drive around with us. For to find even street names once one gets out of the center of town is rather difficult. But once the name Simon Obaseke was mentioned everything began to go smoothly.

To explain this, a short digression into Benin history is necessary. Benin used to be the most powerful empire in West Africa. When the British finally conquered it in the 1890s it had badly degenerated, some say as a result of the profitability of the slave trade. Anyway Benin and Ife were and are not only famous for fabulously beautiful bronzes, but also for cruelty unmatched until Hitler's concentration camps.

The king, or Oba, was removed by the British and exiled, and in his stead the father of the present Obaseke was made Oba. He is of royal lineage, which is important, but rather progressive otherwise.

The present Oba is the grandson of the deposed one. But the antagonism between the two branches of the families continues. The Obasekes are Action Group, the political party in power in the Western Region (of which Benin is a province), while the present Oba has shifted political allegiance several times and just before the last regional elections changed to the NCNC, probably because he expected them to win. There is a ruling Oba to whom the people owe some sort of allegiance, but thus far I have not yet understood how or what, or just what the power of the various kings is. The kings go by lovely names. The Oba of Benin, the Alafin of Abeokuta, the Owo of Oyo, etc.

Well, it appeared that arrangements had been made for us to stay at the Chresbo Hotel, an African hotel run by the sister of Obaseke. That was something to be described in due time. Anyway, it is a hotel in which one can stay if absolutely necessary, in preference to, say, sleeping in the back of one's car. Next we tried the museum, but that was closed. However, we left a message, and were told the man in charge would be there on Sunday morning. Next we met Obabiagbou, and things began to pick up. The name means: the Oba shall rule the world. It seems this particular idea is rather international. The Obasekes, or at least Obabiagbou, seem to be physically different from the other Binis (the name of the inhabitants of Benin). The Binis are related to the Yorubas. They seem to be taller, better built, and stronger, and have very good and strong faces. The English was excellent though with an accent.

Obabiagbou is a historian, and works on the Benin history project, which involves tracing the history of Benin from local records (which hardly exist, the palace having been burned in the 1890s), Portuguese records – the Portuguese have been trading with Benin since the fifteenth century, and writing down oral traditions. This was, of course, fine since it meant that we had a really competent guide. My first wish was to see some modern Benin bronzes. This is actually a misleading term. The 'modern' bronzes are more or less copies of traditional patterns made in the traditional manner by the *cire perdu* process. The arts guild was closed, and the craftsmen who all live along the same street had, with one exception, nothing to sell. The exception was beautiful but too ornate for my taste.

But then we met Chief Inneh, the head of the brass workers guild, a man of perhaps 60–65. He took us to the guild after some persuasion, but told us there was nothing for sale. All pieces were reserved for the Independence exhibition. And the pieces were quite reasonably priced, between £4 and £7. In the States they cost around $300, if you can get them, and old ones – which means pre-British – fetch thousands of dollars. I bought one, a simple mask, the only one on sale, which I liked enormously. The workmanship and design are just beautiful.

There were some figures which just were wonderful, but not for sale. The old man was very pleased at my taste, because the three pieces I liked best were ones he had made. After having seen these pieces, I won't touch any of the other stuff. There is nothing primitive about it, this is really great art. Chief Inneh is a descendant of the brassworkers who came from Ife in the 15th or 16th century. He told me the art was inherited, and all workers came from families who had been doing brasswork for generations. His whole attitude changed. Where he had thought I was just another tourist, he now talked about his art, when he saw that I was interested, he explained what the mask was about, and why the one I had thought too ornate was so expensive, and what was difficult about it. The masks were worn around the belt, different grades of chiefs and nobility wore different masks as identification as well as ornaments.

Having seen this put me into a better mood…These pieces were so beautiful that I became quite cheerful, and began to face the night with equanimity.

With Obabiagbou and the chief clerk of the Obaseke we had a drink in the (all) African Club, where we were introduced to the local grandees: the dentist, the head of the Baptist Mission School, etc. After dinner at the Rest House we went to look again for the Chresbo Hotel, where we had left our luggage. Just to find it in the dark was quite some trouble. There is little street lighting. The Africans whom we asked were quite sure where the Chresbo hotel was, but gave contradictory instructions, without getting into an argument with each other. They then all proceeded to sit in one's car and propose to take one there. Whether they are just friendly or whether they want a ride, or expect a shilling for their trouble isn't clear.

Anyway, we finally made it…The hotel, a one-story, motel-like affair, was not too noisy. The bed was reasonably clean – I think they use poor soap because everything is what our advertising boys call "tattle-tale-gray." There was a bathroom and toilets, but the water had been shut off. Apparently water is scarce in Benin. The next day I was told the waterworks are being expanded, and some bore holes are being sunk. After some arguing we got basins with water and a bottle with drinking water.

At 10:30 PM we went to bed in comparative quiet. At 11:00 PM a terrible racket started with someone blasting a radio. After Arch had shut that off, things were quiet until midnight. At midnight sharp another racket started, which sounded like a religious service of some kind, and was so identified the next day. There was chanting, responses and singing, always the identical thing for exactly two hours, accompanied by drums and gourds. By that time all we could do was laugh. At 2:30 AM there was a fight in the neighborhood. By 3:00 AM I fell asleep.

August 28. At 5:00 AM the night watchman insisted I had told him to wake me, and it took me some time to persuade him otherwise. At 6:30 AM they brought the infernal morning tea, which I had specifically told them I didn't want. By 7:00 AM it was time to get up. The room was reasonably clean except for squashed bugs, leaving the walls red with blood. The toilets were another matter, but we had wisely used the ones in the resthouse. After inspecting the kitchen, we refused to eat in the Chresbo hotel. It was dirty, cockroaches were lying around, etc. The funny thing is that the waiters had been in England on a special catering course, and were smart in their white uniforms with golden buttons. But the training had not extended to the kitchen.

So we had a decent breakfast in the resthouse, and went off to the museum. This was in general disarray, because it had just moved. But there were a few marvelous pieces. The best Benin bronzes are in Germany, Switzerland and England. But they are being brought back. The museum is not as unique an affair as the one in Ife, but it is definitely worthwhile. One piece, a jug in the form of a leopard, was again wonderful.

Next we went to the Oba's palace. First we were shown one of the shrines which had bronzes and swords, one for each generation of Obas. They were essentially shrines of ancestor worship. They are housed in a compound with walls on four sides and a courtyard in the middle. The sword bearer of the Oba, a muscular youth, showed us around. He was one of the few excellent physical specimens, and evidently had both special training and a special diet.

We were then shown into the presence of HM the Oba, an elderly man in simple white gown and cap. I have noticed that at formal occasions Nigerians wear caps indoors. The first thing I noticed was a refrigerator with "The Oba of Benin" stenciled on it. The palace is a huge compound built of mud. We were not allowed to see its historical parts, such as they were. Binis are never allowed in, and others only rarely. There were a few nice statues. Among them one of my favorites, that of an old man, a faithful servant, from the 16th century. And there were quite a few retainers, but who they were or what they had to do I don't know.

Callaway must have told the Oba that I was of German origin, for the first question after an awkward period of silence was whether the Germans were of the same stock as the Belgians. I didn't want to get into a Congo discussion, so I pointed out that they were related, but that all the European races had got pretty much mixed for centuries.

This led to another pause. Since the Oba is a kind of ruling king, it was up to him to discuss what he wanted and when. Next he wanted to know why people wanted to go to the moon, whether I thought there were spirits there, whether I believed in good and evil spirits. Fortunately I had begun to find out that traditional African religion does believe in one God, who however is not really interested in the world where lesser spirits rule. I told him that our business was not to worry about things we could not know anything about, but to do God's will here and now, for example by developing the Second Five Year Plan. The Oba didn't bite. If there was one God, there were also lots of lesser spirits, both good and evil. Did I believe there were spirits on the moon? The Oba was convinced there were, and when we got there we would meet spirits more powerful and intelligent than we are. He always came back to this point.

To me the visit, which the Oba ended after an hour, was interesting for a number of reasons. The Oba not only comes from an ancient royal house, but, in ways that I don't quite understand yet, he is a real power in the country. Many people continue to consider him rather than the British or the present Federal or Western Region Government to be the real ruler. He owns through his position a vast amount of land which is potentially the richest in the country. Yet he believes in the traditional religion with all its superstition as well as good things – and no matter what present-day anthropology says, there is a lot of superstition based on fear – and he showed no interest in development or anything of the kind.

To be sure, an hour is not enough to judge. Obabiagbou thought he asked silly questions, and then added that he was considered too progressive by many Binis. In a way I was glad to escape the royal presence and get back to my friend Chief Inneh. We went with him to the museum to see whether he could make me another leopard. He was very pleased and thought he could by November, not before.

When I get back and have time we will visit him again. I want to watch him work. The method consists in making first a form out of mud. This is then covered with wax which is very precisely molded. The wax in turn is covered with mud. Then the wax is melted out, and the bronze is cast into the empty space. Finally the mud is removed. This *cire perdu* is an ancient process which probably came with the Portuguese, but may have been older and native.

After a friendly goodbye, Obabiagbou showed us two pagan shrines. The first I was permitted to photograph, the second not. There were quite a few rooms, all with open centers. The clay benches on the sides were for sleeping, the center for air and drainage. There were ancestral shrines, with some chicken and goat bones from recent sacrifices, the number of staves indicating the generations of ancestors. There was an altar of the God of Iron with a figure. Apparently one sacrifices to him when driving to Lagos, to make sure the car won't break down. Among the offerings were a broken bicycle chain and an old car jack.

The main room was the Goddess of the Sea, whose worship is associated with fertility – I believe her name is Ohika. Unlike the shrine of Shango in Ibadan, these shrines were bright and cheerful and had a sanctified atmosphere after their fashion. The small figures were made of metal, but the big ones of the Ohika were made of terra-cotta and painted. The goddess has light skin, white being a holy colour. The figure of the goddess was in the middle of a clay bench running all along the wall. Her arms were outstretched and held up by servants. All around were a dozen or so figures of servants. I asked the gentleman who let us in how old the figures were, but he only knew that they were already old when he was a child.

The next shrine was the biggest Ohika shrine in Benin City. Its walls on the outside had animal figures, but I was not permitted to take a picture. Obabiagbou thought that if the priest had been there, a pound or so would have made it permissible. There are lots of things which are forbidden, but suddenly become permitted with money.

There was again the same atrium-like arrangement. We were permitted to go up to the figures but not on the platform. They were big painted terracotta figures of the goddess and her servants. There were worshippers there, women who prayed for a child. The worshippers were painted white. The atmosphere was definitely not unpleasant.

Back to Simon Obaseke, who had returned from his trip...Callaway had been with him all the time, helping him with some business transactions. He is about to go into rubber plantations and processing on a large scale with a foreign partner – for family reasons they never trust fellow Nigerians as much as foreigners. With the extended family system, a Nigerian will always put his big family ahead of the business...

...At the Ileysha farm settlement we met the supervisors, Taio Williams and his wife Caroline, both completely westernized Nigerians with an English education. She is now training teachers, primarily of home economics, an important matter here, surpassed in importance only by his extension and agricultural supervision work. He got a two-year fellowship to Cornell to learn more about agricultural extension work, and she would like to go too, so she can with the farm women. Their work is important if the country is to get anywhere. Unfortunately she is bonded to teach for two more years, the condition for her getting her English education.

At 8:00 PM we were back in Ibadan. Driving in the dark is rather strenuous here. The roads are narrow, one can't be sure whether the wagons will stay on their side, whether goats and ducks are in the road, or bicyclists decide to behave like chicken. And when it is dark, it is *dark*. The rain forest is dense, and houses have no electricity...

Incidentally we heard that most educated women are against polygamy, and that the habit is breaking down. But having as many children as is physically possible is still the ideal.

Also some jujumen will play ball: an agricultural extension worker is said to have thought that stocking the rivers with fish would solve some problems. The trouble was the crocodiles ate the fish, and crocodiles couldn't be killed because they were juju. The extension worker approached the jujuman, who thought it over, and after the appropriate sacrifices (and no doubt transfer of cash) he decided only red crocodiles were juju, and the others could be killed! It seems the religion is as flexible as in the West...

August 31, 1960

It seems that the regular rainy season starts heavily in June. Then there is a dry spell, followed by another rainy one. Well, the second rainy spell has started. It certainly is pouring down now and gives no sign of stopping. Still I am told that the atmosphere is drier during the rainy season than during the dry spell when it is saturated with moisture from the ocean. Lagos is worse than Ibadan. But as soon as one gets away, one gets the Harmattan, the dry, dusty wind from the Sahara, so you can't win in this matter.

August 30. Steward, general manager of the Shell Marketing Co., received me cordially and gave me confidentially their forecasts for the Nigerian economy, for what they are worth. He spoke of their training problems. Shell Int. is a truly international company with no headquarters in the usual sense, and always aims at an international staff. They hope to have 80% Nigerians by 1972, but this will take some doing.

The rest of the day I spent at the Statistical Office. I was rather shocked at what they could not produce. They are supposed to have a census of industries employing 10 persons or more – there can't be more than a couple of hundred firms in this class. Yet they can't get it complete. For example, data from 'Odutola' are missing. He just does not answer. All of this makes statistics work difficult. The balance of payments and capital formation statistics are rather good, though individual items also are defined differently from our usage.

The SO was supposed to do a study of destinations of Nigeria's imports. This is important because import duties are allocated to the regions according to the imports they absorb. In fact the allocation is simply done according to population. Considering that no one knows what the population is, I am surprised that this hasn't caused trouble yet...

September 4, 1960

September 2. My visit reached a sort of climax with the JPC meetings. The session started at 9:30 AM with the Stanford group reporting. After a coffee break, my paper was discussed from 11:00 AM to 2:00 PM, paragraph by paragraph. I think it went well on the whole. Actually, quite a bit was procedural, but I needed decisions on a few points, and in particular, promises of cooperation from the regional ministries.

Chief Dina came for dinner, and afterwards the Stanford people came for a drink; Dina is a very impressive man, a graduate of the London School of Economics, and probably the most important Nigerian in the Civil Service. He told me of Britain's slowness in recognizing the need to train Nigerians. Also, the origin of the political parties was group selfhelp, by way of financing promising young people to study in England and America. He himself was the first of the Yoruba scholars, together with Chief Davis, who couldn't find a job as an economist and was lost to law. He is now a distinguished solicitor in Lagos. I have not yet met him...

My driver lives 12 miles from the car, which he reaches by bicycle. I try to use him outside hours. He told me that he will quit his job in a year and go back to farming, which will pay better. His father will give him land. He wants advice from me but I don't really know anything about tropical farming. He wants to go in for rice and chickens, which indicates he is willing to break with traditional growing of yam and cassava and start new things...

September 7, 1960

September 6. Lyle Hansen arrived and we have been working hard ever since...

September 7. Today we met with the Stanford group and the Dutch consultants on the Niger dam. The issue was to forecast river transport and evaluate the dam's navigation benefits, a tricky problem...At Thompson's request I wrote him another memo about the statistics we will need to do our job. This is actually more troublesome than it seems, because one has to have some idea or at least some feeling for the direction in which the study is to go. And also a feel for what kind of information a government statistical office can get.

Tomorrow we will work out in more detail what Hansen is to do while I am gone, what projects our Nigerian assistants should start, and what I will do in the States on Nigeria – mostly reading. Hansen is a pleasant fellow, middle 30s. Fortunately we see eye to eye on the problems and how to attack them. I hope to persuade him to stay...

September 10, 1960

This is my last letter from here. It rains, the second half of the rainy season is upon us. Since Hansen arrived we have been working to get the next few months organized. Fortunately we seem to think along the same lines. His previous Pakistan experience helps, but I am astonished how little. I mean that I figured out by myself just what must be done. And in many respects Lagos is infinitely better than Karachi. This goes not only for the stores – one can get almost everything here – but also for the quality of the civil service. The present set of PSs is first rate. Undoubtedly with Independence and rapid promotion of young and inexperienced Nigerians, this will deteriorate for a while. Our job is to rescue as much as possible, and in any case it will be substantially done before the deterioration sets in. Furthermore, as the Nigerians get experience, administrative efficiency will certainly improve again. The Western Region is proof. Compared to Pakistan this seems relatively easy, because we don't have to create an administrative machinery on top of the intellectual work, which is really our job.

I had all along the feeling that things are going fine, as my letters undoubtedly showed. Hansen can hardly get over the fact how much better things are here than in Karachi – housing, health, administration, stores, everything. But there is little for recreation and in general facilities for relaxing are bad. But he now wants to come, if he can persuade his wife, who, though she likes to travel and live abroad, is frightened after their nasty Pakistan experience.

Anyway, we wrote two lengthy memos. One to specify in detail what data must be assembled, the other spelling out work assignments. It is also clear that I will have to get from Ford at least one more person for the North and probably one to work in the East. The government has already decided to ask Ford for a man to work with me in Kaduna. They may request another one for Enugu. The job is too big for Hansen, myself and two Nigerians.

Tomorrow I am off to Rome. Then Zürich and London.

September 15, 1960 (Zürich)

September 11. I spent all day at FAO/Rome, finding out what studies had been done on the future of cocoa and oilseeds, and what information I could get. There wasn't too much, but in general the information on cocoa was that production probably would increase 3% per year, that per capita consumption in the US was falling, and that cocoa prices in the future would not be high. With oilseeds, on the other hand, the long-run prospects were good, there would be a shortage, and we should encourage the Nigerians to grow more. I was interested also to find the FAO people on the side of the oil crushers...

Note

1 Stolper presumably means the Western Region; there was no legal jurisdiction named "South".

Chapter 4

February 1–March 8, 1961
Second Tour Begins: Consultations in London and Rome, First Meeting of Joint Planning Committee (JPC) Under Chairman [Prime Minister's Economic Adviser] Prasad, Grubbing for Planning Data, Gov. "Soapy" Williams' Visit

February 1, 1961 (Zürich)

January 25. Met Sir Eric Tansley at the Nigerian Produce Marketing Board, London. He greeted me warmly. The cocoa price has dropped catastrophically by more than £30 a ton. The Nigerians had to reduce the price they paid to their farmers in the middle of the season for the first time since the system of Marketing Boards was introduced during the war. The Nigerians and Ghanaians had apparently decided to withdraw from the London cocoa market altogether, but the Nigerians gave it up after a few days when they found out that the Ghanaians were selling anyway. There is utter confusion. Tansley said they had no inkling from the agricultural statisticians that this year's crop would be so big; and it looks as if future crops would continue to increase as the result, probably, of spraying in the past. This year Brazil had a bad crop. If next year the Brazilian crop is also normal, the price of cocoa will drop even more.

In fact Tansley said that in the past one could rely on one out of three crops being poor. But this does not seem to be the case any more. As far as I can see this is usual in agriculture. With proper agricultural techniques, the effect of weather gets minimized. After all, the proper sunshine and rainfall has effects also on the proliferation of pests which are now controlled by spraying etc. Tansley says he has been selling all along as much as he could. In fact he never sold as much cocoa by this time of the year, and still the stuff keeps piling up. People who before the war got £25 per ton thought of £250 as normal and £200 as a minimum. It may very well be that they will have to get used to £150 or less. After all, industrial prices have about tripled compared to prewar, so a sixfold increase still leaves the Nigerian cocoa farmer relatively much better off than before the war.

Interestingly, the Russians have not yet bought a single ton of cocoa. They are shrewd buyers and evidently expect the price to drop further. As far as dealings with the Russians are concerned, they are tough bargainers, but will stick to their word, once they have signed. However, one has to be extremely careful in phrasing the document to be signed: They are good lawyers who will find any loophole or any sloppy formulation.

About Ghana, Tansley was quite pessimistic, and not merely because he is *persona non grata* there. He says that Nkrumah has lost control internally, and that the internal situation is increasingly controlled by communist sympathizers. The civil service can make no decisions but simply has to refer everything to the President's office. Commander Jackson is out. There is no orderly marketing of cocoa. People who want to buy 10,000 tons go to the Government, offer a price, get it, and the profits go to the party coffers.

Finally, Tansley told me that in Rome, just when I will be there, a study conference on cocoa will discuss all these problems. He suggested that I attend. And I have cabled to Lagos to be attached to our delegation...

February 9, 1961 (Rome)

February 8....At FAO I found a cable from Lagos, to get in touch with the new PS of Commerce and Industry, Daramola, who is leading the Nigerian mission to the cocoa price stabilization conference. Apparently, however, it was preferable that I did not attend as yet...

February 9. This morning started at 10:00 with Hartmans at the FAO. He is a Dutchman from Minnesota, on leave from the University. I got out of him the Report of the Joint FAO/ICA mission to the Northern Region, or rather the first draft. He said the Report was poor and a big disappointment. The purely technical aspects were OK, but the structure of the report feeble and the organizational proposal ill thought through. Also many inconsistencies...

Hartmans also knows a lot about the farm settlements in Western Nigeria, having been a consultant when they were set up...He mentioned that the aim is to set up modern farming units: if you can't make a farm work as well as in Western Europe, when the Government gives you the capital, land, machinery and advice, the thing is a failure. He said he would have preferred to start with three or four pilot settlements, but it was decided to go ahead with 13 in different soil and temperature zones. He said also that further north there were good possibilities for grain production, even wheat, and that one farm settlement produced corn of a Mexican variety – not our hybrid – to feed to poultry, which seemed successful.

Later I saw Dr. Fagundas – I hope I got the name straight – who is an agronomist. I was after information of the type of crops that could be grown in a tropical soil. He differed with Hartmans on the feasibility of wheat. He was more optimistic about the dangers of laterization, but thought that in areas of high humidity and constant heat, the best bet were tree crops which protected the soil, returned some nutrients to it through fallen branches and leaves and brought minerals up from depths where rain washes them. Pasture and cover crops eventually might change the situation, but he doubted whether lengthy fallow could ever be made obsolete.

I raised the question of why there were no more green vegetables grown in the neighborhood of Lagos – where there was a big and sure market. Apparently the soil is too swampy. But there are some varieties of okra, peas, etc. which differ from ours, which could be grown further north, and as skills and managerial abilities improved, would be grown...

February 10, 1961 (Rome)

This was a very busy and on the whole fruitful and pleasant day. I started out with Hartmans. The talk concerned mainly Nigeria's land settlement program and the country's agricultural possibilities.

First it appears that there is some discussion between the FAO team, headed by an Israeli named Gil, and the Nigerians as to whether or not the farms in the land settlement program should eventually become either freeholds or 99–year leases, rather than cooperatives. Strangely enough, even the Israeli is for freehold, while the Nigerians feel that coops are more suitable. The philosophy of the whole farm settlement program is (a) that it should pay for itself and (b) that it should break the traditional low productivity pattern and set an example for others. Hence when the boys who are being trained for two years get to the point of running it, after having been let loose on the farms under supervision for another two years, they ought to get complete control. The Nigerians feel that even after this period they will need direction to prevent them from sliding back into old-fashioned, inexperienced practices.

Gil and the FAO team felt that by that time they can look after themselves. The real issue is whether they should hold livestock individually or cooperatively, and whether they ought to own their own tractors. Since neither exist as yet in any numbers, the issue is somewhat academic. However, it is quite obvious that larger farm implements should be owned by several farms together, while small ones could be individually owned. The Japanese, more even than the Germans, have developed small one-man tractors and cultivators. Hartmans agreed that it would be worthwhile to investigate Japanese machines and agricultural practices in some detail as more suitable to the relatively small-scale farming than even West German or Swiss or Dutch practices.

Halfway through the discussion we were joined by Taiwo's friend and boss Michael Akintomede, who runs all the land settlements and farm institutes. Akintomede felt that land could be individually held, but not machinery, and that there was no point in developing one-sow farms; that if farmers were willing to hold larger numbers of livestock, they should be allowed to hold it individually.

I raised, as is natural, the question of tsetse fly and crop rotation, as well as fertilizer use. It seems African soils are pretty much like other soils in their need for phosphates, potash and nitrates, particularly phosphates. The question was one of price. No crop could do without them. The problem of crop rotation could be licked, they thought, by introducing grass cover and livestock. An eight-year rotation has been worked out, with eight crops for the first four years, two a year, and then four years of grass plus pasture to let the soil recover and add manure. They will try out corn – millet corn, green legumes; corn-legumes for feed; corn-grass. But while they think it will work, it is still experimental.

Both Hartmans and Akintomede thought that, in spite of the present catastrophic price fall of cocoa, cocoa was still the best bet for Africa. The market would increase, there are at present no real substitutes, and no other areas can produce it as efficiently. The fantastic increase in production this year (from 150,000 tons last year to 190,000 tons in Nigeria, and from 250,000 tons in Ghana to 420,000 tons) was mainly due to spraying and new plantings. Next year's crop would increase again though not as much.

Ghana was a lower-cost producer than Nigeria, since they had less problem of spraying. If the price could not be stabilized, production was bound to fall in Nigeria and Ghana, but more in Nigeria. Many farms are owned by older people who hire labor for harvesting, and will find it less profitable to do so. What will happen is that the first four of the six or seven harvestings will be done thoroughly, but the last two or three to pick an already thinned out crop will be omitted, and "then we will be where we were before except at a lower price."

Hartmans also drew my attention to a new Niger Delta Authority which is trying to develop a plan for the Niger Delta jointly between the Eastern and Western Regions and the Federal Government. This seems to be something new. At least I didn't know about it.

Hartmans was skeptical about rubber as a crop. To be sure it would grow well; but the labor to tap it was skilled, and it was impossible for a rubber estate to raise enough income to compete with cocoa. On a plantation with labor being paid 5/- a day it was profitable. But the target income on a land settlement was £700–£1,000 a year for a family of two workers, equal to what peasants earn in Western Europe...

Back to the office to see Abbott, an Englishman and expert on marketing. The FAO has made a study of meat marketing and is suggesting the establishment of modern slaughter houses in the North, with shipments in refrigerator cars of beef and pork to Lagos and other urban markets. This would involve also cold storage facilities at both ends of the line, plus a few refrigerator cars, say three initially. There was, he felt sure, a market for meat of better quality. Whether byproduct plants would pay was another matter.

All of this was seriously questioned by Mittelsdorf, a German who had been all over Africa, and gave me statistics he had collected for FAO for a conference in Chad. He was rather more convincing than Abbott. First he said, everybody talked about the great weight loss of cattle when it is shipped. However most of it does not walk south on the hoof, but is shipped by rail. In Germany over distances of 400 km the weight loss was found to be $2^1/_2\%$ of live weight. In SW Africa the loss in shipments of over 1000 km to S. Africa was -1%, both negligible. Most people who talked about abattoirs and refrigeration plants assumed losses of 50% which was impossible anyway.

Secondly he pointed out that a refrigerator car costs about DM 80,000, against 20,000 DM for an ordinary car. Everywhere return freight was a problem. You could load a cattle car with iron or anything you please to go north, but not a refrigerator car. Thirdly he pointed out that the numbers slaughtered were too small to have efficient plants for byproducts. It was more economical to bury the by products than to make bone meal, etc. In any case the byproducts could be had just as easily after the cattle had been shipped.

Mittelsdorf instead suggested concentrating on increasing first the quantity of meat available. Since Africans boil rather than broil meat the tenderness and marbled nature was not so essential. Anyway he pointed out that the sausage industry was developed precisely at a time when Europe was too poor to eat marbled beefsteak. So they added to tough beef some pork which supplied the softening fat.

He pointed out that, because of malnutrition, cows gave only a tenth the milk of a European cow. This competed with the raising of calves. Hence the 'infant mortality' of calves was exceedingly high. A little improved feeding of oil cake or grains could almost double the cow population. Furthermore because of poor nutrition the cows did not produce many calves in the first place, the majority remaining sterile. Long before one should worry about abattoirs and improving the quality of meat, one could increase its quantity substantially by better feeding. All of which made sense to me.

In the evening the new permanent secretary of commerce and industry of the Federation, Daramola, invited me to dinner. Daramola is a charming and highly intelligent Yoruba who is here to head the Nigerian delegation to the Cocoa Study Conference. Naturally much of the talk dealt with the problem of cocoa price stabilization.

I could not see how this could be done efficiently or even effectively. One plan is a mixture of price controls, establishing a minimum and maximum price, plus the establishment of buffer stocks, to be financed jointly by consuming and producing countries. This plan was put forward by a Brazilian, Tosta. The crucial issues, however, what the prices should be and when the buffer stock authority should buy or sell, is as yet unresolved.

I pointed out that it was exceedingly difficult to withdraw this year 150,000 tons of cocoa into a buffer stock with the prospect of adding equal amounts for another three or four years. It would probably be better to let the price fall and hope that inefficient producers would be squeezed out. Daramola agreed more or less with this gloomy view, but still hopes to be able to establish a minimum price. He pointed out that the American from Hershey's was quite optimistic about the future of cocoa and was surprised that so few agreed with him. He just says they should produce what they can, and they would be able to sell it. Unfortunately he too omits to mention the price at which these sales would take place. Obviously, Hershey and the other major chocolate users have an interest in establishing a buyers' market, though in the long run he may be right.

Daramola asked me to postpone my Lagos trip to Monday night so I can read a draft of the proposals and help the Nigerians work out a constructive criticism...

February 12, 1961 (Rome)

February 10 (continued). I discussed two other major questions with Daramola. One was the possibility of increased trade with Japan, which at present buys little cocoa. I was enthusiastically in favor of this. The Japanese are getting rich, and what is more, they have developed a lot of good small agricultural implements and other machinery which is at least worth investigating. The Minister of Commerce and Industry wants to go to Japan in spring and probably also the Prime Minister.

The other issue was the problem of Iron Curtain trade. Here again I thought that one should try to get more sold, particularly as chocolate was apparently habit-forming and thus might make them more peaceful (!!). But I thought we needed an excellent lawyer to make the contract loophole-free. Tansley had told me that the Russians would stick to a contract which they could not wiggle out of. I was very leery of barter deals and thought we just had to insist on iron-clad, no-resale clauses to avoid competing with our own cocoa. If possible the trade should be in convertible currency.

Daramola asked me what I thought of Iron Curtain goods. I said I knew something of East German and Czech goods; that they were acceptable to good, that they always had been good engineers and designers but had to learn metallurgy where on the whole they seemed behind the West; that machines were still too heavy. And that experiences with Indonesia where the East Germans were supposed to have built a sugar refinery – which to this day isn't finished, the East Germans say it is the Indonesians' fault – suggests that there ought to be penalty clauses of some sort. E.g. if goods agreed upon in a bilateral barter agreement are not delivered at the promised time, payment in convertible currency would become due.

Incidentally I had a feeling that this discussion of Iron Curtain trade earned me Daramola's confidence; I can't be sure why, but he probably expected me to rule out Iron Curtain trade *a priori*, which I would be a fool to do and which certainly would not be in Nigeria's interest. On the other hand I pointed out to him there was no sense in giving the stuff away, since it was easier in this case to use it as fuel at home. Also one had to make sure the quantities sold were additional to those that would have been bought anyway. Finally, I said one could not use cocoa for economic development abroad in the same manner as wheat in India, since it was a luxury good, not a wage good like wheat – I didn't use the term, of course.

The final question was what I thought of shifting the selling of cocoa from London to Lagos. Tansley had told me that this would be quite feasible though less convenient. If he were a younger man, he could easily go there to advise. One would be not quite as much in the center of things as in London, but with teletype and phones that would not be a major obstacle.

I raised, however, another and to me more important point. Thus far, London has been selling both Nigerian and Ghanaian cocoa. For example, responding to my question, Daramola told me that Tansley had always seen to it that Nigeria and Ghana cocoa were sold equally, say in the ratio of their production. If the operation is shifted to Africa it is split between Accra and Lagos. In this case I felt that the sellers would necessarily be in a worse position. Moreover, Ghana now produces twice what Nigeria does. If there are big surpluses, the temptation for Ghana to undersell Nigeria would be irresistible. In fact, Ghana would act against its own interests if it did not do so. There was the further point, that production in the Ivory Coast which to my surprise already is up to 90,000 tons would increase if the prices in Nigeria were raised too much, and the Ivory Coast would have a sheltered market in the Common Market...

It was after all this that Daramola asked me to stay over, if I could, to help him and the delegation formulate a position towards the proposals to be distributed Monday morning...

February 13, 1961 (Rome)

...This morning I met Daramola, who handed me a draft document with the request to study it and give them my opinion at lunch. I worked on this and background papers until 1:15 PM and wrote about $2^{1}/_{2}$ pages of comments, which at the request of Daramola I handed to him. They dealt mostly with the fact that the agreement tried to set up export quotas, but did not discuss prices; did not discuss how prices were to be adjusted when the stock of cocoa increased; allowed for sales outside the agreement without proper safeguards; assumed that all adjustments could come from limiting quantities sold and pushing sales, without spending money on reducing production costs and finding alternative uses for cocoa; and did not consider what to do when stocks accumulate faster than anticipated. There were more points.

They seemed happy with my comments, particularly those which agreed with points they had made themselves. I am to meet Daramola again tomorrow at 10 AM before the next session to see whether there are other matters he wishes me to do.

Lunch was in the Hotel Excelsior, a bloc from the Flora and even more swank. The host was Chief Akin Deko, Minister of Agriculture of the Western Region, a wiry and sharp man, witty and friendly. He and his permanent secretary, Longe, were in native garb, the rest in Western dress. Daramola, Longe and the Chief left earlier for the next meeting of the Cocoa Study group in which the price was to be negotiated.

February 15, 1961 (Lagos)

I finally made Nigeria...Kano was a surprise. The temperature was an agreeable 65°. Unfortunately, we had another unexpected delay, and left only at 9:45 AM. Lagos was about 85° and humid, but after that long flight a welcome sight. Lyle and Peter Clark[1] were there to fetch me; the airfreight had come, and by 2:15 PM we left the airport for the $^{3}/_{4}$ hour drive into town.

...Later in the afternoon Lyle Hansen came back to tell me what he has done, what the difficulties are, what troubles we are in, how far behind schedule we are, how politics are, where he has stepped into hornets' nests, who is who now as against two months ago. I tried to absorb what I could, but I am afraid it was a bit much. Still I got the point...

February 22, 1961

Most things are routine, strenuous routine, but routine nevertheless...

February 20....At 9:00 AM Lyle and I went to the Statistics Office to see what they were doing about our problems. Christopher Pite is the acting chief statistician, a very nice but also ineffectual fellow, later joined by Evans, who is even less effective. We need a chief statistician. The discussion followed these lines: when can we have the national income estimates for 1959? The answer, well, when do you fellows need it? "We need it soon." Would April be soon enough? And so on. Nothing whatsoever had been done on the industrial statistics. The Commerce and Industry man who had talked about their underemployed field staff just didn't know what he was talking about. On the whole it was a fruitless and frustrating morning. We hope we succeeded in building a fire under Pite and Co., but it is pretty doubtful.

After 11:00 AM Prasad[2] called: he wanted urgently a memo on a proposed JPC committee on statistics. He has the sound idea that we have to get the ministries going on collecting the information we need, and should educate them via a monthly two-page review of economic developments in Nigeria, leading to an annual economic review. So Lyle and I sat down and worked out a memo. Today Prasad said he wants to submit it in our name. This wasn't exactly what we thought, but it is OK with us. Pius Okigbo read the memo today and made a number of good suggestions: to reduce the size of the committee, whose meetings are to coincide with those of the JPC, with its regional representatives, and aim first at a quarterly review...

February 21. Dinner with our secretary, Patricia Stonebridge. We drove into real native quarters, and I felt rather adventurous...But Toni's Bar was closed. Apparently, restaurants open and close frequently. The main reason is that non-Africans, who run these restaurants, can't own property. Hence they make an African nominal owner for 2–5% of the property. Every so often the African decides that he is the owner in fact as well as in law, and as a result the place shuts down. So we turned around and went to Maxim's with dance music, air conditioning, decent food, not too expensive. How anyone wants to dance in this climate I don't know. The waiters were Nigerian, the *maitre d'hôte* Lebanese, and the clientele all white. There is no discrimination, but Nigerians just don't go there.

Patricia is pretty, efficient, slightly on the fat side, a friend of the [Toby] Lewis', the new PS in our Ministry. She has secondary school training, plus Pitman's Secretarial School, has earned her living from age 19. Doesn't really like Lagos society, which she says is petty, malicious and gossipy. Probably so, with so few whites and not much to do, this is the only outlet, I suppose.

We are glad we have her. I had told Ford that if we didn't get a good English secretary I wanted money to hire one. Actually the Nigerians resent secretaries more than us, because they underestimate the skill required and consider it more competition...

February 22. Pius Okigbo, Eastern Region Economic Advisor as well as boss of its Economic Planning Unit, came to the office and started telling us about the Economic Commission for Africa (ECA) meetings from which he had just returned. Most talk was political, about minimizing the difficulties of inter-African trade between territories associated with the Common Market and the others. Actually the former French territories liked both the preferences for their products and the easier access to capital. But they see this as a short-term proposition. In the long run, after the infrastructure is built up to the English territories' level and differences between the associated territories and the others have been evened out, they expected to move closer to the latter. I questioned the validity of these 'homogenizing' theories of the French, however the issue wasn't the validity, but rather what was said.

We moved home for lunch and continued the discussion, going first through our questions about the ER fiscal forecasts, which in many respects simply don't make sense. Pius said he had already undertaken steps to get the reasoning underlying the estimates, and we should have them soon. Next we went through the national income tables. We didn't finish and will have another few hours on it before Pius goes back to Enugu on Saturday.

Pius Okigbo is very good; excellent English, very quick. We should invite him sometime to Michigan. The trouble is he is very ambitious, blows hot and cold, is not quite sure whether he really wants to do what he does, *versus* heading NISER,[3] or perhaps even succeeding Prasad, which probably wouldn't be bad. But he should first settle down and do one job well. For us, he is a really lucky thing, because there are not many people with whom one can talk over economic problems on a technical level. As Teddy Jackson said: he speaks our language.

...Later this evening, to prepare for the Feb. 28 JPC meeting, I have to read the Stanford report on transport coordination. What I have read of it is very good, in spite of some pretty wild assumptions on the speed of industrialization. It is said to be full of political dynamite, but I don't yet know enough about these things, and have been unable to spot them so far. In any case that is the reason why the report is being kept secret.

February 25, 1961

...The work is now mostly going through files. Also there are the various estimates of future Government revenues, which are my responsibility, and which I have to make sense of. We had asked not only for the projections, but also for the assumptions underlying them, and those have not been provided. So I have to go through the figures in detail, question their size and trends and write memos to the Regions asking specific questions.

Secondly, we try to meet the juniors daily, get their progress reports and assign tasks to them. I sent Peter over to Statistics to collect data, and he came back without a single figure. Statistics is in an unholy mess. They do not know what they have. On the whole it is an incompetent operation, and Lyle and I will, whether we like it or not, have to be unpleasant to get some work out of them.

Thirdly, there is the Stanford Transport Coordination report. Except for some gratuitous asides, and a few questionable assumptions on the rapidity and composition of industrial growth, it is an excellent report, stressing the need for accurate cost-benefit calculations, making such calculations, and making proposals which on the whole should – but probably won't – be implemented. Primarily they recommend greater reliance on railroads for long distance hauls; concentration on feeder roads; minimum standards of road building, accompanied by prohibition of trucks heavier than 6–8 tons, or 3 ton/axle load (this is politically almost impossible to get through) except where special equipment is needed; charging trucks and passenger cars enough license fees and gas and diesel taxes to recover maintenance cost and interest on capital value of roads; and relying somewhat more on river transport. Unfortunately we will not know for a while whether we will get the Niger dam or not, which will make a lot of difference to many of our problems, from cement to generating equipment, fertilizer production, and transport.

February 24....The day started out with a preliminary meeting of all heads of agricultural research stations – crops, fisheries, forestry, livestock and what have you – presenting their budget requests. All are British and rather peculiar. They sit on their stations, won't talk with the regional research people, who won't take the initiative either. These people deserve our support, but they make life difficult for themselves and for us with their pride.

February 25....Peter Gibbs, Deputy Permanent Secretary from Kaduna, came in, and we had a general talk about the Dam, industrial studies in Pakistan, etc...Tonight there is a party at the Hansens for the junior staff and their wives. If they want to go dancing afterwards they have to go without me...

February 26, 1961

February 25 (continued). Sam Akande was at the party with a most charming wife, the first really good-looking Yoruba woman I have seen. Obineche was there *sans* wife, and Igwagwu couldn't make it.[4] ...Lyle and I decided not only to get to know our Nigerians better, but to have mixed parties and start general discussions. With Sam Akande discussions are easy. He is very westernized even when he comes in native dress as he did. He has broken with quite a few Yoruba traditions. He is not brilliant, but intelligent, pleasant, conscientious and very hard working. He did give up a chance to go to the US to work with us, and we all agree that he ought to have a chance as soon afterwards as possible.

The discussion dealt in part with politics: how popular was Ghana (not very); what about democracy? Lyle and I tried to get across that we didn't particularly care about specific western forms, but felt that decentralization of power was essential, and so was decentralization of decision making. Obineche had fallen for the talk about Russia having been so backward, when they in fact produced $4^1/_2$ million tons of steel before World War I, and had produced hordes of great scientists and writers. And Lyle could disabuse them of some nonsense about China.

Peter Clark is much younger, which comes out in his taking questions and answers very personally, rather than as abstractions. We also said that experts were just experts, and had no right to assume they should run the show. The fact is that in underdeveloped countries intellectuals are, if anything, even more conceited and intolerant than with us, and the British-trained ones seem to have this peculiar mixture of primitive Marxism, Christianity, Socialism and Welfare State characteristic of the British Labor Party. Akande is again rather an exception. Obineche has no PhD so he is modest, but Igwagwu has one from Wisconsin, and I sometimes wonder about his attitudes. On the whole I believe we are establishing good working relations.

I haven't much time to follow politics. But I'm changing some of my opinions. Pan Africanism is popular with the young people. What it amounts to, I can't say. But the situation seems a lot more fluid than I rather naively assumed last summer. The chances are as good that Africa will be balkanized as that there will be relatively few big countries. The only thing I still believe is that Nigeria, and not Ghana or Guinea, holds the key to the future. But even this might turn out to be wrong.

February 28, 1961

February 27....At 10:15 AM we went to Prasad's office for more strategy talks. The first question dealt with an aerial survey which the Canadians have offered to make, and a geological survey that is to follow. There are apparently methods of making electro-magnetic surveys from the air, to detect economically significant geological formations, but they don't work too well in Nigeria where the granite overburden is too thick in places. Also the weather is frequently unsuitable for aerial surveys, which delays the completion considerably.

Next we talked about the agenda of today's JPC meeting. This went quickly. But then we got into a discussion of planning targets where real differences between

Prasad and us appeared. He wants us to make a sort of bargaining plan, which we don't want to do. He claimed that in India the economists made projections regardless of the foreign exchange gap, and the necessary foreign exchange was forthcoming. But this was not really true during India's second Five-Year Plan.

Prasad is also trying to make himself responsible for the plan, which he isn't, and we have to assert ourselves. I fear we will get into some difficulties with him, in spite of the fact that on a practical working level his and our approaches come to pretty much the same thing. This meeting which was to last until 11:30 AM actually went on to almost 2:00 PM...

February 28. Most of the JPC meeting went well and we finished by 12:40. But there were some sticky moments. It was Prasad's first time in the chair. When he came in, everyone stood as a mark of respect. I wonder whether this will be repeated. The first sticky moment came when Prasad wanted a committee on statistics, essentially to get Statistics to produce more. No one could quite figure out what he was after, particularly when he wanted to get balance of payments statistics transferred to the CBN, which could only say that it was difficult to produce them because Nigeria has only a mild form of exchange control.

Prasad got into some trouble when he rather pointedly said he had not been asked to participate in briefing a proposed economic mission, adding that of course he was only an advisor who gave advice when asked. This didn't go down too well. Nor did his frequent reference to how things were done in India or the World Bank. In general I had the distinct feeling that we were listened to with more attention than he. He also had a tendency to lecture rather academically and as Reg Clarke[5] said to me afterwards, "I thought that was what we had you and Lyle for." It was fairly clear that he will have some trouble being accepted. Lyle and I make a point of speaking only when we have a point to make and then making it very briefly.

Our chance came on the issue of free trade between the regions. Lyle and I supported Clarke's and the Western Region's insistence on free trade. The issue arose because the North does not want to sell cotton to the West unless it collects export duty, which it does not collect from its sales in the North. Similarly, the East doesn't want to sell rubber. Clarke and the West, supported by us, insisted on a uniform price (except for transport differentials) within the Federation.

This point of view was accepted, but the North pointed out that they could ill afford to lose even £50 of Government revenues. I tried to point out that their calculation was probably faulty, because sales to the West were in addition to rather than instead of world market sales. That was first denied. But then it came out that the North's losses on cotton are perceived by the Marketing Board rather than the NR budget. But of course, it is all the same in the end, because if the MBs get less cash, the government can borrow less.

Still it was recognized that, while we were right over 3–5 years, the North needs revenue now. It was suggested they could recoup their losses by imposing a sales or purchase tax, as long as it was levied uniformly to all buyers, and other regions were not discriminated against.

The discussion on plantations was postponed at the request of Daramola, who said he had been unable to brief himself since he had only just returned from Rome. This was just as well, because every one sat there with loaded guns to shoot at what was an indefensible paper. Because of the advanced time, Lyle and I didn't get on the program. I didn't mind, though we had really intended to grouch about the lack of capable cooperation from Statistics...

March 3, 1961

The tempo of work is picking up. We were asked by our embassy to prepare a short brief for Gov. Williams[6] on future planning targets and needs. We will do so, though we are not really prepared for it. To extract any statistics out of the Federal Department of Statistics is rather difficult, and Teddy Jackson still hasn't sent the national accounts. We are making our own estimates of where the economy stands now, as best as we can. Jackson's calculations go only up to 1957. It is bad enough to have to invent the future without the handicap of not knowing the starting point. But at least we got the 1957 benchmark.

March 1....Sadler, the UK Trade Commissioner for Nigeria, gave a lunch for us at the Federal Palace Hotel...The only thing making it not a complete waste of time, aside from the food which was decent though not outstanding, was (a) the view and (b) the presence of Murray, Deputy PS Finance, and Phelps, also from Finance, two first class fellows, whom it was good to know better. On the whole we find our relations with Finance to be excellent, which is rather unexpected. Finance is after all a typical "no" ministry, but we find ourselves spending more time shooting down proposals – not too successfully – than developing them. The people in Finance are competent, naturally on the conservative side, intelligent and hard-working. None of these qualities are overly common here. We are lucky in Lewis as the successor of Charles Thompson, but I come back again and again to the view that Charles' leaving was an irreplaceable loss, and that it has changed the picture here considerably.

The afternoon was spent with Lyle in my airconditioned room, trying to update the national accounts, something we have been working on after office hours and will continue to do. In the evening, I was invited to dinner at the Lewis'...There was talk about the riots, the inefficiency of the police, the fact that the riots were organized. Incidentally, all assemblies are forbidden at present. The police chief was on the beach, even though the demonstration had been announced days in advance, and couldn't be reached. Lewis says the police didn't interfere until the demonstrators started to throw bricks. Then the talk turned to the rather frequent burglaries and robberies in Ikoyi and the desirability of having as little money at home as possible...

March 3. Today I'm plugging away on income estimates. We went to see Toby to work out some procedures and a timetable. Many of the expenditure studies are well in hand. I have begun to make some sense of at least the Federal revenues, and have detailed questions of the East. By early May we must have a rough draft plan for internal use and criticism. The question came up when we should start briefing the ministers. We came to the conclusion not later than May, not earlier than April. Toby is taking it from there.

We had also a brief talk with Prasad, whom we now call by his first name – Nahrein.[7] There is some question on monetary policy in Nigeria, and we are backing Prasad on what he wants to do. The first issue is Nigeria's quota in the IMF. Prasad and we want Nigeria to pay its full quota in gold, as long as we have reserves and the

British have no balance of payments trouble. The CBN resists, wants to pay only the minimum, and wants to keep as much as possible in London to earn interest.

Secondly, Prasad wants Nigeria to hold dollars, Deutschmarks, and Swiss francs in addition to sterling, which Governor Fenton also does not want. Fenton is accused, probably quite unjustly, of putting British ahead of Nigerian interests. I suspect that the issue is really simpler: he is a Bank of England man and does what he knows. Being a BoE man also comes out in his and the CBN's resistance to releasing statistics. Nevertheless, from the Nigerian standpoint, if the country is to develop its own money market and monetary policy, both steps are necessary. The hurt to England is negligible. Nigeria would simply do what Australia and other members of the sterling area are doing.

Related to that is the entry of an English discount house, Philip Hill, to do the discounting in London for Nigeria. We all agree that it is good to have access to the London money market, but do not quite see why the CBN should not do most of the discounting right here in Nigeria, particularly as we all, CBN included, want to build up a money market. Why should a short-term bill backed by Marketing Board funds in London have to be discounted in London, then transferred to Lagos, and then upon repayment be transferred back to London at a $1^1/_2$% transfer charge, when this could be done right here by the Central Bank. In addition, the CBN charges only 1% transfer charges both ways, and can save the $1^1/_2$% interest. Philip Hill propose to charge for their services. Under their proposal the short-term money would come to $8^1/_4$%, instead of 5–$5^1/_2$%, which is plenty.

Prasad is so far carrying the ball on this. The trouble is that it is all politically loaded. If any journalist finds out that we propose to pay $8^1/_4$% instead of $5^1/_2$%, you can imagine what outcry there would be about imperialism, exploitation and the rest of it. The facts would be right, though the motivation is, I am quite sure, of the best. Fortunately, the technical stuff is too complicated for a vulgar Marxist, but we have to look out for it anyway.

Prasad, Toby and a few others are going with the Prime Minister to London tomorrow, for a preliminary discussion of the dam. When they return, Lyle and I hope to have something written as a basis of discussion. Also, we must develop a method of working with Prasad. People get confused about all the different advisors. I have no objection if Prasad wants to be the big shot, but I want to keep the identity of our operation separate and clearly fixed. Which means that I think it would be a bad idea to be too closely identified with either Prasad's successes or his failures...

At 7:30 PM supper with the Clarks and then the first Yoruba lesson with Sam Akande. It lasted until 10, and it *is* tough. We spent all evening trying to learn the proper pronunciation. which means basically whether the sound of a vowel is falling, rising high, medium high or low, short or long. "Lo" pronounced with a low voice means "gone;" "lo" pronounced with a high and slightly rising voice means "twisted;" "O" pronounced high means "he," "she" or "it," "O" pronounced medium high means "you". "Lo" with a low voice and falling means either "to grind" or "to announce" according to the context. We spent most of the evening trying to listen and pronounce, and it was sometimes very hard to see why Sam said we didn't do it right and then why he was pleased. It sounded pretty much alike to us.

So now with something new to do, what with blowing the whistle and Yoruba, I won't be bored. Only I'm afraid as time goes on – and it flies here – there won't be time for recreation. The weather is miserable and the office still has no airconditioner. In the morning the air is so thick that one doesn't see across the lagoon when I drive to the office. By the time the haze lifts sufficiently to see across, say 9:30 AM, the temperature and humidity are miserable. Every day I use two shirts and undershirts.

March 5, 1961

March 4. Taking Ebenezer Igwagwu along, we started off at 9:00 AM in the Department of Statistics with acting chief statistician Pite. Later we were joined by Oje Aboyade, who came down from UCI where he teaches. Aboyade is very good, a Cambridge PhD, and we are drawing him into our work, particularly as he worked with Jackson on the national accounts, and probably knows more than anyone else about capital formation in Nigeria.

The talk was mostly about my effort to make a quick estimate of Gross Domestic Product by origin and use. Lyle and I are desperately trying to establish a recent benchmark for our projections. Pite was helpful. He wants to be a statistician and not an administrator, and is happy about us giving direction and priorities...He had a few ideas about our estimating procedures, which we accepted.

At the last moment we decided to look in on Adewolo. I nearly blew my top when I saw him reading a newspaper, I'm afraid I was a little sharp, wanting to know where were the statistics I had asked for. Oh, he had given them to someone to do. He had some at hand, but not anywhere near enough, though I knew they must be in the files. I said, "Look, we are working and we want the statistics. We all just got to work." Lyle touched me on the arm to prevent me from exploding, though he said afterwards that he nearly flipped himself. When I asked whether I was rude, he thought, no, just direct and rather American. Ebenezer commented, "I think Adewolo got the point." I sure hope he did.

In the afternoon we worked over the estimates that Statistics should have done for us in October. All I can say is that at least we are getting something, and know now where the statistical holes are. We also arranged with Pite to have an inventory of all files made, and we will send Peter over to look through them and give an economic evaluation of their content...

March 5. The usual work, getting frustrated about the lack of information which *must* be somewhere...In the evening we talked strategy for tomorrow and the week, also about timetable and problems. This can be done best alone in a relaxed atmosphere. Lyle is now determined to stay as long as I, and is starting to break the news to his college.[8] I feel good about it.

One thing we have to do tomorrow is work out a brief statement for Gov. Williams. I am invited to a lunch given for him given by the Minister of Finance, and we are all going to an evening reception at the embassy. I doubt there will be much chance to talk with Soapy, or whether it is even desirable for us Americans to see much of him. But it ought to be interesting anyway. At least I shall meet our Minister of Finance, Chief Festus, one of our ablest ministers, and reputedly one of the most corrupt! He may get rich, but he serves Nigeria well anyway...

March 6, 1961

The day started out routinely. First we assigned work to all four boys in the office. Sam Akande and Peter went to Statistics to get an inventory of the files. And then I started to write up the GNP estimates we had made during the week...

Onitiri of UCI came and we had a first chat. He teaches international trade, is one of the two really able Africans teaching at Ibadan. He spent one year at Berkeley and another at Yale and is writing his thesis under Meade on Nigeria's balance of payments.

At 1:30 PM Onitiri and I went for lunch and an extended talk on political and economic issues...We want to draw Onitiri in, and he wants to work with us. Lyle felt that Nigeria had greater depth of political leadership than India, while India was quite well off in the number of native engineers. Both suffered from the fact that intellectuals didn't like to get their hands dirty, both literally and metaphorically. Nigeria, at least the South, had more businesslike people than India, where the bulk of the population was really quite uninterested in development.

Onitiri agreed to the latter, but felt there was not enough dedicated leadership here. The government was full of lazy bureaucrats. (After our experience with Statistics we could hardly disagree.) He also felt more central direction was needed, and it was a pity the backward North ran the country. We did not wholly disagree but pointed out that decentralized decision making was in fact getting better results than centralized rulings, e.g. in the US, Great Britain, postwar Germany, Yugoslavia since the reform, or for that matter Russia since Stalin's death.

We also found competition among the Regions to be strong. Thus the idea that each Region should have a university, both the WR farm settlements and free primary education were being imitated. In other words, the North found that it had to move in the same direction as first the West and then the East.

Onitiri said he had made projections of the gross and net barter terms of trade, as well as of the income terms of trade, and felt they were not going to deteriorate much further. Given the fall of cocoa prices, this may have to be modified, however...

Then Peter and Gretel appeared for tea...Peter reported on the mess in Statistics, and asked for advice on how to proceed. Adewolo just isn't interested and won't do a thing. We advised for the time being to continue peacefully with listing files and content. But sooner or later the whole outfit will have to be shaken up, and we will have to go to Toby, if necessary, to throw a bomb under the fellow. Every time I think of them I get hot under the collar, which does, of course, no good and may do harm. The first of the frustrations.

March 9, 1961

March 7.... The big day with Soapy Williams. We spent the morning in the office. Lyle assembled some staff to brief Williams, but we never got a chance. There were about 40 people at the lunch, chaired by the Minister of Finance who is acting PM while Balewa[9] attends the conference of Commonwealth Prime Ministers in London...I sat between the head of the biggest French oil firm, Total, and a Nigerian who works in Posts and Telegraphs and queried me on our race problem. I explained as well and truthfully as I could. Opposite me sat Lyle with Owen Williams from

Enugu, who was down for a meeting on rewriting and unifying the income tax laws. The income tax is to be handed to the Regions completely, except for the corporation income tax and Lagos personal income taxes which are to remain Federal, and the law is to be standardized among the Regions.

Chief Festus made a nice speech of welcome. Politically the only thing worth noting was that along with the traditional friendship with the US he stressed the fact that as Minister of Finance he was going to take money wherever he could get it with no strings attached.

Williams on the whole answered well. He stressed US friendship for new nations and our knowledge, in the case of Nigeria, that even if the Minister of Finance went out with the other girls, he would still come home sooner or later. This went over big...

Incidentally, all over Africa there is strong anti-French feeling. The PM threatened to expel all French if they explode another atom bomb in the Sahara; Nigeria has already broken off diplomatic relations, and no French ships or planes come in, though French businesses still thrive on a relatively large scale. The feeling and threat have not prevented Nigeria from contracting for the Niger Bridge at Onitsha with a French company, which may or may not have been cheaper than others, but which has three Nigerian directors, one of them, I am told, the wife of a Federal minister.

...At 7:00 PM there was a reception at the US ambassador's home...Nancy Williams[10] was there...Nancy wants us to build the women a new market with water and electricity, and better housing. The former maybe, the latter no...I talked with Adebola, the President of the Trade Union Congress of Nigeria – the noncommunist one – who claims to have 700,000 members. The unions are organized like the CIO/AFL. I also introduced him to Williams...

March 8. Met two fellows from Krupp who asked about development plans, since they want to sell us stuff. Lyle was magnificent. They tried to tell us about steel-making processes, but finally agreed that the new Krupp process had only got to the pilot plant stage. In general we told them what we knew, which isn't too much at this point, and we pointed out that whenever the Federal Government was asked to put money into any project we would insist on independent checks and feasibility studies.

Perhaps the most interesting thing they told us was that in Ghana and Guinea the East Germans and Czechs control the telephone system so that when you try to call the West German Ambassador you get the East German trade mission; that the experiences these countries have had with East German and other Soviet Bloc equipment was not too good, and they were trying to buy some in the West; e.g. the road scrapers and heavy leveling machines the Russians sell are OK for the soft Ukrainian soil but not for African laterite.

At 10:00 AM Atta came to see us; he is our very able Nigerian Deputy PS, an Oxford graduate. He liked Lyle's paper on TV, thought we should expand it considerably and felt the issue was not yet closed. There are in fact many ways of saving money and still getting a program. E.g. the Federal TV program could make films to be shown on the regional networks etc...

Peter has been doing yeoman's work at Statistics. I ask him to pave the way, then he goes, digs up files, and brings them. Then I work on them, make my calculations and notes, and he takes them back. You would think that this is a routine chore but it is not. It takes a man with energy and economic knowledge to dig up the right file!

March 9. Today we discussed fisheries with Atta...It takes a lot of money and research to develop the sector. It may be possible to bring in Americans or Japanese to do tuna processing but this requires a fish harbor. We are for that. On the other hand developing inland fisheries requires more research. E.g. it is very difficult to dry fish under tropical conditions so it can be shipped without expensive equipment. Atta thought too much money was being spent on research already, and we don't quite agree.

The next interruption was Wagner of Douglas Aircraft, claiming that Douglas will only sell if the equipment will make money. He tried to tell us that jet operations in the US make money, when in fact they lose except for United Airlines. He was slick and we were tough.

In between I got a good bit of work done, with Peter and Igwagwu running back and forth for material. We are almost finished with the major projections to 1960 of the national accounts, and now must look into the future.

Notes

1 Peter Clark, a recent economics PhD from MIT, was the junior member of the three-person Ford Foundation team in the Federal Ministry of Economic Development.
2 Dr. Narayan Prasad, an Indian staff member of the World Bank, seconded by the Bank to the Nigerian Prime Minister's Office.
3 Nigerian Institute for Social and Economic Research, based in Ibadan.
4 Sam Akande, Cheido Obineche and Ebenezer Igwagwu were Nigerian economist-civil servants assigned to work with Stolper's team.
5 Reginald Clarke, Permanent Secretary of the Federal Ministry of Finance.
6 G. Mennon ("Soapy") Williams, former governor of Michigan, President Kennedy's Assistant Secretary of State for Africa.
7 The given name which Prasad used was in fact Narayan.
8 Hansen had taken leave from the University of San Francisco Economics Department.
9 Sir Abubakar Tafewa Balewa, Nigeria's Federal Prime Minister.
10 Wife of "Soapy" Williams.

Chapter 5

March 9–April 16, 1961
Preparing First Paper for the JPC, First Clashes with Prasad, Initial Estimates of Five-Year Plan Magnitudes, Analysis of Selected Public Investments, Ford Foundation Team Attacked in Parliament

March 12, 1961

March 9. Reception for the Niger Delta Development Board. The NDDB is a new organization, seeking to develop the Niger Delta on both sides of the border. We got invited because as planners we are supposed to give them money. They don't really know yet what they want, and I spent my hour talking with what later turned out to be a Minister and another board member about what planning is, and that we have to coordinate their plans, not tell them what they ought to do. On the whole it was a stiff and rather useless affair, except that it is important for Lyle and me to be seen and to meet people.

At 8:30 PM I went home, changed to my tux, and went off to the Richardsons[1]...I first talked to Dulaurier [of Canadian Aero Survey], because I wanted to know what an aerial magnetic survey could and could not do. Prasad had raised some questions, and I wanted to get technical information. What the survey does essentially is pinpoint the areas into which it may be worthwhile to send geological parties. It eliminates large tracts where there are no economically useful minerals, but even after suggesting areas to be explored geological parties are still necessary. How accurate such a survey is, depends on the grid that is flown. The difficulty in Nigeria is the weather. One must fly at about 150 m., which seems to be very difficult here. The method, which he called a primary geophysical tool only, evolved from submarine detection devices. He also told me that seismic parties used for oil exploration do not use dynamite any more but drop 3–6 ton weights.

I had also a chat with George Dolgin[2] who told me the US had offered to finance the River Niger Bridge at Onitsha through DLF[3] at $3^1/_2$% and had been turned down because DLF procedures make graft difficult. There is probably something in it, but it is not the whole story. I'll come to that presently...

March 10. Obilana of CBN appeared at 9:00 AM. He attended my class in Michigan for two months as a special student, and now works on balance of payments statistics. At 11:00 AM, Hoslett, assigned by the Ford Foundation to work

77

out a management training institute, came to ask about our plans. Our main concern is that the educational pyramid is out of gear: there are too many elementary school leavers, and not enough intermediate trained people. Emphasis needs to be placed on junior and intermediate management. We also feel that new universities would be a waste for another 5–6 years, since the existing ones are not yet filled to capacity. UCI has 1,000 students, and could easily handle 3,000, Nsukka hasn't even opened yet. Even so we will get a University of Ife, but we don't know the details here.

At 1:00 PM Lyle and I went to see Bob Fleming of Rockefeller Brothers Fund. They have lots of feasibility studies of industries, which I want to read through. The RBF tries to develop small industries. They find businessmen willing to invest in Nigeria, accept Nigerian participation, and develop business for domestic and export markets.

Fleming, a large hearty fellow who is nobody's fool despite his Rotary manners, told us something of the frustrations. For example, they set up a radio or TV assembly plant. The US investor wanted to buy flexibly components wherever they happened to be cheapest, and assemble the radios here for export to the US, where they would be distributed through Sears. As soon as a profitable business is in prospect, the Development Corporation wants a share in it, insists on naming directors and determining the location, in short on changing the original idea. And they probably won't get it on these terms. Moreover there is no excuse for a Government corporation coming in, since plenty of Nigerian private capital is available.

This is going to be our major headache: how to mobilize the Nigerian private capital that is undoubtedly available. Every time you try to do something, government interferes. And it is as much a fact that civil servants don't make good businessmen as it is a fact that businessmen are a catastrophe in government.

It also seems that the US is more or less committed to finance a steel mill here. Westinghouse led a consortium to survey the situation, and the Federal Government has given a pledge to delay a decision on steel for a year while the Americans prepare a firm proposal. We are quietly and unofficially told that we will get a steel mill, but that the location is still in doubt. At present 100 tons of ore are being shipped from two locations for analysis in the US.

We are a little disturbed, however, that the Eastern Region will jump the gun, and try to get another steel mill on their own. The Krupp people are trying to sell them one, and they are a little unscrupulous, I am told, not above telling untruths to sell equipment.

At 2:15 PM we had lunch at the Hansens with our junior staff. We will do this once a week: eat together and have a bull session. Lyle raised the question of whether bureaucrats were empire builders, and I said it was a scandal that the Eastern Region Development Corporation had bought cement shares, instead of letting private people buy them. Igwagwu disagreed, insisting that there would have been no private buyers, but that is not so, since the majority of the stock was placed privately in Nigerian hands. The Nigerians also felt it was a good idea to ban foreigners from owning land in Nigeria. We felt there was something to this as regards agricultural land, but not urban land. On the whole, the Nigerians felt strongly that nationalism requires government ownership, and we are trying to convince them that a modern state has plenty of means to safeguard its sovereignty without immobilizing capital in ownership that could be just as well private, and just as well foreign as domestic. We think these discussions would be useful, and perhaps we'll make an impact...The lunch plus bull session lasted until 5:00 PM.

March 10. Dinner at the Kings'. He is PS, Ministry of Lagos Affairs...I had a chance to talk with Reg Clarke, who wants a session with Lyle and me soon about Prasad's latest memo, and in general, relations with him. They are very disturbed about Prasad constantly writing memos to the PM and others, without sufficient factual information. Unfortunately I have to agree. Prasad rubs people the wrong way, which is a pity since he is both able and nice. I hate to be put in the middle, and I shall try to stay out of trouble. But we are asked to give our professional opinion, and I just couldn't make sense out of Prasad's last memo.

I also had a chance to talk to Clarke about the Onitsha bridge. Why the DLF offer was rejected, and contractor financing by a French company was accepted. Which not only was more expensive but subject to the political disturbance that if the French explode another atom bomb in the Sahara, all French businesses will be kicked out. As to the latter, Reg said he had raised it with the Minister of Finance, who shrugged his shoulders and said, they were really dealing with a French firm in Paris – as if this made a difference. Apparently the PM also agreed, all of which is slightly confusing.

As to the former, it is true that DLF money could have been had at $3^1/_2\%$ while contractor financing cost $5^1/_2\%$ – which incidentally isn't too bad. But the DLF loan would have covered only off-shore costs, which in the case of the Onitsha Bridge would have been only 18%. (This seems too low a percentage.) Furthermore, the contractor finance not only will cover 80% of the total cost, but the tender went out separately on a cash basis and on a contractor finance basis to minimize the possibility of a fiddle, as they say here. The French company was a little more expensive but was willing to finance 80% instead of 40% of total cost, for ten years, and probably had a better design. So you see there are all sorts of angles to everything.

There are also plans afoot to have a government newspaper which would give both government and opposition views, and offer a responsible analysis, something which is lacking. It will have pictures and funnies. At present, of the three major Lagos papers one is wholly English-owned, a second is 90% Canadian, and the third and most irresponsible is run by a few people in the NCNC.

On the good news side was that the second mainland bridge has been postponed until we can have a go at it. Festus put his foot down. I wish he had done it on the Onitsha Bridge, which is also absurd; an additional ferry would have been plenty. But then Festus comes from Onitsha, and an election is coming up. If we get a steel mill in the East or the Southern part of the North, the bridge might yet pay off.

Finally we got on to Lagos Slum Clearance. This is another complicated picture which I have not got entirely as yet. When the center of Lagos was cleared, the original owners got paid handsomely, and the law says they have a first claim to build on it. The trouble is they have probably drunk it up by now. In any case, the family-title system causes an enormous delay in getting people to utilize the land. The part which is zoned for commercial properties gets developed, but the part which is zoned for residential stands empty. The first three people of twenty or so entitled to a piece of land get it offered. They have a year to decide whether they want to build, and if so, if they can get the money. If they can't, the next three get the offer, and in the meantime nothing happens.

King would like to redevelop the whole area for middle income housing, and let private capital develop it, but he says his Minister is an idiot, who leans with the wind, understands nothing, cares less since he is from the North, and always agrees with whomever last talked with him. Anyway, this too will come to us, so I'd better read all the files. That brings you up to date...Lyle and I will have finally to talk over our approach to the Prasad problem, which is serious enough that it can't be just ignored.

March 13, 1961

...Today we had a lengthy session with Toby Lewis who had just returned from the London meeting on the Dam...He reported that things had gone fairly well; apparently some representation was made to the Bank. The final representation will come later, and Lyle and I are expected to do some work on it.

We presented our program and some questions. One of the most disturbing is our relation to Prasad. Since Prasad himself asked for a meeting to work out our relationship, we decided to take the bull by the horns and talk things over with him. The fact is that he is irritating not only the British but also quite a few Nigerians, because he wants to change the organizational setup immediately. But even though he is probably right in the long run, if we get embroiled in this now, we'll never get a plan. Toby also says that he gets too close to some Action Group politicians, and if this is true and it gets to the PM, he is a dead duck.

We also talked personnel: we really need at least one more man. We asked and got the OK to start direct recruiting Nigerians overseas. We got a promise that Nigerians whom we had persuaded to work with us rather than to go abroad would get a chance for overseas training when the job was finished. And we gave a progress report on what we had been doing.

In between we got a shock. Patricia was ordered to go to the House of Representatives for one month as a verbatim reporter. We can't do anything about it, but want it in writing that we'll get her back. You have no idea what a good executive secretary means here. I doubt whether I ever will manage to get a phone connection to the States by myself! Or for that matter whether Lyle and I will ever get our car allowances if she doesn't telephone every other day. The payroll department seems to be completely fouled up. It took Toby Lewis' intervention for Patricia to get her three months' back pay! Atta, our Deputy PS, is looking into all these things. It is absurd, but it takes some high-powered officials to get relatively minor matters going.

At 2:30 PM off to Kingsley, to report on progress, ask his advice on how to approach Prasad, and seek his OK for more recruiting. He came up with a good idea: the Dutch consul at one time offered a young Dutchman. If he is still available we'll get him. Kingsley wanted to know whether we could use Ben Lewis from Oberlin. The answer was that we didn't need or want an elder statesman, but if he wanted to get his hands dirty and specially if he could write us a report on industrial development corporations, we would more than welcome him.

...I am now reading a memo from Finance. Also, pressure mounts to write a substantial memo for the JPC meeting in April. I will have to do most of that because Lyle will be busy with the Stanford report.

March 16, 1961

March 14. Lengthy meeting in Toby Lewis' office to consider the Archer report on education costs. Prasad was there, Lyle, myself and Toby from MED. Williams, PS Education, and the Federal advisor on Education, an impressive Nigerian who as head of the Federal Emergency Training College in Lagos had done an excellent job with surprisingly little money. Archer is an Englishman who was asked to cost out the Ashby report's recommendations, and did a superb job within two months. He laid out all his assumptions so clearly that it is comparatively easy to recalculate anything one wants to along more realistic lines.

The results of his exercise were little short of shocking. Capital expenditure during 1962–70 amounts to about £40 million, and by 1970 recurrent expenditure will be £60 mil., an enormous sum. For capital expenditures one can count on some foreign aid, but most recurrent expenditure must be borne by local budgets. The trouble is that Nigeria needs such a big program, but obviously can't afford it. Actually Archer assumed that the West and East would attain universal primary education, while the target in the North was to enroll about 25% of the school age population. In fact, much money will be saved by the sheer impossibility of doing the job! Even so, we did some quick calculations: GNP at present is around £1.1 billion in current prices. At a 4% average growth rate, it will reach about £1.380 billion in 1967. To raise the £60 million would require a marginal rate of savings for education alone of 60/280 = 20% plus! By the time we have added all other programs, the marginal rate of savings would have to be over 50%, something not even the Red Chinese could do with all their troubles.

We insisted, not so much on scaling the aims down, but on looking at some of the implications: firstly, the three new universities would have to wait. The one in the North wouldn't have any students, and Ibadan could accommodate 3,000 students against 1,000 now. Nsukka (about which one hears lots of little complimentary things, but nothing specific, however) would not be filled up till 1967. New universities should be postponed until the next plan period.

We also questioned the need for teacher-student ratios of 1:33 for elementary schools, when in the States or England we can't manage better than 1:40. Housing, especially for expatriate teachers, of whom at least 2,000 a year would be needed, was excessive at £3,000 a house. But that was a question of bringing in housing experts who could advise on getting construction costs down. (Lyle is keen on an Athens firm, called Doxiades, which is doing the redevelopment of Washington, DC.)

We raised the question of increasing school fees and local taxation. It was simply impossible for Regional and Federal budgets to carry the whole load. In Yaba Technical Institute, which took 30 boys out of 1,000 applicants, fees were £8 a year. The alternative would be for the apprentices to pay a master £30 a year for a dubious training. Finally, we insisted that no commitments be made until there was time to weigh education demands against other priorities. We agreed that education should have first priority, but there was also the Dam, and roads, and investments required to employ school leavers.

In short, we earned the economist's epithet as the dismal science.

After the meeting, Reg Clarke came to see us privately. He had written two memos to Prasad in answer to him, and wanted to know what we thought of them...They seemed OK to us. We are a little leery of being pushed in the middle between Prasad and the Ministry of Finance; our good relations with Finance are among our strongest assets.

The rest of the day was hard work at calculations until 4:30 PM when we went out to the airport to fetch Frank Moore. Frank (whose name used to be Moos and who originally comes from Frankfurt) is our man in Enugu...Later Lyle and Peter joined us, for a discussion of his problems, which are many.

The East is a political Hot Potato – with capital letters. Ibos distrust everyone including each other. Okigbo is soft-pedaling his work, and won't come through. They see imperialists all over, insist on government participation everywhere because of this, with the result that they hamstring development. In addition there is, of course, a tremendous amount of corruption by our standards, understandable by theirs. The ER government and the NCNC are mixed up with the African Continental Bank (ACB) and the ERDC, which resists turning over its capital as it should. Undoubtedly, though unprovably, party funds come through the ACB. (Owen Williams was almost fired for insisting that the Bank invest part of its funds in Federal securities; there is a question whether the money is really there.) Whenever you say anything, you touch a political hot potato. Whenever Moore insists there may not be money, he is told, "We can borrow more." When he asks "How much?", sums like £60–£100 million are mentioned.

And yet the Region is fantastically lively, go-getting, and the corruption is probably no greater than what it was 100 years ago or less in the States. Still, people are out to knife each other, and Moore is in the middle. I myself haven't even started to grasp all the political undercurrents. Only one thing I am sure of: there are some very deep undercurrents, a deep distrust underlies the otherwise quite genuine openness and friendliness, a fear of foreigners and white men, of "imperialists and exploitation." And there are quite a few latent Lumumbists there. My summer diary was in this respect quite naive. One consolation is that, at least compared to Iran, working conditions are good. Gardner can be glad that he didn't go to Iran, says Moore. Iran has deep-seated, institutionalized corruption.

March 16....Today I started writing the next JPC paper, which must be ready for distribution by the end of next week. It is on the implications of the past ten years for the future. I have more or less ended the GNP calculations. I did as much as I reasonably can, the rest requires lengthy refinement by the Department of Statistics.

In between, at 10:30 AM Lewis, Lyle and I had a lengthy session with Prasad, which should have cleared the air. Prasad wanted me to take part in current policy discussions on monetary and fiscal policy, and to write the monthly economic review, as well as an annual report, while Lyle was to take charge of agricultural and industrial policy. He, Prasad, was going to be free-wheeling, and obviously we had to see each other.

I said we wanted to see him at least once and preferably twice a week; that I agreed one could clearly separate long- and short-run policies, that the division of labor on the whole suited us and was along lines we had worked out ourselves. On the other hand, I said we were charged with developing the Plan; that I had a reputation of on-time delivery to safeguard, and that he had to understand that the Plan was our first and foremost priority.

As for the economic review, I pointed out that I had myself suggested it in my first JPC paper, but Lyle stressed that we didn't have time to revise the 1959

Economic Survey, nor were we sure that that was what was required. Prasad then said he had something both shorter and more useful in mind, which might come out of the JPC paper we were preparing. This relieved us, because we had something like this in mind. On the whole, Prasad looked tired and somewhat beaten. I like him and think he is good, but he does free-wheel too much and we must first establish a reputation of always basing whatever we say on studies. We agreed to consult mutually and work out strategy.

...Now I have to go off to see the tailor again in a few minutes. This is characteristic here: it just takes endless time to get anything done. My freight also has been on the dock for over a week. It is still not delivered though it is through Customs.

The weather is stinking hot, but airconditioning helps now a lot.

Part of the reason that I am behind in my writing is due to the fact that Patricia is not in the office right now, and Lyle or I have to do a lot of the things a secretary normally does, such as making airplane reservations, calls to Kaduna, or appointments. Jensen – our man in Kaduna – finally arrived, and we have to do all these things to get him settled.

In the evening the Hansens and I gave a party for the Clarkes (PS Finance), Kings (PS Lagos Affairs) and Lewis' (our own PS)...It was a huge success, loosened tongues and spirits, and made everyone comfortable. King complained about his Minister, apparently a dope who doesn't understand anything. The problem of financing sewerage and redevelopment came up again, and King complained that he couldn't get a decision whether or not to let contracts on sewerage. He thinks it's a miracle we haven't had a major epidemic. Clarke explained a little about the PM and the Sardauna of Sokoto. The Sardauna is apparently No. 3 in the Moslem hierarchy, and a real power in the Moslem world. Clarke felt it would be good for Nigeria if he became the Sultan, and our PM, who now is very much No. 2, became the No. 1 man.

I asked to what extent the PM could build himself an independent political base. Nigeria has a parliamentary system, which means every minister really must be elected somewhere. At least the PM must be. Clarke thought that Sir Abubakar Tafewa Balewa was sufficiently independent to get elected as an independent even if the Sardauna should turn against him, but that it would be next to impossible for him to remain PM...

March 17. Lyle and I drove to Ibadan...We saw Chief Dina, Isaak – we are on a first name basis with him. He is now PS Treasury, but continues his interest in planning. Our main concern was to get revenue and expenditure projections, and find out how WR plans were being affected by the fall in the cocoa price. We will probably hear more by mid-April, when Bambgebose and Chukujekwe want us to come up to Ibadan again. However, we found out that foreign exchange receipts from cocoa had not fallen much despite the drastic price fall, meaning demand elasticity is not as low as generally assumed. On the other hand, government receipts from export taxes have fallen drastically, because the tax is progressively geared to the price, and the MBs are cleaned out. Dina promised to send the latest figures, not yet public.

We also raised the problem of the anti-foreign investment bias spilling over into an anti-private investment bias, whether foreign or Nigerian. And we raised the question of government majority ownership as well as the refusal of Development Corporations to turn over their capital. This is a sore spot also in the WR. Dina made a few new points. First he said that they were now discussing the possibility of selling off past investments. The debate on how to do this best is still going on.

The Region is worried about loss of control, which it wants because it does not like to see wealth or income concentrated in relatively few hands. Dina agreed Nigerian capital would take up the shares, but he felt the concentration would be too big. I asked whether Nigeria wasn't too poor to raise this kind of question, which really was a later worry. Dina promised that he and Andrew Wilson, PS Commerce and Industry, would get together on the issue with Lyle and me, and discuss the economics and politics of it with us. Before we left, Dina invited us to be his guests at the State Ball, which marks the opening of the season.

At 2:00 PM we took Chukujekwe to dinner. Ch. is a slim Nigerian, also partially Harvard-trained, shy, and extremely nice and able. Part of our problem was to fix a timetable for the projections. We brought Ch. up to date on what we were doing. We have reached the conclusion that we are headed for a fiscal crisis, interestingly enough, before we get into a balance of payments crisis. Furthermore, it becomes increasingly obvious that the Regions will be completely dependent on the Federal Government for funds, quite a reversal from the past...

At a party that evening I got a chance to talk to...Professor Eggertson, dean of the UCI Medical School...He favored preventive rather than curative medicine. He felt one should attack tuberculosis first, on economic grounds, since it affected people of working age, while anti-malaria had its biggest impact on children. He felt it would take three years to staff the hospitals. He agreed we should not spend much on additional universities, but first build up and expand Ibadan and Nsukka.

There was also some discussion of the proposed Federal TV installations. Everyone shared our dislike of the idea, but not necessarily for the same reason. WR TV loses money as it is. With a Federal TV so close to the West, Mrs. Ademola feared, WR TV would lose all its advertisers and go even more into the red. Since she is connected with radio, which makes money and is coveted by the politicians in order to put it into TV, her fear was understandable.

March 18, 1961

At 11:00 AM I met Professor K.O. Dike, the UCI principal...He is a charming man, about my age, a historian with a degree from Northwestern. He was interested in our work, particularly as it affected education, and I could tell him the appalling cost of the Ashby recommendations. On the whole I found understanding for the fact that a poor country like Nigeria just could not afford teacher-student ratios as in the States...I also mentioned that I was authorized to discuss in a more general manner the possibility of some sort of affiliation between the University of Michigan and UCI. He was very responsive to the idea, but wanted to discuss it further in a few months. He said he had given much thought to the problem of getting first-rate American scholars to come to UCI, and wanted to talk it over. He had a request in with the Ford Foundation to finance inducements to get top people. He was delighted that we were interested and that, as a token, I had recommended Jerry Wells to him..

From Dike I went to lunch with Chuck Brown from MIT and his English wife...Brown wants to be associated with us. I am afraid the CBN won't give him many figures. They probably haven't got them anyway. Brown suggested that perhaps one of the reasons for CBN reticence to release figures was that the Treasurer of the University of Nigeria at Nsukka had told him the university deposited £800,000 with the African Continental Bank over his protest, a bank which is highly political and not exactly sound. The university funds may well be used to cover up misallocation of funds in the bank.

At 4:00 PM Ola Onitiri came. He is also drawn into our planning operation, and expected to write us a paper on balance of payments problems. We talked a little about this, and an article he had written about what he would do if he were minister of finance. This article, which appeared yesterday, is actually quite sensible.

Onitiri drove me around Ibadan. His father was from Lagos, but his mother is from Ibadan and I met her. He showed me where she lived, how the house was constructed. It was pleasant and clean, despite the fact that chickens walked around, and leather was stretched out to dry. We went to the juju market, mainly to take pictures, but this involved buying something. So I settled for two little bells without clappers, which cost 4/-. They are very primitive. They didn't object to my taking pictures, but were disappointed that I didn't want to buy a monkey's head, which is very powerful, they say. I ended up by buying a piece of blue Yoruba cloth. The pattern is traditional.

At 7:00 went to Arch Callaway's, where he had invited a number of economists, some of whom I had met before. Ogunsheye and wife; Beijer with a new English wife; Hogg, an English expert on Nigerian transportation; Sam Aluko, who is more in the public eye than most, and Oluwasami, an agricultural economist. I talked mostly with him.

To his question I responded that our priorities were education and agricultural modernization, but that every time we suggested such a thing, we were given to understand that we were just dirty imperialists who wanted to keep the country primarily agricultural. Actually we felt that the capital and people had to come from agriculture, and one couldn't do a thing without getting agriculture going. What I said is pretty standard.

Oluwasami's reaction was interesting: "You know, five years ago I would have reacted in the same way. But since I have been at Harvard and taken Professor Black's lectures, I have changed my mind." There is now an awareness that the solution lies in agriculture if it lies anywhere and that in any case economics doesn't deal in either/ors, but in "more or less." This, I believe, is being reflected also in changed plans. There is some doubt how far one can get with farm settlements which cost as much per employed person as a steel mill. And at least in the WR we won't have to fight hard to get a vastly expanded extension service...

At 10:30 we went to the State Ball, held on the eve of the budget session, possibly to get everyone into a good mood...Dina took me first to meet Chief Adebo, head of the Western Region civil service, by common consent the ablest civil servant in Nigeria, who looks absurdly like William Bendix in 'The Life of Riley.' Later we were joined by Andrew Wilson, PS Commerce and Industry, a tall Nigerian with an extremely nice wide-open face, very serious and courteous. He had just returned from a Lagos meeting on the forthcoming economic mission around the world, and was quite unhappy about it.

The mission is to leave in May. We are expected to provide some background data, hopefully out of the paper we are slaving over now. Wilson was pretty upset about the mission's composition. It will consist of three Federal and three Regional ministers, one from each Region. But there will be six civil servants, all from the Federation, none from the Regions. They just don't see how a Federal PS can advise a Regional minister. It will in any case be an all-Nigerian affair, with no expatriate senior member. There is no doubt that the mission is badly prepared, and that the ministers probably consider it a junket. But there is also little doubt they will bring home some political bacon, although that from Moscow may look better than it is.

The only other semi-professional contact I made was with Rose, a senior agricultural officer. We talked mostly cocoa. He thinks, probably correctly, that the Ghanaians will never agree to a cocoa price stabilization scheme. They are hell-bent to provide half of the world cocoa production, and likely to get it. If Nigeria tries to withhold cocoa from the world market, this will simply aid the Ghanaians. I did not realize that our cocoa is of lower quality than the Ghanaian stuff, selling at about £10 per ton less. Our only chance is to improve quality, increase quantity and reduce costs.

March 24, 1961

March 19 (Sunday). The Callaways and I were invited for the day by Fataye Williams at the Manor House at Isayin...On the way to Oyo the landscape changed gradually to savanna. It became drier, the rain forest disappeared, and there were fewer palms of various descriptions. After beautifully cared-for cocoa farms, the vegetation thinned out. But poultry is coming in on a fairly large scale. Arch talked about his research with school leavers, and wanted to talk about the farm program. But while he is nice and thorough and knowledgeable, he is also extremely long-winded, and we never got around to the positive program he has developed. It is going to appear in *West Africa* anyway, and he said the WR has more or less decided to accept it. So I will find out in any case. The trouble was that I got a little impatient, which won't do for a guest. The heat does this to one.

School leavers raise a serious unemployment problem. Not serious by Indian standards, but potential political dynamite here. Or so some people believe. The question is: why don't people catch on after a while? Why do they insist on being unemployed in the cities instead of going back to the farms and becoming usefully employed? Arch has done some excellent field research, I believe. As is to be expected, there are many reasons. Parents as well as children see school as an escape from the back-breaking work of farming. That it is not as back-breaking as in India or Pakistan is true but beside the point.

Once they have their four years of schooling, with a new language, they go off to the city to look for a job. Initially their parents or relatives finance them. They may live at first with relatives or other persons who make themselves responsible. If a job doesn't materialize in nine months or so, their welcome usually wears out. But they continue to be supported by their families. And nature is not too bad: they can pick avocados, oranges and bananas. Loss of face keeps them from going back.

But there is more to it than that. Having tasted education, these people feel that going back to the farms cuts them off from the world they have been introduced to. As I understand Arch, the problem could be solved by continuing their education on the farm. Extension service is one method, maybe one could use cooperatives. The farm settlements were an early attempt, but too expensive and too much from above, not enough from below. Making farm life more attractive by spending more, for example, on rural drinking water would help. In part I felt, however, that Nigerians like everyone else have to come off the high horse and adjust to the reality that four years of elementary school doesn't qualify one for a white collar job.

Oyo (which you will find on the map easily) is a fairly big town, with a king who lives in a large palace. It is also a pleasant town with character. To be sure the huts are mud with tin roofs, but there is some imagination. For example, the local bank building has a cement railing in the shape of £££. Also, the country is hilly, and that always adds to attractiveness...

First we picked up a 'guide' to take us to where they make calabashes and then to the leather workers' cooperatives. The guide suddenly informed us that he wanted 10/- because he had left work to show us around. We kicked him out. In the first place 5/- is a good day's salary. In the second place, no one was working, for it was Eid-ul-Fitri, the end of Ramadan, and every one was drumming, dancing, feasting and generally having a good time. Both the calabash and leather workers' co-ops are remarkable in that they have posted prices. No arguing. Unfortunately, the calabashes are rather dull, and I didn't get any. The leather work also was not what I wanted. But there were some wooden sculptures of the god Shango, riding off to war in a pith helmet. It was 'old' all right – Fataye estimated 20 years – and the termites had got into it. I bought a Kola dish in the shape of a dove. It is new and lovely. When I asked my steward how he liked it, he threw up his hands in horror and said, "No sir, it's juju." Maybe so, but it is still graceful, and we will use it for candies and nuts.

Next we went to the palace. On the front wall were paintings of birds. I took lots of pictures, collecting around me hundreds of people who gave advice in Yoruba which I didn't understand. One boy, a printer's assistant, he told me, helped with translating. Drummers pounded away, dressed festively. And they insisted on being photographed. By the time I had adjusted the Leica, five of them were posing in a row. I got them to drum, to make it less posed. The trouble with these posed pictures is that people who normally laugh, get dead serious.

Oyo was worth visiting. We went on to Iseyin, an attractive village about 30 miles West of Oyo. The manor house is on top of a hill. Except for vegetation, the landscape is like southern New Hampshire. And, of course, Iseyin's huts don't look exactly colonial. There are cashew nuts, some palms, and it looks deceptively like an English garden...The house was built around 1916. An uprising against the British was put down, and Taffy Jones, a real character who also built Mapo Hall, the City Hall of Ibadan, built it with what was essentially slave labor. Conscript labor would be a more polite expression. Walls a yard thick, which make it lovely cool inside, huge, airy rooms; and believe it or not, an English fieldstone floor-to-ceiling fireplace. It is now used to weekend big shots. If we come, we can get it for a weekend, including servants, provided Fataye knows four weeks ahead.

The discussion was comfortable and slow. Fataye agreed with me – the first Nigerian to do so – that there was plenty of private Nigerian capital to invest, if it was allowed to do so and we could properly organize the institution. He cited as proof that civil servants had been forbidden to own shares but now were allowed to do so, because of the pressure they had put up. Also, when the Nigerian Tobacco

Company offered shares to its local distributors at £1 a share, they were taken up in no time. All this, because I insisted there was no need to have government money in everything on the ground that no one else would put money into it. Even Arch Callaway argued that way. Fataye's agreement was worth the trip.

He also wanted to know how we were getting through to the politicians. Was our advice taken? After all, decisions were essentially political. If a minister decided that for political reasons he wanted a public work, he would get it even if we protested.

My line was that I couldn't answer, because we had no dealings with ministers directly. But I pointed out that some decisions had fallen as we wanted them. We recognized that decisions are political – one can't have policy without politics. We were not bothered by this, but insisted that resources were scarce, and wanted time at least to start a plan framework, so decisions would not be made piecemeal. We had apparently convinced the PSs, and through them the ministers, not to make large commitments until we had time to organize the plan framework. The second Lagos Bridge was postponed, we were consulted on the Ashby costing though we did not yet know the outcome, and there were other cases.

I said I got a little fed up with people telling me about political decisions. The fact was that politicians wanted to spend roughly three times as much as there were conceivably resources for. No matter what the political 'necessities,' they just would not get more than a third of what they wanted. And it might be time for a statesman to look the facts in the face, talk 'blood, sweat and tears,' and make political hay out of austerity – still raising per capita income by 2% per year, which wasn't bad. I also was fed up with being told there wasn't time. If they don't want to work like mad and wait for the results, then they can't be helped.

I don't normally talk like that, but Fataye is an extraordinary man, and the talk was fruitful for both of us. Anyway he understood what we were up to, and agreed. But then he has a nice English wife, and is completely westernized. Or almost. In May he goes on a pilgrimage to Mecca to become Alhaj. I suspect there are political ambitions behind this, rather than religious motivations. Incidentally, he has two lovely brown children, who don't speak Yoruba, and apparently feel quite superior to their African cousins...

March 21. The morning started off with a briefing with Toby, which we try to have as often as possible. At 10:00 AM we went to Finance to discuss Reg Clarke's and Phelps' paper on resource mobilization. It was a very good, concise paper, written by Phelps. Our questions were mostly factual. The worry is that Nigeria is running down its sterling reserves at an alarming rate. They are now about £160 million against £200 million a few months back. All sorts of problems arise if exchange control is to be avoided. We came out with a maximum of £100 million in Federal resources for the 5–year program. Our estimates of plan requests run £350–£400 million! This presupposes the existing tax structure and rates, but includes a sizable fiduciary issue. Phelps is redoing the paper on the basis of our meeting before he discusses it with Prasad.

I asked Clarke why he opposed Prasad on some issues where we thought Prasad was right. Why shouldn't the Central Bank Ordinance be changed to permit the holding of dollar reserves in addition to sterling and gold? Why should the CBN be limited to a maximum investment of 30% of assets in long-term government stock (this is the British term)? Clarke agreed these changes should be made, but not before the end of '62. The country and currency were new, and it was essential to maintain confidence. You didn't want to monkey with the banking laws right now.

Anticipating our later discussion with Prasad at noon, he agreed to Clarke's points. But he quite rightly said that if you want to change the law by the end of '62, you have to set the legislative process going right now. To anticipate still further, Prasad told me today that peace and love reign, and he and Clarke have come to an understanding, which makes Lyle's and my task a lot easier.

We went then to see Prasad at noon for two hours. First we discussed our meeting with Clarke. Secondly we discussed his exchanges with Clarke on another issue of rediscounting, insisting that the only difference we saw between him and Clarke concerned timing, which we thought could be ironed out easily enough, as indeed it was. I talked about my worries of nationalism spilling over into anti-private sector feeling. I insisted my worry was not ideological, despite my liking for a private enterprise economy, but pragmatic: I thought it interfered not only with getting all the foreign aid we needed, but also with mobilizing domestic resources for investment. Lyle backed me up to a point, but both said nationalism was a phase through which a young country had to go. These things would smooth themselves out in time as they had done in India. I am still only half convinced, but both have more experience than I in these matters, probably they are right.

Prasad then offered some ideas for handling the investment and nationalism problems. He wanted a general development corporation with money from both the Federal and Regional governments, private Nigerians, an international consortium, the IBRD, anyone who wanted to come into the act. This would give Nigerians the feeling of control so important to them. He also wanted to concentrate all reserves and sterling assets in CBN hands. He wanted the CBN to set up a special industrial and agricultural section, which would have research staff, analyze proposals, go out and get industries. To prevent sterling reserves from being frittered away on consumption imports, he wanted to earmark part of them for agricultural and part for industrial development purposes. And he wanted to get ready, quite incidentally but aggressively, for exchange control against the day when we would have to control capital movements. He foresaw an early time when we would have to deal with capital exports and even capital flight.

We agreed up to a point. Lyle and I had discussed the consortium idea before, agreeing that it might get around the wrong policies of the regional development corporations. They would simply be left alone with no additional funds, gradually forcing them to roll over their capital if they wanted to remain active. But I was quite uncertain about having the CBN in the act...I left it saying that I didn't see the point, and wanted to think about it. I think I will continue to argue against it. We both agree with Prasad that we want an aggressive Central Bank policy. But the CBN will have its hands full developing a money market and a statistical service, which is poor beyond imagination. There seem to be better ways of preventing the reserves from being frittered away as they are at present.

March 26, 1961

March 21....In the evening I packed and moved all my things to 18 Ilabere Ave. At 8:00 PM Lyle and I attended a stag dinner at Joel Bernstein's for David Lilienthal. Also present were Reg Clarke, Toby Lewis, Atta (our DPS), Omanai from Finance, and Prasad,...who spoke about the driving forces for economic development, or rather their absence. As yet there is no population problem. Mother nature is bountiful, you just pick bananas or mangos off the tree; unemployment is not yet a social problem. How do you get development if people don't have to work hard? This got a nice discussion going.

Prasad also favored promoting irrigation in the North, and vegetables in the South. But the fertility of tropical soils is deceptive. They lose their fertility and stability rapidly. You see lovely tomatoes and vegetables, but though they have the proper colors, they lack the vitamins and minerals we associate with them, because the soil just doesn't contain them. I told Prasad what I had learned at FAO and the research institutes, which he tended to brush aside. Also, of course, people do work harder than it seems. But he has a point: life is easier than in India, and the need for development is not as pressing. On the other hand there is evidence that the Indians' grinding poverty makes them not so much development-conscious as fatalistic.

March 22....Lyle gave a brilliant briefing to Bernie Jensen, our Ford man assigned to the North. He outlined the political problem Jensen would face: the colonial service set-up, until recently dependent on a very few highly trained and morally upstanding people. I understand there were no more than 300 British District Officers serving as judges, tax collectors and assessors, but not technicians. The technical people dealt with water supply and health, and even the most senior was beneath the lowest man in the secretariat. Economic development, by requiring more and different technicians and a different secretariat, changes things.

Regarding the North's political structure, there is evidence of rapid changes. The North's overwhelming problem and desire is to catch up with the South. On the one hand the North is pathologically afraid of the South and afraid to be cut off from the sea. On the other hand they feel quite superior to Southerners. So much I had gathered already in the summer. The Sardauna is a hardworking person who bullies and cajoles the emirs into changes. There is disturbing evidence of a split between Northerners and expatriates. Except for John Taylor, civil servants don't like to give unpopular advice. When the Cameroonian plebiscite went against the North, the Sardauna openly blamed the British.[4] And now they talk about kicking them all out, if things aren't done the way the Sardauna wants them. All of this is hard to evaluate from Lagos, but we warned Jensen that he would have a tough assignment, tougher than ours in both personal – Kaduna is very small – and political terms.

We also outlined to Jensen our approach: decentralization of planning; emphasis on agriculture, rudimentary input-output. Jensen was three years in Japan and several years in South East Asia. He is a rice expert, which is really fortunate here. He was rather pleased with our approach. We also told him we would come up for ten days to two weeks at a time when he wanted us to work with him directly, but that he was on his own. In general I made it clear to him, as to everyone else on the team, that I was the boss in the sense that someone has to be responsible and make final decisions, but that I considered us essentially a team of equals.

March 23. We took Jensen to meet Prasad, who for the first time talked subdued and sensibly – I wrote before that we thought him good but too free-wheeling for our taste. He is strong for water development and irrigation in the North. Three major river systems could and should be developed: Sokoto, Kaduna and Benue. The farmers have to learn to use fertilizer and irrigation. But irrigation means not big dams but a series of low dams which force the water into the soil. Many wells costing £10 each could be dug, and the farmers should use hand pumps to irrigate. Experiments, Prasad insisted, had been highly successful. Of course, while this raises production and productivity it is also hard work for the farmer and his wife. But this sort of thing, if feasible, makes sense, and is exactly what we would like to see.

In the evening the Dolgins' gave a party for the Jensens. Joseph Palmer, our ambassador, was present. Palmer is a nice and able man, a career diplomat. We are fortunate to have him, I think...I think we shocked the American officials somewhat by telling them about the extremely strong nationalism of young intellectuals. Lumumba is a symbol for them. They are nevertheless not anti-western. We also told Palmer about Archer's calculations *re* Ashby, and that shocked him. We could easily use 2,000 expatriate teachers, 1,000 from the US. Palmer wondered whether we could recruit as many as 500 suitable youngsters. Myself, I am more optimistic.

March 24. More JPC paper. But it takes so long because there are constant interruptions. From 10–12 we had a committee meeting in Prasad's office on statistics, who would collect what and how the collection could be speeded up. The idea is an eventual quarterly or monthly summary I am expected to write for the Council of Ministers.

March 25. Work in the office...Pite [the Chief Statistician] took me home for lunch. He gave me the investment statistics I had requested. I am also trying to argue him into doing an input-output table for Nigeria. Since most of the data would have to be collected anyway to keep the national accounts up to date, he was moderately enthusiastic. I told him about my book[5] and the table Karl and I had done, including all the wild things one has to do.

At an evening party...a lot of criticism of Nsukka came up as well as of ICA. Some of the criticism had to do with Michigan State. Of some things MSU is innocent. E.g. one program they didn't want at all was forced upon them. They wanted at most three people [Nigerian counterparts]. The ER gave them a list of ten and MSU suggested the top three. For political reasons the bottom five were taken. And so on.

March 28, 1961

Work in the office all day. Lunch with Lyle and Nixon (MIT).

March 27....Discussion with Igwagwu and Peter Clark on my draft. Both were rather impressed by it. It is a good paper but unfortunately basically written for fellow economists, and advanced ones at that. Lyle has a major translation job ahead...

March 28. Discussion with Nixon on the political situation. His analysis paralleled ours but in many respects he was better informed since he had been here longer. We agreed that political as well as economic changes were very rapid; that in particular all three regions had for different reasons open societies in which able people could change their minds. In particular in the North the dominant motivation is to catch up with the more advanced South. Although the Action Group did not make any headway in the North during last year's election, it nevertheless had tremendous impact.

Wherever the AG did relatively well, the NR party is moving in to reform the Native Authorities. The NAs themselves are changing rapidly. Originally run by emirs, strictly on an inherited basis, they began with nominated members, and now have elected members. The emirs are still powerful, but power is actually moving into the hands of an educated 'middle' class, mostly people who have gone through teachers' colleges, of whom our PM is an example. He is a commoner and an old school teacher, as well as an unusually intelligent person. The NA structure makes the North still very decentralized, which in the long run is probably a strength. In the short run it means, however, that as the British civil servants gradually leave, Kaduna gets weaker, so central direction is lacking.

March 29. The tailor came with four helpers to finish the curtains! The inefficiency has to be seen to be believed. I let Patricia worry about this. She tells him what to do, he won't, so he has to do it twice, three times. He can't get the hems straight the first time, because he just won't believe that you have to use pins etc...

April 4, 1961

We are just back from Benin, tired in body, refreshed in mind. For the first time in Nigeria I could drop everything connected with the office – which one can't do at the beach because there are always other Americans, particularly Joel Bernstein, the competent director of ICA, wanting to talk business – and now on this trip I concentrated on driving and sightseeing. I needed the rest...

...First we drove to Benin, which is really a hellhole, of considerable historic interest, one of the unhealthiest places in Nigeria, always wet and yet short of water – they are finally building a new water tank – dirty, and evidently not yet recovered from the massacres of the last degenerate days of the Empire of Benin, which in its heyday had extended as far as Dahomey...

We picked up a guide to lead us first to a chief's house, where the floor was inlaid. The floor is actually mud, and the inlay is in cowrie shells. All floors used to be like that, but this is the only one left. The chief showed us the whole house, which is slightly modernized in that it has windows. The old houses are all lit through an atrium-like hole in the roof. Also we noted that the walls were built in a regular horizontal wavy pattern. Apparently only chiefs may build their houses in this manner. Commoners must have smooth rather than beveled walls.

...All chiefs' houses have a big room with a shrine of the chief god (of the sea, I believe) but they have also ancestral shrines, maternal ancestral shrines etc. The chief god shrine usually has good-sized terra cotta figures. The ancestor shrines have staffs, one for each ancestor, and terra cotta or wood heads, one each for each paternal ancestor. The maternal shrines have two wooden cocks. And there are other shrines – one, at least, in each room. This particular chief was anxious that we should take pictures, and he changed into his priestly robes, and his wife – or one of them – dressed up into hers and they posed for the camera. She wanted to be "dashed" for the effort. He was content with a promise of the picture if it turned out well.

Actually the houses are amazingly cool and quite comfortable. But they are also quite depressing, with their unnecessary dirt. It is hard to believe that Benin once was an important and feared empire. One chief showed us his ceremonial robes and put on the hat and held the sword. In the traditional house we were taken to a shrine in the garden.

...We saw lots of dancing and masks on the streets in the villages, as is customary on Easter and Christmas. [See Photo No. 11.] But Alex pointed out that the children's wearing masks was already a sign of degeneracy. When these festivals are taken seriously, women and children not only are not allowed to wear masks, but they are not even allowed to watch the preparations for the festivities, nor are they permitted to know who the wearers of the masks are. And if they find out they must not tell...

Returning home, I found a letter from Max Millikan amplifying his cable. It seems the White House would like to know what we will contribute to a presentation to Congress in connection with the new foreign aid program. Also, Lyle told me that on Saturday we had again difficulties with Prasad, who gave ambassador Palmer much higher figures for aid needs than ours, without being willing or able to tell Lyle how he had derived them. Either he is again shooting off wildly, or our consultation is all one way with us keeping the bargain which I made with Prasad in Washington and once again here, while he does not consult us.

We are worried about it, and Lyle was pretty mad and fed up, particularly as his weekend had been hot and less restful than mine. The manner in which Prasad proceeds is bound to blow up in his face and we might get hit by some of the pieces. His recklessness in giving advice may give the whole economic advising business a bad name. Moreover, we have reason to believe that he says one can't really plan in Nigeria because there are no statistics. Of course statistics *are* rudimentary to say the least. But the point illustrates the difference in approach between him and us. He really is a planner which we are not. He would consider exchange control quite lightly while we would consider it a very serious step to be avoided if at all possible.

And he is still very much an Indian, somewhat anti-English as well as patronizing to the Nigerians. The fact that Nigeria's economy has grown faster than India's, with the Indians trying so much harder than the Nigerians, annoys him and fills him with disbelief. And still, he is a good, competent man, a most unusual World Bank type – we expected trouble from the fact that he as an IBRD man would be more conservative than we are – a man of many insights, from whom we try to learn what we can. But we refuse to work in a sloppy and haphazard manner.

I reworked the whole 27-page JPC paper on the basis of Prasad's comments, most of which were either matters of formulation or unacceptable to me as the senior author. Then I wrote a two-page summary and another page. Lyle is in yet another transport meeting and Patricia has to work overtime to put the blasted paper – which Lyle and Toby say is very good – on stencils, so it can be distributed at Thursday's JPC meeting.

This week we have a JPC meeting, Lyle more transport meetings, and I one on statistics with Prasad. No rest for the weary.

April 23, 1961

I must write my diary, but can't do it any more day by day. The last weeks were awful, and I still don't know how to handle some problems that were raised. The week April 4–8 was full of the JPC meetings.

April 4. The JPC subcommittee on statistics met. Everything seemed to go well. When it was over, and coffee was being served, Prasad wanted to know whether there would be a paper. I said I had rewritten the paper allowing for all his comments except two. I left in the view that development in the fifties had been held back more by executive ability than money. That, I explained, was based on rather extensive studies I had made while at MIT. Prasad said he disagreed, and in any case, why did I say there were no investment opportunities. I answered that I had said nothing of the kind.

Prasad then said the British could have done more. I said, to be sure they could, but then they had been here only 100 years. Prasad said in India they had spent $100 million (!) on a technical college in the 'nineties, why had they not done so here? Instead of refusing to discuss the reasons for the lack of executive ability, I let myself be boxed into defending the nasty British imperialists. Well, I said, in India there has been a literate class for a long time, and then I turned to Okigbo, and asked "How widespread was literacy in the traditional culture?" Pius, obviously offended, said, "What are you implying?" I answered that for economic development you had to have a fairly large group which could read and write and cope with modern things. Both Pius and Vincent, the able SAS Finance, were obviously offended by this.

The second point I didn't change was the estimated foreign exchange gap. I had it at about £200 million in 1957 prices, Prasad at about £300 million. Prasad absolutely refused to say how he got his figure, and I refused to change it without knowing the basis. I pointed out to him that I had arrived at my figure as part of a consistent set of assumptions which would have to be changed. I said I probably agreed with his figure after adjusting for past and expected price changes and inventory accumulation. I should have had a forewarning of what was coming, but was too naive.

April 6. The meeting started with a change in the agenda. Prasad wanted eliminated from the minutes some things he had said which did not look so good in black and white. Then consideration of the Stanford report was postponed and my paper was put on the agenda. Prasad wanted to discuss it right away. I asked to be allowed to make a preliminary statement first since MED's inefficiency was such that the paper had been distributed only the night before, and then without tables. I pointed out that the paper was an intellectual exercise, looking at implications of past developments for the future under various assumptions, and individual figures were not to be taken seriously, but trends and orders of magnitudes and relations were probably meaningful.

Then things got really interesting. Prasad objected to the reference to lack of executive ability. This time I was forewarned, and pointed out that I wasn't discussing the reasons, only the existence of the lack. He and Okigbo objected to the assumption that foreign aid had to be matched by local funds. We had written that it was safe to say as a rule that not more than 50% of projects could be financed by foreign aid. Prasad and Okigbo hit into this, pointing out there were exceptions. We said, "Yes, that is why we say 'as a rule'." (The absurd thing was that after that elaborate attack, Prasad told the Regions to assume that for each £ they raised they could get £1 from abroad. I didn't want to point out that this was 50/50.)

All this was preliminary. Prasad then said it was strange that his views were not represented in my paper. (They were except for two points.) The paper was fine, but we obviously had no notion of how to plan, and his method should have been presented. (We had no inkling what it was.) He then launched into a 45-minute speech, misrepresenting our approach. He claimed it was financial and aggregative only. What with bad statistics, that was obviously not worth a damn. For example, we had assumed a 2% population increase but it probably was $2^1/_2$%, and all our calculations were off. The thing to do was to string together a series of projects, and that would be the plan. He then proceeded to tell the Regions that they should get their expenditure programs lined up and he would be around by August to collect them.

All of this was rather nasty. I held back as much as I could and then said I was upset that the chairman should think there was such a big difference of opinion. In fact, if he had read my JPC paper of September and Lyle's of October and November, he would find that we had stipulated that the expenditure programs were the heart of the plan, and that we had not only requested the figures but had asked for them by the end of April, rather than August. I insisted our paper was a forecast rather than a financial paper. The difference, if there was any, was that we felt we had to have a framework within which individual projects and programs could be placed. How else could one decide which projects to omit in case resources were not forthcoming? How else could one ensure consistent programs and projects?

Although I was really upset and mad – the attack had come out of the blue sky, and was a violation of our agreement in Washington not to have public differences until we had ironed them out in private – I was rather mild and tried to play it down. Prasad made outrageous statements – how the Colombo plan had been initially done in one week by telegram, etc.

Another disturbing thing was the shilly-shallying of Okigbo. The two had somehow got together in trying to shoot us down, with Okigbo's motives being quite unclear. I told Toby that I was not going to stand by while Prasad tried to wreck our operation. – then I went home, took a bath and tranquilizer and played all afternoon *Die Meistersinger.*

That evening MED gave a cocktail party at the Federal Palace for the regional visitors. I avoided Prasad. Reg Clarke came up and said, "I hear you have an acute attack of Prasaditis." I said, I felt better, having played *Die Meistersinger* all afternoon. Reg Clarke said: "My hate music is the *Ride of the Walkyries.*" Peter Gibbs said: "Your fight reminded me of the battle of Britain. There were two fellows up 40,000 feet in the air, you didn't know who was who or who won. None of us really knew what was going on this morning." On the whole some of the sympathies at least were with Lyle and me...

April 7. Another JPC meeting. Lyle and I wanted to talk with our regional counterparts. Prasad invited himself and tried to take over again. But this time I said we wanted to talk calendar, not planning methods, which we had fixed, for which there was JPC approval, and to which we would stick until the JPC gave different orders. This time I got really mad when Prasad kept interrupting the two of us and I asked to be allowed to finish my sentence. We asked the Regions how far they had come. Much to our surprise the North said we could come soon. Okigbo again blew hot and cold. It was quite clear that he had not done a thing and wouldn't, and was laying the groundwork for explaining why. We fixed dates for our Kaduna visit, and tentative visits to Ibadan and Enugu.

April 8....Ogunsheye dropped in from Ibadan. He had to write a newspaper article on the budget. Finance had told him our paper contained estimates of the savings gap. Could he get a copy? Since we had been ordered by Thompson to make friends with the economists from Ibadan, I saw no reason not to give it to him, pointing out that no figures must be used. This turned out to be another mistake. Later Okigbo dropped by. It was all amiable again...

April 10. At 8:00 AM Toby called and showed me a letter written by a Dr. Okeke, accusing us of transmitting secret research information to Dr. Aluko who was using it to run down the efforts of the Federal Government. The letter had been sent to the Minister for answer in the House of Representatives. Fortunately there was not a shadow of truth in it. Toby wrote a categorical denial, praising our devoted service etc. The Minister felt this was too strong, and the final statement simply said he was not aware of any information having been passed, but the appreciation of our devoted service etc. stayed in.

This raised the questions as to just what was behind this attack. The whole business took more or less the whole week, and it is still not clear. Maybe Okigbo is behind it all. This hurts since we treated him as a friend, but Ibos are more difficult than even Bengalis, and only the Hausas and Fulanis are worse. Just what he hopes to gain by it is quite unclear. Lyle still sees Prasad's fine Bengali hand behind it, but I don't believe so. Igwagwu, who works with us and knows Okeke, was shaken by the attack. Okeke has an American degree. He collared Okeke and demanded an explanation. Okeke said the government was against Nigerian intellectuals, and hired foreigners when Nigerians were available. Maybe, but no Nigerian economist with a BA or PhD is unemployed...

When the attack on us was actually made in Parliament on the 13th, it went much further than the letter, suggesting that the Ford Foundation had planted us as spies to tell our government Nigeria's secrets. Since we were making a point of staying away from the American embassy, this hurt. Kingsley said not to take it seriously, it was word for word the same attack made on Ford in Ghana and all the other Casablanca-Afro-Asian countries. It was a communist-inspired attack. So there is another explanation. Probably all four are partly true. I am losing my political naivete fast. Toby obviously was and still is shaken...

April 11–14. Three days of discussions with Hayne, PS Labor, frequently interrupted by the Minister calling his PS for answers to parliamentary questions. We had equally good discussions with Daramola and his staff in Commerce, outlining studies to be undertaken, and the reorganization of the ministry which Daramola proposes...

...I called Ogunsheye, asking him to return the paper I had given him if he didn't want to cause trouble for me. He did so and was nice about it. His article was quite good, quoted only one paragraph of mine, without figures. It attacked the Stanford report, saying how much it cost. Fortunately, I didn't know that, so no one can accuse me of having given him the figures – which apparently are correct...

April 14. Since the Ford Foundation had been attacked and we sensed an underhanded attack on us to change our Ford contract, we felt Kingsley had to be told. Also we valued his shrewd judgment. He said that when Prasad was named, Kingsley had gone to Washington to see the Bank and ask whether they wanted to do the planning. The answer was a clear "no." The IBRD was sending an advisor only; they did not intend to give Prasad any staff. He was not to do the planning.

Kingsley said he was prepared to pull us out and send us to Ghana, which had asked for a planning operation since the haphazard project approach advocated by Prasad had got them into trouble. Kingsley offered to talk with Prasad but I asked him to postpone this until after a peace-making attempt by Toby. I told Toby I hoped he would set the record straight. And I would do anything to establish good working relations, but would not take orders from Prasad.

Another matter which not even Lyle knows: on the 11th, Toby showed me in strict confidence a long letter from Prasad protesting our bringing differences of opinion into the open, instead of discussing them with him beforehand, and accusing us of not consulting on anything with him. How Toby took the inference that he should report to Prasad, I don't know. I did not and do not take kindly to the flagrant lie. It is quite clear that Prasad wanted to cover himself by accusing us of doing what he had done himself. I told Toby I hoped he would set the record straight...I also told him I would resign rather than take orders from Prasad. No one knows of the letter. I have no trust in Prasad, have ceased to call him by his first name and resent if he calls me Wolf, which after my pointedly addressing him as Prasad he has ceased to do.

April 15. The day started with yet another statistics meeting chaired by the "Great Bengali." Since I agreed with what he had to say, I backed him up. From 11:00 AM–12:30 PM we met in his office, Lyle, Toby and I. We accused him of muddying the waters, not giving us an inkling that he wanted the paper withdrawn, and giving us no idea that he disagreed with our approach until his 45-minute harangue. We wanted to know where the differences really were. I was quiet, having promised as much to Toby, and it was not too unpleasant. But Prasad is a Bengali, and wants to be a big shot. He is afraid of losing face even in a small meeting. We agreed to meet again the next day in Toby's house, "on neutral grounds."...

April 16 (Sunday). We went to Toby's at 5:30 PM. Prasad was there already. He jumped to the attack. He would let us proceed as we wished, but he didn't think we would get anywhere. I flared up, that he was in no position not to let us proceed as we wished. I was responsible for planning and he was responsible for short-term advice. And if we were to work together it had to be a two-way operation. He shot back that no one had told him to stick to short-term advice. I said I understood this to be our respective terms of reference. He said I was wrong – which may well be true. In any case, why could we not proceed together? I said I thought we were not so far apart as he suggested; that we had no illusions about how far we would get with our systematic approach, but felt it essential to try. Indeed that was what we were hired to do. The civil servants were smart, and could handle the project approach very well without benefit of economists. Where they needed us was to bring in consistency, and a set-up that could make best use of the available knowledge.

It was a standoff. Neither side wanted to let it come to a break. But while we separated reasonably amiably and on speaking terms, it will be difficult to work. I just don't trust Prasad. He is a bureaucratic infighter of considerable ability, very conscious of his status, milking it for all it is worth. We will always have trouble with him. I am not too unhappy to see it brought out in the open that we don't agree. He is tactless with the Regions. But it is a pity that he gives the whole business of economic advising a bad name.

In the evening I broiled a steak for Patricia and me...It was good and relaxing. No alcohol with it. I simply wanted not to be alone so as not to have to think of all the implications. These last two weeks are like a nightmare...

Notes

1 Canadian High Commissioner.
2 George Dolgin, US Embassy economic officer.
3 The Development Loan Fund, at the time the lending arm of the US foreign aid program.
4 In early 1960 the British Southern Cameroons voted to join the former French colony of Cameroon, while the British Northern Cameroons voted to join Nigeria's Northern Region.
5 *The Structure of the East German Economy*, Harvard University Press, Cambridge, 1960.

Chapter 6

April 17–June 6, 1961
Rivkin Mission on US Aid for Nigeria's Plan, JPC, Trips to Eastern and Western Regions

Lagos, April 30, 1961

April 17. We started early for Kaduna…It turned out that with us there came also a party from the International Atomic Energy Commission in Vienna, seeking to find out what they could do for the Northern Region, and the poor Northerners had everyone on their hands…

The weather was hot, about 100°, but really dry. It was hazy, but the haze was dust from the Sahara. The eyes smart after a while and I had to buy eyewash, but otherwise one does not feel as uncomfortable as in the great humidity of Lagos…On the 18th we started work in earnest. Working hours in the North are from 7:30 AM–9:30 AM; then a break for breakfast and then from 10:30 AM–2:30 PM. About 1:00 PM a man comes with some coffee. I was terribly thirsty. There is absolutely nothing to drink, no running water of any kind in the Government buildings. By the third day we learned to do what everyone else does, and bring water along.

Jensen had confirmed what Lyle told me himself, that he [Lyle] had offended the Northerners, and he advised me not to press them. So I took the lead instead of letting Lyle do it, as usual. [See Photo No. 12.] Actually things went extremely well. Gibbs showed us a list of projects which the ministries had prepared as a 'plan,' but the whole thing was really just a collection of things to do, put together for election purposes. The total expenditures amounted to £82 million, but Gibbs doubted whether they could in fact spend that much. I offered my services to make the revenue forecasts for them, and did so during the week. It involved first two lengthy sessions with Dick Latham, the NR tax expert, on the determinants of individual tax rates, expected changes, etc., a study of the past budgets, and some calculations.

In the evening we went to Gibbs for dinner…John Glass stormed in. Gibbs and Taylor had made him responsible for the Atomic boys, one of whom was a Russian, Kaylov, who tried to recruit Glass. But he handled it well and said, "Sir, I am a Nigerian Civil Servant and an American Citizen." Then the Russian became abusive and talked Cuban aggression. Glass shot back about Hungary and Tibet and denied in any case that we had invaded, pointing out that the absence of a free press in Russia hardly enabled Koylov to know the truth from propaganda…Most of the talk was business in one way or another, but small and rather witty. Drinking was moderate, at least by Kaduna standards, which are high, and we got home at a reasonable time, having a good day's work behind us.

April 18. We went to the agricultural research station at Samaru, about 9 miles north of Zaria...We wanted to know about their research plans, their reaction to the FAO/ICA report on the Northern Region, and also the present knowledge of agricultural techniques. I wanted to know in particular what could be done about expanding agricultural output, how far research results were proved under realistic conditions, and I wanted to convince everyone, not only that we were sympathetic to their needs but that we looked upon planning as something more than a collection of real estate projects.

Actually we went into such detail with them that we not only did not see anything but spent most of our time around a conference table, and only got through half their program. This in turn pleased the director and the staff, who had enough of people who just come, look, take their time, eat, and disappear. We were particularly interested in fertilizer research and cattle. The Samaru people agreed with ICA and FAO that wheat should not be extended, while cassava and yams should be reduced.

But there were sharp disagreements with the FAO/ICA recommendation to reduce staff on seed improvement and fertilizer trials, and assign half the staff to the land survey section. They felt they could hardly cope with the work with seven people, and to have only one would be absurd. On the other hand, for many purposes a fairly rough soil survey was sufficient, followed in specific areas by detailed ones as needed. We found out that cotton yields per acre could easily be quadrupled but that it took seven years to introduce a new seed throughout the country. Actually with cotton it is quite easy to improve the strain, because the farmers don't keep any seeds but get all of it at the ginnery.

The weakest man was the one on livestock, he obviously knew little. The only good thing was a lovely boner, during discussion of the ICA/FAO proposal to put the livestock division administratively into the ministry of animal health: "If we do this we lose the manure to another ministry!" The fisheries man was extremely interesting. The problem is to develop fishing on Lake Chad, where fishermen don't even have nets. The Fisheries Division has brought in nylon nets, and is trying to introduce powered canoes. There is fish in the lake, but that is about all one knows. There is also the problem of drying under tropical conditions – air drying means infection by maggots. Finally, Lake Chad is in a God-forsaken spot.

...On the way home we stopped in Zaria, a walled town...[See Photos Nos. 13 and 14.] The landscape up there is very different. Apart from being dry savanna and mostly bush without real trees, it is all wilder. And the villages are very primitive. There are apparently many pagan villages around, though I will see them only when I get there on my next visit.

April 20....I saw K.E. Baldwin, a senior assistant secretary, a walking encyclopedia about the North, who should really be in a research institution, not government. Apparently Jensen had some early difficulties with Baldwin, whose promotion had just been blocked. Baldwin felt that Jensen was brought in to ease him out, which of course was definitely not the idea...

To explain what follows I have to describe, or at least try to describe, the atmosphere in Kaduna. Kaduna itself was nothing until Lugard moved his administration there. It is still as he laid it out, the only tall trees are the ones he planted. It still has the atmosphere of an army camp about it. There are relatively few women there. In fact, it is a toss-up whether it is better to have your family with you or not. There is nothing to do but hunt or visit villages, drink, or work. Most people are bachelors. There are no white secretaries to take out, and anyway no place to take them to. The Club is the only center, with movies, tennis, games and drinking. You have to be quite self-sufficient. It helps if one is an outdoor type, for riding and hunting are good.

There is also a certain amount of hazing, like in basic training in the army. They sent Glass out to Lake Chad, as an assistant district officer, to investigate a murder! Without previous training, without help. He acquitted himself magnificently, and as far as America is concerned is worth his weight in gold. And of course all the resources of the service would have been there to pull him out if he had got into trouble. Still, there is glee in Latham's voice when he tells how they put Mott and his starry-eyed young wife into the bush and make them collect taxes. But they are nice people, educated, not brutes. Still, there is this army smell about it...

By 8:00 AM [the next day] we were at the airport, where we were to fly to Sokoto in the Government's private plane. It turned out to be a new Italian plane, which has the propellers behind the wing, and is an ideal plane to observe from. I hope very much the whole family can fly around in it next year. It's a nice way to see the North, which is big and hot. The plane went up to 10,000 feet – non pressurized of course. But at least it was nice and cool up there. The visibility was quite good...

We wanted to see the Sokoto-Rima rivers, where a hydrological survey is going on. There seems to be plenty of water up North, but all the rivers are silting up. The water not only goes underground, but when the rainy season comes, the silted-up river beds cause larger and larger floodings. Despite the water we saw hardly any green, but the area seemed fairly thickly settled.

Approaching Sokoto from the North, the pilot went down to 1,000 feet, where it was a lot hotter. He circled around some lakes, and when he did so at a 45° angle, I got airsick. So when we landed in Sokoto, I was not quite myself...The whole far North – the Holy North – has an Arabian Nights quality. "Of course, no irrigation project we have tried ever worked," the Resident, Purdy, told us. Why? "We don't know. People don't want to work. Perhaps they are undernourished, perhaps they have no motivations."

It's the 12th century all right. The few cars and roads and the airport don't seem to make much difference...Where the British lived it was pleasant, with trees planted and cared for. The rest dry. Lots of camels, donkeys, thousands of people...

After two hours we went back to the airport and took off for the site of the proposed Niger dam. The pilot went down to 2,000 feet at Yelwa, north of Fogge Island, and flew south at that height to Kurwasa. [See Photo No. 15.] This is really wild country, miles from nowhere, with rapids, few villages, dense jungle forest. The rising heat bumped us around quite a bit, but the Dramamine did its trick...Back in Kaduna I had about 2 hours sleep, when Glass and Latham came at 5:00 PM to take me shooting. So I went along, walking six miles through bush and cassava fields, while the others tried to get some partridge, Glass actually got two.

I must say, I enjoyed the whole thing. I didn't think I could take so much with so little sleep. The whole performance served also another purpose: I am now accepted as a good sport who can drink and go without sleep without complaining. Obviously

I was treated relatively mildly, being [at 49] by far the oldest – even John Taylor is only 47. I liked these fellows, they are professionally able. And African game hunting was a new experience.

In fact, Gibbs and Taylor tried to persuade me to stay till Monday, and go hunting seriously – about 15 miles walking – on Sunday morning, but I couldn't get on the Monday plane. Next time I will do it, though.

April 22. we worked at the office. John Taylor invited me home for breakfast...He wanted to talk a little about persons and problems. He said he was sorry their feeling about Lyle had ever gone to Lagos. They would have preferred to talk with him on his next trip North. He was surprised to hear that Prasad's performance in the JPC meeting had come out of the blue. He felt Prasad underestimated the strength of the Regions and wanted to strengthen the Federation too much and too fast. Compared to the Fulanis and the Hausas, Ibos and Bengalis were simple. No one ever knew what was in the mind of the Sardauna. For example, a minor file got displaced, which with the inefficiency of the junior staff can easily happen. Much to the surprise of Taylor, there came back a handwritten, full-page memo from the Sardauna ..."I have noticed several times that you are trying to obstruct me..." Taylor wondered whether this was a Northern way of asking him to resign. Purdy, the Resident inquired. "No," replied the Sardauna, "it's just to keep you fellows in check."

Taylor is about to retire in March. But he may come back on contract, and I fervently hope so, at least for 5 years. The Northerners certainly need people like him.

In general the North presents a startling contrast between extreme political shrewdness and backwardness in every other respect. Moreover, it is not quite clear why any one in power wants development, unless out of fear of the South and its growing economic power. The whole problem of economic development in the North has a certain fairy story quality. And still the place is moving. Food production is unquestionably up. Every time a feeder road is built, more land goes under cultivation, and the acreage per cultivator seems to have increased from about $3^1/_2$ to 4 acres, the maximum he can handle with his techniques.

We flew back to Lagos at 2:00 PM, arriving at 5:20 PM…

April 23 (Sunday). I spent the day mainly resting. In the evening I went to the airport to see the FAO's Viton off to Rome. I wanted to see him badly, to find out about the cocoa conference in Accra, and the outlook for prices, which have risen from a low of £150 per ton to £180, where they are likely to stay. This is a lot lower than the £225 people got used to, but still quite good. The only good thing is that prices rose before the Russians came on the market. This time at least they missed the strategic moment.

April 24. Started off with a visit from Ann Arbor – Sandelson of Ford Motor Co accompanied by a Herr Schmidt from Ford-Köln. They wanted our opinion of the country's future. Ford is considering putting up a local assembly plant for the Nigerian market. They wanted to know land and labor conditions, prospect of nationalization, conditions of Nigerianization etc. We answered as well as we could, that we were optimistic about the future, that we saw the main problem to be executive capacity, followed by getting enough foreign capital. We said we felt foreign capital would be forthcoming, if we could produce a halfway decent plan; that labor was willing but very inefficient. That Ford undoubtedly knew better than we how to train really unskilled people; that as long as the present Government was in power there was no danger of nationalization, notwithstanding a strong undercurrent of nationalism. That we felt it desirable for Ford (Nigeria) to offer shares locally which would certainly be taken up to some extent; and that the Nigerian Government probably would insist that Ford commit itself to train Nigerian managers as far as possible.

We later saw Toby. The damage done by the JPC meeting and the attack on us in the House of Representatives is becoming clearer. I am not allowed to send Max Millikan figures on possible aid needed by Nigeria. I know from other sources that Prasad has been talking with ICA and others. How much is personal jealousy I don't know but it is felt that I should not send the figures. So I won't. Though it is a pity. How often does one get a direct line into the White House? Secondly, when going up to Ibadan – where we were yesterday – I am not to give a lecture at the University, even on such a harmless topic as factor price equalization. I must not be seen with the 'boys' at present, not till elections in the North are over. I am furious but behave like a good civil servant should. The thing just has to blow over, we must not be seen with the Yorubas from UCI.

April 25. I am now mostly reading, trying to project revenue, savings and exports. So I have to become a cocoa and oil expert, which is slow. Cocoa is easier though...

April 26. Work, interrupted by Dean Stone of Pittsburgh University, who was interested in the teaching of foreign administration. Toby came in to talk Peace Corps with us. Everyone is worried. It has not been handled too well on our side, and to say that English civil servants don't have imagination may be true but does not meet the point, which is very serious shortages in absorptive capacity of the host countries. Also some of the preparation (e.g. learning the native tongue) won't work with Yoruba or Ibo, though it might with Hausa. Still, the reception has not been too bad despite the promoter types that came with Shriver.[1]

Joel Bernstein gave a cocktail party for Shriver. I accepted on the mistaken assumption that there would be perhaps two dozen people. There must have been 150! So I shook hands with Ambassador Palmer and Shriver, exchanged a few words, drank three orange juices and walked home in disgust...

April 27. Our staff luncheon talked mostly staffing problems, future of the ministry, of professionals within an administrative civil service; our counterparts worry they will lose out in the race for promotion. Still, we could point out that Toby has assured us he will personally see that each one of them gets his chance; Sam Akande is being sent to Paris for a long weekend, and Ebenezer is going as our representative on the economic mission around the world...

April 28. To Ibadan for an intensive work session with Chukujekwe in the planning ministry. We were there at 9:30 AM, worked till 2:00 PM and from 3:30 PM to 6:00 PM...The meeting was fruitful, all technical, and slower than anticipated. We had intended to go to Enugu next week, but Pius – not unexpectedly – called it off. He wants us together with Prasad. I called today and was polite, particularly as there is nothing we can do about it, but I am furious and disappointed. I can guess the game Pius is trying to play and he may even get away with it for a while. I intend not to let on that I am very much on to him.

May 8, 1961

April 30 (Sunday). I took Patricia and Jean Lewis to Abeokuta. Toby was with Prasad in the Delta. The sun was shining and it was hot with humidity to match. (Enugu feels cool but the thermometer in the room in which I am writing says 88°!)...The road west really turned out to be lovely. It was well paved, through good cocoa country, much of it open country which almost though not quite looked like an English garden landscape...We finally got to Abeokuta at about 1:00 PM in the worst heat. It is rather famous for its wild history.

There are some rather spectacular granite outcroppings, and we wanted to have lunch there. To find the right place we picked up a policeman, who took us to the highest 'juju rock.' There a typical Nigerian comedy started, at least in retrospect, but very annoying while we were there. We were immediately surrounded by about two dozen Africans, ranging in age from perhaps 8 years to 25. It is very hard to tell their ages, and they may not know it themselves, of course. All of them wanted to be hired to carry our food and the two reed mats and preferably also cameras etc. They fought with each other, tore stuff out of our hands and were generally a nuisance.

We took two, but all the others kept following us, wanting money outright or because their mother was dead or because she was alive. So we ascended some pretty steep steps with two dozen Nigerians on our heels and in front of our feet. There was a gate, and we had to pay 5/- entrance – an outrageous price. People insisted on guiding us along a perfectly obvious and well laid-out path. We found a place in the shade underneath a rock and tried to sit down. The place was hot, swarming with flies and smelled like most of Africa, but it had a magnificent view of the town, with its rocks and greenness around it. All other places smelled worse. We finally got the Nigerians to stay about fifteen feet away from us and ate in peace. But then they wanted our food. We could take it for about 30 minutes and then descended. Jean asked me to keep some of the more importunate Nigerians off her back. They all wanted to touch her hat and carry her purse, no doubt to disappear.

In retrospect the thing had its funny moments. But at 100° in the shade it was irritating. I didn't take as many pictures as I wanted and we never went to the top of the rock. Just the same it was beautiful and very different from anything I had seen before. In the town itself, there were also some noticeable differences: first, there was some sawn timber, something you rarely see, and huts made of wood, which you see even less often. The shops along the road also seemed to have different things to sell: hurricane lamps (which means that people are relatively well off, using kerosene rather than palm oil), a big variety of caps, flat irons using charcoal, but nothing, absolutely nothing even remotely resembling art, nor any household article which was even remotely aesthetic.

We returned *via* the direct road to Lagos. There were not exactly meadows, but there was grass. Pineapple fields, citrus trees, well-kept cocoa groves, and a village just about every mile, most of them well-kept mud huts with tin roofs, slightly off the road. The whole trip took me by surprise, because the contrast with the Lagos-Ibadan road was enormous.

About 20 miles north of Lagos there were big fruit stands with avocados (8 for a shilling) oranges, tangerines, pineapple, lemons and a fruit I don't know, which looks like a big pear-shaped grapefruit, has a sweet juicy flavor, the color inside like a watermelon and a rather firm, fibery flesh. Mangos, too, but I don't like them. So we bought baskets full for £1.

There were also lots of poultry farms; the eggs are fresh, hardly bigger than dove's eggs, but things are improving with American aid. Poultry has caught the imagination on a large scale. About ten miles north of Lagos is the Ikeya Industrial estate, with mattress factories, a brewery, etc. I am going back again sometime with Onitiri, whose father comes from Abeokuta...

May 1. Lunch with Daramola. The object was to meet a Col. Hardy, who was being considered as economic advisor/industry to Commerce and Industry. Daramola wanted me to chat with him and give my opinion. Hardy turned out to be nice and competent. He is English, ex-India army, was in Southern Rhodesia as a businessman, is *persona non grata* there and wants to get out because he is out of sympathy with the policies both towards the African population and industrialization.

The Public Service Commission meeting next day was very interesting. The PSC is the highest civil service commission, passing on all top appointments. It consists of three Nigerians. One of them, a doctor, wanted to know whether I was related to a famous yellow fever expert named Stolper. I said I was not aware of it. The questions asked Hardy were intelligent without being searching. They dealt mostly with his academic qualifications and his experience in industrialization of underdeveloped countries. The only outsider besides me was Daramola. I was asked to give an opinion after Hardy had left but I was cagey, I just did not know how I could in fairness say much more than that he had impressed me favorably.

At 11:00 AM Phelps came over from Finance. That Ministry is charged with organizing the around-the-world Economic Mission which leaves May 20 and they just don't know what to do. I said we had a notion of the size of the development program, an unevaluated idea of the projects, a notion of the balance of payments gap, but no real notion of priorities except for implementation of the Ashby plan and the Niger dam, on both of which Cabinet had committed itself. Also, because of the work of the Stanford group we had reasonably clear notions of the transport program. Both the agricultural and industrial programs were still too vague though in 3–4 weeks we would have sufficient details for briefing.

I argued that the mission should not try to go around with a shopping list, offering various Governments to pick up a piece of road here, a bridge there, two schools, or part of the Niger dam, but should go out for general balance of payments support, to be followed by specific negotiations, and should emphasize trade. I was afraid that by going in for project support and project financing, we would not only overlook the indirect repercussions on the economy, leading to balance of payments trouble, but would get into an administrative mess since it was very difficult to mix aid from different agencies or even governments. We talked for about 3 hours and I agreed to write an internal memo on what I thought the Mission should try to accomplish, giving figures for them to talk from, and where we knew we wanted aid.

At 2:00 PM Lyle and I went to the Federal Palace Hotel to have lunch with Sandelson of Ford, along with the managers of his Nigerian and Ghanaian agencies. It was worthwhile. Sandelson was more open than most businessmen, and we told him that we had material he wanted, but he would have to get it through the minister because after the discussion in the House of Rep. we were under strict orders to be careful. Sandelson was not in a position to tell us much, but he said he would recommend establishment of an assembly plant in Nigeria, location unspecified. Being an economist he doesn't have to tell me that the location must be in Port Harcourt or Lagos. Further inland just can't be economic. Perhaps the most useful result for me was the introduction to the local manager, because I will want to talk to him sometime on inventory policy and problems of labor productivity...

May 3. Talked with Hardy about his prospective job. He had good ideas about establishment of small industries, advisory services, and the role of development corporations, which agreed with our hunches, but he had more experience than we...Later I dictated a letter to the Public Service Commission giving an extremely favorable opinion of Hardy.

May 4. We went to Ibadan,...where we met again with Chukujekwe, Bamgebose and staff, to talk expenditure programs, priorities, financing and executive capacities. The Western Region is not yet finished with its plans, but much the most advanced.

At 12:15 PM Chukujekwe and I went to Finance, to talk about revenue projections which are becoming quite urgent, while Lyle and Peter continued their discussions with the rest of the boys on expenditure programs...At lunch the talk got onto personalities, among them Egnatoff, the Canadian education expert. Gretel Clark made a comment that I was very different, a mixture of American and German traits. This turned out to mean that I invited other people's opinion and free discussion but then asserted my authority. This gave me a chance to say politely something I had wanted to say for a month. "If you mean that I want to finish my sentences without being interrupted, yes I do." The result has been healthy; though both Lyle and Peter have become more self-conscious, neither of them listens well and I am having trouble. More of that later. But at least now, if they interrupt, they check themselves and apologize...

May 5. A hectic day...Prasad came at 9:00 AM to discuss my memo on the economic mission. This was something of a triumph for me, for Prasad not only was sweetness itself, he accepted all my ideas, though with skepticism on the feasibility of some (particularly general balance of payments support). Even better, he accepted all my estimates as to orders of magnitude. He even reversed himself on the issue of quoting figures. In the JPC meeting he had objected strongly to quoting specific figures on the grounds that once quoted they would cease to be flexible. I have no such fear, since within two weeks people forget anything and everything.

Then Toby broke the news to us that on May 16 an American mission is coming, headed by of all people Arnold Rivkin! Ambassador Palmer had brought the news from Kennedy to the Prime Minister, that the US was willing to commit itself for a number of years to sizable sums, subject of course to congressional approval, that they wanted to send a mission to negotiate, and that they hoped to hold the negotiations in Lagos, so that the Nigerian economic mission, when it came to the States, could concentrate on trade rather than aid. This was obviously what Millikan had wanted to say, and I was furious that I had not been permitted to send him my paper and write him. This makes both my memos more useful and urgent as well.

I later took Toby aside and tried to persuade him to let me send the paper now, or at least to write Max Millikan personally. He agreed to the latter but not the former. His argument was not unreasonable: the paper had not been approved by Cabinet, and it had not gone to the Nigerian embassy in Washington. It would be disastrous if the embassy found out the Americans had internal stuff that had been withheld from

Nigerians. He finally agreed that I could talk freely with Dolgin, our very nice and able Economic Officer, and that he would do the same.

A sidelight on the general disorganization: if Dolgin had not copied Toby and other permanent secretaries, they would not have known about the American mission. The Prime Minister's Office and the Foreign Ministry forgot or neglected to inform the ministries of development, finance and commerce and industry.

In any case it was agreed that we should carry the burden of negotiating with the Americans...

Back at noon to Toby's office, where Prasad had returned, and Phelps and Omanai from Finance and Johnson from Commerce and Industry came to discuss my memo. Finance clearly did not know how to brief the mission, which was headed by its minister, Chief Festus. Johnson thought the mission should be headed by his minister, Dipcherima, who was not very intelligent, and that it should concentrate on trade and attracting private investments. Omanai on the other hand wanted detailed briefs on individual projects. Phelps also reported the view of Fenton, Governor of the Central Bank, who felt that if we asked for too much we would get nothing, and wanted to play it very soft. The discussion was further handicapped by the obvious fact that Omanai was out of his depth, despite the fact that he is able and intelligent.

Finally we agreed that I would write a brief for the Minister – not to be handed out to foreign governments – on trade and particularly bilateral and barter agreements; that Lyle would rewrite my memo at greater length and prepare one page descriptions of the major projects about which we were sure; and that Toby would then take the whole works and rewrite it in the proper language, allowing for diplomatic and political idiosyncrasies and pitfalls, which we could not know sufficiently, and for which he was after all a Permanent Secretary...

At 10:00 PM I went to see Sandelson at the Federal Palace before his return to Ann Arbor via Ghana. He told me confidentially, but not to my surprise, that they would try the Lagos-Ikeja location, if they could get land at reasonable cost, that he had made some approaches through politicians, that he had found the attitudes reasonable, felt the country was a going concern, and thought it was worth risking an investment in Nigeria. He would recommend this to his bosses in Michigan.

May 6. A little less strenuous. I worked again on Toby about the American mission...Over dinner I outlined to him what I thought it would want, and gave him an idea of what kind of a fellow Rivkin was. Toby in turn said he had had lunch with Dolgin casually, liked him and decided to play it straight. I was authorized to see Dolgin (I noted above that Lyle and I had been scrupulous in staying away from Americans) and tell him what I knew, also that Toby wanted to talk, that we wanted to know the composition of the Rivkin mission, and what they might want to know...

My Sunday evening talk with Dolgin was very useful. I like him a lot, and was glad that I was allowed to talk. The mission is headed by Rivkin; then there is Geber on it whom I know from the East German project, a professor from George Washington University named Schmidt, and a man from ICA whose name I can't recall. It is not quite clear whether the mission is ICA, State Department, or White House. I suspect the latter, but Dolgin isn't sure. The mission will stay 3 weeks.

What they want to know and what they are prepared to offer is something of a triumph for me: it is just what I have been arguing we should do. This is perhaps not too surprising, because I was after all at MIT, and it is ideas from the Center for

Foreign Studies which are now coming back at me. In a way Kennedy is trying to jump the gun on Congress. Congress has not yet authorized the money nor has it authorized long term commitments. The Mission will want to know our resources, what we can finance ourselves, how many grants and loans we need. This makes my labors on revenue projections even more urgent, because it will take me another week at least to answer these questions even approximately. The Americans will *not* talk individual projects. In fact Dolgin said to me that they want to pump in money in sizable amounts fast and one can't do that on a project basis. Hence we can expect general balance of payments support. Dolgin also told me of the order of magnitude of the possible commitments, but asked me not to reveal it. I had guessed it anyway, but will keep quiet.

May 14, 1961

The work continues to be routine, but one constantly interrupted by rather surprising things. It continues to be hot and humid, one doesn't get used to it but it becomes a part of the landscape and one doesn't notice it anymore, just as one no longer notices the palm trees, nor much of the dirt or the really astonishing absence of aesthetic or artistic values.

Prasad and his secretary were on the same plane with us to Enugu. All was sweetness and light. We arrived at about 11:00 AM. Frank Moore, the Ford man, briefed me on what was going on. I also wanted some direction on how to proceed. The situation in the East is complicated by many facts and personalities, and I am far from understanding the situation, but I got enough help. In general, there is a power struggle within the NCNC, the ruling party, between Azikiwe, the Governor General of Nigeria, and Okpara, the Premier of the Eastern Region. This struggle has resulted in splitting the party and keeping the government disorganized and inefficient, led to misuse of funds, etc. For example, the University of Nigeria at Nsukka is Zik's baby. The education ministry has nothing to do with it. Worse, funds are appropriated there without asking anyone, and millions of pounds which are badly needed go into what is not a well thought-out project. Marketing Board funds, which were supposed to go into agricultural production, are being diverted into the African Continental Bank, which probably helps to finance the party as well as the intra-party fights.

The organization itself is inherited by Okpara from Zik, who liked to keep control of everything within the Premier's office. It means that liaison between ministries is absurdly bad. Some are not on speaking terms with each other. Communications should be quite easy, as ministries are in two blocks. One just walks to another floor or another building. When I as an outsider come, I can get files which Frank Moore has in vain tried to see.

Moreover, there seems to be great drive, but no conception of what development means, or that funds are scarce, that you can't borrow from abroad to make up for ordinary budget deficits, that loss-making operations don't contribute to economic development, or for that matter, of just what planning is supposed to do. Yet the possibilities are there.

Okigbo is stuck in the middle of all this. He played his cards somewhat too well, and is now scared that he can't quite deliver the goods. On the basis of an excellent and well-deserved reputation, he as an outsider was installed as Economic Advisor and Permanent Secretary over the heads of career people. Thus, the fact of his both being an advisor and having administrative and executive powers (which Lyle and I don't have), which could be a source of tremendous strength, is offset considerably by the resentment of the (African) civil servants. (The Europeans don't care; they leave anyway within a few years.)

I asked Frank why Pius Okigbo postponed my visit, and a few other matters of personal behavior. Apparently Pius was genuinely scared, after the last JPC meeting, of getting caught in the Prasad-Stolper fight, and so wanted both of us there. Actually, Prasad and I had composed our differences. The blowup had apparently served a useful purpose, and sweetness and reason prevail. Pius also was genuinely and quite reasonably worried about duplication of effort, since Prasad and I would be asking similar questions. Finally, and this worried me most, Pius told Frank that he found it easy to work with me but just couldn't work with Lyle. It is true that Lyle's undergraduate teaching makes him more didactic. Also, he is a much more assertive person and I tend to play everything much more softly – that is, until I really explode, then I am much sharper than he is, and then I can get really impatient.

Lyle is assertive in day-to-day operations; he probes more insistently, and asks questions which I leave alone as soon as I feel they are embarrassing the respondent because he does not know the answer. Yet all these 'shortcomings,' if they really are that, are petty, and somehow the complaints coming to me from various sides make me uncomfortable. In the first place, it is not that serious, secondly, I don't want to hurt Lyle's feelings. He is much too nice for that. I shall talk to him about it and in such a manner that it comes naturally, or else it will be blown up beyond its worth. I have a suspicion that all this is used to split Lyle and me, to make us ineffective. Prasad's case is particularly relevant here.

Still, even Frank, who is definitely on our side, told me to speak to Lyle (as well as to Peter). I must do it just to maintain Lyle's effectiveness.

Frank doubted that Pius had anything to do with the unpleasantness in the House of Rep, which incidentally has blown over completely. After all, it would backfire on Pius, and he would not do such a thing unless it furthered his interests. Frank gave me a few briefs to read, and told me about the waste of funds on hotels, which should simply be left unfinished in order to cut losses, as well as on the farm settlements, which are completely ridiculous in the East. He also urged me pry some files out of the ministry of agriculture.

By 12:30 PM I was in Pius' office. I outlined what I wanted to do: revenue projections and evaluations of the expenditure programs. I said I didn't want to press him unduly, that I was willing to be another body on his staff, that I wanted to go just as far as we could and then see how we would proceed, and that time was short. At 1:30 PM we went to his house, where he had invited Prasad, myself and two Nigerian physicians to lunch…Talk was small, as Okigbo had intended; he obviously was afraid of getting too quickly into business. I found out that Prasad was to see the prime minister and the minister of agriculture. I asked to come along to the discussion with the latter, Okeke. There was no reason why I should see the premier.

The talk was partly about the Americans in Cuba, and the smallness of the space effort – but it was good-natured. I ribbed the Nigerians about their irrational fear of fallout from the French Sahara explosions. The talk got halfway serious only when

Pius and the other Nigerians said they were pleased that Tshombe had been arrested. They hoped he would be shot. To them Tshombe is a traitor and a colonial stooge, and they hate his guts. I said I had no feelings one way or another about hanging or shooting Tshombe, but I thought it a bad idea if people coming in good faith to a peace conference could not count on safe conduct. Obviously, no one would come to such a conference anymore. This did not go over so well. But I said as tactfully as I could what I believed.

There were drinks – I try to stick to non-alcoholic whenever possible, and no food was served till 2:45 PM. Incidentally Frank Moore was ostentatiously not invited. Pius likes to keep him at a distance. So Frank refused to come to the cocktail party at Pius' house in Prasad's and my honor. Most of the PSs were there, and two ministers. Men and women stood in separate clusters. My attempts to break this up were unsuccessful.

I walked up to Prasad and told him I was happy that our differences had been ironed out. Prasad's answer startled me somewhat. "There never was anything between us. I told Toby that Wolf [Stolper] has a heart of gold, I can get along with him, but Lyle is just different," implying he didn't trust Lyle. I said I was glad to hear that he felt that way about me, and sorry that he did not have the same feelings for Lyle, who was straight and absolutely reliable. However I would try to straighten things out in due time. The fact is that Lyle has gotten on his nerves, and he finds disagreements easier to take from me, only a year younger than he – Prasad looks 60, is 50 – than from Lyle, who is in his thirties. But it also happens that the attack in JPC was on *my* paper and on *me* and that *I*, not Lyle, carried the debate. Obviously I had to, as head of the team.

Again I got the uneasy feeling of an attempt to split us. I am sorry that my normally trusting nature becomes suspicious, but in the jungle warfare of government you become this way. Anyway I will talk to Lyle – as his friend I owe it to him. But I am also more determined not to let anyone split us, or to take our minds off our urgent business.

For the rest I talked mostly with Philip Barton, the PS of Finance and successor of Owen Williams. Williams has returned to the British Treasury, which seconded him to the Eastern Region. Barton is very able, however, so Williams' leaving is somewhat less of a blow than we had feared. He is an ex India-Burma civil servant, speaks Chinese and Burmese fluently and has a distinguished record of fighting in Burma behind the lines. He is a chemist by training, Baliol College, and we enjoyed the kind of intellectual small talk about Don Glaser's bubble chamber, highbrow music etc., which led to an invitation to a most delightful dinner two evenings later.

May 9. The first real working session started with Barton and his principal assistant secretary, about revenue projections. I find myself becoming something of a fiscal expert on underdeveloped countries and their budgets. The three Regional budgets differ in their setups. The simplest is that of the Western Region, the most complicated that of the East.

At 11:00 AM, Prasad, Pius and I went to see Dr. Okeke, the minister of agriculture, along with his PS, an Englishman, and his chief inspector of agriculture, a Nigerian named Okie. Prasad led off the discussion. I was determined to follow his lead, not to contradict him in public and in general to play second fiddle, all the more as I had invited myself to the interview. It was quite clear that Okeke had no notion who I was.

I am rather pleased about this: the less I am in the limelight the more I like it. Publicity here is even more dubious than at home. One never knows when things take a 180° turn, and everything one says which is at one moment applauded, is eventually turned against one. Still, I found it amusing that no one introduced me as an advisor, but instead used the title Professor, which has here, of course, an English connotation.

Okeke talked mostly about farm settlements. He is a businessman and quite intelligent. The farm settlements are Okpara's idea. Everyone is worried about increasing unemployment and a drift to the towns. Okpara ordered Okeke to get the settlements going. Six settlements plus two institutes to train farmers will cost £12 million plus! – all for the sake of hiring 5,400 people, 10% of the development plan budget for 5,400 people! This is bound to backfire politically; it isn't going to solve the drift to the towns, it isn't going to make a dent in the unemployment problem. It is ill conceived, much too luxurious, hence it won't even have a demonstration effect. People will say, sure I want to be a farm settler, but not a farmer. Give me £3,000 capital – that's what it costs – and I like it. Things are even worse: land is supposed to be cleared while the settlers learn to be farmers. I asked why they can't clear. Well, this is the hard work they don't want.

I pointed out that in 1945 and 1946, when Germany was bombed to pieces, German students had to help rebuild the University with their hands for half a year, before they were admitted as students. Why could one not ask something similar from Nigerian farm settlers, and cut the outrageous cost for clearing and building? That was news. The notion is that the prospective farmer goes to school for two years on salary, and then moves in to a beautiful settlement with housing, barns, machinery, social rooms, movies etc. Ten per cent of development funds for a privileged minority. And the minister thinks this sort of thing must have political priority. I quite bluntly pointed out that I didn't think much of the economics of the scheme, and that it was bound to backfire politically in no time if carried.

Then it turned out that there was indeed substantial popular opposition to the scheme, particularly in the Premier's own constituency. In the Western Region, which initiated the idea of farm settlements, there is plenty of empty land, so this is no problem and people from overcrowded areas are settled in new areas. In the East there is little empty land, and the settlements are not located there, but on land already overcrowded and farmed. Naturally the community resists giving up the land, and they are catching on to the fact that only a few of the displaced farmers will be reabsorbed in the settlements.

Obviously the whole thing won't be a dead loss. Land will be cleared, a few privileged people will learn how to farm, but how much more easily all of this could be had by reorganizing the high school system with added agricultural courses. I raised the question of substantial enlargement of farm extension work, the obvious place to get results. There is virtually no such service in the ER unlike in the WR. Yet with existing and proven knowledge, an investment of £400,000 on new hydraulic presses would increase output of palm oil from existing trees by 50% within a year. Spending less than £1 million on palm grove rehabilitation could double the output of kernels and oil within eight years. It all depends on organizing co-ops, getting credit going – the money is there, but the supervision isn't – and on vastly increasing the extension service. They have now one extension worker for 50,000 people! In the States we have one for 300 farmers, in Nigeria they would need more. It would cost about £2 million to get one extension worker per 1,000 farmers. The planning horizon for training extension workers is currently two years and they plan for an annual output of 50 starting two years from now.

I was appalled. The ER plan asks for £12 million for these idiotic farm settlements, which won't pay off until six years from now, and benefit no one, but only £200,000 for presses instead of £400,000, £700,000 for extension workers instead of £2 million (I made rapid calculations in front of the minister, who was delighted), £300,000 for co-op credit instead of twice that amount; and £200,000 for palm grove rehabilitation, enough for 10,000 acres, instead of £2 million, enough for 100,000 acres, which is the minimum they should aim at.

I think I began to make an impression. Prasad and I talked in tune. We asked what their plan was. The minister didn't know, never heard that he was supposed to work out the needs. Prasad said he had asked for it 3 months ago. I pointed out that I had asked for it in August of last year, Lyle again in October, and again in February. There was something of a plan, but we had to trace the file. Prasad said: don't plan with a money limitation in mind, just plan your need. There is going to be plenty of foreign aid. I was a little appalled at this, but said nothing.

The truth is that the ER has a plan costing £123 million without putting in a red cent of its own funds, and hasn't a ghost of a chance of getting outside finance for more than half of any plan. The PS said that last year they worked out a complete reorganization of the extension service on the assumption that money limitations didn't matter, but Finance had shot it down, and they were sick and tired of doing academic exercises. The fact is, one naturally plans what one thinks one can get. It was an open secret that such a file existed, and I got it – something Frank Moore had been unable to do. (He is in the middle, between Pius and the rest of the PSs. What a mess politics is.)

I raised the question of executive capacity. How fast can you train extension workers? That depends. It takes a month to train a man for a specialized task, but he won't be good for anything else. E.g. the WR had trained people in cocoa spraying techniques that way. And, of course, cocoa production had increased as a result by 15%. Could you do that for palm grove rehabilitation. Yes, but. But what? Well the staff would know nothing else. Could you train them later for another month in something else? Yes, you could. Frank Moore pounced on this at a later meeting, and we persuaded them to work out crash programs in addition to the school that was to train only 50 people in two years. I'll come back to this later.

Altogether the meeting was somewhat depressing. Afterwards I saw the Englishman, Coatswith, and asked Frank to join us. As a result, Frank will finally get the files he needs, and Coatswith set up a meeting for me with Okie to discuss the agricultural program…

In the afternoon Frank took me to Nsukka, about 50 miles north. The drive was along good roads, through lovely, hilly country. Incidentally Enugu is both cooler and drier than Lagos, and you are quite comfortable without air conditioning. Nsukka is even higher, about 2000 feet. The location is lovely. A high plane surrounded by hills. But the site is ruined by the most unimaginative architectural scheme. In fact, an Israeli architect did an imaginative master plan which was rejected, probably because it allowed for less graft. It is questionable whether any architect was used for the dull concrete buildings going up. Moreover the costs are staggering. Faculty housing is OK, but £5–£8000 apiece.

We visited Edwards, the American Negro from MSU who heads the economics program. He offered us water, which was a help, but otherwise made a poor impression. Frank says he is lazy, and does no research, which is badly needed. He offered to help me in my work, but Frank afterwards said he had no intention of doing anything involving work. And these damn fools talk about a Center or Institute for African Development Problems, in the middle of nowhere. Well, this one I can shoot down, even if ICA and MSU try to set it up.

They are also building a stadium for 40,000 spectators in the middle of nowhere, at a fantastic cost and with appalling lack of imagination. They could have built it into the hillside, and got a beautiful Greek-style stadium. Instead they built it up in the flattest part. Similarly, the homes are not on the lovely hillside. It is a pity. And, of course, MSU sends, with one or two shining exceptions, only expendable faculty. Since the whole is Zik's baby, no one can do anything about it. He has committed so much money to it, that he figures someone will bail him out. The millions for Nsukka are, by the way, *not included in* the £123 million development program. The planned departmental set-up is also questionable: a school of theology, and one of secretarial arts, but no agriculture as yet! Oh, well. There is always Ibadan, which continues to be impressive.

In the evening we read files. The file on extension was the most acrimonious I have ever seen. The PS had drawn up a sensible plan while his chief inspector was on leave. The latter not only disagreed with the plan, which was his privilege and duty to say so if he so felt. But he implied that the present organization was the same as in the WR, which isn't true; that it was the same as in England, Wales, and Belgium, which is neither true nor relevant; that it works, which is nonsense; and that the PS had drawn it up during his leave to bypass the chief agricultural inspector, because the PS was English and the CIA Nigerian. I begin to see why Coatswith was beginning to be cynical.

At 11:00 AM Frank, Ebenezer and I went through the detailed and as yet unevaluated ministry programs in Pius' office. I tried to get as much detail as I could on capital and recurrent costs, priority from the viewpoint of us 'experts' *versus* priority in the political view. (The stadium and farm settlements rank low from our standpoint, high from the political standpoint.) Had payoff studies been made? What about foreign exchange content? Were the projects suitable for grants or loans? Could they be suitable for ordinary bank financing? What was the lead time? What was present executive capacity, could it be raised, how fast and at what cost? Needless to say I did not get many answers, but it was an exceedingly useful exercise all around. Pius, by the way, is in Lagos now and we must work on all this in more detail here.

We worked into the afternoon to get the overall picture straight. Later I wrote up the whole thing with my comments, so that Pius could take it to the Premier in the evening for policy decisions. Pius told me later that he had had some success. The Premier promised to back substantial increases in funding for extension work, palm grove rehabilitation and hydraulic presses. He could not be budged from the farm settlements, since he had announced them with fanfare. They can be executed at a slower pace, thus absorbing relatively few resources while grandiose announcements are made, and we may even be able to convert them into plantations, which would make more sense.

There are other hot potatoes, about which we could do nothing as yet. Government participation in industry is one. Over £5 million for no good reason, wherever a foreign investor wants it. But the Eastern Nigeria Development Corporation has as its director a crazy American Negro who is an empire builder, and I think a catastrophe, but is shrewd politically and, incidentally, wants to become a Nigerian citizen.

May 11. Three intensive hours with Agriculture. Frank and I raised technical questions about their program. Had payoff calculations been made, and why not? Why did they request only £200,000 for palm grove rehabilitation? They didn't know. Would the poultry scheme pay off? Yes. How did they know? They didn't. How much did it cost to feed the damn chicks? They didn't know but could find out. How many extension workers could be trained in crash programs? Apparently quite a few. They could use the facilities of their various pilot farms, etc. It was again depressing to see how much knowledge went to waste, because they had no idea how to organize it. I pointed out that Frank and I were no technicians. We didn't know how many eggs a chicken laid and how much it ate. But we had to help them in getting their priorities straight. Frank thought the meeting went well. I hope so…

May 12. Back in Lagos…The JPC meeting was at 9:00 AM. I was apprehensive, but it went very well. Prasad not only stuck to our agreement, it was all sugar and honey. Moreover, he completely reversed himself, and took my line on planning throughout! So the blowup had some good results. It helped even more that the US mission is coming, that I know two of its four members, and that I had guessed right what they would want to know. We went through the Regional Development Plans, possible local funding, and the gap. The North wants £82 million, can finance about 30, the West wants £95 million, can finance 50, the East £123 million but can finance nothing! Actually, only the Western program is thought through and feasible. In the North they spend at the rate of £5 million per year now, can raise it to perhaps £6 million, meaning they will be lucky to execute £30 million in five years, in which case their deficit disappears. The East spends at the rate of £6 million per year now. If they can raise that to £8 million, it means £40 million in five years, which is still a hell of a deficit.

The discussion focussed on the Stanford Report, the overseas economic mission, and what to tell the Americans when they come. I hope I won't be put in the embarrassing position of having to advise the Nigerians *vis-à-vis* the Americans. That would put me on the spot. Not that I wouldn't be true to Nigerian interests as best as I could, but who would believe me…

Lyle and Chukujekwe came for lunch. Ch. is very able and nice. He is a Western Ibo, from the proposed Midwest State. When that comes, he and most other Midwesterners will go back there. That will create lots of problems. Aside from making whatever plan we come up with urgently in need of recasting, it means that the most efficient civil service in Nigeria will be split into two mediocre ones. But there may be a long-run political payoff in further decentralization…

May 13. 8:00 AM at the CBN, at their request, to discuss the American mission. It was quite useful, because they were going to duplicate our effort. I got them to do other things. I was naturally tired,[2] but surprisingly alert, unlike Lyle who, despite his younger years, was knocked out for the day. I am constantly surprised how much latent energy I have, or perhaps I am burning it up without noticing it. In any case, three hours teaching is a lot more strenuous for me than what I am doing now. For an academic I really take to the action life so called.

Actually no one can tell me stories any more about action *vs.* ivory tower. Civil service is just as much ivory tower. One gets action only once in a while. Instead of writing signed articles, one writes signed memoranda. One is just more anonymous. But I understand why Dick Musgrave[3] used to yearn for Washington. I am afraid that I have also 'licked blood,' though I don't think I am going to be spoiled for academic life.

The birthday party night caught up with me, however, later in the morning. The JPC met for three hours on statistical issues, under the chairmanship of Prasad, with me being a sort of vice chairman...The meeting droned on, with reports about balance of payments statistics – a wrangle between the Central Bank, Statistics and Prasad, on who should compile them – terms of trade, on which I reported, etc. It got duller and duller. At one moment I must have conked out, without being aware of it. I said something about wage rates vs. weekly earnings, when Pius leaned over to me and said, "We don't talk about wages any more!" Fortunately everyone thought it was funny. Gibbs winked...

May 14 (Sunday)....Toby dropped in. He knew I wanted to talk with him alone. He agreed that Lyle is first rate, but needs a little relaxing. He says we should take Lyle and Prasad out to Maxim's [restaurant] once in a while. Also to play it quietly, draw in Lyle even more, and talk to him when the occasion comes. Toby was on his way to see our Minister, Jaja Wachuku, to find out whether he will stay with us, and whether he is going to do any work. Tomorrow we have a meeting with Finance and Prasad about the overseas mission. It's everyone's headache all right. (I found out that one of the reasons Charles Thompson preferred to leave was that, as a DO in the East, he had arrested Jaja Wachuku. It would have been a little embarrassing to serve the same man as a PS, particularly as Charles seemed to have a low opinion of Jaja, whether correctly, or not, I don't know yet.)

May 21, 1961

The US mission's impending arrival has speeded up the tempo. On May 15 Toby called me in to talk about anti-American intrigues underway – privately, of course. The minister, Jaja Wachuku, a member of the Public Service Commission and a third person whose name and position I have forgotten, have begun to worry that there are too many Americans around. Why was the planning done by Americans? etc. Toby told me not to take it seriously and to keep my sense of humor. The whole thing had really nothing to do with us personally or with us as Americans. If we had been Poles, they would have raised the same questions. They really want to get rid of 'foreigners' – understandably if foolishly. We just happen to be here and to be Americans. Jaja is anti-American, apparently the only one of the ministers. Actually the whole thing has ceased to bother us, and isn't worth taking seriously at our level.

At 9:00 AM, Pollock of the Economist Intelligence Unit appeared to find out what we knew about transport planning. Since everything is now up to the Cabinet, we told him nothing, and were cagey like old bureaucrats. Actually, he was a silly young man.

At 10:30 AM we went to a meeting chaired by Prasad in the Cabinet office. Present were Toby, Lyle and I from our ministry, Keep, the Deputy Governor of the Central Bank, Rice, his American research advisor, and Murray and Phelps of Treasury. The problem was how to handle the American mission, what to give them, what papers to write.

Prasad was excellent. Ever since our blow-up we have been getting along fine. He has talked our line and I believe he means it. Partly this may be because Keep, an Australian and a very nice but primitive man, takes the old Prasad line, but in such an unsophisticated manner that it becomes simply idiotic – which it never did with Prasad. We decided to prepare five papers for the mission. The first, to be written by Lyle, essentially a rewrite plus refinement of my old JPC paper, adding a brief description of the major projects about which we know enough. I have to write two papers, one about available financial resources, aided by Phelps, and another about balance of payments. The Central Bank is to write something on capital markets, and Commerce and Industry on the industry program.

We also decided to be absolutely frank with the Americans, tell them everything, but not give them everything in writing. There were some other questions about publicity, which thank God no one wants. And of course, we were worried just what the Americans wanted and would offer...

May 17. Phelps was back to discuss an excellent paper of his, which will go up to Cabinet now, and which I must use in my paper on mobilization of foreign resources. The picture is grim: the problem is first to find out how much of our financial resources are left, and secondly, how to centralize them. Our only request was to show things on a cash-flow-basis. Phelps had deducted all commitments against available reserves to arrive at free reserves for the next plan. But some projects – mainly the Escravos bar and the rail extension – are scheduled to go into the next plan, and the reserves won't be spent until then. It'll add £108 million, but even then the picture is far from reassuring.

The rest of the day was spent calculating and helping out Lyle when he wanted to discuss a point in his paper...After squash we went over to Toby's and had supper and then discussed the paper and the problem of negotiating. Toby said the paper was "bloody good." I had produced a two-page summary and we agreed that Igwagwu would write another summary based on my summary of Lyle's paper and my four-page discussion paper from two weeks ago.

Then Toby began to open up about the troubles he has with Jaja. "Every time I take a file to him, it disappears. He just won't take decisions." Apparently Jaja is playing to get Foreign Affairs, held at present by the PM himself. So nothing gets done. To this day, Jaja has neither ok'd nor vetoed our ideas on how or what to negotiate with the Americans.

May 18. We went over Lyle's paper and my suggested changes. Most changes were simply editorial – long live Sir Ernest Gowers' "Plain Words." It probably helped shorten the paper by 20% or so. Lyle's paper was $^2/_3$ a rewrite of mine but still it was his work and my job was primarily to make sure that he said what he wanted to say and to check the logic. Then we went to Prasad to go over it again. He took the total figures to the PM for approval, so we have something even if Jaja doesn't make up his mind. Prasad was pleasant and Lyle relaxed. Except for the horrid week I usually am relaxed anyway. I suspect that inviting Prasad's daughter to my birthday party helped a good deal.

As soon as I got back from Prasad, I got the manuscript out again and rewrote it, feeding it to Patricia to put on stencil. She worked over lunch, while we went home. I had to make peace because there were again interruptions from Peter Clark and others, which were not necessary. I finally threw Peter out, telling him to apply some planning to the planning unit also. In fact, Patricia sat for two hours doing nothing and fuming, because Lyle hadn't finished some calculations because of Peter, etc. Lyle stayed until 5:30 PM, but I had to stick it out until 7:30 PM to proofread the stencils and make sure my handwriting could be read.

Cocktail party at the Sadlers, the UK trade commissioner, described by Toby as "Now you know why we lost the Empire."...I stayed only for 20 minutes, because Toby invited me to Antoine's for dinner, with dancing at Maxim's later.

Entering Antoine's we walked right into the American mission. I handed out some Brazil cigars to them. The evening was not a success as far as I was concerned. I was simply pooped and could hardly keep my eyes open. I left 'early' at 12:15 AM.

May 19. Another meeting at Prasad's office to approve our paper. Strangely the Central Bank objected violently. So did Finance somewhat less violently. Keep said it was too theoretical, and based on weak national income estimates. He produced an outline, which on the face of it looked like an old League-of-Nations outline: past performance, discussion of sectors, means of financing. I pointed out to him that our paper contained two of the three things he wanted, and that we had agreed that the financing would be dealt with in a separate paper. He insisted that we should add up the projects, then see how much money was available and so calculate the gap, including the foreign exchange gap.

I wanted to know how he would calculate future revenues. He looked for help to Finance. I asked how he would catch the projects' indirect impact on the balance of payments. I don't think he understood the question. I'm afraid I was a little rude, pointing out that he was just as theoretical about the future as we were, just less elegantly so. And then, to my regret, I said, "Why don't you write *your* own paper, instead of ours. Why don't you tell us how much savings we can get out of the private sector, and how. What institutions we should have." He stared at me – Prasad felt it necessary, quite properly, I might say, to protect poor Keep from me. I asked: "Well, aren't money and capital markets the business of the Central Bank?"

Prasad was diplomatic but firmly on our side. Finance had objections but most of them had been taken care of by my editorial job. Only at one point was there an outcry of anguish. We had been talking about the need for sacrifice, and Murray, the PS Finance, thought that Festus understood what was involved. But when it came to our paragraph that Government would have to tax away 4/6 of every additional pound of income without interfering with the private savings effort if our proposed program is to be financed, Phelps said, "At this moment the Ministry of Finance may be permitted to faint." We said, "Go ahead, we'll join you."

We then agreed that the five-year program of £600 million government plus £550 million private investments was not feasible; that we could squeeze water out of it, but that we should show the implications to the minister. The program is feasible only if taxes and private savings are raised substantially and the composition of investments is shifted radically to the directly productive sectors; if social overhead is developed only where it contributes directly to production – as certain kinds of education will – and if unnecessary expenditures such as TV are cut out. Obviously we won't get it; but the Minister ought to know what the choices really are. The paper was approved to be handed to the Americans, but only to two or three people in the Nigerian overseas mission. It was agreed also that Lyle should write a 4–5 page jazzed-up version of the project description for both missions. The Central Bank left unhappy in general, and Finance unhappy on specifics.

When we left, Toby said: "How did Keep get in here? This guy is Deputy Governor! Why, if we merely wanted to do what he wants, we wouldn't need you fellows here. I could have done it as a bush DO." Actually I find Keep rather funny. He is a lively little man, nice, obviously not very bright, with a heavy Australian accent. His notion of development obviously is: add up the projects. Then open up the cash register, and count the pennies. If he were black, people would say that he has only recently come down from the tree. He sure is primitive.

May 20. I got Sam Akande to do calculations and I did a lot of telephoning. The nice thing in my position is that if I want to know something I can just telephone. The problem is projecting marketing board receipts, etc., which involves among other things breakeven prices, farm prices, etc., which are laborious to collect, and in any case the reports are two years out of date.

At 1:30 PM we were invited to Dolgin's for lunch with the US mission…We sat around until 4:30 PM telling them what we knew in general. They got the papers. I explained why I was very leery of seeing them. I was now a Nigerian civil servant, and I did not want to be put in a position where there would be a conflict of loyalties, or any doubt would be raised about my discretion as far as the Nigerians were concerned. Within these limits I would be happy to see them and talk. Rivkin understood, I hope, in any case he said so…

Afterwards Toby and I had a ginger ale at his place. He told me his woes with Jaja. He not only won't make a decision, he is currently very anti-American and afraid of criticism from the left wing elements in his party. He won't make any decision which might be criticized later. Toby is so fed up that he has pushed his leave ahead by a few months to August or September and may not come back. Nice prospects!…

Today at 5:00 PM I will take Rivkin to the beach for a walk, while Lyle takes the other three for a swim. Then they all come for a steak dinner to my house. Toby promised to brief Rivkin on the political situation, and that should be interesting for all. I am so steeped in the more technical aspects that I have neglected study of the political forces.

June 1, 1961

Life is very hectic here. I should finish two papers by the end of the week. May 21, a Sunday, I offered my house as a sort of neutral meeting ground between Toby and Arnold Rivkin. In the afternoon we took him and Wilson Schmidt for a walk at the beach. The evening was a big success. Rivkin was impressive, short and to the point. Both he and Toby decided to be perfectly frank. Rivkin took a risk and so did Toby.

I can take some credit for any success the American mission will have both for the US and Nigeria. Rivkin explained what I had guessed from Millikan's cable and letter, that the Mission was preparatory to making a congressional presentation on the new foreign aid policy; that Nigeria had been picked along with Tunisia as the two focus countries in Africa, and that he was instructed to find out as best as he could the country's needs and priorities, foreign aid gap, attitudes towards receiving aid through a consortium, etc.

Toby on his side was frank about the difficulties here. The latent anti-Americanism, the fears of a 'new colonialism' through accepting too much foreign aid, etc. The main point of the meeting was to establish a feeling of confidence between Rivkin and Toby, which is rather essential. It is easy to say things to one man which one could not say in front of four. Toby also showed Rivkin his paper on the dangers of the Peace Corps, on which Rivkin also was skeptical. This is a good example of the injustice done to the British Colonial Service. Back home no one raised any questions about the Peace Corps, about the problems it might raise in the recipient country, about the possibilities of it backfiring on the US. No American here did, either. Toby in the course of his duties did. This is now used to show how conservative the British Colonial Service is because it cannot grasp the great new ideas!

May 22. Lyle had prepared the first paper for the Mission, based on my original JPC paper. I was charged with preparing a second paper on available resources, on which I had done a substantial amount of work since going to the Regions. I not only made revenue forecasts for each of the Regions, based on the best information available today, but had estimated possible revenues from Marketing Boards. I worked like a bear from 8:00 AM–11:00 AM. Afterwards I was told to attend the negotiations with the Americans as advisor to Toby. It was a strange feeling to sit on the opposite side from the Americans as a Nigerian civil servant. Toby chaired the meeting, flanked by Prasad and myself. On his left hand sat our party – Finance, Central Bank, Foreign Affairs and Commerce, on the right hand the four members of the American mission, Dolgin of the embassy, Bernstein, the head of ICA, and two younger embassy staff whom I have met only casually and whose names I can't remember.

Rivkin began by outlining the mission's aims, and then asked each of its members to fire questions about the paper, which I answered. After this each of the ministries added some explanations, and the Central Bank added its two cents worth. Everything went well. I carried the ball, but that means only that the discussions were essentially economic and academic, and no policy or political questions arose.

Then I spent the afternoon working on my paper on resources…After dinner [at Prasad's] I worked in the office until 2:00 AM on that d... paper. The Federal ministry of finance had been a little late in getting me the necessary data to make the export revenue projections. But I wanted to get things done in time, so I could go off to Ilorin with a good conscience.

May 23. Worked all morning on the draft, got it done by 1:00 PM, went through it with Lyle and Toby, made corrections and adjustments, brought a copy to Prasad for his comments…At 4:30 PM the four of us met again at my house for tea and talks. I was not in on all of it because I had to go back and forth to the office to hand over the manuscript. (Office is about 5 miles from my house.) Apparently Prasad cited ministerial resistance to the idea of an international consortium providing assistance, and there was some talk about our ambassador, Palmer, having been able to prevent a deterioration of the situation since the riots, but not really having caught the Nigerians' imagination in the manner of Chester Bowles *vis-à-vis* the Indian people. This is of course unfair since there are not many people of Chester Bowles' type.

Patricia finished typing my paper at 8:30 PM. I invited her and Rivkin to dinner, which was excellent for a change. Unfortunately they wanted to go to Maxim's, "for just one brandy." So after two dances it was again 1:00 AM when I got home. I think I am through with Maxim's and dancing for the rest of the tour. Rivkin got a typewritten copy of my paper, while the rest of the team had to wait until the next day when the mimeographed copies were handed to them.

May 24. Meeting with the American mission. Two points were discussed. Rivkin asked how the Nigerian government would react to an international consortium in the manner of the "Aid India Club," possibly chaired by the IBRD. Prasad had done a considerable amount of evangelistic work with the Prime Minister, so the ground was well prepared. The man from the Foreign Office thought this would not only be acceptable but positively welcomed by the Government, provided it did not preclude Nigeria's accepting aid from any source that offered it. This assurance was given. There was much agreement and the discussion on this point was very brief. Rivkin told me later that he was taken aback and had expected to talk at length to convert the Nigerians to the Kennedy point of view. As Rivkin is going on to London and Bonn, to talk things and get money out of them for Nigeria to match any American contribution, this is quite important...

The discussion next moved on to my resources paper. Most of it was again technical economics: how I had done it. Where were the omissions, etc. I said I had assumed current tax rates, and presently visible resources; that I had projected Eastern Region revenues on the assumption that they would spend major sums on palm grove rehabilitation, and the introduction of hydraulic hand presses; that if they did not do so, revenues would be drastically smaller; that they had not yet agreed to this major program, and that I did not want to say so in the paper, but that I had assumed their agreement in order to put pressure on them...

In the evening Minister Wachuku gave a party at the Federal Palace Hotel for some New York University professors. He wants something from them, they want something from him, and both will be disappointed, according to Rivkin. Just who wants what from whom is apparently unclear to everybody...

May 25 and May 26. High Moslem holidays, Eid-ul Kabir, the birth of the prophet. Lopashish, Patricia, Ann Hansen and I including Felix – got away at 8:00 AM. Lyle did the babysitting to give Ann her first chance to go on a trip...[After Ibadan and Ife] we went north via Ede Oshogbo, Oton-Ila-Oro, where we made our next stop. [See Photo No. 16.] Near Oro is a small town called Esie, not on all maps, where Lopashish wanted to see and show us stone figures dating back to the Middle Ages. Apparently there was a pagan temple in the bush where these figures were shown in their natural environment...

We got back to Oro at 3:30 PM for a picnic lunch in the pleasant yard in front of the Catholic church. Surprisingly the Catholic mission students obeyed Felix (who is Catholic) when he sent them away and let us eat our lunch in peace. We were in Ilorin by 6:00 PM...and took a drive through the town. The only electricity is in the Emir's palace, and a few private houses. The rest had kerosene lamps only. The absence of electricity has at least the one good result: the noise level is kept to what people can do unaided by loudspeakers. There were people on the streets, and some drumming. The Emir's palace was lit up, and people were gathered in front, but there wasn't much going on. The night was cool – i.e. one needed a sheet for cover, and we slept under mosquito nets. Ilorin province is Yoruba, but has a Moslem Emir, and belongs to the Northern Region, with its noticeably different vegetation.

May 26....We got away at 10:00 AM to a town named Share, about 40 miles from Ilorin, three miles off the paved road. It turned out to be an interesting village, half Yoruba, half Nupe, with two chiefs, one for each tribal group. The Nupes had originally conquered the area, and still behave differently from the Yorubas. They look different too. They are Northerners, as black as Negroes, but with more hamitic than negroid features. The behavior is also strikingly different. They treat whites as equals, with no inferiority complex. They know they were conquered by the White Man, but these are the fortunes of war. They know they were originally masters, not slaves, and act accordingly...

Lopashish went in first to see the Nupe chief, whose title is Alhaji Sule Mdakpoto, Chief of Shangi, who had four chairs brought out, and then received us in style. His English was perfect, and it turned out that he had been a school teacher before he was elevated to his chiefdom...

Next came picture taking ceremonies, for which Ndakpoto dressed up in his official robes. [See Photo No. 17.] Picture taking was almost too easy. Once the people saw that we were accepted by their chief, everyone wanted to be taken and it became hard to photograph just the compound. There were skins stretched on the floor for drying, but otherwise the compound was meticulously clean, and did not smell. When we took our leave after two hours – everything has to go slowly and in a very dignified manner – we got a leg of lamb wrapped in newspapers as a farewell gift. I promised to send the copies of the pictures when they turned out, in about three months.

From Sh. we went to Jebba, where there is the famous railroad-road bridge...[See Photo No. 18.] On Jebba Island in the Niger was a bronze figure we wanted to see. This turned out to be very beautiful, dating back probably to the 16th century. There were also chains that were supposed to have been brought by Cedre (?), the founder of the Nupe empire, but which according to Lopashish were much newer and undoubtedly of Portuguese workmanship. There was a trumpeter with one of those long African trumpets. Everyone wanted money, and having taken a picture of the idol which was taken out of its hut, we hurried on...

We were back in Ilorin by 6:00 PM, and went to the market to buy pottery. I got two big water jugs of traditional design, for 2/6 or 35 cents. The Ilorin pottery is famous, handmade without a wheel by women, hardened over an open fire, and according to Lopashish of interesting similarity to Peruvian pottery. I am sending the pots home...They are pretty, even with all their crudeness.

After dinner we went once more back into town, to watch festivities. These consisted mostly of people dancing to drummers, but it was all quite subdued despite the fact that there were huge crowds. The crowds were rather friendly, even though they always asked for money, which we didn't give them.

May 27. This was the big day, when we saw the real Africa for the first time. It was still Mohamet's birthday. We left at 7:30 AM for Shara. We picked up our guide, Mallam Mohamed Halim, an agricultural officer, who spoke in addition to his native Nupe, English, Yoruba and Hausa. We took a dirt road to Ogudu, a little village on the Niger, downstream from Jebba, about halfway between Jebba and Lafiagi. On the way we got a lecture on the millet fields and other crops.

In Ogudu the village head appeared in full dress. They had prepared two canoes for us, constructing a sunroof of reeds. Everyone was courteous. The son of the Etsu of Shonga, who did not speak English, came along, and another man, whose role I did not understand, who was a healed leper, at least I hope he was healed. We walked down to the river, followed by the whole population, but *not* the chief...There were three pole men, who sometimes also rowed, particularly when the wind got too strong, or they wanted to sit down. One of them startled us when he got thirsty and simply drank the filthy Niger water. His stomach must provide an excellent sample for a bacteriological laboratory.

Tada, which is not on any map I have seen, but which must be about seven miles upstream from Ogudu and which can be reached only by water, is not directly on the river, but on high ground about $1/2$ mile from the river beyond the flood plain. It is rather romantic looking, a real traditional African village, practically no modern influence. For example, almost all houses are round mud huts. There are only a few rectangular buildings, none of concrete, and no tin roofs to speak of, but all thatched. Our guide took us to the community hall, a biggish round mud hut, scrupulously clean. In it were four chairs for us. Opposite us the village chief and the elders sat on skins, and the hut was filled with people sitting on skins.

There was silence for perhaps a minute, although it seemed longer. Then the village head, all dressed up in his robes of office, and with his staff of office, asked us through his interpreter what had brought us to Tada. After a ceremonial pause, I said in my most formal manner and being scared to make a *faux pas* that we came first of all to visit with them, and secondly to see their famous images. After another ceremonial pause, we were told that we were welcome and asked to follow the chief.

We then walked after the chief and his elders to the hut, which housed the images, followed by our own interpreter, the son of the Etsu of Shonga (who was rather useless), and the whole population at a proper distance. It was all very polite. Unlike in Abeokuta there was no pushing, no crowding, but polite curiosity.

The images were very beautiful, all bronze. There were 4 figures, two of which were of Cedre (?), the founder of the Nupe empire, or at least were called that...Three were elephants, kept against the wall. We asked whether the images could be taken out into the sun to photograph. We were allowed to take out all but one, which had never been removed from the hut, and we were politely asked not to remove it. We respected the request...

Then the village head asked us to take our meal in another hut. We were led to it, which incidentally not only was clean, but cool. We spread my mat, and had our picnic. It was lovely. The politeness extended to leaving us completely alone. All children were sent away. The gates were shut, and we were left in peace, with our mat, and a few chairs brought specially for us. This, said Lopashish, was the traditional Africa, now being ruined by economic development...

We asked to make a gift, and were told that the village wanted a tin roof, since the building with the statues would become important. We contributed 10/-, which was accepted as a big gift, shown to the assembled people and handed to what I presume was the village treasurer. The elders accompanied us to the edge of the village on the bluff. Another pose for a picture, and then we entered the canoes.

The trip downstream took almost as long as upstream, because a strong wind had sprung up, and the river had waves, and white caps. Back in Ogudu...we shook hands all around, and went off to Shonga, five miles or so on a bush road, to thank the Etsu himself.

In Shonga, we had to wait until His Highness the Etsu had changed to his ceremonial robes. Then we were led into what might be described as the throne room, a largish round mud hut, which was really cool. In the center was an iron bedstead, covered with carpets for the Etsu. Beside him stood his Kadi and elders.

Our interpreter and the others who came in prostrated themselves and sat on the floor. (Prostration is a common form of greeting, not only from lower to higher, but among all social strata.) All discussion went through the interpreter, of course. The Etsu wanted to know where we had been. We told him and thanked him...

In Shara we wanted to thank Ndakpoto. He was in the village hall, which doubled as a Mosque. The place was crammed with people celebrating the birth of the prophet. Ndakpoto was in beautiful white robes which would have pleased the Archbishop of Canterbury, underneath a canopy of red velvet...In his beautiful voice and excellent English, Ndakpoto asked our forgiveness for not coming out to meet us, but tradition forbade that. We equally ceremoniously but with much less dignity asked his forgiveness for disturbing their ceremonies, and expressed our thanks...

It was a big day. We will do this as a family trip. It is not too strenuous. The canoes are quite safe. The lack of comfort comes from the fact that one sits on a mat on the flat bottom, but in part it was because the son of the chief of Shonga took too much space...

May 28 (Sunday). Back in Lagos. It was a magnificent trip. I feel I have seen Africa for the first time.

May 29. The American mission is in the Regions and won't be back until Friday, June 2...Worked with Peter Clark on export forecasts and import substitution effects of proposed factories.

May 30. At 9:00 AM, UCI vice-principal Bevin brought us the University's request for money for the next five years...

Later I saw Toby, and got my first shock. I told him Ben Lewis was coming on June 22nd. Toby asked who Ben Lewis was. I said, why the distinguished American professor whom we had asked to join us at no cost. Toby said he knew nothing about it. I said I remembered distinctly that we had discussed it and got his OK to go ahead. Toby said probably so, but it would be catastrophic to add another American at this moment. Jaja had calmed down. Our relations with Prasad were smooth. Another outsider would blow us sky high.

I got red in the face with embarrassment. I had written Lewis after clearing with Toby. Kingsley is embarrassed. The Ford Foundation higher-ups had asked him whether we could use Lewis. After clearing with Toby we said yes. We have to work out something to save the situation. I am disappointed that I can no longer rely on Toby's word, even though I know now that everything has to go through channels. That I should have put it on paper, that the paper should have been initialed by him and the minister and put on file, etc. Well, we will get over this somehow.

In the afternoon, Toby picked me up to inspect a small fishing pier together with the Ministry's fisheries expert. There is a small outfit, Dutch, which catches fish, puts them on ice and sells them in the evening. They want to expand. They need more land to do so, and have negotiated with UTC for a plot, but the local manager must wait for a decision from Basel, the headquarters. If they can't get the plot, they must get permission to expand the pier into the water. They now have just an ice plant, but they want to open a small cannery for processing and possibly exporting the fish. The manager said that just that morning he had concluded a deal for a £1 million investment: £150,000 from the Dutch company, £150,000 from a Japanese fishing company, £200,000 from the Western Region Development Corporation, and on the basis of this equity a £500,000 loan from the Japanese government. Toby promised to push the matter as soon as the land question was solved.

June 13, 1961

June 2. I worked from 8:00 AM to 7:45 PM and finished a paper for the American mission which will be used also for the next JPC meeting on June 23. It is about balance of trade forecasts, and was extraordinarily difficult to prepare. In the evening we had dinner with the American mission which had just returned from their tour of the Regions...

June 3. I had the mission for lunch with all our Nigerians...

June 4 (Sunday). Toby had organized a Ports Authority launch which took us around the harbor and to a beach across the harbor where I had never been before. The mission enjoyed it. In the evening all went over again to Toby's for one of those informal talks. Prasad was also present, Murray of Finance and myself. My opinion of both Prasad and Rivkin rose considerably. Both were to the point, with no nonsense about them. Prasad had done his homework, and told Rivkin what we would like to see, what the problems were. Again he sprang a number of things on us without previous consultation, but on the whole he stuck to previously agreed matters.

He was particularly critical of the very high degree of corruption, which would complicate the giving of aid. After all we wanted to avoid a Laos situation, where corruption was as complete as it can be. But he also pointed out that Nigeria had to be seen in an African context, and that made their report rather positive. He insisted that the country was not taxing itself enough – which shocked Murray – and that there were also rather tricky and dangerous foreign policy situations. If the Nigerian mission now traveling abroad got a lot of Iron Curtain aid, it would almost certainly discourage American or British private investments.

Moreover, the Regions could go abroad and negotiate anything they liked, leaving the onus on the Federal Government to say "no." Constitutionally the latter has to approve all foreign loans and aid, and distribute the money among the Regions. But the system has never really been put to a test, because money was easy, and the Western Region, run by the opposition party [Action Group], has not yet applied for any sizable allocation. I was a little shocked that Murray, whom I liked, did not follow all the political arguments, and sought comfort and refuge in administrative rulings. As if those could undo political realities.

June 5. Final session with the mission. It was friendly, and we parted with good feelings all around. That is, the embassy and ICA people were a little sore, because Rivkin had been treated so much better than they had been, and had got so much more information. But I think from now they will get it too. The rest of the day I worked on the paper.

At 9:00 PM was an official black tie dinner for the mission in the Federal Palace for 90 people...Jaja came late, because of a Cabinet meeting. He gave a short speech which I did not understand because of the acoustics, but which I was told was just this side of insulting Rivkin, whom I did not understand either, who apparently spoke well.

After that a few of us went to the private apartments of Clegg, the Hotel Manager, to drink a few bottles of Veuve Cliquot, and from there we went to Maxim's, the inevitable, where we stayed until 3:00 AM.

June 6. At 5:00 PM we all went to the airport to see the mission off in style. I was rather offended that no one came from our embassy, only Bernstein of ICA. On the whole the embassy treated the mission rather shabbily, perhaps because Ambassador Palmer was away.

Notes

1 Sargent Shriver, President Kennedy's brother-in-law and first Peace Corps director.
2 After his 49th birthday party the night before, which he celebrated until 3:00 AM with lots of Moselle, accompanied by the Federal and Regional PSs of Finance and Development. (His actual birthday was May 13.)
3 Professor of Economics at Harvard, WS' one-time classmate.

Chapter 7

June 12–July 24, 1961
Federal Investment Program, World Bank Mission, Managing the Ford Team, Malaria, Preparing Introductory Plan Paper for JPC and National Economic Council (NEC)

June 12. Subcommittee meeting on statistics in the morning. I was irritable with Peter, who had not done what I asked him to do while I was away; but it was really the aftermath of the 'restful' weekend [in Dahomey and Togo]...

Now a completely different work schedule begins. We have to start pulling the expenditure projections together. I have put everyone on notice that we have to work overtime regularly from now on, at least for the next month. I was disturbed by a lot of things, but I now understand that no matter how I try, I am the boss and I alone, not Lyle and I together as I would have wished, must deal with Toby and Prasad. I just have to get used to being a bureaucrat, working in a government machine.

June 17, 1961

I got a dreadful cold and stayed in bed. I had worked with Lyle on the expenditures programs. What with the continuous coughing I probably was less friendly than I might have been, but I don't think Lyle minded. He was perhaps a little surprised that I could drive and boss. We have now to check back with the various ministries, and either get quick answers or write letters over Toby's signature requesting them.

Haven't yet finished the Addis Ababa paper. I find that I am happiest when I can work with figures, push a slide rule or a calculating machine and make endless details fit into a grand pattern.

June 23, 1961

Beginning of the following week we had a rush job at the office to finish the detailed list of Federal ministry plans. We had a discussion with Toby and Neil Morrison, the DPS, who isn't much good. Apparently the purpose of the exercise was to get an overall view of the magnitude of the problem and see what projects the World Bank mission which is about to descend on us might pick up for financing. I had a hard time keeping my temper because the subject matter constantly shifted. Toby's temper was also raw because he had an attack of malaria with 102° fever. Lyle was his didactic self which did not help.

The real reason for raw tempers lay, however, in the political sphere. Our Minister, Jaja, left for the Congo for a week, having raised hell because he was given only a small plane for the trip. No one knows why he is going. In any case, he has about 30 files requiring his decisions, which he just hasn't taken. Toby can't get anything out of him. At the same time, while we are working on a national plan, individual Ministers go around announcing great plans, sometimes without even consulting their PSs, certainly without telling us. They sign contracts and commit us to spend money which we don't have. So we are sore, but cannot ride herd on them, and an uncomfortably large part of the Government plan is prejudged for us.

We are now trying to pull together what we know of individual projects, what we can say about payoff, what the remaining problems are, what questions we are to shoot back to the individual ministries, where we do this on our own initiative, and where we need Toby's authority. The imminence of the IBRD mission makes all this urgent. The procedure will be identical with the one used with the US mission, and Toby and I will be expected to carry the major burden.

The state of our files is shocking. Lots of information that we asked for last year, in February and again in April, has been slow in coming in. Even collecting what we have is a miserable job. Theoretically it could be done by a junior, in fact Lyle and I have to do most of it. I have surprised my staff by my turnaround from an easy-going man to a taskmaster. But my patience got exhausted when I couldn't get results, and people couldn't understand that we have to do a limited job, and do it fast. We haven't even started writing the plan yet.

Yesterday I got everyone running and some progress is being made. More letters are going out with questions and deadlines...

In the evening I took a break and went to Victoria beach to see what the weather has done. It is rather frightening. About 30 yards of beach have been washed away. Trees which were way back of the water are in it now, and the erosion has been incredible...

Today things are calm, but it is the calmness before the storm. I am writing up the railway program, looking at the papers submitted for JPC tomorrow, and trying to make sense of the Ministry of Health program. Tomorrow till Sunday is JPC again, with the Regional people coming in. I have two papers in for discussion.

It is now really raining, and rather cool, but it means one has to be indoors most of the time.

July 2, 1961

There are deadlines, I am being drawn in to some near-top-level meetings, I have to give opinions on memos of others and at the same time we are so understaffed that we all have to do glorified clerks' work. Our Nigerians continue to be nice, and they work reasonably hard. They come to the office in the afternoon and evening if asked to, and sometimes even without being asked. But I have to check all their work and it often is simply useless. Also in the British civil service it is not easy to delegate anything to a junior. There are few grades: Assistant Secretary, Senior Assistant Secretary, Deputy Permanent Secretary and Permanent Secretary, and the jump particularly from AS to SAS is very big, involving a tripling of income and power. Hence our ASs, who will talk freely with Lyle or me because we are not in the hierarchy, hesitate to say anything to a superior. I can call a PS in another ministry and get a quick answer over the phone, but Sam Akande has to call another AS.

June 23. Another JPC meeting. The agenda was long, including my two papers prepared originally for the American mission. One of those was finished only a few days before the JPC meeting and had to be sent to Rivkin in Washington.

Prasad handled the meeting beautifully. He put me at the end, which shortened the discussion. Before that, the Regions attacked the Ministry of Commerce and Industry (MCI). I kept Lyle from speaking. The Easterners had tabled a memo on pioneer industry status, the spirit of which was good, but which was nevertheless silly, because pioneer status doesn't help much to attract new industries when at the same time more difficult obstacles are placed before private industry, both domestic and foreign. Also the idea that some subaltern should decide whether Nigeria already had enough factories in a given industry seemed rather absurd, considering that there is no industry worth speaking of. Since MCI had prepared a sensible answer, there seemed to be no need for us to talk. It is better to be quiet unless one wants to make a point strongly.

The discussion of my papers pleased me very much. I was attacked, all right, but quite justly. The Northern Region pointed out that I had made a boner in my revenue projections for the cotton crop. This was not simply a difference of assumptions about which one can argue, but a really obvious mistake. When writing my paper under considerable pressure, I had telephoned the MCI's Marketing Division, Barker, to give me breakeven prices. Cotton is so complicated that I got fouled up. Yesterday it took me two hours at Barker's plus some afternoon work to get it all straight. Anyway, the difference is considerable. Instead of a profit of £2 million, there are expected losses of £9 million. The rest were minor points making little difference in the end result. In my export projection, for example, I had forgotten groundnut cake, which now amounts to about £1½ million. But given my method of estimation that won't alter the results much. Anyway I don't know the future any more than the next man.

The afternoon I spent with papers Pius Okigbo had given me to read; first, he gave me hell – not unreasonably so – because over the phone I asked him to get me the promised Executive Committee paper. Only Ministers see those, not even other civil servants, and he pointed out that he could be fired. He nevertheless let me have it with the promise not to show it to Lyle or Toby or anyone. The information in it was pretty much what I had worked up with him when I was last in Enugu, but it was a courageous paper, laying down the law to the Prime Minister, pointing out that the ER financial situation was going to be desperate, that the Plan had to stress high and quick payoff projects, if the Region is not to bog down, and that more taxes would be needed.

I hope he has influence. Unfortunately there is some evidence that Daniel, an American Negro who is taking out Nigerian citizenship and is literally mad, is more influential. He runs the industry section of the Eastern Region Development Corporation, is an empire builder and wants to sink lots of money into crazy industrial undertakings, when it should go into palm grove rehabilitation and hydraulic palm oil presses. They should expand cement production, and they might get a steel mill, which with luck might even pay off. But then they do funny things, like developing an industrial estate at great expense and setting rates so high that no one can afford to lease the land. But it looks good on the books that they will have 1,500 acres at £6–£6,500 per acre!

The second paper was a somewhat expanded version of the ER paper, with a slightly different breakdown of the figures. Pius also asked me to comment on a paper he had written for a conference at Northwestern University...It was a good paper, though too orthodox for my taste. I have never believed that underdevelopment creates a need for more rather than less state action, and the Nigerian experience confirms my prejudices. The less capable administrators one has, the more important it is to use them intelligently and the more they should be concerned with general policy and giving direction to the economy, while execution should be left as much as possible to 'automatic' forces. Things may be different in India or even East Africa, but in Nigeria it would work, I am sure.

In the evening there was the usual cocktail party for the JPC. I met briefly Lord Head, the British High Commissioner, who seemed to suffer through the affair. Some journalists were a pain in the neck. I am getting fed up with these parties. But I had to go. In the first place Toby was sick, with the bug I had – which has now got the DPS – and I had to take Jean along. And then, as a member of the Ministry, I have that kind of duty too. I only wish there was more than one caterer in Lagos! The stuff is always the same.

June 24. JPC Statistics meeting. Again we got only part of our job done. The census people were there to tell us their plans. It is clear that the census will not give much information besides the number and sex of the population, and perhaps the tribal and regional composition. Even age distribution raises questions. The UN expert thought they should have 5–year age groups. First they wanted to record ages 0–6, 6–12, 12–20, 20–50, 50 and over, corresponding to preschool, school-age, labor force and electoral ages, but samples indicated that no one was under 20 or over 50!

The WR representative wanted each individual's age to be enumerated. But in the absence of birth and death registers, this data will be almost valueless. In any case the census people were adamant that they could not ask any more complicated questions. They would need 50,000 enumerators and they had trouble getting that many qualified people to ask even simple questions. Questions on employment and economic status were left to a post-enumeration sample survey. How you get a sample without having a good census first was left unclear – perhaps the experts know what they are doing, but then perhaps they don't!

The statistics subcommittee, as I probably wrote before, is concerned with getting the data needed for planning. One of my jobs will be to write a first economic report to Cabinet, and organize the Statistics Dept., the ministries and the Central Bank to get them to collect the data we want, and speed up its collection, dissemination and publication...

June 25 (Sunday). I worked through the files which Ken Baldwin had lent me. Baldwin is also from Kaduna, about to be made economic advisor in the North, with a separate planning unit in the Ministry of Economic Development, or Planning, which has just been set up. There used to be a planning unit in Finance under Peter

Gibbs. Taylor, who was PS, is on leave, and will come back for 6 months to help his Nigerian successor get organized. Peter has been Nigerianized. His successor as PS is a nice and apparently able Northerner. It is a serious blow to us to lose Gibbs, with whom we had developed excellent personal and working relations. We will have to start all over again with his successor. This fortunately will not involve heavy drinking, because he is Moslem!

Baldwin used to be in Ibadan at the Nigerian Institute for Social and Economic Research (NISER). He is able, a co-author (with Chief Dinah) of the monstrous cocoa study in my office, but he is also something of an old maid, blows hot and cold, and is one of those people who can never say anything good about anyone.

Anyway he left me his file, including a lot of stuff on Marketing Boards that I had been anxious to get my hands on. I spent hours reading and copying. Then I went over to see him at the Pites, where he is staying, to get his criticisms of my JPC papers. Except for the cotton boner they were all minor. He wouldn't let me see the file where he had written his comments. The mistakes were minor, but it was characteristic that he had to write them assertively. And this does not change the fact that he knows an enormous amount about Nigeria in general and the North in particular. Or that he frequently contradicts himself.

But I did get important information out of him, such as the plan to establish two more groundnut oil mills, that crushers had taken only 125,000 tons of nuts out of their quota of 140,000, that the quota has been increased to 200,000 tons, while the capacity for crushing at present is only 170,000 tons. I also got a list of industries and plans – one can count them on the fingers of one hand. And there they worry about control and dispersal! I am going around preaching the doctrine that one doesn't have to worry about control and dispersal until one has something to control and disperse, but that is too subtle.

I forgot to mention that one of the subjects discussed at the JPC was the reorganization of NISER and its divorce administratively from UI, though it would remain there physically and retain close relations with the University. A committee was set up to report, and I am on it. I am pleased with this, because it is something semi-academic. Also, I want NISER to be something like the Brookings Institution, crossed with the Center [...] and an Institute of Applied Economics, and I will try to get the University of Michigan to backstop it, if it turns out to be something sensible...

The week just ending was our hardest so far. I made myself unpopular with everyone, yelling at them, losing my temper, being impatient and behaving like a boss. I myself worked every night until 1:00 AM, starting again at 8:00 AM. The point is that we *must* get as much of the Federal ministry expenditure and development programs as possible into shape for the Bank mission. I had laid out the work. Originally, Lyle and I had agreed I would do the revenue side, he the expenditure programs, and we both would work on the final resource allocations. Well, I didn't, except in a general way, inquire how the expenditure work was going, but I had told Lyle three weeks ago that we had to have it, holes and all, by the time the Bank Mission came. Lyle came in quite depressed, saying the files were in much worse shape than he realized. The ministries had not met their deadlines. I was quite sympathetic because this isn't anybody's fault in particular. One has to be careful how one puts pressure on the various PSs. But I thought the time had come to put it on. Toby had told me the work was essential, and I agreed with him.

I pointed out to Lyle that there were two other good reasons for taking stock now, and following up as much as we could. First, the ministers keep on making commitments, and if we don't stay a jump ahead of them, there won't be much to plan by the time we meet our own deadline. Lyle not unreasonably said that our deadline was tight, and agreed to by JPC. [...] My answer was that this was true, but couldn't be helped. Secondly, to have any influence we have to be ahead of Prasad – with whom everything, by the way, is milk and honey now. Prasad *is* Advisor to the Federal Government, we are only advisors to the Ministry of Economic Development. He has access to the Prime Minister, we do not. Toby works with Prasad, and so must we, directly and through Toby.

Lyle kept lecturing me about not jumping to conclusions until all the facts are in. I agreed, but pointed out to him that we had discussed this and agreed, and there was no need to go over the same ground again and again. L. has a tendency to talk to everyone as if they were undergraduates. It was beginning to get on my nerves, because every minute counted.

I said I wanted tables laid out giving for each ministry and program annual capital requests; annual recurrent expenditure arising from the new programs as well as from old programs and general administration; payoff data either through income and revenue where applicable, or physical output such as numbers of doctors trained or school leavers. I wanted expenditure broken down by location, since this is politically important. I wanted labor, material and import content. And any other relevant information.

We had been asking this kind of question since February, I had started already in September 1960. Lyle agreed. I said after we had the information together, we would see the holes, and get a preliminary sense of priorities and questions yet to be asked. And we would write a two-page memo on each program, with our comments and questions, to be shot back to the ministries with a covering letter from Toby. For in this system one gets action only when there is a letter from the PS – unless they like you personally, of course. We also agreed that I would take Sam, and Lyle take Peter and Obineche.

What caused my irritation was that, after explaining all this to everyone three weeks ago, and pointing out that everything except this work had to be dropped, I had to explain again what I wanted. I finally lost my temper and said I didn't want to say it again. I had laid out a master table, and they should use their heads to modify it for different ministries, I didn't want them wasting time by discussing problems not relevant to the task at hand. This was directed particularly at Peter Clark, who is fascinated by the problem of industrial incentives, and always wants to talk about that rather than the more boring work we have to do. I'm afraid I was pretty rough on him.

After the easy-going atmosphere, everyone was taken aback. But I had pressure from all sides: Toby, Prasad, the Bank mission, and I had politely asked them to do specific tasks. Lyle said: give me a deadline, and you'll get the work. I said: you have one: June 30. Lyle wanted to know the long-run deadline. I pointed out that this could not be answered until the present exercise was finished. Lyle said he couldn't work that way. I said, I'm sorry, but how the hell can you make a timetable if you don't know where you stand. First we have to take stock of where we are.

After a week's struggle and very hard work on my part, I not only got the action I needed, but Lyle now agrees. And since he has a considerable amount of gamesmanship in him, he not only is tougher on Peter, Sam and Cheido, but acts as if he had thought of everything from the beginning. Which is fine with me as long as I get the work done. Actually, Lyle is damn good, but he is at times pedantic, starts with Adam and Eve, and must have general principles specifically laid out for him before he can set up a table. Usually I take this in my stride, because I esteem him highly and like him a lot, but I know that he irritates everyone else. I get this from all sides, and he got under my skin this time. But I did talk with him, pointing out that Toby, for example, was intellectually perhaps not systematic, but he was very fast and if you told him something once, you need not repeat it.

Well, enough of that. It was a struggle that will continue from now on because the tempo is rapidly picking up. Also, I am essentially a lone wolf. I treat everyone as an equal, expecting to be independent, and then I am disappointed. If they don't perform, then probably my failure to give direction is at fault. From now on I must be the team leader, whether I like it or not. Again the British system forces me into this. I am the senior, and Toby deals with me rather than us. It does no good to want to treat everyone as an equal. In the office I can't escape being the boss, even though I try to.

June 26. In the afternoon I saw Hill of the Timber Association to get a forecast of timber sales for my revised export projections. Hill turned out to be a retired Brigadier, with military bearing, and very nice. However it took me a long time to get him to promise the figures. He said it would be like a military paper, what would happen under certain assumptions. I said this is how economics papers worked too. Hill spent most of the time explaining the industry's woes. Nigeria probably has great timber reserves. The demand for the hardest woods is small, but for the softer hard woods it is excellent. They could use their forests better, but it takes large enterprises with foreign connections. There was a danger that government intervention would ruin everything. I said – several times – that I didn't have to be sold on the desirability of private enterprise.

There is some urgency in this question. At present African Timber and Plywood, a subsidiary of UAC and the biggest timber company in Africa, is threatened with loss of some of its concessions. One needs at least 100,000 acres to have a good harvest and get the necessary equipment. Unscrupulous European firms are now trying to break in, bribe ministers and cut existing concessions to 50,000 acres. If this happens, timber resources will be depleted fast, instead of being built up. Furthermore, unless there are sales connections abroad, exports would suffer. German firms, lacking these connections, have failed badly.

At present, exploitation of top-quality wood is only 53%. The rest is sawdust, or bark. This is absurd. Only recently did they start making block wood. According to Hill, they could make Kraft-type paper – though not writing paper – from the local wood; they could also make pencils and matches, which are now imported in large quantities. For railroad sleepers, instead of wood they use imported steel, even though there are vermin resistant woods. They use little wood for building, even where the wood is vermin-resistant or could be vermin-proofed, because they don't season it. Huge trees are towed by water to Lagos and lifted out with as much water in it as wood. The wood is sawed up and the next day used in a house "No wonder they don't like to use wood." And so the tale of woe continued.

An amusing sidelight. Hill's office had a picture of a magnificent chief in full regalia. "He is one of the shrewdest traders and businessman," Hill said, "but if you see him in Port Harcourt don't go to his house after 5:00 PM. You won't come out again." "Why not?" "He will eat you." This was said in all seriousness. I knew that in Abakaliki cannibalism still prevails. But apparently it is more common than we suppose. Hill said that he asked his steward whether he had ever eaten human flesh. He didn't deny it, but said he preferred goat! It is awfully hard actually to find out whether cannibalism is widespread, whether it is mainly ritual or what.

In the evening I worked until midnight trying to make sense of the Ministry of Health's program. This took me the better part of the week, and several phones to d'Astigne, the PS Health, who also came several times to the office with corrections. Even though it is essentially clerical work, I find it useful to go with a fine-tooth comb through at least one important program to see what is involved. I have an urgent need to know what I am doing in detail. So I spent hours calculating for each doctor, nurse, cleaning woman, how much their income will increase. I finally came up with phased recurrent expenses, and a phased capital program. Health should really have done it. But it is no use complaining. If I don't do it, it just won't get done.

Actually it was just as well, for I found out that Health had made serious errors – aside from the many unavoidable mistakes of addition which don't amount to anything but are always used by fools who can't think of anything else to discredit a man. Health had added the *additional* cost of new hospitals and staff to the *total* cost of the number of beds. It made a difference of £1$^1/_2$ million a year. Also the staffing problem is formidable: 161 new doctors, 1200 nurses, and worst of all pharmacists, radiologists and lab technicians. Where are they supposed to come from? I requested d'Astigne to provide a paper on staff training. I told him we would support strongly any capital expansion which he could staff, but I was against building useless hospitals. There is also a discrepancy between Health and the University on pre-clinical training, which we have to straighten out. I also asked d'Astigne to prepare a separate paper for the World Bank on training of doctors and expansion of the Mainland Hospital to a full teaching hospital, which I think is an excellent scheme.

Doing this work involves endless arithmetic, rather boring at times. I can see why Peter is more interested in policy questions of a grander nature. But we just have to do this now. I guess as one gets older, one gets reconciled that 90% of whatever one does is more or less glorified routine, and one doesn't expect any more. Or perhaps I am a sufficiently well-trained theorist not to lose my sense of where I am going when I calculate what the Mainland nursing staff will cost in each of the next five years. Whether Peter, and Lyle for that matter, lack sufficient theoretical training, I don't know. But I couldn't do without them.

However I am discovering some things about myself I didn't know. The idea was that I am the economist while Lyle knows his way around government, where I had no experience. It turns out that I, the theorist, can suspend theory more easily than Lyle, tackle a specific problem with a specific deadline and get along much better in government than he. I'll come back to this when I report on my conversation with Kingsley. Part of it is undoubtedly due not to any special personal qualifications, of course, but to the fact that I have no previous experience in this kind of work, hence I see Nigerian problems completely afresh and not through previous experience in Pakistan or India. I have always suspected that what counts is good training, tact and a willingness to tackle problems on their own, and that experience may not always help in different circumstances. I am now convinced that I am right. Although I must qualify this. Prasad's experience makes him a superb chairman in a manner I could not begin to approach. But even this is true only since our blowup.

June 27....The only 'outside' event was that, of all people, Tommy Balogh[1] appeared in the office, greeting me as an old, long lost friend! I invited him for lunch at the house, and threw him out of the office until then...

Tommy says he is economic advisor to FAO, trying to make economic sense of their technical programs...He was scathing about the FAO/ICA Report on the Northern Region, which is lousy and internally inconsistent – people have a bad habit of forgetting to add up their recommendations and seeing whether they are mutually consistent. He claimed that FAO had successfully eradicated rinderpest in a section of Abyssinia[2] only to cause overgrazing and serious soil erosion, which is undoubtedly true...

Tommy wanted to know where he could buy old Benin bronze. I asked whether he had £35,000 or so, and was willing to smuggle it out. If not, he should spend £10 on a new one he liked. We talked about an article of mine, the one with Paul [Samuelson].[3] I said I would give a lot to write another one like that. But now I was only good for quantitative economics. I actually liked, metaphorically speaking, getting my hands dirty. Then Tommy inspected the house, decided it was nicer than the hotel, and said he was going to stay here on his return from Ibadan. There was nothing I could say after this but that he was welcome! Considering that he is the only person I ever had a serious acrimonious controversy with, in which I accused him of intellectual dishonesty, his behavior was – well – Tommy Balogh! Actually I was quite amused. He left at 3:30 PM, and I went back to the office and slavery.

June 28. First I got the office organized, gave Sam some work, and saw the rest of them to make sure they didn't go off on tangents...

At 10:00 AM we had a meeting with Prasad. He is going to India for a month with ER Premier Okpara, so I asked what line I should take with the IBRD mission during his absence. The major problem is the Niger dam. We must get straight what the damned thing will cost, and how they estimated benefits. The reports I have read in detail just don't tell. And somehow I have to be ready for any disagreeable questions. We all agree that in the short run, the dam will not pay, but that as a long run proposition it is probably better than marginal. The opportunity costs are probably not as great as one might think because "the wretched Nigerians" (as Prasad says when none are present) won't have any industry worth talking about for a long time.

I also told Prasad what we were currently doing, and said I expected to have a first detailed look at the Federal Program by the time he returned from India. I thought we should then sit down together and hammer out any differences. We should go after the Federal ministries to finish their work. Lyle wanted to know strategy. Should we first get each minister's approval of his part in the final plan, or should we submit the program as a whole.

Prasad thought we should wait until the program as a whole was ready. He would talk with the Prime Minister, who would then put it through the Cabinet. If we went to the individual ministers, everything would be ruined piecemeal. I must say I agree with Prasad completely. Toby didn't say anything then, but later pointed out that no matter what Prasad said, one had to inform the individual ministers ahead of time and get their approval. After all we had a system of ministerial responsibility. He obviously has a point, but I suppose what it means is that the PSs get their ministers to OK the program. Anyway all these things seem to have a habit of working themselves out somehow, and usually in a way which is quite planned...

In the evening I went with Toby and Jean to the airport to see Prasad off to India. He had reserved the VIP room, which was just as well, because the airport seemed to be full of Prasads and their friends...He was pleased to be seen off, and it helps in relations. Besides I begin to like him quite a bit and will invite him when he gets back. I think I have learned from the fight that it pays to try to resolve one's differences openly...

June 29. The only non-routine event was a visit with Kingsley, partly on business, partly to say good bye to him before he goes on leave today. He started by telling me I had done a superb job, that he gets it from all sides. I think I blushed, but I can't say that I disliked the statement. He thought I handled personal relations well. In particular, when I arrived, there had been some boiling problems in the Regions which I had smoothed out. Apparently it was touch and go whether we would establish working relations with the Regions. I said I was very happy to hear all this. I was aware that we didn't do too badly. I had not been aware that there had been particular problems with the Regions as distinguished from the general and eternal problem of federal-regional relationships which continue to be delicate.

He wanted to know how I felt about Lyle. I said he was damn good and useful, and I would be sunk without him, but that he was pedantic and repetitive at times. He is also very assertive, which I am not. I tend to play things down, which goes over well with the English and Nigerians, while he – and until recently Prasad – irritated both English and Nigerians by assertiveness and arguing that they knew everything better. That they really do is beside the point.

I was also disturbed that I had had to straighten things out in both the East and North. Pius and Frank Moore don't get along. My academic position means something to Pius, but that is about all. The rest is that I assume Pius to be intelligent and well trained (which he is) and understands things the first time, while Lyle can't leave off lecturing. And Frank gets so involved with the local situation that he is upset – rightly, too – for the East is quite irresponsible. I get the same thing in the North, where there was a complaint. I straightened that out with Peter and John Taylor. Now Peter Gibbs has told me to come up and straighten out Jensen-Baldwin who get on each other's nerves. Jensen is in his fifties, and irritates the British by complaining about living conditions which the British feel are much better than what they had 50 or even five years ago.

Kingsley said he was aware of all this: Lyle did bore him sometimes. Prasad told him that he liked and respected me, but that he disliked Lyle, which I both understand and find quite unfair. Lyle's assertiveness does not bother me as much as it does others. But this seems to be oriental status consciousness. I have the same rank as Prasad, and what is more, I am only a year younger than he, while Lyle is in his thirties. Prasad told Kingsley that he could work well with me.

I find it amusing that I am a success politically. Particularly as it seems entirely due to the fact that I can drink like a fish if necessary, and go out to Maxims in a tuxedo! The world is really quite absurd.

I raised a number of questions with Kingsley. First, if the planning operation is not to collapse, there must be some people here who overlap with us and can carry on. Lyle has written a draft memo on staffing which I have not yet read. (It is too long.) I also talked with Toby about the problem. Until now we could have used one more man but now we should really double our staff. I want only MAs or PhDs, no more BAs from second-rate British universities. And we need a senior Nigerian to boss us. Even if he doesn't work, as might be the case with Pius, he would be a net gain. Toby was formerly the DPS in the Ministry of Establishments. He promised to get us people fast by direct intervention with the Public Service Commission. Once that happens, I told Kingsley, I'll come back to him as to what Ford can do.

Secondly, I said, if Ford had a continuing interest here I would be interested in backstopping it, in the manner of Ed Mason in Iran, etc., provided this was agreeable to the Foundation. Kingsley said the Foundation would be more than happy and anxious to use me, and he felt the Nigerians would too…

June 30. I relaxed for the first time. The morning was as full as usual until 2:00 PM. Then we had our staff luncheon at my place. I felt anxious to have it because in the office I had discouraged all talk not directly related to the immediate job at hand. There was an urgent need for an informal get together, where everyone could relax. I also invited Ben Lewis and Otto Königsberger, partly to entertain them, partly to give our junior staff a chance to meet visiting firemen, a chance they do not normally get except at cocktail parties where one really meets no one.

Ben Lewis from Oberlin was finally and happily placed in the Ministry of Commerce and Industry to investigate Pioneer certificates and the working of the pioneer law. We are trying to persuade him to broaden his investigation into the problem of industrial incentives. We originally wanted him to evaluate the working of the regional development corporations, but this is politically too hot to handle. In my opinion, which I state quite frankly, the reason is that these corporations are thoroughly corrupt and ineffective, squandering money which is urgently needed elsewhere, on ill conceived industrial projects, and they hide behind nationalist slogans. As usual, patriotism is the last resort of the scoundrel.

Königsberger is Lyle's triumph. A Berliner by birth and a British citizen, he is an engineer and architect, and runs an institute of tropical architecture in conjunction with the University College, London. He is here under UN technical assistance. He is investigating how the phenomenally high cost of construction can be brought down…

July 1. I spent most of the morning at the Department of Marketing and Exports trying to establish where I had fouled up in the cotton accounts. It took four hours to figure out how to project cotton marketing board losses. (I think the many days of sleep deficiency must have begun to show, for I feel I should have gotten the point faster…) The meeting brought out other interesting things. The Marketing Division is being abolished, amid violent criticism of the London office, and propaganda for setting up terminal markets in Lagos. I don't think anyone understands here what this means. I really think the politicians – specifically the Minister of Commerce and Industry, Dipcherima, a Northerner, neither Hausa nor Fulani – wants to get a hold of the company first. But they also think that somehow cocoa is shipped to England where it is stored by the nasty imperialists, who won't allow anyone to come to Lagos and pick it up here!

There were two major items in the press, both obviously planted by someone, I suspect Dipcherima himself. First, the Russians and other satellites told the Nigerian mission how much they would like to trade with Nigeria, but directly in Lagos, not through London. This is not true because the Russians have an organization in London, and not here. However in any case it stirs up nationalist sentiment.

I told the Marketing people I had written a memo strongly advising against shifting from London to Lagos, which at best would make no difference, at worst would be a catastrophe for Nigeria. Then they showed me a Hungarian file that Barker was just answering. It started with an inquiry by the Hungarian foreign trade ministry seeking to buy 500–1,000 tons of palm kernels. They wanted to deal with Lagos directly and requested an offer. Lagos cabled back OK, offering 1,000 tons at the world market price f.o.b. and requesting an irrevocable draft on a Lagos bank. The next communication was another cable from Budapest: we are interested in buying larger amounts against sugar sales! I.e. they are not interested in buying, they want to sell. Most of my memo dealt with bilateral agreements.

The second incident dealt with a letter to the editor. Someone had offered to buy 100,000 tons of groundnuts for cash in Lagos, and the Marketing Company had refused. Which proved to the papers – all of them carried the story – that the Marketing Co. was missing out on sales. The story was obviously fishy. 100,000 tons is a sixth of this year's crop, an enormous amount. Secondly, the Marketing Co. sells all its groundnuts – and miraculously even its cocoa! So one could hardly say they had missed any sales.

I asked what was behind it. Apparently an American Negro had come into the office, stated that he wanted to buy 100,000 tons for an unnamed American firm, that he had cash to pay. Quite legitimately the company wanted to know who was behind it,. If this was a speculator, 100,000 tons could play havoc. The American refused to say. Well, the company declined the offer, but the papers didn't mention any reasons.

Elder, the director, told me another story. Ghana bartered cocoa to the Russians on a c.i.f. basis (i.e. Ghana arranges the insurance). The Russians sent a freighter built in 1902. The insurance on such a boat is £5 per ton more than on a new ship, so Ghana got £5 per ton less than they thought they would! It seems people don't want to learn from Nazi and Communist experience…

July 9, 1961

July 2 (Sunday).…I went to the Federal Palace Hotel to have dinner with the IBRD mission. The team leader, Bob Skillings, whom I had met first in 1958, had invited me. Only two other members had arrived, two Norwegians, Froland and Ardvisk (?), two deadly serious young men, incredibly stiff and formal, almost what the Danes say about the Swedes. Prussian-like but obviously intelligent, highly trained and probably very nice once one penetrated that armor of Nordic ice.

After the food we retired to Skillings' room. He bombarded me with questions. The team had all the papers we had prepared for the American mission. In general, the same procedure was to be followed, with the same panel, which meant myself. Skillings wanted me to know what questions they would like to raise about our papers and the "plan," and wanted me to say whether it would help or hinder me.

I'll try to reconstruct the talks as best as I can, which is not easy, because the discussion was freewheeling. Also I don't quite believe everything that was said, though I'll put it down.

First, the size of our program and the foreign gap were too big. I said, I couldn't agree more. Was it true that Prasad had insisted on the bigger numbers? I said yes, that we had a fight partly over this issue, and I wish now that I had not spoken out. Skillings shook his head. I said the fight was patched up, but the controversies would come up again in another context. Skillings said there were a lot of things the Bank would find it difficult to live with. For example, why did we not raise the question of additional taxation? I said we did both explicitly and implicitly.

He liked our emphasis on investment in the directly productive sectors. Was it true that Prasad wanted more expenditure on social overhead. I said yes, and that I was against much of it. But I pointed out that it was in fact difficult to spend money on agriculture in a sensible way, also that the kinds of social overhead that could be sold, like electricity or railroads, or where cost could be recovered, like water and sewerage, were in a different category from schools or hospitals. Was it true that Prasad wanted the Government to participate in the oil refinery and was against the Ports Authority going to the Zürich and New York financial markets? I said yes and I was against it and at Toby's request was just writing a memo against it for the files.

So it went. I defended Prasad, and what's more I meant it. I have not only got to like him, but while I think I am much the better economist, he is superb as a negotiator, and much better than I can ever hope to be as a political and policy center. But there is more to my defense. I agree with Prasad that a plan should not initially be based on availability of funds. People should think what they would like to do and in what sequence if money were no object, and then availability of funds should separate more from less important projects. Prasad himself refers to this as the coupon method.

Where I differ is firstly a matter of principle and secondly one of tactics. Regarding tactics I believe it highly dangerous to tell politicians who can't tell the difference between £10 million and £100 million that somehow the money will be forthcoming, as I heard Prasad say to Eastern Region agriculture minister Okeke. The principle involved is the question of macro *vs.* project planning. I also said Prasad was convinced that the British had held back the country's development, while I was convinced this was not so. I told him how Prasad had boxed me in into defending the imperialists. But I also said Prasad had come around very much on our side, partly no doubt because of the American mission.

Skillings was disturbed because the papers gave no indication that we were worried about inflation and exchange controls. Was it true that Prasad...[4] I said yes, that Prasad thought the politicians would never learn unless there was a crisis first, and that I was determined to avoid both if I could, but that I had serious doubts about my ability to do so. Prasad had the ear of the Prime Minister, whom he had more or less sold on the larger program, while I had mainly the backing of Toby and the PS Finance, Murray (acting during the absence of Reg Clarke). Obviously I can work only through Toby to Jaja, and through Toby via Murray to Festus, who fortunately is a powerful minister. Jaja isn't really interested in Economic Development but wants and probably will get Foreign Affairs.

I told Skillings I had written a sharp comment against exchange control in connection with a brief put up by Prasad, who wanted to forbid trading in British securities on the newly opened Lagos Stock Exchange, which has just two issues listed so far!

All these were things the Bank could not live with and made the mission unhappy. I said, look if that's how you feel, why did you send Prasad? The answer was that the Nigerians had asked for either Prasad or John Adler by name, and there was a sigh of relief when Prasad left. I asked how the hell the Nigerians knew Prasad – Adler is different, he had led the first mission in 1953. Skillings said that Udoji, the Chief Civil Servant in the Eastern Region (who incidentally hates Pius Okigbo), had known both men at the Bank's Economic Development Institute. (Toby later said this was incorrect. He used stronger language: the Bank just sent Prasad.)

The rest of the evening was spent on details rather than high policy and personalities. I pointed out to Skillings that the general paper had been written by Lyle on the basis of an earlier paper of mine which had been attacked and not approved, and which had been much better and had made many of the points he, Skillings, had suggested. I said that in the resources paper I had made a major boner, not just a difference in assumptions: the NR marketing board would lose £9^1/$_2$ million instead of making £2^1/$_2$ million, as I had suggested.

Skillings had two comments on my balance of trade paper. He accepted all my long-run prices except cocoa, which was still too optimistic. The London office had projected £200 per ton, I had assumed £180, Skillings thought we would be lucky to get £150, and might get only £120. This would really be a catastrophe. We agreed to exchange my suppressed paper against his secret one on Ghana. He wanted to know what had happened to the Stanford report, and was happy that it had been accepted in principle, meaning acceptance of the principle that road users should pay for the roads through taxes and fees. When this will be put into practice is another matter.

I left about midnight. We agreed not to publicize the meeting but that Toby had to be informed. I pointed out to Skillings that the size of the plan was to some extent phony. Not only was the price tag merely the sum of unevaluated ministry plans, they could not possibly execute all of it. A good example is the Ministry of Works road plan. They gave us detailed proposals for £96 million worth of roads and bridges, but stated in the accompanying letter that they could not execute more than £50 million. We put in £56 million, because for some bridges outside contractors could be used. Also, the plan was inflated by such items as buying out BOAC's stake in Nigerian airways and buying new airplanes, all of which costs a lot of money but does not require executive capacity. It was an altogether useful but rather disturbing evening, I thought.

July 3. The meeting with the IBRD mission took place in Finance as the responsible ministry...John Murray was in the chair, next to him was a secretary and the Bank people starting with Skillings on one side and the Nigerians starting with Toby on the other. Two more mission people had arrived that morning, with one more to come. One of them, Sadoff, told me I was his tutor in Leverett House[5] in 1938! As it turned out the Mission consists of two Americans and two Norwegians, both students of Ragnar Frisch. Two of the Americans are Ben Lewis' students, and one is mine. Which goes to prove how restricted a circle we move in.

After introductions, Skillings went to town. The Bank is going to be a lot tougher to deal with than the American mission. Of course its purpose is different. Skillings hammered away at exchange control and inflation, the size of the program, etc. I pointed out – and I carried the burden of the technical discussion, firstly because Prasad was away, secondly because I had written or supervised all the papers – that he was criticizing our first paper, which outlined the size of the problem, and did not go into solutions, for which we would not be ready for a while. Finance was quite aware of the need to raise taxes, the Central Bank I hoped would come up with ways to collect small and big savings, and we, I hoped, would come up with reasonable priorities and cuts in the present program which would be politically acceptable.

Most of what was said followed the warning I had had the day before, so it was not a surprise. Skillings asked whether a member of the mission could see me in detail to discuss the papers sentence by sentence. Froland was delegated, and I invited him for lunch on July 4. We broke up at noon. By 1:00 PM Toby, Lyle and I had to be in the Federal Palace for a luncheon which Daramola was giving in honor of Ben Lewis. I don't really like these affairs where you get aperitifs, sherry with the soup, and two wines with fish and duck, as it turned out. But this was nicer than most. In the first place I like Daramola a lot. He is the PS in Commerce and Industry, charming, absolutely straight and a hard worker. He obviously returns my liking for him. In the second place it was a relatively small crowd.

I sat beside a man who does credit work for John Holts of Liverpool, the other great trading firm besides United Africa Company, which is in turn part of Unilever. The trading companies finance the traders. Now banks are taking over this financing and thereby increasing their business. Holts (and other trading firms) would have six-month lines of credit outstanding, worth up to £$^1/_2$ million, to women traders well known to them. The man described a woman trader in pots and pans who regularly got three-month credits of £50,000. No papers, it always worked. She had started small and by work and shrewdness built herself a big business.

The way such people then often lose money is that a pots and pans dealer – this is an actual case – would try to get into another line. In this case the lady decided to go into stockfish, about which she knew nothing. She went to a bank for a large credit which she got on the basis that she obviously was a successful dealer – in pots and pans. It was assumed that she could also trade equally successfully in fish. As a result both the bank and John Holts lost money. There was not sufficient clearing of information. Also bankers did not know their customers sufficiently well. The expatriate bankers had not grown up here the way the traders had, and didn't know the individuals.

The John Holts man regretted the passing of trade financing to banks though he felt it was a natural and eventually necessary development. I was beginning to feel funny – I thought from the wine and food, but it turned out to be the beginning of malaria – so I wasn't as quick as I should have been to point out that the banks could finance trade indirectly by giving credit to Holts, who would finance the trade in return. Murray said that two years ago, the big expatriate banks had lost £2 million, which wasn't generally known. The indigenous banks had lost substantially more. The banks had been told to go easier in granting credits.

The lunch broke up about 3:20 PM. By this time I felt funny, but blamed overeating and drinking for it. Normally I have a very light lunch and of course nothing to drink. Toby insisted in taking me home for a rest. I said the pressure was on, that I hated to feel the indispensable man, that no doubt I wasn't a good team leader because things turned at this moment too much around my being in the office, answering this question and that, giving instructions, yelling at poor Peter for not using his head. The fact is if I am not there things don't quite get done right. I work, for a theorist, with imagination – not intuition, but just imagination. I have the ability of being able to extract a maximum of information from scanty data, but this requires the painstaking study of detail. Lyle and Peter don't quite understand yet, how the detail is used in a general context...

The work is really nerve-wracking now. We are getting all the ministerial programs ready, and analyzing capital and recurrent costs into material and labor, and on-shore and off-shore, as well as revenues and other payoff data, and the Federal resources required. This is where I am a slave driver, for I have to keep sending Lyle, Peter and Cheido back again and again to ministries to request the information or uncover it somehow. Sam Akande has turned out to be quite useless, though he is the only one I don't yell at. First it wouldn't do any good, and secondly he is such a gentle soul that I haven't got the heart. Anyway, I am trying to pull it all together, which will take the better part of two weeks if I can only get some peace and quiet.

The pain got worse and spread to the shoulders...Nonetheless I went off to the Minister's cocktail party in honor of the Bank mission...I didn't drink or eat much, and tried to introduce people to each other. Various PSs wanted to meet Skillings to interest the Bank through him to finance their pet projects, among them d'Astigne who wanted money for the Mainland Teaching Hospital. I am all in favor of building it with Federal funds, as the cheapest and fastest method of doubling the number of doctors that can be trained every year. But Skillings told me there wasn't a chance the Bank would finance any social overhead without direct payoff, except roads and sewerage, neither would IDA, and he told me to tell d'Astigne so. I believe d'Astigne's reaction was "bugger the Bank," not polite but expressive...

July 4. Economy measures have decreed this year that only American and foreign officials are invited to the Embassy 4th of July party, and I being neither fish nor fowl wasn't invited. Except for the Dolgins I have no desire to know anybody better at the embassy...

[After seeing a doctor for the malaria] I couldn't quite go home yet...Toby asked me to accompany the Bank people on their official visit with the Minister. When I asked him for a briefing he gave me the brief he had written for the Minister, and added: "When you see Jaja, you don't worry what to say. You worry whether you get to say anything at all, and when you get away." And so it was.

We all sat in front of Jaja's desk, who was in his splendid robes and cap – his pajamas as Toby says irreverently – and listened to Skillings tell him about the Bank's program in Nigeria, and that they were here to help and that they hoped they would be considered partners in the great enterprise of Nigeria's future. He gave us a nice boost, telling Jaja how impressed he was with the planning that was going on. Privately, and then also in the meeting, he said that our model of the economy was the most sophisticated model of an underdeveloped economy he had seen. I don't know whether this is true or not, or whether he meant it, but I'm afraid I lapped it up. I am quite impervious to the usual flatteries, only to fall for this kind of professional flattery, hook, line and sinker. Must be some professional inferiority complex somewhere.

Then Jaja started speaking in the voice that earned him a prize in oratory at Dublin University. (BO – bachelor of oratory, as one Nigerian paper put it innocently.) He was in good form, friendly partly because he was dealing with a UN agency group, partly because he had his mind on Foreign Affairs. He gave a lecture on economic development, stressing the need for higher education to produce leaders to stir up things. The Belgians had wanted a literate but uneducated mass, Nigeria had not made this mistake, and they wanted more universities. He cited the need for agricultural research and the rest, all very sensible, all common knowledge. He stressed road links with neighboring countries, etc. I sat there as straight as I could although I felt like doubling up with pain, and just waited for him to finish. My temperature went up, I am sure, to 103°. (I was sweating in a room with two airconditioners.)

Finally he stopped at noon. A press photographer was called in. We all had to group around the great man, sitting at his desk while he showed Skillings a document, which he said he had written himself. Then there was another picture, with us grouped around Jaja in front of the map of Nigeria. [See Photo Plate No. 19.] He showed the dam site, but the photographer's bulb didn't go off. So he showed the proposed road to Chad, and then started on another lecture about possible extension of the road from Maiduguri to the Sudan and across the Continent. By this time I was desperate, but we finally got out…

July 7. I went to the office, Toby wanted me home by 10:00 AM but I got away at 1:00 PM. It sounds conceited, but I was needed. They made poor Patricia type empty tables, and when I remonstrated they told me: I thought you wanted the tables, and the choice was between getting the tables done and chasing the information. I almost exploded but held on, explaining patiently that I didn't want empty forms but information, and going through it for the umpteenth time that part of the exercise was to spot the lacunae in our information. Even the information which we have isn't ready made. We have to get it together.

At this moment I was pretty disgusted with the staff. Everyone wants to deal in grand policy, no one wants to do the dirty work, which just has to be done. I don't mind it myself. In fact, I rather enjoy it. They were, I think, a little afraid of me, which is just as well. I hate to give the same instructions fifty times. I have to be nicer to Peter though. He is now almost like a puppy needing a pat. He is very good, but he needs some discipline. The stuff which Sam had done we had to do together again. Perhaps he learns that way. Yet we are committed to enable him to go abroad for a year. He is so nice that on this account alone it is probably right to send him…

July 8. …I dropped in at Toby's on the way home. Toby told me that the DPS, Neil Morrison, had come in in the morning white as a sheet and shaking as a leaf because the Minister wanted to see the plan right away. Actually Toby and Neil had come to my room and I had handed them a document we had prepared for just such an eventuality, which consisted of about 25 pages, giving a list of projects and their cost by Ministry. It meant nothing, but it kept Neil happy, and Prasad before him. Toby told me: "I said to Neil, calm down. Just give Jaja a piece of paper. He won't read it anyway. He has still thirty of my files which he hasn't read."

Jaja wanted the piece of paper because he had the Canadian High Commissioner with him to negotiate the aerial survey and mapping of Nigeria at a cost of £1.5 million, which the Canadians have offered to give us. Jaja had the file on his desk for 6 weeks without reading it. And there he was in fine form, telling the Canadian High Commissioner how he had worked on the file until 3 AM!…

In the morning I wrote a memo on financing the Ports Authority Dock Expansion. I had to take a line against Prasad, who felt that Ports should be internally financed at 6% instead of externally at $7^1/2$%. I disagreed sharply, my only regret being that I had to do so before being able to discuss the point with Prasad. It was quite a good memo, I thought, short and to the point. My point was that Prasad assumed there were idle resources that would earn 2% in London while by repatriating they could earn 6%. But the fact is that everything will have to be used soon, and if Ports can go outside to the market that means additional capital.

July 9 (Sunday).... Next there are three things to do: the expenditure program, revision of the aggregate model in the light of the disaggregation we have done, and a letter to the chairman of the Western Region Development Corporation, who wrote a very confused article in the paper defending WRDC's refusal to turn over its capital. This is a dangerous thing, and requires a judicious answer.

As Alex[6] told me before, malaria is really no longer much of a problem. Nothing to worry.

July 16, 1961

Your letters come regularly, and I am surprised that you haven't heard from me since June 22.[7] I don't seem to be able to write more than once a week. The diary I sent should make clear why. Even when there is a moment, I tend to collapse. But I wrote a very long letter on July 2, which I gave Kingsley to mail in London...The letters contained a large part of the diary which I should hate to lose, and which I would have a hard time reconstructing. The value of the diary to me is not so much that everything I say is correct, but that it gives the thoughts of the moment. It indicates what I thought of things before they happened. It will be interesting to see how often I guessed the course of events right...

July 10. The Prime Minister, Sir Abubakar Tafewa Balewa, is leaving for the States on July 22, and the burden of providing the background paper for Toby to brief him is on me. This has made me into a slave driver as well as a slave myself. Sam Akande turned out to be quite useless. Everything he did had to be thrown away and Lyle or I have to do it ourselves. Obineche is performing well though he needs direction. We got a new man Steven Mbananawa who is as yet an unknown quantity.

Our best Nigerian, Ebenezer Igwuagwu, is still on the around-the-world economic mission. Peter has been working with me and by now must hate me thoroughly. I keep his nose to the grindstone. He is rather rude without realizing it, not doing things I ask for and doing other things I ask him not to do. He tries to do the sixth step before the first and won't believe this can't be done. If ours were an academic exercise I would let him find out for himself. But we have deadlines, which keep being pushed closer than originally agreed, and I just can't let him waste his and my time. He wants to evaluate individual programs before we have an overall picture of requests. Lyle is directing the evaluation while I have pulled Peter out to help put the overall picture into shape.

At 2:00 PM, our closing time, Barbara Ward[8] appeared and I took her home for lunch. Lyle came, and Peter asked to come too, promising he would not say much. I first said no, because I thought it was bad policy to discriminate between him and the Nigerian junior staff, but he was so hurt that I reconsidered...

To my surprise Miss Ward stayed until 6:00 PM, talking. She is writing a popular book about Africa, as a kind of companion volume to her book on India. We talked mostly about local problems. But we also asked her about Ghana. Her husband is Sir Robert Jackson, who was or still is the driving force behind the Volta Dam. There are all sorts of rumors, that he is out, that he has been fired, that he has lost influence, that he is looking for another job, possibly to run the Niger Dam if we ever get it. It is hard to disentangle truth from gossip, and not really very interesting. I didn't ask.

Ghana is slowly getting itself into a mess...I said I thought Sir Abubakar in his quiet and responsible manner did more for African unity than Nkrumah with all his great speeches. He sees to it that international road links are built and that communications are improved. As far as I can see Nkrumah's announcements are all phony. Take the announcement of the customs union with Upper Volta. The only trade between Ghana and Upper Volta is transit trade on which no duties are ever charged in the first place.

Barbara Ward laughed, and said that Ghana and Upper Volta first had to construct a customs barrier in order then to hold a ceremony taking it down. Or take the union of Ghana, Guinea and Mali. Nothing has happened to implement it. Quite the contrary. The recent strengthening of Ghana's Central Bank and the centralization of her sterling reserves – which incidentally could make sense – work in exactly the opposite direction. Nothing much except talk happens at the conferences of the Casablanca group, while under the leadership of Abubakar the decisions of the Monrovia Conference are being implemented.

Miss Ward insisted that Nkrumah was not a communist, which I believe to be true, but an African nationalist who wants to lead the Pan African movement. Both she and Lyle insisted his actions and speeches were shaped by his political aspirations. I agreed, but pointed out that actions speak louder than words. The fact is that Pan Africanism is simply not in the cards. Far from balkanizing Africa as is so often asserted, colonialism has for the first time provided a really centralizing force. But violent tribal feelings still abound, and only a few intellectuals feel strongly about centralization, most of them with insufficient training to carry through.

I know only Nigeria – which I am getting to know quite well – and even here the North-South as well as the Ibo-Ibibio-Yoruba antagonisms are strong and hard to overcome. I am told that Bantu influence starts in Cameroon, and that this is in general a biological divide in the ethnic and every other respect. Nigeria was willing to sell its cocoa cooperatively with Ghana from London, but Nkrumah split this up. We are willing to have the West African Cocoa Research Institute (WACRI) in Ghana, administered jointly, but Nkrumah wants to split it up. Africans are not stupid, they can tell who is for African unity.

I think I made some impression on both Miss Ward and Lyle, but am not sure. Political scientists take speeches much too seriously compared with actions, and feel that when they have – perhaps correctly – analyzed the reasons behind a politician's stand, they have found an answer. But I can explain the pressures on Nkrumah to make his Pan African speeches and still argue that the same pressures could have led to more constructive responses. Moreover, I still insist that Nkrumah's speeches and actions will backfire on him, while Abubakar's have at least a chance to succeed.

Miss Ward said she had friends in the White House, and if we had something we wished to get there she offered her help. She'll come again today. I asked who the friends were, but she wouldn't say, except that it isn't Walt Rostow or Max Millikan. Still, I have my own connections in the White House, and so, it seems, does everyone else. It is a fact that the White House has become quite accessible to academics, but there is absolutely no evidence that access is the same thing as influence. Quite the contrary. The smart men seem to be pointedly ignored. Perhaps it is just as well. Our horizon tends to be much too long-range for day-to-day or even medium-range decisions.

Balogh had invited himself for tea at 5:00 PM...I called him at the hotel to shift him to supper at 6:30 PM. He came at 6, thereby breaking up the lunch party.

Then we got down to business – or shall I say semi-business. Balogh said he was greatly impressed by my memoranda. Coming from him this is a dubious compliment. He is personally nice, but unreliable in his judgment, and I found it disturbing that this time he agreed with too much of my proposals. Perhaps when you get down to business and become technical, ideological differences vanish into the limbo into which they belong in any case. I had to defend almost every well-known economist. The only person he really liked is Louis Lefeber,[9] where I agree. He agreed on the need to push agriculture, but did not realize that this was a Regional matter, where we in the federal government could only make proposals.

Why did we not have a strong industrial program? I said we were proposing £40 million for a development corporation, but that productivity problems were fantastic here. I related my hassle in getting my piano moved, as well as the experience of Kaduna Textiles and Nigerian Tobacco, both relatively well-run enterprises. As a practical proposition, industrialization was a very long-run proposition, except for such things as cement, possibly fertilizer, perhaps even more textiles. We had hopes of getting a steel mill. But for the rest, I didn't believe the nonsense engineers spread that productivity was determined by machines. It was determined by management, foremen, and the labor force, which was miserable here.

The split personality in people like Balogh is a funny thing. *In abstracto* they are for industrialization and the rest of it and think it is easy. Yet in daily life when they run against the unbelievable inefficiencies of the locals, they talk about "niggers" – a strange word a left Laborite like Balogh to be using – or "wretched Nigerians" *à la* Prasad, who on the whole is quite realistic. But somehow they can't put the two together.

Balogh also held forth on the African Common Market. I said I was all in favor for reasons opposite to his. It was of course completely impractical because the West African countries had little to trade with each other, but as a free trader I wanted them to get used to the idea that we might import aluminum from Ghana once the Volta project works, and export steel if we get a mill. If you have to call free trade a common market, go to it.

He said there should be steel mills in Liberia and Nigeria with iron ore coming from Liberia and coal from Nigeria. I almost laughed. Nigerian coal is lignite, lousy stuff. Americans can deliver good coal cheaper in the Ruhr than the Germans can produce, and to ship Nigerian coal anywhere is a sheer waste of resources. Besides the Nigerians are fighting over whether the steel mill should be in the North or East, and they sure don't want it in Port Harcourt where it would have to be if the ore came from Liberia. If it were in PH, incidentally, Enugu coal couldn't compete with the landed cost of Virginia coal. Balogh's argument was both politically and economically unsound.

Balogh said he had advised Nkrumah to join the European Common Market, but not alone, only together with everyone else. The trouble was that if every country joined alone, as the French African states had done, they would lose influence, and the imperialists would keep Africans from industrializing. He actually said this in a document which he gave to Jaja. I said I was all in favor of joining as a unit. But I didn't see that it made that much difference. Protection – I didn't really think it would do much good – could be applied anyway. He had completely forgotten that a major advantage for African countries in joining the ECM is access to the European Investment Bank. Far from preventing industrialization, we could hardly, even in a planning unit with no responsibility for specific projects, keep the damned equipment salesmen off our neck. Germans and Americans swarm all over the place trying to sell steel mills and jets from which I pray God will spare us.

Balogh wanted a reform of the tax system. I agreed. I was for Marketing Boards as a taxing device to catch low-income receivers, and import duties as a means of catching the richer ones. I didn't believe moderate duties would protect, and any industry which required high duties impoverished the country and wasn't worth having.

The evening was quite pleasant. I didn't agree with him any more than I ever had. But we buried our hatchets – not in each other's skull – without either of us taking back anything we had said before. He left about 10, announcing himself for supper again two days hence…

July 11. I asked Peter to come at 10:00 AM and not before, but he came anyway at 9:00 AM, and talked with Lyle. In the first place the office becomes more and more like Grand Central Station with *necessary* visitors and talk, but anything unnecessary just adds to the state of nerves without compensation of any kind. In the second place we just can't afford to waste time now. At 10:00 AM I gave Peter what I thought were clear instructions. He either didn't understand or I lose my ability to express myself clearly. Then I went to see Toby…I told him I was slowly going crazy in the office, and just had to have a place where I could hear myself think. He called the PSs of Lagos Affairs and of Communications, and arranged for me to use as needed the office of the deputy director of PTT. This is a relief.

At 11:00 AM I met with the FAO team. They had all our papers. Their chairman was Krishnaswami, an Indian, former Cabinet Secretary, ex-ICS and a very good type. It was soon clear that he and Balogh disliked each other heartily. Balogh, who the day before had said he would keep quiet since he did not believe in talking in public meetings, soon interrupted Krishnaswami, going off on a tangent of – one can only call it 'Klugscheissen.'[10] K. was miffed and would say nothing more. Neil Morrison, our DPS, who was chairing the meeting, simply couldn't handle it. Toby would have made a crack and in a jiffy got the meeting on an even keel again. I tried my best, but wasn't up to it. Morrison simply had no feeling for what was going on. I could feel it but just didn't have Toby's experience to do the needful.

From then on things went badly. Krishnaswami sulked. I said I needed help and advice and wanted his badly, but he refused to talk. I asked what assistance FAO was willing to give, and whether they would pay on-shore costs. Before K. could say anything, Balogh interjected that onshore cost could not be paid, and anyway we really could not discuss the point!

Then Morrison invited team members to ask questions. First came a nutritionist with penetrating baby blue eyes who was evidently absorbed in his topic. He wanted to forbid the import of wheat flour. I said that we all knew about the nutritional deficiencies, but had trouble doing something about it because of social resistance, which however was fading with rising income. Nigerians were beginning to distinguish cuts of beef, etc. I also pointed out that the ICA/FAO Report on the North was a lousy document because its nutritional and production recommendations were inconsistent – someone had forgotten to add things up. Something that happens with disturbing frequency to people without theoretical training who view consistency as a hallucination of theorists! I also said that, when it came to FAO advice, people interested in production of cattle and selling of meat were giving contradictory advice. Perhaps FAO could coordinate a little and so help us poor planners who were dependent on expert advice.

Next, a German manpower expert from ILO read a prepared statement on manpower problems, raising questions about farm settlements and determination of rural employment and unemployment. We knew all the problems, and he didn't know the answers. Not that I blame him. How can one after two weeks in a country? I am just beginning to know instinctively what makes the country tick, down at the grass roots.

Altogether the meeting went badly, though I doubt any actual harm was done. I asked Krishnaswami to come see me for tea, which he accepted gratefully…

K. congratulated us on the basic paper – Lyle's rewrite of mine. "This is the way to go about it. Make a survey of resources and allocations. No project approach. That is all nonsense." I said, "Shake hands. Do you know Prasad?" K. said he was a friend. So I asked, could he convince Prasad, who was already half convinced, that my approach was right? The trouble with P. is, K. added, he is really a banker. Then he complained about Balogh. FAO's Director General, another Indian, sent him to help, but he just throws his weight around, treating everyone to lectures. I said Balogh had been the only economist with whom I ever had a controversy in print, but that we had made peace on a live and let live basis. K. then gave me his draft notes with suggestions to FAO what to do about Nigeria.

His main point was coordination. Not only did he agree with my complaint about lack of coordination within FAO, but offers of aid were coming from all sides, each agency having a different procedure, each having a little empire builder at its helm, none knowing what the other does. He would suggest a UN ambassador through whom all international aid should be channeled – a very sensible suggestion.

At 11:00 PM I went to Lyle's for supper. The main object was to go through the economics of the Niger Dam with a fine-toothed comb. Toby had arranged a meeting next day with the General Manager of the Electricity Corporation (ECN), in which Lyle and I were to think up all possible objections which the World Bank could raise. Because if we ourselves were not convinced of the desirability of the dam, how could we negotiate with a skeptical bank? We worked until midnight. This on top of several hours in the afternoon. Another lousy night.

July 12. The meeting with ECN General Manager Wyatt took place at 9:00 AM in Toby's office…Our objections centered around points of vagueness. We did not understand how costs had been calculated. Further, in comparing hydro to thermal power, the report on the dam had assumed the Federal Government would contribute £17 million interest-free during construction, while interest would be paid on the full capital cost of the thermal alternative. I made some rough calculations indicating that proper accounting would raise the dam's cost considerably. However it was still preferable to the thermal option.

The second objection centered on the high cost of thermal power. The labor cost per KWH was 100–150% higher than in England or the US. Why? Wyatt said, "I'm not trying to say what the power should cost. I am telling you what it will cost. Nigerian labor is extremely inefficient and overpaid." The gas price, quoted by Shell, is also high, about 85% above US averages. Why? Apparently they have to drill expensively. But Wyatt added, *entre nous*, that he didn't think Shell would want to quote so high a price as to make the Dam unprofitable, since the project was dear to the Prime Minister's heart, and Shell wanted to remain in the country.

We asked about technical coefficients – e.g. how much gas was needed per KWH – which "everyone knows", except, of course, us poor economists. The meeting lasted two hours. Afterwards I wrote a four-page memo, outlining questions about the dam which Toby used as a basis for a letter to Balfour-Beatty in London, ECN's consultants…

July 16 (Sunday). I went to see the Hansens. Lyle told me politely that I was too much of a one-man show, which was bad and lost even him occasionally when my brain was evidently racing like a greyhound. I agreed, but said that when I had explained something once they should get it. He thought it was bad for morale; that I lost the juniors regularly; with juniors it took more then one explanation, preferably in writing. I said I didn't want to be too detailed before I knew exactly where I as going. That I had found that writing too much detail in advance killed off the development of ideas. He has a point. I am like a highly trained race horse, Lyle is a reliable war horse, and the rest are beer horses at best. They must have more direction. The trouble is that I am not an organization man, though also not exactly a lone wolf. I can work with a team that pulls its weight.

July 23, 1961

I am glad that the letter I have given Kingsley did finally arrive. There were too many indiscretions in it to get lost, but for God's sake, be discreet. I can get into serious trouble if some of the stories spread. Besides, I am rethinking some of my impressions of the moment. In retrospect and as new facts come out, things may look quite differently.

Jaja got Foreign Affairs and we have a new minister.

I have been working like a dog and have made everyone else work like one too. As I leave for Addis tomorrow night I had to get as far as possible on a major policy paper for JPC, and ultimately for the National Economic Council, the JPC's Ministerial equivalent which meets in September under the PM's chairmanship. Prasad is still in India with Okeke, and Toby is off to Rome and London on Thursday to meet him and start some financial negotiations. I have so far done about 20 pages and three tables. Toby will take the paper with him and discuss it with Prasad. I have also instructed Lyle on what I want prepared. Then, when Toby and Prasad are back, we will get together and see what we want to present to JPC and then to the Ministers.

The paper first discusses the development plans of all federal ministries, departments and statutory corporations, adds them, phases the expenditure over the next five years, and estimates financing needs. This involves basically systematizing submissions to us. Even there, however, we had a lot of work to do. But whenever one works one influences. The bulk of that work was done by Lyle. E.g., the Lagos Town Commission and the Lagos Executive Development Board, both of them pretty grim outfits that don't know what to do, basically had their submissions framed by Lyle. My own export and import projections come back to me in the form of revised submissions by the Ports Authority and the Railways. Both the hard work and the personal relations we have built up are beginning to bear fruit. We have the deputy directors of Ports and Railways constantly in our lap. The office continues to be like Grand Central Station, and last week I sometimes could hardly take it, but the results are worth it. And the cement plants expand as we want because of us.

The second part of the paper works out the implications of the proposed capital expenditure on recurrent expenditure, adding in recurrent programs. I did most of that work. The results incidentally are horrifying. We still don't have the implications for debt service, which Finance must do for us. Only they can work out the timing and nature of borrowing. I showed this to John Murray, the acting PS Finance. As a result, they asked me Friday evening to prepare a paper for them on the next budget: how much surplus do we need if we are not to jeopardize the next program.

This again is a lot of work. But I am exceedingly pleased by the request. First, they are taking us in the Planning Unit seriously. Second, we have influence where it counts: in budgeting. Anyone can make a beautiful plan, which then will likely be irrelevant to what happens. This may even be true for what we come up with. But if we can establish intimate working relations with Finance, we are all set. So I spent all day yesterday and probably will work more on it this afternoon and evening.

The paper's third part estimates how big a program we can afford. The submissions are much too big, the balance of payments gap is too big even with the most generous help from America, and not all programs make sense. Intellectually, the exercise is fascinating. It means putting the detailed figures into our aggregative model, which we have thus far revised twice, and which must be revised again. This also has considerable academic interest.

These three parts are more or less drafted. The final part is the crux of the plan: an evaluation of the submissions with a view to cutting the program to the maximum feasible size, showing how much revenue must be raised and where and how to find it. I have done the telephone and telegraph system, which is a government department rather than a statutory corporation, and whose apparent surpluses turn into huge deficits when it is put on an approximate business-like basis as it should be. And I have done the road system, which is also heavily subsidized.

The points I must get across and on which I need ministerial direction, if necessary from the Prime Minister, is the principle that wherever payoff calculations can be made in money terms – as they can for phone or road users – the users should pay their way and help finance expansion. That subsidies should be used only where such payoff calculations cannot or should not be made, as for education or health, or where the economic calculations give different results from private profit calculations.

Incidentally, I am not sure how the external economies so dear to economists are really relevant to economic development. But I am reserving judgment. The difficulty, of course, is that everyone will agree in principle but not on specific cases, and the job is to accumulate such a mass of specific cases with specific proposals adding up to so much money that the calculations simply can't be ignored.

I think I wrote before that I have now found my feet on the ground, and my staff who got used to my being very easy-going are now getting used to my pressing for results. But I also keep them informed of the progress. We have Toby completely on our side. How far this will change when Prasad comes back, I don't know. I know that there will be serious disagreement with him on the size of the program, the amount of aid we can get, some priorities, the precise role of government investments, the size and location of a development corporation which he wants inside and I want outside the Central Bank. But fortunately our personal relations are now excellent and likely to remain so, there is mutual respect, and we see eye to eye on many issues.

Based on my memo to him we form a united front against ministries and occasionally against nationalization of certain properties. I have convinced him that we must cut down the plans substantially to levels which incidentally correspond pretty much to my original aggregate estimate. I now know what I am about and feel sufficiently sure of myself to fight for what I think must be done. If only my nerves hold out. On other issues I expect a fight: inflation and exchange control, both of which I would consider catastrophes while Prasad would take them in his stride. Not that he thinks they are any good. But he is more cynical and believes that no one learns from other people's experiences, and every country must go through its own crises before it believes they can happen.

Anyway, I am deathly tired at times, but also elated because of the progress we are making, both in developing the plan and in getting our views across.

I am now also convinced that my approach to development is right. It is nonsense to start a development program separate from day-to-day operations. One has first to get a total picture of the economy in some detail. Development is just using resources well. One can have the most beautiful development program and ruin everything by wasting resources in everyday administration. Cuts are not made in routine things but in development. People just won't accept that money and resources are just money and resources wherever they are employed., and that every program competes directly with every other program. I have gotten *that* across by now. When the present exercise is finished the same thing must be done for the Regions, which will be even harder work, and politically more tricky. But even here I have had success: the Eastern Region has accepted my revenue projections, and the other two are making only minor adjustments.

But enough of the general tenor.

July 16 (Sunday).…Supper in the evening for Barbara Ward, who wanted to pick our brains and get some of our papers for her Africa book. Toby gave his OK. As he said to me: a little judicious leaking is necessary to get proper publicity for our program and mobilize western aid. We expressed disappointment in Roggely's *Economist* article on Nigeria. It was wishy-washy and in part inaccurate. We were all the more disappointed as Toby had arranged for the young man to see Sir Abubakar and Jaja, and I had spent some time with him too. We agreed that Barbara Ward would write a better article in September and that we would keep her informed of our work. Obviously, Toby will decide what can be sent to her. Countries in the English tradition have strong budget secrecy, an excellent tradition which I hope to make use of in enforcing plan discipline, and obviously nothing relating to the budget can be sent. I wouldn't even put it in this diary…

Toby said he would send me to London at the end of August, partly to discuss the Niger Dam with Balfour-Beatty. (This came out of my memo about the dam report.) All this is exciting.[11] Whether it really will work out we don't know. I have learned to believe nothing until it happens. Just as malaria and Jaja's wishes interfered with our going to the Niger dam site, so all sorts of things might happen: e.g., our new minister, Waziri Ibrahim, might interfere and not approve my going. He has a strong mind and a reputation, deserved or not, of being anti-white and anti-Southern [Nigerian]...

July 17. Lyle gave a hugely successful lunch for Barbara. He had invited all our staff, plus Atta, our former DPS and now PS Defense. Atta wishes he was back with us, and so do I. A Northerner, he is not only a most charming man, but also a most intelligent and highly trained one: a First from Baliol is OK, after all. Vincent, formerly of the Ministry and now of the Central Bank, was there. Vincent is a Lagosian, also a highly intelligent man who was in line to become, say in four years, PS Finance. But as a Yoruba (and Yorubas are politically *non grata*) he was kicked sideways into the Central Bank. (At least for the time being.) Pity. Every time something like this happens I get upset. Not so much the politics of it. This is to be expected and is part of the game. But it is so awful that every time you have built up a good working relation with someone, you go back and someone else is there. Altogether we were 16 for lunch, all but five of them Nigerians.

What made it such a success was that everyone talked freely, and even our staff joined in the discussion...It dealt with the European Common Market, Nigeria's interest in joining or not, and a possible African common market. What interested me most was that Nigerian distrust of the Common Market is entirely directed against the French overseas territories.[12] They feel Nkrumah is right in describing the French Africans as mere stooges of the French. Algeria and the dropping of the atom bomb have less to do with it than one would think. The argument is that the French not only pay all development expenditure, but even government operating costs, which is true. Since these new countries are entirely dependent on France, how can they be independent? Which may or may not be true, but at least it is a sensible argument. Atta then chimed in: he just does not trust the French Africans. "I know, I have dealt with them. They will agree to something one day. Then comes a phone call from Paris in the evening, and in the morning they break their agreement because Paris says so. They are not independent." Since Atta *has* negotiated with them, he was listened to with respect.

It was also clear that the Nigerians rather like the Commonwealth, as it appears everyone else does. It is startling to discover that Nigerians or Indians, in whose interest it is to join the Common Market, don't want to because it might destroy the Commonwealth.

They also feel that the French territories don't want the British territories in because it would mean giving up their privileged position. This is probably true. On the other hand they are a bit inconsistent in their fear that joining the Common Market would condemn them to be raw material suppliers, and interfere with their industrialization. I could recognize some of Balogh's arguments in Atta's, who studied under Balogh at Baliol.

As I had with Balogh, I sharply disagreed. Industrialization is a long way off, and in any case only makes up the visible seventh of the iceberg. The important six-sevenths represent less spectacular agricultural development and general improvement in productivity. I cited our access to the European Investment Bank, and said that the German industrial structure depended on export of investment goods. The trouble was not that Germany did not want Nigeria to industrialize, but that they wanted to sell us all sorts of things that we really didn't want or need. Atta agreed, and argued that France's monopoly in her overseas territories could not be broken by anything Nigeria did, but only from within the Common Market.

This led to a discussion of Nigeria's foreign policy compared to Ghana's. One reason why I enjoyed the discussion was that the Nigerians disagreed among themselves. Vincent, a Yoruba and Southerner, defended Abubakar, a Northerner. Atta, a Northerner, attacked him. Nigeria is beginning to be a nation after all. Atta's attack was directed primarily against the lack of incisiveness and of ideas in Nigeria's present foreign policy. It follows, it doesn't lead. The Monrovia papers did not make as much impact as the Casablanca papers. The mere fact that people could believe the Monrovia Conference might have been financed by 'certain' Western powers indicated what people thought. The fact that it was not so financed was irrelevant. Nkrumah's Pan Africanism spoke much more to the people. In any case, we should not associate too closely with the untrustworthy French-speaking territories.

Vincent, on the other hand, said that Nigeria did not want to get into the internal mess of Ghana with its loss of civil liberties. That in fact there was not much collaboration among the Casablanca powers, it was all talk, while we actually did things. As you gather, the discussion was along the lines of Lyle's and my earlier talk with Barbara Ward at my house. I chimed in that I thought Nkrumah was talk, and negative action, while Abubakar was doing positive things which I admired. Vincent was grateful; Miss Ward and Atta argued that in a new country, a little shouting was needed to get unity and get things done. Soft acts and harsh words, that sort of thing. I didn't agree. Nkrumah wants Pan Africanism, but he is breaking up the West African Research Institutes, or would do so if not stopped by us. He broke up the West African Currency Board. His customs union is phony. Nothing whatsoever has happened to unified Ghana and Guinea, etc.

What would I do? I said we are already doing the international road links to Chad, Niger Republic and Dahomey. The Niger Dam has transport implications way up to Timbuktu. I would immediately try to form a West African Airlines. Ghana is losing £3 million a year on hers, which is a little expensive for prestige. So far we have kept Nigeria from going in for jets, on which everyone loses. But if West Africa got together, communications might improve, there would be West African cooperation, and it would pay. We should ask the other West African countries to join our national shipping line, research on cocoa and palm products should continue to be interterritorial. Commercial agreements with Ghana and Guinea could be made where we would buy their aluminum, they the steel from our proposed mill. In fact all we needed was free trade and to hell with the rest.

Barbara Ward chimed in. Free trade was OK but just not fashionable. You had to call it something else like common market. It was like women's fashions. It was no use to say dirndl when it was Dior that year. I pointed out that fashions returned. After all, all that the fashion designers could do was to lower or raise hemlines and waistlines. So everyone agreed to call free trade common market. We did not agree on whether Nigeria was dynamic enough, but everyone agreed they did not want to be like Ghana. And everyone was for closer inter-African cooperation. Everyone agreed that until the Congo and Angola were settled – Mozambique was strangely not mentioned, but this may have been an oversight – it was difficult to get responsible politics elsewhere in Africa. These two problems, plus South Africa, would disturb peaceful development everywhere, and be food for demagogues.

Barbara Ward also made a point which I believe is valid at least in part. She thought we were much too preoccupied with the forms of democracy: two-party state, opposition, parliamentary forms. So Nkrumah's suppressing his opposition upset us. Yet she pointed out that Tanganyika had no opposition and Nyerere had a good press. The point was that we should have safeguarded civil liberties. Suppression of civil liberties and parliamentary opposition is not the same thing. She has a point. Back to the office at 5:00 PM. And again in the evening.

July 18. Main item was a visit with Murray of Finance. I wanted him to look at my projections, he also had some problems to discuss. I was working on a memo for Toby to brief the PM before he left on July 22nd for the States, and had to clarify our sterling reserve position and some budget plans. Murray was sure we would not permit deficits in the future and would raise taxes sufficiently to provide at least as many surpluses as in the past.

Then he showed me a memo from CBN calculating our sterling reserves available for development. According to the Bank there are none. I just laughed when I saw the memo. The Bank is playing the same cat and mouse game as Prasad, only on the other side of the fence. Prasad wants to have a 10% or 20% currency reserve, the CBN has 100%. I support having enough reserves to avoid exchange control. Prasad argues that you don't need reserves, and exchange control, while an evil, isn't the worst in the world. The Bank came up with the following. They not only calculated legal reserves of 40% plus 10% for fluctuation, which is legitimate. If they had argued for a 50% reserve their available resources would have come out a little higher than my estimate. I put in as the minimum desirable reserve the equivalent of three months imports, which turns out to be a little more than 50% with the present money supply.

Then, however, the CBN's Rice – an American advisor – adds the three-month import reserve to the legal reserve. Murray was troubled by this procedure. I told him it was double counting, that the reserve was meant not only to control the amount of money in circulation but to finance trade. He first wanted me to come with him to the Bank but then changed his mind, and just had me go over the argument again.

Back in the office...I continued on the JPC/NEC paper. I went to the retreat which Martin Hall had made available to me to work quietly. The office was again a madhouse. The Deputy Director of the Ports Authority, Clark, came to revise their traffic forecasts. I fled, my nerves on edge...

July 19....At noon Hendricks came over from Statistics. He is on loan to set up agricultural statistics. My job was to outline what we needed. Much of what we need is actually collected already but lack of staff has prevented its analysis. I went back to the office in the afternoon, and took the Niger Dam file home to read at night. I was rather upset when I saw it. I should have read it before. It contains at least some answers to questions on the Dam which we sent off to London. Worked until midnight, which I don't do often any more...

July 20. Instruction to Lyle and the staff on "the plan," a revised list of projects for Jaja to take to the States. It is still unevaluated. Squash at 7:30 PM. To bed at a reasonable time. But I wake at 6:00 AM. Actually it now gets light about 6:30 AM, and dark at 7:30 PM, unless it rains heavily. I miss the seasons. One loses a sense of time, with the constant work, the constant temperature, which varies between hot and very hot, with occasional warm in between, and the constant length of the day.

July 21. The office was relatively peaceful. Ebenezer Igwagwu came back from the economic mission. I invited him to our staff luncheon and briefed him on what we had been up to. He was the guest of honor at lunch at my place. We had also our new man for the first time, Steven Miramara. I am not yet sure of his last name.

The mission had a rough time. Since Ebenezer had been the only one of us who had been or was likely to go to Peking, he was asked about that. The mission was received everywhere except in Russia by the top boy. In China, Chou En Lai himself came to the airport. There was always a general meeting with Ministers, then they split up into a trade and a general economic committee to work on the official level. There was always an *aide-memoire* – the Ad-Memo Ebenezer called it – and a communique. Our boys were also supposed to look into planning methods, but this was much too technical for 2–3 day visits.

The reception they got everywhere was excellent. But the Chinese themselves said that, much as they wanted to help, they needed everything themselves. They were interested in trade – bilateral of course – even in cocoa. Oilseeds we had expected. Ebenezer said he raised the question of no-resale agreement, but was stopped by our own legal counsel from discussing it further. Whether our legal counsel felt this was too detailed or unimportant Ebenezer did not know. The Chinese admitted that they had trouble in planning and in their economy. But the hotel was good, the town crowded, the road from the airport to the hotel very good, and they saw little else. No factories or collective farms were shown them.

They did not particularly like what they saw in Moscow or Prague. The reception was friendly, but the only communists who impressed them were the Poles. They were not only friendly but lively. In Prague rebuilding was still lagging. Moscow and Prague were stuffy, Warsaw lively. None of the communists were willing to discuss credits, but they were willing to accept installments. The exact difference must be looked for in Marxist ideology. They expressed a willingness to accept Nigerian products in exchange, but again the important question of no resale outside the bloc was not raised. On education the bloc promised gifts and aid, and was willing to give a trade school here or send teachers there. But on anything else they insisted they had first to send a mission to investigate the feasibility of particular projects, which is legitimate. So the visits were not fruitless from the Nigerian standpoint, and from the West's standpoint they made clear that Nigeria could not count on much from the bloc. In Moscow they were always asked first whether they were from Ghana, and there was a little disappointment that he was from Nigeria.

I told Ebenezer to take a few days off from the office and write a report for internal use only. The chances that the fellow from Foreign Affairs would write a decent report were slim. I had seen one done by a Foreign Affairs fellow for an ECA meeting in Addis, which was lousy, while Atta had written a brilliant one, which was transmitted to the PM. So I may get a chance to draw the PM's attention to Ebenezer – anything we can do to build up our staff is good…

At 7:00 PM I had to go to a cocktail party…in honor of a UNESCO mission to study the setup of the proposed University of Lagos, which is supposed to accept students next year though as yet they have no site or plan! The mission head is a French educational administrator, Capelle, and there is a Russian on it, whom I did not meet. But I did meet the charming Russian *Chargé d'affaires* who is to set up a Russian embassy here. I wish we had someone as effective as him. Most of our people seem to be rather stuffy, except Dolgin and his wife…

The Russian expressed his quite justified horror at the cost of the Federal Palace Hotel in Lagos. "I can live in Moscow in my 3-room flat for three months on what I pay here in a day." I was too polite to ask how many others had three-room flats at six rubles a month!…

At 8:30 PM there was a drink at the Halls. The Halls are retiring after 28 years here, and glad to get away. Mrs. Hall felt it was a mistake to stay on after independence; there should have been a clean break.

July 22. Peter and I went over the work he had done for me. The rest of the boys are working under Lyle on pay-off figures. We can't reconcile the figures of the Marketing and Export Division in Lagos with what the Northern Region Marketing Board gives us, and what is worse, we can't make sense of the NRMB's data. The various sets of figures just don't add up right. Things aren't what they seem to be. One would think that prices received by farmers are just that. But they aren't. They include export duties which are collected before the farmer gets his price. Everything has to be done all over again because of such things. But at least we are getting nearer to the goal of knowing what is going on and what to do…

Notes

1 Thomas Balogh, later Lord Balogh, a Fellow of Baliol College, Oxford and activist in Labour Party affairs.
2 Pre-World War II name of Ethiopia.
3 Wolfgang F. Stolper and Paul A. Samuelson, 'Protection and Real Wages', *Review of Economic Studies*, 1941.
4 Elipsis in the original.
5 An undergraduate hall of residence at Harvard, where WS was a nonresident tutor after taking his PhD in economics in 1938.
6 Dr. Alexander Gotz, my Ann Arbor physician and a personal friend.
7 The letters referred to in this paragraph reached Ann Arbor after an unexplained delay.
8 Also known as Lady Jackson, a staff member of *The Economist* magazine and prominent Catholic laywoman.
9 An economist of Hungarian origin, formerly on the faculties at Brandeis and Harvard, most recently at York University in Canada. Author of *Allocation in Space; Production, Transport, and Industrial Location*, North-Holland, Amsterdam, 1958.
10 Literally, being 'a smart shit'.
11 WS is also referring here to an invitation from Barbara Ward to write a piece on the East German economy for *The Economist.*
12 Nominally most of these territories gained independence shortly before Nigeria, but it was largely formal. The French in fact continued to run the show, had troops in many countries, and controlled the budgets and development expenditures. I remember that when I tactlessly made this point in Addis, there was an audible gasp from the interpreters. The French were in fact very generous, and it was always nice to work in francophone Africa for that very reason.

Chapter 8

July 24–August 28, 1961
New Minister (Waziri Ibrahim), Macroeconomic Policy, Consultations with World Bank and IMF Missions, JPC Discusses Stolper's Paper, German White Elephant Factories in Eastern Nigeria

July 26, 1961 (Addis Ababa)[1]

July 24. A hectic day in the office. I got my memo ready for Toby...We were told our new minister, Waziri Ibrahim, wanted to visit our office at 10:00 AM. He is a Northerner. Unlike Jaja, he lost no time in meeting his whole ministry. He is said to be anti-white and anti-Southern. Obviously a man of strong opinions. Some that he expressed in favor of private development are all right with me, if he means them. A strong minister with the right ideas can make a lot of difference. But we have to wait and see.

He asked each of us about his background and the planning operation, but spent most of the time interviewing Ebenezer Igwagwu about the mission to China, Russia and the US. Most of the questions were rather simple: would Igwagwu prefer to live in Moscow or Washington, etc. But it was good to have a minister take interest...

[On the ECA conference.] Apparently the two weeks of meetings prior to my arrival have produced a certain amount of fatigue, where everyone has said what he had to say and then repeats himself...After lunch we had another meeting, led by a Frenchman, Mr. Roland Pré, on mining. He was good – the only Frenchman who is! In the discussion we were treated to more facts which aren't so. A Russian, Gavrilov, claimed that of course capitalist oil explorers did not find oil in many countries because they did not want to find it. Russian geologists came and *did* find it. He mentioned Pakistan as a case in point, and unfortunately the Russians haven't found anything there because they haven't yet started to look. Mr. Gaston Ledue of Paris produced the wisdom that no one had found oil in Africa South of the Sahara, because there wasn't any, despite the fact that we Nigerians export 1 million tons!

Today that sort of nonsense continued. Hans Singer didn't do too well with the discussion on industry *versus* agriculture. The most sensible man was Mamoun Beheiry, Governor of the Bank of Sudan, who pointed out that the question wasn't agriculture or industry, but what and how much of each. Also he felt protection could be carried too far even for consumer goods. If one kept competition out, one would not get development, just high-cost and low-quality industry. Coming from a practical man, this warmed my heart. Everyone seems to feel that if one only makes enough losses, somehow one will develop. The logic of this isn't quite clear. I felt it was a mistake that no African had been asked to prepare a paper. Onitiri or Okigbo would have done well. I also found out that Austin Robinson is going to introduce my paper, which I suppose is some sort of honor, since he is president of the meeting and the IEA.

At lunch I told Robinson a little of what we are doing and what I couldn't say in any paper for obvious reasons. He seemed impressed, but felt I was trying to do too much. He recounted some of his experiences in Whitehall, and asked: "Which kind of planner are you, do you want to prevent things from happening or push them into happening? You have to make a choice." I declined to accept the question as posed, said I wanted to prevent some things, make others happen, and had the backing of Beheiry.

July 28, 1961 (Lagos)

The afternoon session was devoted to my paper, the last.[2] It turned out to be a perfect conclusion though I had not seen any of the other papers. Austin Robinson introduced it, flatteringly, in 30 minutes, but the discussion had little or nothing to do with what I wrote. Everyone had had enough of conferencing – even I got sick of it after only two days...A Czech economist, Vopicka, dean of the Faculty of Economic Planning in Prague, thought that perhaps Africans could learn something about foreign trade from the socialist countries. That gave me a beautiful opening to point out that the shoe was on the other foot, and that the East Germans traced their difficulties to foreign trade. The discussion of my paper broke off early, because we were summoned to an audience with His Imperial Majesty at 4:30 PM...

Dupriez called a meeting to discuss the conference, but only French-speaking economists turned up, most others had enough of themselves and even more of the French-speaking economists, who had talked more volubly and less sensibly than anyone else.[3]

...I had a lengthy dinner with Austin Robinson, we discussed the shocking state of French academic economics...He described his interview or rather audience with the Emperor, who had requested it because he wanted advice on the planning organization. According to Robinson, Ethiopia's political set-up is close to Elizabeth I, with ministers all the time in attendance on His Imperial Majesty, and deputies running the show. Abyssinia makes Nigeria look like an advanced country. As some of the Ethiopians wistfully said, they never had the advantages of British colonialism.

I went to bed about 10:30 PM and read. In Addis I got some economic articles read, here I can't do much reading beyond what I have to. The tropics are odd. Addis of course has a wonderful climate. But back here the constant heat, the lack of variation in the length of the day, makes one lose all sense of time. I am not exactly drifting – there is the work and there are deadlines, but I find the sameness of every day nerve-wracking.

August 6, 1961

July 31. A hectic day. At 11:00 AM Waziri, our new minister, came in and talked with us for three hours. This was one of our most interesting and useful mornings. He asked our plans, what precisely we were aiming at, timetables. Often we had to say we didn't yet know the answer. I explained my concept of development planning. Suddenly he asked us to come to his office. It became clear that he wanted to talk with us privately without Patricia overhearing Waziri is a very intelligent man and no one's fool, he was quite capable of understanding professors.

W. started by saying he assumed we knew our stuff better than he. The ministry was new to him, and he was working through the files. He was glad we were Americans. He had seen Kennedy on TV and thought that he was a great man with a lot of right ideas about foreign aid and foreign policy. Just that we should not follow too much the lead of the English. He had a book by Sterling Morton, which urged America to cut loose from British apron strings. As Americans we had a tremendous opportunity to help his country. The British were all right, but a lot of them had no imagination and couldn't be clerks in their own country (there is an uncomfortable amount of truth in this).

We were to consider ourselves as his advisors and have access to him at all times. If we disagreed with anyone – Prasad, Lewis, anyone – we should come directly to him. He would listen, and if he agreed with us he would fight for us against anyone and in Cabinet. The country had been doing fine under the British, but he felt it would have done about as well without them. There was a great deal of inefficiency, which had to be changed. He had been a businessman – the first African to be made a manager by UAC, I later found out – you either performed or went broke. He had his annual sales quota of £2.7 million and always sold more.

I had already said we believed very strongly that the country had to develop a strong private sector, not for ideological reasons, but to make maximum use of the scarcest resource of all, trained manpower. I also was skeptical of a rate of education/training, which absorbs so much capital that nothing is left to employ them productively. He grinned and said he couldn't agree more. If the telephone service were private, maybe he could get through to Kaduna and Kano when he wanted to, instead of waiting for hours. He had also protested against the purchase of foreign companies by Nigerians. I said that made me happy, I had written a strong memo against repatriation for phony nationalistic reasons. He said he hadn't seen my memo but had argued similarly in Cabinet, to my knowledge successfully. I said I was very happy to have this agreement.

Lyle pointed out that he had put us in a difficult spot by suggesting we go directly to him over Toby Lewis. We had decided that since we were here for 18 months, we had to work through the PS – I added that the PS agreed completely with us. We felt we could not simply ignore that. I was really grateful to Lyle for the manner in which he raised the problem. Ibrahim had put us in a ticklish spot, and I couldn't think quickly of a way of dealing with it. Not only am I a friend of Toby's, but he is good, does agree, and I don't like to do anything underhanded. Ibrahim said he understood our view, but he would not turn around and scold Toby if we saw him (Ibrahim) directly.

Ibrahim wanted to know what we were going to do about agriculture. We said the Federal Government was responsible only for research, that all we could do was persuade the Regions to do sensible things. Also, we could work through the National Committee on Agricultural Policy. The minister thought that was fine, but not enough. He would write to the Sardauna when we went North so that coordination of plans could proceed smoothly – I had said I was probably going north right after the JPC meeting – but he also wanted the Federal Government to go in for agricultural projects directly, not just research, and the Prime Minister agreed with him. We had talked of a large development bank or corporation and he thought it could go into joint agricultural ventures with the Regions.

We came out of the discussion feeling elated that we had a strong minister who took an interest in the ministry, knew his own mind, to whom we had easy access, and who saw eye-to-eye with us on the major issues. The elation was somewhat clouded by his distrust of the English. In general I understand this, but I want to keep Toby, and must speak to the Minister about it. Even if Toby were not as good as he is, continuity in our Ministry is essential and I don't want to spend energy on having to get used to another PS. I am also a little uneasy about the Chicago influence. But his liking for Americans seemed genuine enough, so did his admiration for Kennedy, and his preference for a private sector. On balance the meeting left me with a very warm feeling...

August 2. Dolgin called and when I got there, showed me two cables from the US on the Balewa talks, which have a bearing on our timetable. The visit of our PM went extremely well. Both sides were pleased. He was told confidentially that by the end of the month Congress would have passed the foreign aid bill, and we would be told immediately how much aid we could expect over five years. It would be substantial. He was also told by all means to go ahead and talk to other prospective donors. He was pleased with the idea of a consortium, but wanted to be free to have bilateral talks in addition. Kennedy assured him that was fine with America. A little more disturbing is that he wants aid from us for the Air Force. Air forces are too damn expensive.

Rivkin wants to come back in October for the next round of negotiations. This is most inconvenient. Toby wants to go on leave in mid-September. I think he is essential for the negotiations. I told Dolgin I thought we could shift our timetable ahead to mid-September, Dolgin should try to persuade Toby to postpone his leave by two weeks and Arnold should come back about Sept. 20, right after the NEC meetings.

The day before, we were given a confidential version of the Rivkin Mission Report, a cleaned up version will be given to the Nigerian Government. Most of the Report is favorable and very complimentary to us. Most of it plays into my hands very nicely in stressing the need to avoid inflation and exchange control at any cost.

There were a few things I disagreed with, and I immediately wrote Arnold privately to see whether they could be changed. Actually they don't make that much difference. The question is one of determining the desired amount of sterling reserves. I disagreed with the reasoning, which is similar (though I believe superior) to the Central Bank's. I came out with about the same figure. Also, Arnold had not mentioned financing education by a separate consortium, as Prasad suggested very sensibly, and I asked him to reconsider. The parts of the report that will probably be cut out in the cleaned-up version deal with the alarming spread of corruption, which makes lending and grants difficult.

I told Dolgin he should talk with Toby as soon as he comes back from Europe tomorrow morning. I have invited them all for dinner tomorrow so these matters can be discussed privately and efficiently.

In the evening was a farewell cocktail party for Ben Lewis and his wife, both of whom I like very much. (Johnson took me aside to say how delighted they were with him. "Have you got more like him at home? If so, send them along.") Also present were ICA head Joel Bernstein and his wife Merle. Joel I like somewhat less. Both are very nice, but he is dead serious and always wants to talk business. For an ICA man he is a very good economist, but we need more than that here, just as we need an ambassador like Chester Bowles. The sixth guest was Bloomfield of the Marketing Company.

The party was a mixed success. Even with so small a number it broke up into three groups. I hate parties with no center. First Joel came and immediately started to ask how we proposed to raise domestic savings. He proposed to give us a good man as advisor for that. The name of Al Hirschman was raised, which would indeed please me very much, though I doubt we could get him…

From Bloomfield I learned…that we sell quite a bit of peanuts to Russia and the Iron Curtain countries and to France. The reason is odd. Russia had bought 40,000 tons of groundnuts from Mali, as had France or so they thought. But when Mali and Senegal split, Senegal slammed an iron curtain of its own down, refusing to have Mali's groundnuts shipped through Dakar. Now only a trickle gets out through Cotonou.

Russia and France have to buy from us to make up for it, which also accounts for the fact that the price remained higher than anticipated. Bloomfield also told me that Hungarians did finally buy 500 tons of palm kernels in Lagos and on our conditions. Also that groundnut crushers are having a hard time. The Iron Curtain countries in particular don't want to buy oil, but only nuts, which is understandable, since groundnut cake is important cattle food, but also amusing because they always accuse the west of imperialism for insisting in buying nuts instead of fostering a crushing industry.

August 3. I worked all day in the office with Lyle. During the morning there is usually a lot of interruption by staff. We have started a serious evaluation of the Federal programs. In the afternoon there is peace. We have a particularly difficult problem with the Lagos Executive Development Board, responsible for housing, etc. Their program was lousy. Lyle worked out a really beautiful program that not only will provide more houses, but also pay for itself eventually and get a building society going. Unfortunately Lyle writes badly. He feeds me the stuff, I rework it to fit my ideas of what should be done. Actually his part is very much the work of both of us, but for LEDB, the basic credit must go to Lyle…

Skillings of the World Bank, who was back in town, came over for supper. The discussion was very important to me. He threw some cold water on our planning operation. He said we were isolated in Lagos. I said that we wanted to get the Federal program into reasonable shape, but then we were going to the Regions to do the same. He said we would find difficulties. The Regions were flexing their muscles. At the civil service level things were reasonable, but the ministers were going to assert their independence of the Federal Government.

In particular, the North was set on a £82 million capital program. I said they hadn't a ghost of a chance of either financing or implementing such a large program. Skillings agreed, but said it wouldn't stop them from trying. The £82 million had appeared on the political agenda just before the election and they were hell bent for it. Moreover they didn't have any money. Only the Eastern Region had some Marketing

Board funds. I said the groundnut price and other farm-gate prices had to come down substantially, and farmers would react as everywhere else by increasing production. He agreed but said I would have a hard time persuading ministers to reduce prices as long as there were any Marketing Board reserves. He may be right on this.

He also said he had some bad news for me on my price and output projections. Fortunately it was partly a misunderstanding. Prices were going to be lower than anticipated, but the base for projecting output was too low. It turned out he was talking about the IBRD London office's estimate, not mine, which agrees with IBRD/W figures…On cocoa he agreed with me and disagreed with both the London and Washington people. He thought my output projection was right, but my price perhaps a little low.

I explained to Skillings my approach to planning and my use of macro models as a frame to ensure consistency but not more. The crucial bottleneck, aside from executive capacity, is recurrent expenditure. Initially I am reducing it to what I believe is a tolerable level of Government consumption in the national accounting sense, and as indicated by the model; then I adjust capital expenditure accordingly. I explained that I was going on the assumption that it was comparatively easy to get aid for capital, but except for education and health next to impossible to get aid for recurrent costs. He wished me luck, but said that after touring the Regions he was a bit pessimistic, and would advise the IBRD to be cautious. He hoped I would carry my plans out, but wasn't so sure I could. Well, we have to see. Maybe having access to Waziri Ibrahim will help.

Skillings also raised the corruption issue. He thought the idea of pumping public money into the private sector was fine, but he didn't think I had much of a chance to get lots of capital for that unless corruption could be substantially checked. Rivkin made similar points. Corruption in the Regions is worse than in the Federal Government.

August 4.…At dinner I spoke with Bernstein about a possible association between [University of Michigan's] new Development Institute and Ibadan, my original idea last summer. Possibly things will happen. I was scathing about MSU's effort in Nsukka. Joel said they were thinking of sending Edwards home. I said it was irresponsible of a university to accept an ICA contract unless they were willing to send their best people…

August 5. I worked first on the education ministry's program, trying to save money on capital by reducing building costs, and on recurrent expenses by raising student teacher ratios from 37 to 40. A poor country can't afford better ratios than rich countries. Besides, they won't get the teachers anyway. Also, building costs are higher than in England. There is no sense putting up American-type structures in the tropics, where there is no problem of snow and ice. Actually, this is a very tough program to evaluate, and when I am through I'll show it to Lyle for another go.

At 1:00 Skillings and Hamilton came for lunch and stayed until 5:30 PM. Skillings brought me the marketing board stuff, which I have to work on later tonight. Both of them wanted to know why I wanted a big development corporation, how I envisaged it. My main reasons were: (a) to pump money into the private sector, (b) to find a receptacle for foreign funds that would not raise nationalistic antagonisms, (c) to kill off the Regional development corporations, in my opinion hopelessly corrupt and impossible to reform, and (d) to provide general balance of payments support in the hope that the private sector will behave better than anticipated.

I had to expand on points (b) and (d). Both men thought less money than I wanted would do, which is probably true. Hamilton thought the difference between a development bank and corporation was negligible and shouldn't concern me. They agreed with (c) but raised again the problem of corruption. I thought this could be met by giving not only capital to the proposed bank but also managerial services and supervision. In this area I learned more than they did. Skillings also was skeptical of crash programs for agricultural extension workers, and thought it was like a man who had an affair with nine women and expected a baby after a month. The story is nice, but I am not yet convinced that our ideas of crash programs are wrong...

August 13, 1961

There is a short break now following the Bank mission's departure, but there won't really be a let-up until October when the Americans have returned and left again...Tomorrow is another JPC meeting in which my paper will be the major object of discussion. It is 41 pages and goes a long way towards writing the Federal plan. But it raises a number of policy questions, and we need JPC decisions so the ministers can in turn decide. The national economic council (NEC) meets early in September, and if we are to negotiate with the Americans later in the month a number of points must be cleared up...

August 7. Toby and Prasad arrived from London in the morning...In the office I could start rewriting my paper because Prasad hadn't read it yet and was tired...Later he told me over the phone that he was in agreement, but wished me to put things more positively. That was all right with me.

Then the party in the evening. The food was good, but Toby was tired and Dolgin insisted on talking business. Questions came up about the Peace Corps, about a Nigerian selection committee to be sent to the US which Toby thought he could do in five minutes but which Dolgin thought would take longer. The timing of the Rivkin mission's return came up. It is of course somewhat too early for us. Also I would like Toby to be here. To me it seems important that the same team, which worked so well together previously, should continue the discussion.

Toby saw the PM, who was exceedingly pleased with the warmth of the reception he had got. Also he had been told that US policy was now to aid, not those countries which got into a mess, but those which did a good job in helping themselves. Kennedy told the PM that his advisors – meaning Rivkin – had told him that the Nigerians were doing an excellent job of planning, which not only pleases Toby and me, but also raises the Ministry's importance in the PM's eyes, and strengthens our hand. Because of all this Toby has decided to stay until after the negotiations with the Americans are finished.

However all of this raises the pressure on us. The last missions were exploratory. The next mission is negotiating for keeps. We must be ready with enough facts and plans, to allow negotiations with Rivkin about money. If we are not ready in time, Nigeria will not get its slice of the pie Congress is going to appropriate. We will be told what the minimum is we can expect. Rivkin will be authorized to negotiate actual amounts. I have been explaining to my staff why I have to drive them, and I must do the same selling job to the Regional representatives. This is nerve-wracking and tiring. I have had several sessions with Toby about timetables, etc. Dolgin also raised the question of an international consortium, but we just can't see that happening by the middle of September...

August 8. The day was spent with Skillings and Ardsvik, a Norwegian professor of agricultural economics. We tried to straighten out my export and agricultural production forecasts. This was important for both of us. Skillings had brought lots of new data from the Regions, and also quite a bit from Washington on future prices of oils and fats and cocoa, and we were trying to establish common ground for both sides to use. All of this is rather detailed work, not suitable for inclusion here. It will all appear in the Bank mission report and our papers. But it is important, and not uninteresting when one is working on it. Lyle was also present.

In the evening Skillings and I talked quiet shop over a bottle of wine at Toby's. Most of the more important business takes place in this manner. Skillings spoke about his relations with Prasad. Prasad outranks him in the Bank, and that colors their relations. Whether Prasad wants to stay is unclear, and whether he'll rejoin the Bank is unclear. His children don't like it in Nigeria, nor does his wife enjoy going to the innumerable official parties. The children are completely Americanized. Bob pointed out that he agreed 90% with Prasad but there were some residues of disagreement which were uncomfortable, and which are basically also mine. I really think inflation and exchange control would be catastrophic in Nigeria, and I am prepared to defend these points on purely scientific grounds. None of the pro arguments usually applied are relevant to Nigeria. I had made these points as strongly as I could in the paper to be discussed tomorrow,

Prasad thought my paper was fine, so apparently under the impact of the changed American policy on long-term aid Prasad has come around to my position. Unless, of course, he is giving in because either he doesn't care or because he thinks in the end it won't make any difference, he will have his say anyway. (When one is shuffling papers and making projections as much as I do one can't help thinking from time to time that all this is futile, and the real decisions will all be different, made by people one doesn't even know.)

Skillings found morale in the Western Region to be very low. The politicians did what they wanted, paying no attention to the civil servants. This was quite different from Rivkin's report, but I am sure equally accurate. Both in the East and West people are hell bent on farm settlements, about which all of us are skeptical. They are trying to get the cost down, but that is all. The North is hell bent on its £82 million program, which it hasn't a chance of executing.

But Skillings said on the whole he would write a favorable report, and he became a little more optimistic as the evening rolled on.

August 9. Official meeting from 10:00 AM–12:30 PM in Finance with the Bank mission...Dinner with Peter Duncan, down from Ibadan...Duncan confirmed a little the relatively low morale of the WR civil service.

The creation of the Midwest State was discussed. It has been the policy of the West and East to try to break up the North into a number of smaller states, making a total of perhaps six. However the West got itself boxed in, and the first new state is being carved, not out of the North, but out of the West itself. I still think the West played it badly, and should have acted like the Americans, who insisted that either both Hawaii and Alaska become states, or neither. The West and East clearly would love to see a middle belt state where the unruly Tivs live, the fellows who in some exuberance of energy keep rioting from time to time. The catch is that the Tivs don't really want a state, since they are better off as unruly citizens of the Northern Region than as responsible citizens of their own state.

In the meantime everyone including the Western Region has voted to carve out the Midwest State with Benin as the capital. However the catch is that the local population itself must vote by a $^2/_3$ majority to become a state. The Action Group, the ruling party in the West, is working very hard to organize the Midwest so it will vote against becoming a state, and chances are that the necessary majority will not be forthcoming. The larger the local majority against the new state, the bigger the political boost for the West. But if the margin is small, I think matters will be much worse than they were before.

August 10....Toby is not too happy with our new minister. He is not strong in Cabinet, and as a result we may not carry anything even if we get him on our side. He seems to meddle in other ministers' affairs, which not only makes them mad, but the PM had to give him a dressing down. In general, Cabinet does not seem to be a happy family. Toby didn't want to say what it was that got our minister into trouble with the PM, but it had something to do with internal security.

On the more cheerful side, Toby said he was working to get Atta back as Deputy. Toby would be leaving for good next year, and Atta could take over. Lardner, who is slated to come back from Addis as DPS, is known to be anti-white, prejudiced, and inefficient. When he left last time, they found 250 unattended files in his office.

Atta is good – a Baliol man – and absolutely straight and honest. He comes from a somewhat wild, highly aristocratic, middle belt family. His father, a local king with some power, was deposed by the British. But he had all his children including his daughters educated in England. Atta himself is a tall, handsome man, and so apparently are his sisters. One was the mistress of the Sardauna, another first the mistress and then the wife of the top British civil servant in the North, who left then for Ghana. His brother is Nigeria's High Commissioner in London. If we got him back, it would really be a boon. It was a blow when he transferred, against his will, to the Ministry of Defense.

Much less agreeable was the discussion of the Ministry of Foreign Affairs. Until Jaja Wachuku became Foreign Minister, the PM ran the office. The Ministry's PS, Lawrence Inionaru, also a friend of Rivkin, is rather weak. Toby said the papers prepared for the discussion on the Common Market had been shockingly bad, had dwelt on such matters as the 9% tariff discrimination against cocoa, had not gone into political questions, and were inconsistent, as every assistant secretary seemed to make his own foreign policy. With Wachuku as Minister things may improve – if he stays in Nigeria long enough. As a traveler he bids fair to outdistance Dulles. He still hasn't returned from Washington.

August 11....The day started with a subcommittee meeting on the Nigerian Institute for Social and Economic Research. We proposed doubling the budget, and insisted that (a) NISER should have academic freedom, (b) the Executive Committee should be chosen on merit and not because people represented a government or university, and (c) the location should be near the center of economic and political decision making...

At 5:00 PM Ken Baldwin came to discuss agricultural production in the North with Ardsvik. Jensen is making good progress and we should have the stuff in a week...

In the evening a mediocre, typical Federal Palace dinner for the Bank mission. Festus made a good speech, Skillings, who had lost his voice, answered nicely, then Ibrahim talked glibly but what he said was terrible and came out all wrong. I could see that Chief Festus was furious, and I understood what Toby had meant about Ibrahim being a dangerous man.

Afterwards, I repaired to the bar with the mission and some others...Hamilton, the mission's industrial expert, was quite interesting. He was depressed by what he had seen in Ibadan. In three years the Lafia canning factory lost as much as it had cost. "It is too big. Rats run around, the manager is discouraged." The WR Development Corporation is really a management company. The real investment decisions are all made politically in the ministries. WRDC is told where to invest and when, what to buy, whether to lend or buy equity, and how to manage. And Hamilton had been told that he had seen the best, that the ERDC and the NRDC were much worse. It depressed me too, because we need a big development corporation and won't get the money for it, what with the Regional ones being so inefficient and corrupt.

August 12. I tried to clear up a number of files, but they were too important to hurry. The transport ministry wants to spend millions on jets, and we have to stop them if we can. I shoved that one onto Lyle's desk. Toby wants me to study the Common Market file so I took it home over the weekend, together with a file by the Central Bank on sterling reserves. Pius Okigbo, Ardsvik and Lyle were in the office, estimating the impact of the palm oil presses we are keen on, but I withdrew from that, too...

August 20, 1961

From now on the tempo will rise, not slacken...

August 14. JPC meeting. Our 41-page paper had been distributed only on Saturday and people were angry about that. It had 28 pages of tightly reasoned text, the rest tables. Members had so little time to read and think about it. But in addition there was, for the first time, an undercurrent of hostility in the discussion, which came, of all people, from the Ministry of Finance and the Central Bank. The former was represented by Omanai, a junior official, the latter by Rice, an American seconded to set up the research division and not a great light either.

As usual I was slow to comprehend the political undercurrents. I was somewhat upset, because both Finance and the CB should objectively have been happy with the paper. I had taken their line completely, arguing for fiscal soundness, the futility of inflationary finance, the need to meet all recurrent costs plus aiming at a surplus to cover at least half the cost of the capital program, and the necessity of avoiding exchange control.

The objection was twofold. First, half of the paper comprised a general discussion of the size of the proposed program, along with an estimate of what size program we could support without inflation. I was rather proud of this part, because I had tried to relate the program in fiscal terms to the implied national income magnitudes. This, as far as I know, has never been done. By translating government recurrent expenditure into national income terms I had put it into the context of our original model, shown how I intended to use simultaneously the macro- and micro-economic approaches, and how the two fit together. The objection to this, which came mainly from Andrew Wilson, the WR's planning PS, was that it was too technical for simple civil servants, which may be so. Obviously Pius or Philip Barton had no trouble.

The second part consisted of an economic analysis of four ministry programs, which we used both to illustrate the kind of problems to expect and as a peg to get the JPC to make certain policy decisions. The objection to this was that we had not consulted the ministries, and were washing dirty federal linen in public.

Now both these objections were demonstrably false. We had practically sat in the laps of the ministries we discussed, including Finance. But I got up on my hind legs when it was suggested that any ministry and particularly Finance could veto a paper of mine. I said that my function and that of the Economic Planning Unit was to analyze objectively so that ministers could make rational decisions. We were not committing any ministry to anything, but were posing specific questions to them. Prasad backed me very strongly – in general our personal and working relations are now excellent – and so did Okigbo and Daramola, the able and honest PS of Commerce. As far as washing dirty linen in public, how could we get the Regions to submit their programs to our analysis if we were not ready to discuss the federal program in the JPC?

Of course, what really lay behind this discussion was a serious power struggle within Cabinet. We are a new ministry and the concept of planning is new. In the past, Finance has been all powerful, and has even kept the Central Bank under its control. C.B. Governor Fenton used to be JPC chairman; now it is Prasad as Economic Advisor. Neither Finance nor the CB has any decent staff, so much so that it is worrisome. They used to have Vincent in Finance, but because he is a Yoruba he got bumped and shoved into the CB Reg Clarke will come back in September, then go with Festus to the Commonwealth finance ministers' conference. Then Festus is off on the second leg of the economic mission, which is accomplishing very little.

At the same time, the PM comes back from the US with a glowing account of our work, which he got from the Rivkin mission via the President, and directs the Ministry of Economic Development to negotiate with the US mission, which is asked to return to Nigeria as soon as possible. Festus wants to be there, but has his economic mission scheduled. So he creates difficulties. Little Henry Omanai, who is not very competent, calls up all the PSs to create trouble for us. Toby said if that keeps up, he will step on him hard. All of this is really an attempt to shift power back to Finance. In the meantime, the PM has ruled a second time, this time in no uncertain terms, that we and not Finance are responsible for negotiating with Rivkin, while Finance will carry the burden of negotiations with the IBRD.

All of this is quite clear to politically clued-in members of JPC, but even I found out fairly soon what was going on. I react sharply when my integrity is assailed, or when little people try to tell me how to do my job. I got quite a bit of backing in JPC without at the time understanding just what was going on. The upshot of the discussion was that JPC would meet again on the 25th to consider my paper, by which time they would presumably have had time to study it. It's a good paper, though I admit somewhat technical in parts.

The rest of the meeting dealt with our report on NISER's reorganization. We got our principle across, which was primarily that we wanted an independent institute of applied research. Prasad was excellent in suggesting reformulations of what we had done, and Finance as usual objected when we stated that Government had to pay for ongoing research, even though it initially endowed the Institute.

Andrew Wilson and Chukujekwe came home for lunch. Wilson is a Yoruba, a big man with a broad open face and very pleasant manner. He is intelligent but slow, and as honest as they come. In general the honesty of the Civil Service is in the best British tradition. The honesty of the ministers leaves something to be desired. Chukujekwe is a Western Ibo from what might or might not become the new Midwest State (with Benin as its capital). He is quiet, slow, and very able. His honesty too is beyond doubt. He is also overworked, as is every able man here, and worried about the turn things are taking politically within the Federation.

These luncheons are important. In fact I could kick myself for never having invited Governor Fenton. More of such social life would smooth over a lot of things in JPC. In any case, both Wilson and Chukujekwe were worried about the necessary cuts in the program. They agreed with my analysis that the program as it now stands would have to be cut by about £100 million, but wanted to know where it would be cut. In particular they were worried that the cuts would be made in the Western Region program, simply because the Western Region is run by the opposition party and a ruthless drive is underway against the Action Group.

I obviously could not assure them this would not be so. But I did assure them I was not going to sidestep the issue. The cuts that the Economic Planning Unit would recommend would be based on economic criteria alone. What the Council of Ministers would do with it, we could not tell. We could not make recommendations until the Regions had given us their programs in as much detail as the federal program.

We intended to analyze all federal and Regional programs, recommend coordination where there was overlapping – e.g. between the Federal Government and WR on housing in Ikeja just outside of Lagos – and recommend cutting where it would cause the least economic harm. Furthermore, I thought the very fact that we were negotiating with the Americans as Nigerians rather than as representatives of the Federal Government was a safeguard. It was also a safeguard for the Regions that American aid depended to a large extent on the quality of the overall plan, which itself tended to reduce the amount of political boondoggling.

Actually, the Region has something to worry about. The NCNC in particular is trying to stir up trouble in the West, by walking out of councils and issuing statements that law and order has broken down, that the FG should interfere. Festus has written Okpara, the titular leader of the NCNC, to come home from Germany where he is at present negotiating, so that the Federal Government can restore law and order in the West. On the other hand the Prime Minister has stated that all this is nonsense and that he does not intend to interfere.

Lyle and I asked whether the Midwest State would come into existence. Wilson and Ch. thought not...

I had Pius and Philip Barton for dinner, together with Lyle. We thrashed out some of the JPC discussion, and I also wanted to find out when I would be welcome in the East. I didn't get very far on this. I now know why, too. Pius, who was to have gone back to Enugu last Thursday, is still around. Not much work is getting done.

1.   Camels at Kano Airport, July 16, 1960.

2.   Ghanaian fishermen on coast near Lagos, July 22, 1960.

3. Ibadan, August 1, 1960.

4. Yoruba market woman,
    Ibadan, August 3, 1960.

5 and 6. Two scenes of Kano, August 9, 1960. The panorama is taken from the city reservoir.

7. **Emir's Palace (opposite mosque), Kano, August 9, 1960. "When I tried to take the same picture on a visit after a series of military coups, I was not allowed to do so."**

8. **Installing a tarpaulin on groundnut pyramid, Kano, August 10, 1960.**

9. Just Faaland, Director of Christian Michaelsen Institute, Bergen, Norway,
    in a village near Enugu, August 13, 1960.

10. Port of Lagos, Apapa, August 18, 1960.

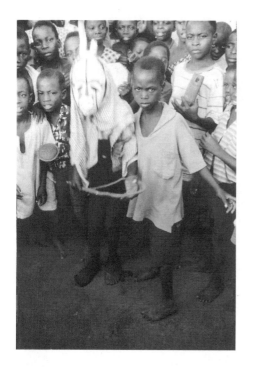

11. Easter celebration near
Benin, April 4, 1961.

12. 'Briefing', Kaduna, April 17, 1961. Left to right: Peter Gibbs, Bernie
Jensen, Lyle Hansen, Sam Akande.

13 and 14. Two views of Zaria, April 18, 1961.

15. Aerial view of site of proposed Niger River (Kainji) Dam, April 21, 1961. The dam was commissioned in 1968.

16. 'Sacred grove' in Oshogbo, May 25, 1961.

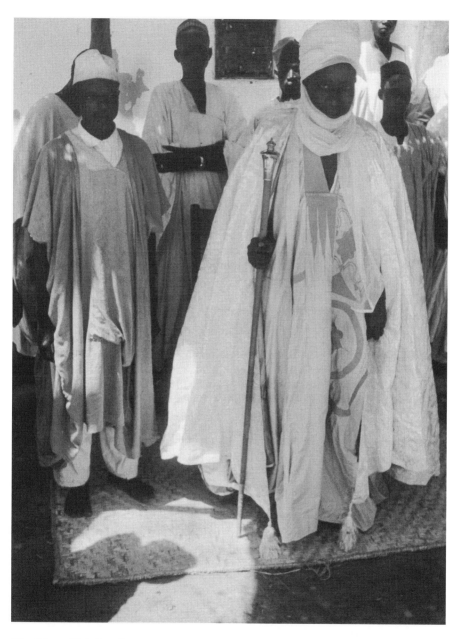

17. Nupe Chief at Tada Island in the Niger River, May 26, 1961. WS: "This village was divided between Nupes and Hausas, each with its own Chief."

18. Jebba, view from railroad bridge, May 26, 1961. Background: Niger River, 80 miles south of future Kainji Dam site.

19. *Lagos Times* photo of WS (2nd from right) and his then minister, Jaja Wachuku, with World Bank delegation headed by Robert Skillings (2nd from left), July 9, 1961.

20. Kano, August 31, 1961. Left to right: WS, Northern Region Marketing Board (NRMB) secretary Fenn, and two NRMB assistants.

21. Maiduguri market with 'a Kanuri beauty', September 3, 1961.

22. WS duck hunting near Lake Chad "while others dig out the truck" (WS). September 5, 1961.

23. Lake Chad, September 7, 1961. WS and Peter Drew in papyrus boat, "exactly as pictured in some Egyptian tombs. Lake Chad has now shrunk to one fourth of its 1961 size because of irrigation projects along the rivers that used to feed it" (WS).

24. WS: "Felix Oguala was my very intelligient and trustworthy steward. Picture of him and his family on the porch of my house, January 1962."

25. Cross River at Itu, en route to Calabar, Eastern Region, March 7, 1962.

26. WS: "Akuon Fulani ladies – high aristocracy! Taken in market in Wum, Cameroon, on March 11, 1962. I promised to send them copies, and I did."

27. WS (standing) and Lyle Hansen, FMED/Lagos, March 16, 1962.

28. Amalgamated Tin Mining Company of Nigeria (ATMN), Jos, May 3, 1962.
     Left to right: Permanent Secretary of Northern Region Mines and Power,
     Mallam Musa Dagash; WS; and ATMN general manager Farmington.
     WS: "My interest in taking this picture was to combat the nonsense
     rampant at the time, that less-developed countries should have only
     labor-intensive industries."

29. Richa village, on Jos Plateau, May 4, 1962. WS terms it "primitive, perhaps better aboriginal. The route to it was a path, more like something cattle might have produced than a road."

30. Left to right: Andrew Wilson, WS, WS' older son Tom, and Steven Chukujekwe. Taken in government building in Benin, June 1962.

He has of course a tough position...Pleasant though the evening was, it was also evident that Pius and Philip don't particularly like each other.

August 15. All morning was spent in the JPC's Statistics Subcommittee meeting. There was the usual wrangle over the forthcoming census, which has been going on for a year...On the issue of age-group enumeration, a compromise was reached that the regional census officers would be free to ask specific ages if they thought it would get them a correct answer, but that the general aim would be a census by 5-year groupings. This agreement had been reached some time ago, but it always gets re-opened again, mainly because there is no ruling as to who will pay the extra cost. I understand that in meetings of the Census Committee, of which I am mercifully not a member, this discussion continues endlessly. For the rest, matters went according to plan. The major point was a program of agricultural statistics suggested by Hendrix, about whom I wrote once before, which was accepted and which ought to give us the basic information we need.

For lunch I invited Baldwin from the North, and Koenigsberger, the UN construction expert, together with Lyle. It was one of my slowest lunches ever. Koenigsberger and Baldwin were trying to draw each other out, and both were too cagey to get anywhere. The only way to find out things from others is to tell them something. By that time I had my fill of economic development, JPC and the rest...

August 16....Meetings at UCI with vice-principal Bevan and his colleague Dr. Brown, MD. Discussed problems of preventive medicine with Dr. Brown. This was essential for me, since all our criticisms of the health program is that too much is spent on curing people and not enough on preventing illness. Then Bevan took us around to look at the dormitories. In the old ones students double up in relatively small rooms. In the new ones the rooms are designed for two people. The cost is still £700 per student which seems excessively high.

We then discussed approaches UCI might take to get as much money as possible. I suggested they should say they would try to further simplify building designs and make any adjustments, which the forthcoming Koenigsberger report might suggest. Regarding annual faculty home leave, I agreed with Bevan that past contracts giving every faculty member, expatriate or Nigerian, first class passage to England during vacation, had to be honored. I agreed that this was essential if first class people were to be attracted.

He replied they had already agreed that passage need only be economy class, and there was a voluntary agreement to go to the UK only three years out of four. I asked why students could not live in town, why dormitory space had to be provided to everyone. Bevan answered that the town was hellishly noisy and the students would have no place to study. He also pointed out that Northerners would have a terrible time finding any suitable accommodations. If day students were admitted, they would all be local or at least Southerners, and UCI would lose its character as a federal, national institution.

Returning to the office, I found it in a panic. By Saturday we had to get a progress report on the planning exercise paper to the National Economic Council. Moreover, it had to be simple. We agreed to meet in the evening at Toby's to do some first drafting on the basis of ideas that we would collect in the afternoon. So I assembled all the golden words that I had committed to paper in one form or another, and looked at what could be done...

August 17. Lyle and I worked like mad, each on our own draft, to have it ready for discussion with Toby at noon. My draft was accepted with modifications, and I proceeded to rewrite and dictate it. By 2:00 PM we had it and a copy was sent to Prasad. P. had valid objections that the paper was too technical for ministers. He pointed out, very reasonably, that to write that the rate of savings had to increase from 10% of GNP to 15% would sound perfectly easy to ministers who had no notion what GNP was in the first place. "In India we have been trying for 15 years to raise food production by the 1% needed to overcome starvation." He suggested a revamping of the paper in budget rather than national income terms, and asked me to prepare that...

Dinner at the Federal Palace with Hamilton, IBRD expert on development banks. My minister has been after me to discuss development banks with him. I know little about them. In any case, Prasad is carrying the ball, and I don't want to gum up the works.

Hamilton came back from the Regions rather depressed. ER Premier Okpara had brought back from Germany a contract for a new brewery and bottle factory. As regards the brewery, it is not simple to establish a new brand. The Germans will provide a brew master for five years, but training of local staff is left in the air. It takes 20 years to train a brew master, yet the East wants to take over after five years, and thinks it can easily hire an expert after the initial five years. As for the bottle factory, it can't pay unless all beer imports are forbidden. At present no bottles are produced in Nigeria. Local breweries and soft drink plants depend entirely on re-using bottles from imported drinks (a side income of waiters is selling used bottles to the bottling plants). The cost of producing bottles is about three times the cost of re-used bottles. So there goes £1$^{1}/_{2}$ million urgently needed for reasonable projects. The Germans did a beautiful job of salesmanship and the Nigerians in their nationalistic urge fell for it.

Incidentally I forgot to mention an amusing incident in Ibadan. Some months ago, WRDC head Chief Rowane wrote an outrageous article on the corporation's policy. I took the trouble to write him a personal four-page, single-spaced letter, objecting to his statements on purely analytic grounds and making policy suggestions. I hadn't heard from him since.

Arch Callaway told me I had given them a hard time. The letter has sat on Chief Rowane's desk since it arrived, and they don't know how to answer it. Apparently the chief had spoken out of turn and Chiefs Adebo and Dina had both stepped on him for making policy privately. Now the WRDC could neither ignore my letter nor find a reasonable answer, and they had asked Callaway's advice!

Back to Hamilton. He pointed to four distinct problems. First, the problem of small agricultural credit, which was one of supervision rather than money. At present supervision is lacking. Moreover people did not understand what the credit was for, and used it for housing, debt repayment or anything except production. Moreover it was politically impossible to collect outstanding debts, the same as collecting taxes from one's political friends. This sort of credit had to be linked with agricultural extension, and was not really suitable for a development bank. (However one might finance agricultural co-operatives in connection with credit and such a bank.)

Second was the problem of experimental industries or plantations. A development bank had a function there.

The third problem concerned large-scale industry. Here too a development bank had a role to play by providing insurance for the foreigner who wanted it, rather than establishing a socialist industry. Hamilton had noticed, as had we, a strong socialist bias based solely on nationalism. And it is a bias which hampers development.

The final problem was that of small industry. This was akin to agricultural credit. It was a problem of showing ten or 15 small fellows a year how to hire and fire, how to keep books, how to sell, etc. This too was not suitable for a development bank. Medium-sized business incidentally hardly exists except for a few Lebanese and Syrians.

The evening was useful, though slightly depressing. Too many development corporations exist, buying out existing businesses for no good reason except to gain control. We must try to do something about this.

August 18. Prasad wanted another rewriting – quite reasonably so, I might say. But I said it was useless for me to do it. I had rewritten several times, I could not think of new words, and my mind now ran in a groove which it could not jump out of. Could he please do the next draft? Could we discuss roughly what should be in it? We agreed to meet at 7:30 PM at Prasad's...

By 5:30 PM his draft was ready, and between Toby and myself we dictated from P's draft a new version, which turned out to be the final version.

August 19. I spent the morning with Hamilton in Prasad's office discussing a possible new development bank for Nigeria. Also present were John Murray, the CB's Graham Keep and MCI's Daramola. I just listened and tried to learn. I also tried to stay awake. H. outlined the four problems mentioned above. We discussed what he would put into his Bank report. ICON, the Investment Company of Nigeria, has done a reasonably good job, but is not politically accepted in Nigeria. This is due to (a) public relations ineptness, (b) the overwhelming majority of the capital is English, and (c) the Nigerian directors are part of the 'old gang,' whatever that means, therefore not considered representative of the new Nigeria. On the other hand ICON has momentum, and the problem is how to build on it, how to change it into an accepted Nigerian corporation, how to give it sufficient capital and power to establish in the Regions commercial in lieu of political criteria for investment...

Hamilton left and we stayed on to pass finally on the NEC paper. Much to my surprise, Murray had only a minor objection, with which I happened to agree, and we cut out the offending sentence. He also wanted an additional reference to Chief Festus and his economic mission. Toby made the final adjustment and the paper is now being stenciled.

In the meantime we received the Westinghouse report recommending a steel mill for Nigeria, a monstrous document which Igwagwu is studying over the weekend. We heard that the Eastern Region Government has received another report from Ferrostahl (Germany) which it prefers, but won't show us. So I wrote Guenther [Harkort][4] whether he could get it to us in strict confidence. In the meantime Lyle found out who has it in the East and where we might get a copy. We have a report by the Rockefeller Brothers Fund on a cement factory in Sokoto, which it claims is a fine location, except there are no transport facilities and so the Railway must be extended. Well there is coal at the South Pole! So I am trying to read something on iron and steel over the weekend...

Early next week Prasad, Toby and I, and Lyle when he returns from Lokoja, will sit down to discuss the plan outline. From now on it's going to be a marathon.

August 26, 1961

Life has been hectic here, in part miserable, in part quite enjoyable. The weather at least has been unusually nice. No rain, and positively cool, say like England in August. The work consists mainly of an attempt to get ready for the American mission. I tried to go to Kaduna, but was told in no uncertain terms not to come yet. So on Tuesday I am going to Kano to spend two full days trying to straighten out the marketing board accounts, something I have been unable to do so far. They just don't add up right. Also I want to see some of the oil seed crushers, and some of the new small industries, such as soda water and candies. Fenn of the Marketing Board, whom I met last summer, is making the arrangements.

There never is a dull moment…In the course of the morning Lucien Pye from MIT called, and I invited him for dinner with Toby. He is a well-known political scientist, a Far East specialist, nice and good company. He had just come from East Africa, where the MIT fellows had met…The talk turned around the future of East and West Africa, and more specifically the relative future of Ghana and Nigeria. Ghana is obviously more in the news, things happen there or so it seems, they are dynamic, while we seem always to be reaching to what goes on outside, never really to be leading. We all agreed that in the long pull, Nigeria would be far ahead of Ghana, but in the short run, leaders like Nkrumah (who now claims divine birth) can do an awful lot of silly things, which look good before you have a chance to analyze them. And they can be an attraction to the younger and somewhat confused intellectuals. I have written about this theme before. It constantly recurs and worries Nigerians. It also worried Toby, who felt that a little more political imagination was needed if the Monrovia powers were to pull ahead of the Casablanca powers. They undoubtedly will in the long run.

But in the short run there will be quite a bit of trouble, particularly coming out of East Africa. There is a good chance that Nyerere will put in his lot with the Monrovia group. But what will happen in Kenya or the Rhodesias is not nice to contemplate. Apparently Mau Mau oath taking is on the increase again. Pye felt that Kenyatta was a Castro type. He is now free though not in power yet. He is saying all the right things, no racial discrimination, brotherly love etc. But once he comes to power, as he undoubtedly will, there will be trouble. I felt that Pye is right on this. Just what the effect will be, is hard to see. East Africa is a long way from here, yet even the confused Lumumba had serious repercussions, and Kenyatta does not seem to be confused. He will not come in with us, I am sure, but whether he will come in with the Casablanca group is not certain. If he does, that group will have a number of megalomaniac leaders – Nkrumah, Nasser, Touré – all vying with each other to prove they are more nationalistic and more pan-African than the next. We have already seen in Bizerte[5] what that kind of nonsense can lead to…

August 23. We assembled at 11:00 AM at Finance to meet the IMF mission, headed by Mladek, an American of Czech origin, and consisting also of a Vietnamese, Oanh (a Harvard PhD), and an Indian, Bhatia…I had intended not to go, but Toby sent me as our representative since he was involved in a parliamentary crisis. The House of Representatives is now in a supplementary budget session, two of our bills came up, our Minister was in Maiduguri, there were several questions to answer, the file was lost, the parliamentary secretary had lost his brief, and Toby had half an hour to prepare an answer to be read in Parliament. He was in a foul mood, and I had to hold the fort at Finance.

Nigeria has just joined the Fund and Bank, and the purpose of the visit was essentially to get acquainted. But the IMF had sent a brief of about 50 pages on which they wanted our comments and corrections, and we had given them our papers. They sprang a request for an oral briefing. Prasad started off for 20 minutes, outlining our general thoughts. I agreed with most of it, but felt he was still pushing in the direction of a project approach. Next I talked for 20 minutes about what we were doing. I took my cue from Prasad, but tried to bend the approach somewhat more to my way of thinking. Ken Johnson of Commerce and Industry talked next. Finance and Foreign Affairs had nothing to add. It was agreed to meet again in Prasad's office on Friday for further discussions, when the mission would have read our planning papers and those of the CB and Finance.

We then adjourned to an excellent lunch, quite unusual for the Federal Palace. It turned out that John Murray had himself taken a hand in planning the lunch, for, as he said, he liked to be on good terms with people who could give an overdraft. Since the IBRD dinner was lousy, I suppose he preferred overdraft bankers to hard loans.

In the evening Lucien Pye invited Patricia, Jim Coleman and me to dinner. Coleman is a professor at UCLA, probably the best informed political scientist on Africa. He is now doing research here at Ibadan…We talked about the speed with which the Northerners are kicking out the expatriates. When Nigeria was federalized, the Northern Region was set up covering more than half the country. There were rumors that was done because the British were convinced the Northerners would need them, thus they would stay in power longer. I don't believe the more Machiavellian implications of this, but it is certain there was a policy of keeping expatriates rather than bringing in Southerners.

However things have moved incredibly quickly. John Taylor is back for six months, and it is rumored he won't last even that long. Peter Gibbs will come back but definitely not to his old position. Suddenly a whole new group of Northern Permanent Secretaries has appeared (I have to start all over again building relations with them.) Likewise a whole new middle class which shares power with the emirs and may yet take it away from them. It was significant that when the Sardauna was in the US he said he expected to return as the head of the UN delegation. Our PM quietly said that it was he who would appoint the delegation, and the Sardauna did *not* go. This would not have happened five years ago…

August 25. The JPC met, primarily to discuss my paper. Finance had been the main troublemaker two weeks before, but this time Henry Omanai, their representative, drew in his horns, and said he agreed completely. Apparently he found out that we had after all consulted every one. From the Ministry of Communications we got a reaction in writing, exactly what we wanted. For the rest Prasad said he wanted to go ahead with a major agricultural survey, to take two years, which FAO was willing to finance, and also a water resources survey. I had had only an inkling of it, but it makes good sense. We also pointed out that the Americans were coming back soon, and asked everyone for God's sake to cooperate with the Federal Government in preparing for the negotiations.

The meeting went rather well. Lyle had reported on the trip to Lokoja, which incidentally confirmed our suspicion that, for a long time to come, expected traffic would not justify major investments in waterways – unless of course we got a steel mill. The Westinghouse Report is in, but I haven't had a chance to study it. Igwagwu has been made responsible for it.

From then on things deteriorated. Toby was in with the minister, who yelled at him and accused him of disobeying instructions. As it happened, Toby was innocent, he was livid, said he had had enough, and was going to see the PM this afternoon to hand in his resignation. It all had to do with the Peace Corps. The former minister, Jaja, had insisted that Nigerians participate in selecting the Peace Corps volunteers. A panel had been picked to go to the States. Then Jaja went to the US as Foreign Minister, decided it wasn't necessary for Nigerians to go, and promised to tell Waziri Ibrahim, our minister. But he forgot. In the meantime, Ambassador Palmer cancelled the trip. So Toby couldn't send them if he had wanted to, because the Americans were not ready to receive anyone. So Ibrahim accused Toby of intriguing with Jaja behind his back!

This naturally rather upset me. We wouldn't get another PS half as good, but I could see Toby's point. Still, I pleaded that, as apparently our minister was unstable and even Nigerians didn't get along with him, Toby might outlast him. Anyway, I went home for lunch with Lyle depressed and upset, on top of my tiredness which does not seem to leave me. We both wished we had Kingsley here to advise us. Obviously we can't resign, but without Toby our effectiveness would be seriously hurt...

In the afternoon we joined a meeting underway with the IMF. The IMF – specifically Mladek – was hammering away at Prasad and John Murray (PS Finance, about to leave Nigeria) on why we wanted exchange control legislation.

I must say, the Fund people were excellent. (Mladek is acting director of the Africa unit. The IMF's policy is to appoint a native of a region as the unit director, but they couldn't find an African. Hence he is only acting director.) I was in a spot because I completely agreed with them that exchange control would be a catastrophe for Nigeria. However I did agree with Prasad that we ought to have standby legislation for emergencies. In my view such an emergency would obtain only if our export prices dropped precipitously without increase in quantities sold, or if a war in Europe halted foreign aid.

Prasad however wanted to go further and control outflows of short term bank funds, and in general use control of capital movements to ensure an independent monetary and fiscal policy for the Central Bank. I was in a spot because I did not want to disagree with him publicly. I did try to bend the discussion to my view, without much success. The notion that a country so dependent on imports could run an independent policy strikes me as unrealistic. As usual I am caught between the Central Bank, too stodgy for my taste, and Prasad, who advocates policies that are bound to cause major trouble.

It is true that the expatriate banks shift funds back and forth on a large scale, but that is part of the business. As the IMF team stressed, this could be influenced easily by talking to them. Moreover, this is a game that can be played only once. If one doesn't let them take funds out they won't bring them in, much as I ask you [WS' wife] to send me only what I need. (By common consent Nigeria is by far the most expensive country in Africa. Lucien Pye was startled at the contrast with East Africa.)

Prasad was pushed into a partial corner. He insisted that we did not plan to use the controls but only to have them for an emergency, and that they were necessary to free reserves for development and allow Nigeria an independent policy. Moreover we were planning something quite harmless, not of the Latin American variety, where exchange control takes the place of economic policy. This was a gain, but despite my and Murray's attempt not to undercut Prasad in public, disagreement was evident. My own feeling is that Prasad will win out all around. He has the ear of the PM, who seems increasingly to listen to him, after a period of skepticism. The fact that British civil servants don't get on too well with him does not hurt him, quite the contrary.

In one matter I did disagree openly with him. Prasad said the plan would be essentially a list of projects, and then attacked the Jackson-Okigbo national income estimates.[6] He did not believe that the economy had grown at 4% per year or more. This was just a British hoax to prove that their colonies had done well. Nor did he believe the 15% investment/GDP coefficient. When I pointed out that Pius was Ibo, not English, he dismissed him with a sneer and a shrug, which is unfair to Pius as a scholar, though possibly not too unjust to him as a civil servant, in which role he is unsure of himself and, as far as I can tell, lazy. Why, continued Prasad, are growth rates more or less the same in East and West Africa. Everyone seems to have 4% growth, etc.

Part of this was, of course, directed against our approach. Part was undoubtedly due to Prasad's prejudices as an Indian against the British in general and frustration over India's inability to grow at such a rate, and part must be due to his contempt for the "wretched Nigerians," as he calls them, who seem to do well despite their laziness. Still I could not help but point out that statistics on export crops and imports were very good, and that the modern sector had grown at over 5% pa.

Mladek and Bhatia, the Indian, pointed to general agreement that (a) the population was growing at $2^1/_2$%, (b) the average standard of living had improved, and hence (c) 4% GDP growth seemed necessary to accord with observations (a) and (b). I think I got much the better of that argument, without of course convincing Prasad. I am happy to say, however, that all debates are now good-humored and lack the acrimony of the first attacks.

When we left, I was somewhat disturbed and continue to be so. I am quite reconciled to being Prasad's staff, and even to have him produce a project plan for bargaining purposes instead of a straightforward feasible plan. But the exchange control debate is more serious. And I also fear the anti-British, anti-colonial bias will play into the hands of more irresponsible Nigerians.

After the meeting, Toby, Prasad and I had a friendly chat about Toby's problems. Fortunately Toby had not succeeded in seeing the Minister. Clearly a feud is underway in Cabinet. Our own ministry has now had four ministers in its short life. Considering it is an important ministry, where continuity is essential, this is too much. I asked whether Festus of Finance was behind it all in an attempt to keep our ministry weak and his own strong. This seems to be generally assumed to be so, and only my own political naiveté had prevented me from catching on earlier. Toby still was fuming, however.

Apparently even Nigerians have trouble with Ibrahim, and can't figure him out. Quite possibly he won't last long, given enemies among his fellow ministers, in which case Toby might outlast him. I said I found it difficult to work with someone with whom I couldn't have a personal relationship. But Toby turned this around, saying he couldn't work with a minister who was suspicious of him and accused him of intriguing against him. Then he said Ibrahim had called him in to explain that it was the Americans, not Toby, who were intriguing!

August 28. All morning in the office, first rewriting some stuff Lyle had prepared for me. Then I dictated a letter to Prasad explaining in detail why I disagreed on exchange control and asking for a meeting. This is a really important point that I am ready to carry to the PM if necessary – if I can get access to him, that is. This by no means certain...

Later finished a memo on nationalization of Cable and Wireless, a British Govt. Corporation responsible for international telephone and telegraph communications in Nigeria. The government, not unnaturally, finds this unsatisfactory and wants to take over. I wrote as tactful a memo against it as I could because it would involve us in too much capital export when we are trying to import capital. Not that it will have any impact.

The other thing I had to do was to get four program evaluations ready for Toby. One of them won't go to the Ministry, Patrick says, because it was too caustic. The Railway program begins to make sense, the Ports are fine. They are a really efficient outfit. The Airways could be all right provided they don't buy jets and don't buy turbo props before 1963 or 1964 when they have an engineering base ready. But what got us was the National Shipping Line, whose balance sheet was messy. They claim they made money on purchased ships, which wasn't true, though they did make money on charters.

There is also some trouble brewing with Prasad. It isn't personal, of course, but an important policy difference is brewing. Earlier I mentioned my memo about exchange control. He wrote back a letter which, while polite, was nevertheless somewhat biting. He tried to pull his experience, and also some nationalism. But I question whether the experience proves a mild form of exchange control to be possible in Nigeria, or even desirable. Anyway it gave me a headache, metaphorically speaking, and I decided to see Toby about it.

At 2:00 PM I went to lunch with the German ambassador, a friend of Guenther Harkort and Heuss (Count Posadowski-Wehner). His wife had committed suicide a few weeks ago because she thought she had incurable cancer. He had just returned from Germany and brought along his 18–19 year old son to keep him company...He asked me to let him know if I heard of a man named Voss, who was to come under technical assistance. He was not the type he wanted to see, being an ex-Nazi. He also told me the Germans were going to finance the second Lagos bridge minus approaches, and were going to give the North a major hospital in Kaduna and 12 regional ones. He wanted to know the foreign exchange content, so he would not be too far off in his recommendation to the German Government.

And I want from him the Ferrostahl Report. Ferrostahl did one on a steel industry for the Eastern Region Government which it won't show the FG. They are equipment suppliers and need scrutiny but how can we advise sensibly if we have only one proposal. He also wanted to know what we thought of our minister. I said he seemed pro-American. The Ambassador replied, maybe, but when he talks with me he is pro-German and when he talks with Yavor, the Israeli ambassador, he is pro-Israeli. We left it at that...

In the evening Lyle came over. He is counting on staying on. Also the problem comes up of writing a draft of the plan. It ought to be about 60 pages. And fairly non-technical, with the more technical stuff in appendices. But I balk at making it merely a project list: this is definitely not what we were supposed to do, though Prasad begins to push again in this direction. I will actually be in a fairly strong position because it will be I who will have to do most of the writing. Lyle was worried about the editing. We would prefer to have Toby do it because the thing is basically intended for the ministers. Possibly we might get Kingsley to do it, since he has a lot of *savoir faire* in these matters.

At 9:00 PM I went over to Toby's for a drink and a quiet chat. He had told the PM he was ready to resign. Fortunately the PM had not accepted it, but told him he would talk with Jaja. Stanley Wey, the PM's new PS, a Yoruba, shrugged his shoulders, commiserated with Toby and thought he should stick it out. Toby was quite fed up, and told both Sir Abubakar and Wey they could have his resignation at any moment. On exchange control Toby is pretty much on my side. He wondered, though, whether I would let all the football pool money, estimated at £2 million a year, go out. I said no, but this was not a question of exchange control but of simply not allowing English pools to operate in Nigeria. After all, the Government could decide what businesses it would permit. In the North one can't slaughter pigs because it offends Moslems.

I also said I hoped to be able to write the plan my way, with an overall chapter, something to make plain that we had given thought to consistency, indirect effects, and pay-off. I didn't want just a list of projects, and I did not want goals just in physical terms. Furthermore, I insisted that exchange control would be a catastrophe and had to be avoided, and if necessary I might ask to see the PM on this. To me that was a fundamental point.

When I left we were both fairly cheerful though neither of us had entirely overcome the strain and disappointment of the past few days.

August 29. Today started as usual with routine. At 10:30 AM we met with a Swiss firm of considerable reputation to discuss the possibility of setting up an aluminun smelter here, even before the Volta River smelter in Ghana. This is strictly confidential and must not go further. What the Swiss wanted was a letter from the Government, giving them the exclusive right to make a feasibility study. Nigeria is attractive because of political stability. The Guinée participation has broken up and Ghana's policies drive business out. If we stay politically sane, we will get every business in Africa.

The Swiss were, of course, also interested in the cost of power – it had to be two cents or less to make up for the cost of transport. They are thinking of a 10,000 tons smelter at the start, which would need protection and could be opened before the Dam is ready. Once the Dam produces electricity cheaply, it might go up to 50,000 tons unprotected, mostly for export. If bauxite is found in Nigeria, the situation changes further, but as 6,000 ton freighters can go through the Escravos Bar, this would do. In any case, a 50,000 tons smelter would use about a fourth of the Dam's capacity right away and might make it profitable much sooner than anticipated.

This is, of course, a very exciting prospect. Toby promised they would get their letter, and Lyle is doing considerable work on power and shipping cost in the meantime. I made a minor slip in saying we could supply power cheaper in Ghana from our dam than they could from the Volta. After all, while the Aluminum people are impressive, they are also in business and are negotiating.

After the meeting I saw the Minister to tell him I was off to Maiduguri, his home town, and ask whether he had mentioned to the Waziri that we would come. He had also written me a letter dealing with a proposed development corporation that is dear to his heart. I read it in my office and then come back to discuss it, but Ibrahim had left to take his son to school. So I dictated an answer. Actually the letter was sensible, but it disturbed me that it was addressed to Prasad and me with a copy to the PM, but not to Toby. This lack of confidence between Ibrahim and Toby is unfortunate.

I had a short rest, then we went off to the airport, taking the London plane to Kano. Fenn was at the airport and brought us to the Central Hotel, where the air conditioning worked this time. Kano was unusually green, as the rains had been heavy. And I understand this year we may have a record groundnut crop of 800,000 tons as a result. Though this seems high. Last year's crop was 620,000 tons, the past record was 715,000 tons.

Notes

1 WS was on mission to Addis Ababa to deliver a paper on planning in Nigeria at a conference of the Economic Commission for Africa.
2 On 'Comprehensive Development Planning'. It was distributed as a UN document and later published in the *East African Economic Review* (1964).
3 I am sure that Dupriez didn't like us anglophones. I was supposed to be on an advisory-planning committee for another conference chaired by D, but I got the invitation to attend by sea mail, long after the meeting had taken place.
4 Guenther, at the time an official in the German ministry responsible for development aid, was one of my closest friends during the Schumpeter Seminar days in Bonn. He eventually rose to the equivalent of our Undersecretary of State for Economic Affairs.
5 WS refers here to an altercation between Tunisian president Bourgiba and the French government over the Bizerte naval base, which France evacuated only in 1963, seven years after Tunisian independence.
6 P.N.C. Okigbo, *Nigerian National Accounts 1950–1957*, published by the Federal Ministry of Economic Development, Enugu, 1962.

Chapter 9

August 30–September 22, 1961
Visit to Kano, Maiduguri, Lake Chad:
Plan Drafting Begins, Regions Pressed to
Submit Their Investment Proposals

September 1, 1961 (Maiduguri)

We arrived here about one hour ago. We probably won't be able to make Lake Chad. This year's rainy season has apparently been very wet. Even the paved road from Kano to was impassable last week – and the last 16 miles to the lake, normally passable by Landrover or jeep, is just a swamp.

The drive from Kano to Maiduguri is uneventful, but rather beautiful, and long – 372 miles. The weather was good, occasional rains, always clouds so it wasn't too hot. It is pretty flat up here, with occasional outcroppings of rock, once a ridge, but the rest is just savanna, beautifully green at this time of year. In fact it does look like an English park even from the ground and it got to be more so the closer we got to Maiduguri. M. is the seat of the Waziri of Bornu, a real high potentate. He has to be addressed as high as possible: at least Your Excellency, preferably Your Highness! It seems that in Kano only the emir is allowed to own camels. In M. only the Waziri is allowed to use an umbrella or parasol. Everyone of the high and mighty has his own status symbol! I shall try to see the Waziri tomorrow; my minister told him I was coming, so I have to try at least.

The most fascinating thing to see was the birds: cattle egrets in droves, birds which looked like – and may have been – ibises, very large, like Marabous. My driver – the same I had last year, Baba Dihwa – said they came from "Egypt-side." Red Birds, blue birds like pheasants with their tails but larger beaks and a shiny, steely blue. The closer we got to M. the more camels appeared. The people here are Kanuri with a different hair style. Amazingly they still have swords with them and lances against thieves. I think they are not allowed firearms. Only the police.

The resthouse is lovely. We had coffee in a resthouse on the way, but were warned to take our own lunch as the food was bad. An Englishman complained that the meat tasted of kerosene and was inedible. But the place here is clean, has electricity and hot water (I just washed my shirt), but one sleeps under a mosquito net. And just by writing this letter I am getting bitten. But back to the diary.

I'm just back from the standard British Colonial Resthouse Supper: unidentifiable soup, fairly hot, a cross between oxtail and mock turtle, toasted sardine on toast $1/2$ inch by 2 inches, warm, lukewarm lamb, quite good plus cold vegetables, and a custard. I shouldn't have eaten it. There are also lots of bugs about.

Lake Chad area is famous for them! I am told that the DOs on the Lake go to bed at sundown to avoid being eaten.

August 30. First to Fenn's office at the Marketing Board. I tried to straighten out the groundnut accounts, in particular find out how to learn what farmers actually receive. This is very tricky and can be done only very approximately because there are about 250 buying stations with numerous middlemen and different prices. But I got a method of doing it approximately at least.

We then discussed the possible future of groundnut crushing. The industry has a hard time now, with nuts bringing a premium compared to oil and cake. Some crushers want to get back to the old system of crushing for the Marketing Board for a fee, and the MB would export nuts, oil and cake, thereby reducing competition. There are some obvious drawbacks to this. There is also the question of the price at which the crushers can buy nuts, which is decided by a fairly tricky system, which however has frequently worked in the crushers' favor. By the time I had straightened myself out on that issue it was 2:15 PM and we went to the hotel for lunch.

At 3:15 PM Baba Dikwa came to take us through Kano and the market. This time it was leisurely, and I saw parts I hadn't seen last time. It was very muddy, but it didn't smell. I bought a Hausa jacket which I may give to Matt eventually to smoke his cigars in, and some slippers for Tom.[1] There was suddenly quite a bit of excitement, because thieves had stolen Baba's driver's license, two pounds, his references and his army discharge book. That cut short the visit at the market, and we went to the Native Authority Police to report the theft and see what could be done about getting duplicate documents. I replaced the £2.

After dinner at 8:30 PM Fenn came to the hotel with the cotton file to help me understand how the price of cotton is fixed. The trouble is that the MB buys seed cotton and sells both lint and seed, has development expenses and hands back seed to the farmers free of charge. After that Fenn told us of some appointments next day at oil millers etc.

September 3. Plans have changed, we are going on an exciting four-day expedition with Landrover and truck to Lake Chad with the local agricultural officer.

But first all about Kano:

August 31....At 9:00 AM we went with Fenn to inspect NICCO, the Nigerian Confectionery Company. [See Photo No. 20.] This firm started only about 18 months ago and I had heard it was in trouble because of new taxes slapped on by Festus. This turned out to be wrong. The plant is airy and modern, with German machinery, a German production manager and a Sudanese General Manager, and it seems efficiently run. They employ 150 people, run 3 shifts. I never heard that of a candy factory before. They now produce six tons of candy a day, and will go up to 12 tons within a year. They could double and still not satisfy the market. We got fresh samples which were very good indeed. Only, the German manager said sadly, they don't like chocolate toffee, though it is the finest one can produce. There is about £20,000 of NRDC money in the plant, the rest is distributed mainly among local investors (Northerners).

The next stop at 10:00 AM was Mandrides, the Cypriot owner of Nigerian Oil Mills, and a rather sad gentleman. He was one of the first groundnut crushers who always believed in working with the Govt., even when it was hampering the industry's growth. This year they are all losing money, and just this year the

Sardauna extracted a promise from two of the oil millers to set up crushing plants in Gusan and Maiduguri. Mandrides declared himself ready to set one up in Maiduguri, but lots of things remain to be ironed out.

For one thing, it will take the railway two years to get to Maiduguri. Secondly, electricity here comes from a so-called amenity plant, which makes losses even though it charges 5d/kwh compared with 2d/kwh in Lagos and a fraction of that in the US or UK. Thirdly, Mandrides wants a so-called pioneer certificate which gives him tax exemption for a number of years, but has been told the law won't permit it. "If setting up a plant in Maiduguri isn't pioneering, I don't know what is." I promised to talk with Commerce and Industry about it, although if the law says he can't have the certificate there isn't much he can do about it.

Mandrides said the future of the industry had to be decided now. He felt they should go back to the old system, when the MB marketed nuts, oil and cake, and the crushers crushed for a fee. Three of the four crushers would like this, but as crushing is unprofitable right now, I don't see there would be any crushing at all. Mandrides felt Nigeria should not try to export whole nuts. As long as she did, crushing would not be profitable. The European firms, mainly Unilever, would always pay a premium for whole nuts to keep their own mills busy, so why should Nigerian oil have to compete with her own nuts. The situation would get worse, as less nuts would become available for export.

I mostly listened, letting him talk. But I did point to other countries selling whole nuts, notably Senegal and Mali, while US soya beans were making increasing inroads, so Nigeria could easily lose out all along the line. Moreover, the situation would be different if Nigeria consumed lots of groundnut oil and cake, but it didn't. Mandrides himself is the big exception. He has been trying to develop a local market and sells groundnut oil in the South under his own brand name.

We went then through the mill, idle because it was the weekly maintenance day – exactly as I hit it last summer. I tried some of his oil cake, which is quite good and has 56% protein. There is some thought of grinding it into pieces, mixing it with a flavoring agent, and then feeding it to a protein-starved population.

At 11:00 AM we saw Spinney, the general manager of Kano Oil Millers, owned by Karami, a Lebanese. This time I saw finally a mill working, and it was quite impressive. Spinney felt the price fixing at which oil millers could buy the stuff from the MB was unfair now, though it had worked to their advantage in the past, but he had no substitute to offer. And since you have to buy at the same price, the criticism alone is not much good. On both millers I tried out Fenn's idea of allowing the crushers to buy what they wanted on the open market. Neither liked it. Mandrides thought it would be unfair to the farmers, Spinney that it wouldn't work. Fenn had warned me the crushers did not like the idea.

Some of the machinery was German, some American (Armstrong from Cleveland). The German machinery was disappointing, big and requiring too frequent spare parts. The US machinery was better than expected, and in the local climate they needed one operation less than in the US – some press drying was unnecessary. Karami is the fellow who promised to put up a mill in Gusan. He also owns the biggest transport business in the North. He has the Shell (?) contract right to the Chad Republic, and also bottles Pepsi. At 12:00 PM we were due at Marani, another Lebanese crusher. Actually, only Mandrides has all his money in crushing.

His enterprise is now £1¹/₂ million, and he recently made it into a public company with shares held by local Northerners. All other millers are still closely held family corporations, with substantial other lines of interest. Marani has quite a few, and we wanted to see them.

The first was a shoe factory, making rubber sneakers and plastic sandals. We were greeted by a Lebanese general manager and an English CPA, Robertson, who had come just the day before, apparently to bring some order into the business, and looked discouraged already. The plant made a bad impression. They employ about 150 people when working full-time, mostly during the groundnut harvesting season. The stuff is all for local consumption and rather shoddy. The machinery is partly German, partly English. The molds of the plastic presses were worn, with the result that workers had to snip the excess off with scissors. The people stamping out the rubber soles could easily have got 2–3 more soles out of a sheet. When I asked the manager, he said it didn't matter, since there was no real waste: the excess rubber was reused. He didn't see that labor was cheap while heating, pulverizing and electricity cost a lot of money. No wonder R. was discouraged when he saw that lousy outfit.

The final stop was a piggery, also owned by M. and run by a Danish couple and their son who showed us around. They have 48,000 pigs, all going to Lagos since Moslems won't eat pork. M. uses some of his oil cake for feed. He would like to grow his own fodder, but is not allowed to lease the land. He would like to open a slaughterhouse in Kano, and cure the meat there – according to the Danish manager, the climatic conditions would be unusually favorable – but the Emir won't have it. The blood of pigs would pollute the water, and Moslems couldn't drink it. The piggery was efficiently run, and obviously a money maker. M. has his own outlets in Lagos and I have eaten his product. Incidentally both pigs and cows have less diseases here than in Europe.

Lunch at 2:30 PM and a short rest. At 4:00 PM Fenn came for another sightseeing tour through Kano. We drove around the wall, to find a little gate, which still had an iron door with bullet holes in it. I took pictures from a hill, where it was grey and misty and looked like the Arabian Nights...Later in the evening Fenn and his Scottish wife came for dinner. His contract runs out in April, he wants to farm in East Anglia but she doesn't...He also preferred the open life in the North to Lagos, which he hated when stationed there.

September 1. We drove to Maiduguri. Sept. 2 we went first to pay our respects to the Resident, Arnold, thank him for his arrangements and request interviews with the Waziri and with the agricultural officer. Arnold showed me a map of an artesian well program which is transforming the economy of the Lake Chad area. This is good drinking water which needs neither filtering nor boiling. Troughs for cattle are set up, and the problem now becomes one of overgrazing. Some sort of cattle control will have to be introduced. Also some sort of water legislation.

I also found out just what the Waziri is. He is a very nice man, and head of the Native Authority – the real power. But he is not a traditional ruler. Waziri is his title – wazir of 1001 Nights. The traditional ruler is an emir who is also spiritual leader of his people but who is old and takes therefore less part in local affairs.

The agricultural officer, John Goss, is a young Englishman, who does extension work and everything else...He suggested we accompany him to Kabba and Abadan, both on Lake Chad. The former is the fishing center *cum* experiment station, the latter a wheat experiment. Getting there will take two days by Landrover and lorry. The first night we will sleep in the truck. The second night we will have a bush rest house. We may not get there at all because of the rains. But it will be worth seeing the conditions under which work proceeds here...I am of course jumping at this opportunity, though it takes more time than I really have.

Goss took me to the Waziri, who was impressive and pleased to have me see Lake Chad. (With luck I'll see a hippo. Elephants are almost impossible to see.) I then went to the local veterinary officer, also English. Cattle is the thing here. There is a slaughterhouse, killing about 50 cattle a day, before 7:00 AM to get it to market. As there is no chilling, the beef does not get hung for a few weeks as with us, but is just bled. They will experiment with chilling and fattening. Eventually they hope to slaughter 400 cattle a day, operate a by-products plant, and ship the stuff by plane to Lagos.

A Texan has been in, interested in the flying operation. No one knew the economics of this, but in Fort Lamy, the capital of Chad, there is a slaughter operation with the meat being flown profitably to Leopoldville and all over the ex-French territories; and conditions there are pretty much the same as here. The vet officer doubted whether the region could supply 400 head a day, but both the slaughter house and the by-products plant would be profitable at 200.

Both cattle and people in the province number about $1^{1}/_{2}$ million. There is overgrazing, and attempts are being made at ranching and feeding to take cattle off the land. The average weight of beef cattle is 500–600 lbs., half what it is in Europe, and it takes four years to get cattle up to that level compared to two years in the US. Still, this is good for the tropics. The slaughter weight is about 51–55%, also good...

I meant to write last night, but got talking with Lawson from Colorado...He is trying to persuade some Fulanis to let him have cattle for feeding. At first the response was enthusiastic, until they learned the cattle were to be slaughtered at the end of the trial. Several then withdrew; what is the point of getting the cows really pretty, and then slaughtering the best looking ones?!

So these are some of the difficulties. Still, everyone agrees that Fulanis will settle down when conditions are right for them, as will Kanuris.

The proof is that on Aug. 31 we visited a settled Fulani village about 2–3 miles outside of Kano. It was clean, rather comfortable and didn't smell. Fulanis sleep on beds which have mats on them, and eat out of calabashes. They are cattle people and hence drink milk, which seemed to be sour, however.

I went to bed at 9:30 PM; everyone else was either in bed already or at a dance at the club. The bugs are pretty fierce in the evening, not as bad as in Vermont, but more dangerous, and it isn't good writing in the evening.

I don't know how long this letter will take. The next plane out of here is on September 6, but it will go by truck to Kano before that. The rest house manager, Reynolds, was rather dubious about the trip. He has been expecting people from Fort Lamy for a week, and they haven't been heard from yet.

September 3 (Maiduguri).... Yesterday evening I went to the local market, much more colorful than the Southern markets, or even than Kano. [See Photo No. 21.] The hairdress of the Kanuris is quite different from either the Fulanis or the Hausas. The men actually shave their heads. There was quite a bit of leatherwork, some blacksmiths making daggers and implements, using goatskins as bellows over a small fire, all sitting down. I bought two knives or daggers, quite good, both for 8/-. They use them for everything: butchering, cutting leather, anything. Hordes of tailors, under trees, were busily making gowns with Japanese or Chinese cottons on their Singer sewing machines. There were the local butchers. And hat makers. The local hats are quite distinct, looking something like a pagoda. But the fellow wouldn't come down from 7/-. It was all fascinating.

Later I saw the first draft of Lawson's report. The land is being depleted rapidly. Everything is lush now, but rainfall is only 25 inches, and from October to May there isn't a drop. In large sections the land is infertile because fallow has disappeared. The problem is how to control numbers of cattle to prevent overgrazing. This could be done in part if they started ranching and fattening with fodder instead of letting the animals just graze on pasture. But this is expensive and not only goes against present habits, but runs into serious difficulties with land tenure. Until freehold is introduced not much can be done. In the meantime there is large-scale soil erosion...

At 4:00 PM Goss, the agricultural officer, appeared with his beat-up Mercedes 190, and he, Lawson and Long, the veterinary officer, took me to the cattle market. It was quite interesting watching them look for the right animals: 4-year old steers with capacity for fattening. I was surprised to see the bulls mixing harmlessly with the populace, unlike in the US. Apparently, when not segregated from the cows, they behave quite well. The scene was somewhat improved by the riders in flowing robes with swords on their sides, in a Western-type saddle, from which they couldn't fall off if they tried. The main object of the visit was not yet to buy, but to see what there was and find out prices: about £12–15 for a 600 lb. bullock.

At 5:15 PM we went to the experimental farm, about 6 miles outside of town, where the main object is to teach mixed farming. They also have rice, a kind of bean, some citrus fruit and bananas...

The next stop was the slaughterhouse. It is quite modern, but much remains to be ironed out, as it is the first one in Nigeria. They make £10,000 in fees, with about £5,000 running cost. Whether it is profitable or not depends on capital costs, which are not clear...The slaughterhouse was started by the NR Govt., then handed over to the Maiduguri Native Authority, which put £65,000 into it. The NRDC has invested probably an equal amount.

The meat is all for local consumption, and slaughtered according to Moslem law. When they start exporting to the South, they may mechanize. The by-products plant stands idle. The experts claim it doesn't pay to send cattle on the hoof 1,000 miles to Lagos. I raised the question why it was possible in the US – see all our Westerns! The answer is that all our cowboys had to contend with was the Indians. Forty cowboys would take a year to run perhaps 45,000 head through green pastures and at the end of the trail they were fat. Here there are no pastures, but plenty of tsetse. The whole business centers on the cost of air shipment, which a Texan thinks he has all figured out. Seeing the place and talking with the local people doesn't make it all look as hopeless as it does from Lagos. But there is a problem of getting 400 head of cattle a day. The breakeven point is probably 200 head. It might still be better to have a bigger slaughterhouse in Kano and ship from there. Lawson thought the problem would get worse, as overgrazing and erosion would reduce the number of cattle.

September 10, 1961

...Even under the best conditions, the trip to Chad is rough. It was successful, though, from every standpoint: as adventure, as economic research. We went first from Maiduguri NW to Chobol, and from there to Gajiram, but not on the green road, which is a dry season road and quite impassable at this time of the year, but along camel tracks on an arc between the Gubio and Gajiram roads. From Gajiram we went in as straight a line as possible NE towards Kauwa. We spent the first night in a village called Gezeriya, which is not on the map, but is halfway between Bulabulin and Lagerete on a different camel track.

The next night we spent in Kauwa. Then we went to Baga on Lake Chad, retraced our steps halfway to Kauwa and followed a track along the lake to Arege. From there we went to Abadan and South to Yo where we spent two nights. On Friday we left early, got lost but on the whole went down the camel track from Arege to Gajiram, and straight down (not on the green road) to Maiduguri.

And now for the details, as the newspapers say...Apart from myself our party consisted of John Goss, principal agricultural officer of Bornu Province; Wally Price, Bornu's agricultural supervisor; Peter Ward, a research scholar from UCI doing a piece of research on qualea, the weaver bird and one of the biggest pests in this area; and Patricia...The distance between Maiduguri and Gezeriya is about 100 miles. It took all day until 7:30 PM to get there. The reason was first that the road – if one can call it that – was frequently under one to two feet of water. Then the truck got bogged down twice to its axle...and the gearbox appeared to be broken.

The landscape was beautiful: green with deceptively soft-looking grasses, lots of acacias with sharp and long spines, but the country was flat and only a little rolling. The wildlife also got more interesting. The "Egypt side" birds I mentioned before I could identify as crown birds. Trees which looked to be in white bloom turned out to full of cattle egrets' nests. There were the enormous Marabou storks, and somewhat smaller Abdin storks. And of course, geese, ducks and a sort of wild turkeys, as well as bush fowl, a variety of partridge.

When the gearbox could not be fixed, John decided to leave the truck where it was, and seek out the next African village which turned out to be Gezeryia. Peter Ward and Wally Price went ahead in their Landrover to negotiate with the village chief. They all speak Kanuri and Hausa, which is quite essential when working up there. When we got there, we had permission to sleep in the entrance to the chief's compound, and also to use his cooking hut for our cooking. The huts are like beehives, made of strong reed, clean, but rather stuffy, but the entrance hall, though fairly waterproof, had at least two openings instead of the usual one, and the sides were not tight either but mats were brought out to make it more private...

September 5....The truck was fixed in half an hour, and we set out on the second leg of the journey. We had intended to accompany Peter Ward to Kauwa, help him get settled and then push on to Baga. It didn't work that way. Progress was very slow. The track was either too wet, or too sandy. The truck got bogged down twice, and each time took almost 3 hours to get out: one digs under, puts boards and strips of perforated steel under, jack it up etc.

While we were sitting there, a Ministry of Agriculture vehicle came chugging along. A 'Unimog' is a Landrover-jeep type vehicle, made by Mercedes, which unlike other Mercedes products is no good, though it looks fabulously efficient. The unimog had been sent down from Yo to Maiduguri and was supposed to carry nothing but a drum of gas. Instead, the driver, counting on the negligible chance of meeting a Ministry vehicle, had got into business and was transporting about 1 ton of dried fish from Lake Chad, 5 bags of reptile skins and 14 people – all in a vehicle the size of a jeep. John stopped him, kicked off the passengers, unloaded their stinking fish and reptile skins, told the driver he was fired, and ordered the vehicle to turn around and come back with us. Since everyone knew that they were in the wrong, there wasn't a peep out of them. That was already the second one we had stopped. John Goss said, "Now you see why we have trouble maintaining our vehicles when they are overloaded like that."

All the while, we met camel trains with dried fish, each train of 4–5 camels carrying about a ton. They take the stuff down to Gajiram where it is reloaded into trucks. The only trucks we saw north of Gajiram were Government special 4-wheel drive vehicles. Also underway were numerous donkey trains and Fulani herds. Tribesmen wandered around, armed with spears and bows and arrows, and the men on camels all carried swords. No one had rifles, which are strictly controlled.

The second breakdown came at a lovely wide spot where the rains had formed a good-sized pond. There were plenty of wild ducks around, and I was handed a shotgun and told to try my luck. [See Photo No. 22.] So while the rest dug at the truck and pulled it out I tried my luck, stalked a flock of geese and with beginners' luck got two with one shot. But they were sitting. I never got within range of either a sitting or flying duck again…

We all looked forward to Kauwa, where we had decided to stay the night. It was getting late, and at Kauwa was a borehole in the system of artesian wells the Resident had mentioned. We got there just at dusk. Peter Ward and Wally Price had found a place to pitch Peter's tent…, when a messenger from the chief came asking us to stay in the village, because where we wanted to stay was a bad place. It had been a cemetery. Also there were plenty of bugs. So the tent was folded again, and we rode into the village, where two compounds were put at our disposal…

The goose had gone bad in the heat, but we had partridge and the ducks I shot for dinner. We also had a bottle of wine I had brought in the hope that Peter Duncan would be there. However we found out later he had got bogged down further south and arrived two days late. I am beginning to see why time doesn't mean much up there. One just can't tell when one is going to be where; not even to the day, to say nothing of the hour. Some trucks take a week for the journey that we made in 3 days, mainly because without Europeans to drive, the Africans take it easy when they are axle deep in the mud. And who is to blame them.

The borehole, about 1,300 feet deep, turned out to be a godsend. The temperature all day must have been well over 100° in the shade, and we were dusty and sweaty and muddy. The water was perfectly safe to drink, but it smelled of sulfur and was too hot to stay under while washing. Still we all had a bath and felt at least temporarily refreshed.

The evening was hot and there wasn't a breath of air…In Maiduguri the average annual rainfall is only 25 inches, though this year it was more. We now were in an area of 15 inches rainfall. In two out of three years the millet and guinea corn harvest fails: we are now in the third year, when there is sufficient rain for a good harvest.

...Gezeryia was a good-sized village. Since the borehole had been put in, it had grown. I was again impressed by the cleanliness of the huts and compounds. The new feature was ostrich eggs on top of the huts. I was told they are fertility charms which the Chief distributes. Some huts had beer bottles in place, possibly as decorations.

September 6....We left Kauwa for Baga at 8 AM...The landscape changed again slightly. It looked like an orchard, and indeed this type of bush is called Orchard bush. But it is all hardy, thorny stuff. The villages all seemed to live on fish, and were noticeably more primitive if this is possible. Then, when we got to the peninsula where Baga sits, the landscape changed again. It became completely treeless and bushless, with lots of water in between, absolutely flat, with fishing villages dotted along the shore at greater intervals than one would get at home – the latter a reflection of the unbelievably primitive fishing methods which will not support more people...

At Baga is a research station of the Northern Regional Government and also a fairly new research effort by our ministry. The place is so inaccessible that previously no one could stand it for long. Ray Cross, the present fisheries officer, is there with his wife and a healthy looking $4^1/_2$ year old son...Cross showed us what they were doing. The problems are (1) to teach the locals how to fish and (2) to cure the fish so that it will get to the market without spoiling. As to (1), the traditional method of fishing is to put out a line on which hooks are spaced but not baited. They wait for the fish to get caught in the hooks, yielding a very poor catch.

The fisheries people teach the locals how to make 6-inch nets with nylon and use them efficiently. This takes about 6–8 weeks. However a fisherman with 3 nets can catch £1 worth of fish a day. Since a net costs only £12–£16, he can pay off the nets in 6–10 weeks. This is the kind of investment I like. Officially, only 8 fishermen are taught the method. But I noticed nets drying all along the shore. The success of the scheme is shown by the fact that about 100 fishermen now use nets, having learned it from the few trained by Cross. They still fish from their traditional reed boats. The experiment station has not yet found a satisfactory motor boat. A scow-type boat is not satisfactory because of sudden storms. The local reed boats can't take an outboard motor and aren't much good anyway. An English boat is on order costing about £150–£160. If it works it ought to be economical.

The traditional drying method isn't much good either. The fish is cleaned and cut into pieces of about 1–2 lb size – no one bothers about weight, only size – then it is smoked until a hard crust forms, and finally sun-dried. This is when flies get at it and lay their eggs, so the quality deteriorates and the stuff rapidly goes bad. The fisheries station is salting fish, but Southerners don't like salted fish. Sun-drying can work if netting is spread, but the stuff gets re-infected in transport – one could smell the Unimog with its illegal load for a hundred yards. The problem is one for entomologists and perhaps for packaging experts. The traditional packaging is a straw mat, transport a camel. Local employees smoke and dry fish on their own account, but with superior methods and their products command a premium price.

The fish we got was a type of perch, and very good. They hope to build up the industry from its present 12,000 tons a year with primitive methods to about 250,000 tons with modern methods. But both drying and transport problems have still to be solved.

Next Cross took us out on Lake Chad to see where the (more or less) open water begins, and also to see local fishermen at work. There certainly are plenty of fish in the lake, something disputed by some people. Even at the heat of 11:00 AM, plenty of backs were visible as they arched out of the water. There is plenty of papyrus around too, forming floating islands which are a nuisance and a danger to nets. We saw a huge one that hadn't been there the day before. The only wildlife we saw were pelicans. Elephants live in the water during daytime and come out at night to feed, but all I saw was a skeleton less tusks. The same is true of hippos...We left at noon and none too soon. We tried to follow the Lake shore, but it turned out to be impossible. From time to time we tried to cut back to the Lake, but were always stopped by swamps...We saw many birds but didn't come across a single mammal. We did locate a qualea breeding ground. The weaver bird is only sparrow size, but there are literally millions of them in a spot. Normally they eat grass seeds but every so often they descend on crops and they have been responsible for famines...The only known method of eradication is dynamite. It is a fantastic sight to see heavy branches bend – and I am told break – under the weight of sparrow-sized birds.

It was dark when we got to Arege. In the dark the landscape completely changes its character. The occasional trees seem like forests, the puddles like enormous swamps. The only lights one sees are fires of the Fulani herdsmen, which make the longhorn cattle look enormous. Some mammals appeared, such as hare and rabbit. And a kangaroo-mouse...Five miles before Yo we got stuck in the mud, but really good. It took over 2 hours to get out...

At Yo (or You on some maps) is an irrigation project for wheat. It is run by Peter Drew, whose father is Chief Engineer of GM International, living, of all places, in Bloomfield Hills, Michigan...The guest house is just ten feet above the Yobe River, which forms the border between Nigeria and Niger Republic. The river is used for irrigation...

September 7....Later in the morning, Peter Drew took me to Abadan – we got stuck only once, and were pulled out by local talent. There is an interesting market there. All northern markets are much more colorful than the southern ones. It is partly the robes, partly the camels, but the people have a dignity and politeness completely lacking in the South. They are dark, but have more semitic than negroid features. Most of them are Kanuri, some are Shua Arabs. Their dignity and politeness does not prevent them from being swindlers and rogues if they can get away with it. But one does not hear the constant "dash me, dash me" as in the South, and while hordes of people always gather around you, they keep a polite distance and don't push and rush you...

Drew then took us to Mallam Fatori, on Lake Chad, not on the map but due east of Abadan. Here also Fisheries is trying to establish net fishing. It is an important market for dried fish. The Lake is open there and looks quite different. There were reed boats – I took a ride in one...[See Photo No. 23.] They are really quite uncomfortable, being very close to the water and absolutely flat. They are just reed bundles tied together with reeds, plus a curved bow...

The irrigated wheat scheme is successful as far as I can tell, yet it is rather puzzling. The farmers grow wheat, and the politicians have decided to grow up to 10,000 acres. Abadan is in the very Northeast corner of Nigeria, absolutely nowhere, and I have just described the difficulty of getting there in the wet season. In the dry season one can make it from Maiduguri in a day, but one still must have four-wheel-drive vehicles. The farmer gets an unsubsidized market price in Abadan of £50 per ton. It costs £10 to bring a ton from Abadan to Maiduguri and another £5 to bring it to Kano, where people are willing to pay £65–£70 per ton for a wheat which is nothing special, and could be imported from the US for £35. No one knows the answer to that puzzle.

The soil there is not laterite, but impermeable clay, of a relatively high salt content, which is OK for rice but not wheat. Lake Chad is too salty for irrigation, even if this were not too expensive. But the river Yobe is completely salt-free, and like Lake Chad reaches its crest during the dry season...The scheme started with five acres, last year was 80, this year 200, and within two years will be 1500 acres. The soil is cultivated for the farmers after it is dry. A farmer with a hoe could do at most $^1/_3$ acre, it is that hard.

They have now 1-acre farms, but want to go to 6 acres. It costs £2 per acre to plow, and £2/acre for water, but the politicians won't allow a charge of more than £3 for both. No one counts interest and depreciation. Yet we made a rapid calculation that even if true cost were charged, the farmer would make lots of money even at a wheat price of £40 or £30. Without half trying he can get 1,200 lbs per acre. With better methods of cultivation he can easily get 1,500 lbs, with some fertilizer he can get a ton.

Since the soil is impermeable, once it is plowed by tractor, the farmers form beds of 6 x 6 ft. with ridges. Once a week the water is let in and kept there. It penetrates about one foot but no more, enough for the wheat, then evaporates. As the crop is irrigated, weather does not affect the harvest.

One of Drew's chief problems is salt content. Apparently, the irrigation process itself leaches the salt out. One reason John wants to proceed more slowly with the scheme than the politicians is that the salinity varies, and generally declines with distance from Chad.

He is also experimenting with alternative crops, but has to keep this quiet, as the politicians want wheat only. But it turns out that one can have rice as a wet season crop, so that for three years running one can have two crops, followed by three years fallow. Also, legumes and onions can probably be grown, and will eventually be more profitable than wheat.

What fascinates me about this scheme and others John Goss has developed is that they all start small, are highly successful, grow to be self-supporting and self-financing, provide for their own expansion, and seem eventually to grow to substantial size, much faster than the originally much more ambitious large-scale and fabulously costly farm settlements of the South. I think Jerry Wells might like to make a comparative study of the Bornu Province schemes and the Western and Eastern Region farm settlement schemes.

One would have to look carefully at cost. The Southern schemes include a lot of roads and social overhead absent from the Northern ones. Yet a crude calculation I made with John indicated that the latter are still by far more successful. How far this is because in the North, but not the South, one can have mixed farming, is a question. But tree crops such as cocoa are on the whole more valuable.

It may be that John Goss or Wally Price are better people. They are not only unusually nice, but dedicated and obviously highly competent. I again raised the problem of a crash program for extension workers with him. Extension work, not capital, is the key to agricultural development. No one likes the word 'crash program.' Yet John Goss thought it would work and it is the only thing that would.

The way he put it, though, was that one should concentrate on an area, so that people could see results for imitation. For example, they now had too many mixed farmers for individual supervision. So they pick a model farm in an area, work with it, and run a sort of group extension by organizing continuous visits to that model farm. Also he felt it was important to give an extension worker a specific task to do, again so he can see results. This would also help overcome the general apathy of the locals to extension work. Most of them just sit in the bush and draw their salary. They try to make extension prestigious by sending fellows off to conferences and courses abroad. Every time a man comes back he has more authority and enthusiasm. But this idea of a specific task is exactly the heart of a crash program. So is the idea of group work...

September 8....We didn't get stuck, *mirabili dictu*, but we did get lost trying to find the camel track leading due south along a line of boreholes to Gidam Bari and Gajiram. We suddenly found ourselves near Arege again, then near our weaver bird colony. The landscape was spectacularly beautiful – grass coming to the windows, views of Lake Chad and wonderful wildlife, including Thompson's gazelle and the very rare Dama gazelle with a beautiful white belly and rear...We saw hyenas, and I thought I saw an ostrich, but it was just a Denham bustard. Still, it was damn big. We saw a huge flock of pelicans standing in the water.

We tried for a while to cross a largish plain but were always stopped by swamp. Finally John decided we had chased enough gazelles, took out his compass and we finally found our camel track...The millet and guinea corn was high. We drove two in front, two standing on the tail board, and I chatted with John and Wally about costs of agricultural production and development problems.

I said I liked the idea of schemes that could finance their own growth and keep their profits rather than handing them over to the central, i.e., Regional authority. They liked the idea too, and confessed they were doing this behind the back of Kaduna. I would have listened more attentively had I not worried about running out of gas in the middle of nowhere. To be sure we met plenty of camels, but they don't carry gas. We also met plenty of cattle moving north to French territory to evade tax. The jangili, the cattle tax, is about to be collected...

We made Gajiram, and luckily our bird control truck was there. We got gas from it, and pressed on...In Maiduguri...everyone was surprised that we had succeeded in reaching Abadan and getting back in time...Apparently most people think the trip is too strenuous. I really had forgotten how much I enjoy this sort of outdoor life. Of course it also depends on the company. Competent and friendly companions like John Goss and Wally Price are rare.

Both asked me to come back soon. They were enthusiastic about the possibility of Jerry Wells doing a study and they thought the Ministry of Agriculture could find funds for it, as well as the necessary vehicle. John hoped I would bring the family. He would fix something up so we could make the trip without danger. He would just take a few extra days and drive slowly. With a few DDT bombs it ought not to be too uncomfortable. The camp beds are OK. But a camel track just isn't a super highway. Perhaps we can fly over the area in a small plane.

September 9....We made flight reservations home. Maiduguri has only two planes a week but a huge airport. It was an American base during the war, and a staging area for the Middle Eastern theater...At 2:00 PM we finally left with the good wishes of the skeptics, who thought we wouldn't get to Kano, because the rains had washed bridges away, and no truck had been in from Kano for days. They turned out to be half right. Two bridges were washed away, but two Bailey bridges had taken their place, and light vehicles were permitted.

Even then the misadventures did not end. In Potiskum, we gassed up. The local yokel put the oil into the radiator instead of the motor, and it took us almost an hour to drain and wash the radiator. But for the rest, we arrived in Kano at 10:30 AM after $8^1/_2$ hours driving, which isn't bad for 372 miles.

...The plane from London was on time, and got us on time to Lagos, at 7:15 PM...We went first to see Toby, who also returned only yesterday night. He was fed up with the minister. Apparently everyone except the Prime Minister was crazy, and things are somewhat disorganized. He said he will go on leave by the end of the month, since he hasn't heard from Rivkin, and must make arrangements...

Lyle appeared happy to see me...He said he had noticed that I got fidgety about once a month and needed to take a trip once in a while. Maybe. He had held the fort alone...

I am doing most of the final writing. Lyle is superb in organizing the staff, getting them to turn out stuff. Two of them are good, one of our bad ones, though personally the nicest, got promoted out of the planning unit, and two are not too good. We will let Peter supervise those two. He has improved tremendously.

Well, now there is no more time to collect more facts. And we must come to a judgment.

September 11, 1961

...At 12 Booker appeared from the UN to inquire what they could do for us and our statistics. I told him the UN had promised us a chief statistician for two years, and we still had not got one...He wanted to know what I thought of Martin from Kenya. I said I had met him only once at MIT, and in one hour he had not succeeded in saying a kind word about anyone I knew or didn't know, for that matter. (Toby told me afterwards he had been rejected on security grounds.)

Did we need a demographer? I said no. We needed a staff leader who could organize the work and get it out. A lot of our data never got analyzed. I also thought someone should come and construct a really useful Statistical Abstract...Booker thought that could lead to a 2–3 months assignment. Altogether not a very satisfactory meeting. We obviously won't get anyone decent, unless we find him first and suggest his name to the UN. Only I don't really know anyone.

At 2:00 PM, three fellows from Toronto University appeared, on their way from Sierra Leone to East Africa...They had been under UNESCO auspices in Sierra Leone, without clear terms of reference. Typical UNESCO...

At 6:00 PM I went over to Prasad with Toby to work out a timetable. We must have a 'plan' for the National Economic Council meeting on Nov. 22. This means it must be in their hands by Nov. 5, and in the hands of the Council of Ministers by Oct. 15, so our deadline is Oct. 7. The Regions must come across in that week or else. Rivkin comes back Sept. 25. Wilson Schmidt will be with him, but a new man from ICA and the man from State haven't been named yet.

I told Prasad we had done better on the Federal level than anticipated, but much worse Regionally. The Regions just hadn't performed. He agreed, but thought it was due to their fear of putting anything on paper not already OK'd by the Sardauna or Okpara, the Premier of the East. Frank Moore called to tell me that Pius had done nothing beyond what we had done together a long time ago. He had just added figures horizontally instead of vertically.

They talked a little of the NEC meeting, which must have been something, with the PM a rock of sense in the middle of the madhouse. We had been attacked for trying to spend too much money federally, and there were clamors for changing the Federal-Regional allocation of revenues. In fact, Philip Barton was charged with preparing such a paper, and he called me about it. I had to refer him to the Federal Ministry of Finance, since I took their revenue projections, only making the Regional ones. As Toby pointed out, the constitution settles that, and it can't be changed overnight. In addition, not only had the Federal Government prepared all the papers for JPC in the last half year, but all had been prepared by us, specifically by myself. Let them submit papers for discussion…

Prasad then suggested I draft a plan-outline to discuss with him, Toby and Lyle. I agreed, but wanted guidance. He said it should not be too technical, 50 printed pages, readable for ministers. The technical document would be written later. I said I knew he distrusted national accounts, but I felt we had to have a chapter in national income terms. To my surprise and relief he agreed.

How did he envisage the chapters on the Federal Plan? He thought we should have targets of X kwh of electricity produced, etc. I agreed but felt the chapter should contain some of our payoff calculations. He felt that was too technical for the Oct. 15 document. I said I didn't want to be too technical, but thought it must be shown that we had made payoff calculations, and would get more resources back than we put in. I was very leery of physical planning, possibly resulting from my East German studies. We agreed to that. I asked where policies towards the private sector, exchange control, fiscal policies, surveys, etc. came in. His suggestions were vague – he thought I should try an outline which we could then discuss.

I have learned that Prasad gives in easily when he doesn't think it matters, then makes you do the work, and then changes everything around. Sometimes I don't mind, sometimes I do…

September 12.…I saw the Minister twice to report to him. For the first time I saw him relaxed in Western dress – shirtsleeves without necktie. He puts his native dress on as soon as a visitor appears. He was pleased that I had been in his home district and was enthusiastic. I said I was particularly proud that, being nearly 50, I could still take the reasonably rough life and in fact enjoy it. He was surprised at my age. Afterwards it seemed politically astute to have mentioned it.

He was going to see the Sardauna and see whether I could work out a farm settlement plan for the North. This scared me. I am not an agricultural expert, and Regional-Federal relations are delicate. I said Bernie Jensen in the North was an agricultural expert and I was afraid to step on Regional toes. His eyes darkened as if I had said something displeasing. He said if I had attended the NEC meetings at Enugu, I would know that the Regions wanted the Federal Government to do more. This is exactly the opposite of what I had heard, but I said nothing.

The Minister also wanted a list of projects with my sense of priorities before he left on September 22 on Phase Two of the Economic Mission. I promised to do what I could but pointed out I could not be specific where we had not yet made payoff calculations.

I then wrote an outline of the draft plan, a job I don't particularly like. I hate outlines, period…Toby had a number of good suggestions. He had studied our Rand Corporation pamphlet on 'The Failures of the Bank Mission', and used it now to criticize my outline and suggest amendments. We then called Prasad, said we were coming with the outline and to have a drink ready. I had followed Prasad's suggestions for the first five of nine chapters but he had quite different ideas, unaware that they contradicted his ideas of the day before – which I had in writing. This didn't quite surprise or bother me. He wanted to sleep over it and then meet on an outline prepared by him. I haven't heard yet, and it is now five days later.

I went with Toby to his place for a drink, and we discussed the situation. I pointed out that Prasad had changed completely what the draft plan should look like, and I would continue revising the figures until I heard from him…

September 14. The Ministry of Finance forwarded, for my comment, the export projections sent them by Skillings of the IBRD…Mellanid was here to study the location of a refinery, and told us one of the pipelines works much below capacity because the oil is too waxy, but the other hopefully will go up to capacity…

September 15. Work, work, work, without necessarily getting anywhere. Toby is nervous that we haven't got all our ministry programs back to the ministers. So am I…

September 16. Not having heard from Prasad, I started dictating a first chapter of the Plan anyway…

At noon Robinson of Shell came…Our refinery isn't in the bag yet, apparently because Okpara makes difficulties. Everyone is worried about selling crude oil: there just is too much around. Though Nigerian crude is sulfur-free, making it desirable because it can be more easily and cheaply refined – sulfur-containing crude requires equipment of special steel – it is really most suitable for the American market with its high gasoline needs. But the US market is quite isolated and separate from Europe, where our crude will have to be sold.

Robinson said Shell is a deficit company which has to buy crude from other oil companies. In particular they are committed to taking Middle Eastern oil from Gulf, which has surpluses. There isn't much money in oil these days. Particularly as the old cartel-like arrangements are rapidly being eroded. Almost all of Shell's exploration team are Swiss.

…At 6:00 PM I went to a cocktail party for a Gray, a young man just out of Harvard, who is with ICA…

The second part of the rains has come. It is wet, but pleasantly cool. On the whole this was a reasonably dry and cool summer. Cool means about 80°.

September 18. Work on the Ministry of Health submissions. They don't make sense, aren't thought through. I'll see their PS tomorrow, also the one in Education.

September 24, 1961

It is finally Sunday again, the only day when I have an iron rule to see nobody, absolutely nobody before afternoon…There is considerable tension in the office now, because of the incredible deadlines we have to meet, because of general confusion, because the Regions have not come through with their stuff, because of personality clashes. I am told I have not given sufficient leadership, which may or may not be true. But the fact is I have been protecting my outfit the best I could, and when they get on my nerves, I go into the wilds to recover. In any case, I am now hanging on desperately, trying not to say words I would regret later, not to stoop to the level of others, to remain faithful to my own conception of what I am about: to let people have maximum freedom as long as they meet the deadlines – which they don't always do.

Toby Lewis goes on leave today…He has been a tower of strength to us. He will return in November via India.

I don't look forward to the next two months. The tensions in the office, and between us and Prasad, are bound to rise. Thus far, Toby's tact and efficiency has smoothed everything over. I have the efficiency, but not the tact. Lyle has neither. Th deputy who will take Toby's place is not up to the job, and will lean heavily on us, which is all right on substantive, but not on administrative points.

On Oct. 18 we will get a new Deputy Permanent Secretary, Lardner, a Sierra Leonian with a reputation for inefficiency and anti-European feeling. We will also get a young man, Shaddock, from the Cameroons who worked with Toby in the East and is to help us write the final document.

Prasad will work three-quarters with me, while keeping one quarter to himself, to maintain the mystique of the all-knowing advisor. If I disagree with him in public, the whole planning operation will break down. But we are bound to disagree sharply on substantive points: program size, inflation control, exchange control, where I take a conservative line as the only one appropriate to Nigerian circumstances. I may have to go to the PM, but don't quite know how to do it without creating bad feelings, and only Toby could have helped.

Meanwhile we had some more minor successes. I had been objecting to nationalization of profitable enterprises as capital exports when we were trying to attract capital imports. The Government's legitimate wish to exercise some control could be met without investing funds urgently needed elsewhere. Well the Cabinet agreed to my line, and Toby showed me the file where the Minister says specifically he agrees with my arguments and would ensure Cabinet got them. This is a personal success, moreover I have saved the economy about £6 million.

Toby just dropped in. I was happy to hear Prasad has been saying he and I have to stick together if our operation is to succeed. He and Lyle sometimes tell me how things were in India or Pakistan, Nigeria is nothing like anything they knew, we are further along in five months than they were in India and Pakistan after three years. Therefore we should do things as in India and Pakistan.

My response is: (a) I don't know India or Pakistan but only Nigeria, (b) I am the best economist in West Africa, (c) I know where I am going and have tried to explain it dozens of times orally and at least twice in writing, (d) my strength is a combination of seeing detail in a general context, and insisting on both, (e) our success in being ahead of India and Pakistan is due to excellent cooperation all around, which is Toby's merit, hard work which is Lyle's and all our merit, and a sense of direction and ability to pull together detail, which is mine.

Well, enough of complaining. I just had to get it out…

September 18. Work to draft a chapter, and in the evening a cocktail party given by the US Embassy for an American trade mission. Since I hadn't gone for some time I felt I had to go – it was dull as expected.

September 19. First an interview with the PS Health and his chief medical advisor. I explained our criteria for programs lacking payoff in money terms. We wanted to know doctors trained, patients served, beds supplied. Was the program of national interest, such as doctor training, or purely of local interest? If mainly local, we felt that even with the Ministry of Health in charge, local Lagos rather than Federal funds should pay for it. We wanted to know where staff was expected to come from, and it was not an adequate answer to say you could always get staff if enough money was available. I knew differently from staffing problems at the University of Michigan.

We wanted to know whether hospital sites had been found, and why costs were so high. And we opposed budgeting large token amounts, e.g. £500,000, on the ground, first, that every crooked contractor in the country would read it and make sure the cost was no less than that, and secondly, that, rather than reserving funds for the ministry at a later date, or saving money in a general development fund, underspending would lead to execution of lower-priority projects which happened to be ready.

After getting some answers, I went back and dictated some of the program evaluation, calculated some more, cut altogether £7 million from the submission as low-priority and/or not sufficiently thought through, and got the revised program ready to send the Ministry for their comments in less than 24 hours, something of an efficiency record. The next day I did the same thing for the education program. In both cases I came up against a linguistic problem. When I asked: where are the pre-clinical students going to come from?, I got the answer: "from all over Nigeria," when what I meant was: have you provided for the training of sufficient numbers of pre-clinical students to fill your classrooms?

In both cases I also ran into some misunderstanding of planning. Again and again, people felt that once a plan was agreed upon it would be inflexible. The PS Health, Lawson, a Nigerian, asked me: "What assurance have I of getting the money needed for a children's hospital, if you only allow me a £100,000 token budget, in lieu of the £500,000 I requested?" I said, he would have none. The point of planning wasn't to foretell the future, which I knew no more than he, but to provide a sense of direction and an overall view, to assure consistency. When his project was ready it would be considered in light of the then available resources and the competing claims on them. If the cocoa price stayed up, lots of things would become possible which would have to be cut out if it fell.

In the evening I had the German ambassador, Count Posadowsky-Wehner and Toby for dinner…Both showed great diplomatic tact, which means to be judiciously indiscreet. I am learning a little about it…The ambassador told us £2 million a year for 10 years would be available for long-term, low-interest loans, not tied to purchases in Germany…

I also learned about the Ferrostahl steel mill proposal. We now have it officially. It is more honest than our Westinghouse proposal. The ambassador said it was deliberately pessimistic. The cost is larger than either the company or the German government want to finance. Moreover, after bad experiences with steel mills in India and Iran, the Germans are extra careful.

The Indians insisted on getting the most modern steel mill, even more modern than anything in Germany. It was therefore not fully tested – something which scares us about the Westinghouse proposal, which uses an untried process. Thirty-six German firms participated in building it, without proper coordination, nor any provision for training Indians to take over. I had also heard from an Indian that the local engineers were too conceited to want to learn, and took longer for repairs than would have been necessary had the Germans – who weren't too sure of themselves either – had their way.

I think the evening helped to smooth German-Nigerian, German-English, and German-American relations. We have established an informal confidential contact. I shall invite Rivkin and Posadowsky together...

September 20. Work on the Ministry of Education program. Given a Cabinet decision on overall size and direction, there was no point in challenging it directly. I made a number of suggestions and changes. First, I shifted all provision for scholarships and subsidies to the Regions out of the recurrent into the capital budget. The reason is, first, that they are *au fonds perdu*, and really in the nature of a capital cost. Secondly, education and, to a minor extent, health are exceptions to the general rule that aid is available only for capital, not recurrent, costs. Third, Prasad had the excellent idea of separating education from the rest of the development program, forming a special international consortium.

Secondly, I insisted on making student-teacher ratios less favorable. Even in America or England we don't hold elementary school classes down to 37 pupils, and I suggested planning for 40. Even this is unrealistic, as teachers just aren't available. I made similar suggestions for high schools, but not for so-called Sixth Forms and Universities, where a reduction in teacher-student ratios is not really feasible. I calculated recurrent cost savings, and capital cost with fewer teachers and classrooms – and drew attention of the M. of Ed. to the Koenigsberger report with its suggestions for keeping down construction costs...

September 21. The morning was full, with one interruption after another. At 12:30 PM we discussed the American mission...It was agreed we would be as frank as ever, but we were also as little ready as ever. In addition Toby, who was supposed to stay, won't be here. But I am getting the Central Bank to provide something on increasing small savings.

Taxation is the really tricky problem. Specific proposals can't be discussed in a public document because of budget secrecy, and yet revenue targets must be indicated. I just have to wait until Reg Clarke comes back, to take my cue from him. Finance now has an interregnum. Murray is gone, Henry Omanai goes today, and Clarke won't be back until the end of next week. Meanwhile there is no one around.

I drafted a second chapter in the afternoon...At 9:00 PM I was at the Hansens for supper with Jensen, who needed cheering. I seem to have done something to offend him. If so, I don't know what it is. In any case, he brought the unevaluated figures with him and gave them to me, at the request of Alhaji Ali Akilu, the successor of Peter Gibbs. While I can't do much with figures lacking explanatory text, I appreciated the gesture. Jensen said the three new PSs – Development (Akilu), Finance (Talib), and Agriculture (Lawan) – were good but inexperienced, and wanted to find their feet first. This is fair enough. My offer of help was appreciated but premature until Akilu was firm in the saddle. He would call when he wanted me to come. I took note...

I was quite impressed by what Jensen had accomplished, and told him so. He brought tables showing the probable effects of seed improvement, fertilizer, expansion of acreage, and weather on all major and most minor crops. Agriculture being the key sector, this is a major achievement. The tables also show possible increases based on Samaru experiment station results, against probable execution with limited extension staff.

Jensen also had details on capital and recurrent costs, foreign exchange component, and manpower requirements of numerous projects. Some of the data required for payoff studies was missing, but he was well on the way. The program was too large, but Akilu knew this and wanted to cut it down himself.

September 22. We had our JPC meeting, the main outcome being an agreed timetable for getting the Regional plans. I was put on the spot twice. First Prasad made me secretary of a subcommittee on Federal subsidies to the Regions. The Regions were asked to send me their views, I would circulate them and write a report on the subsequent discussion. I protested that the day has only 24 hours, however Lyle has too much to do as it is. So I am it.

I was asked about the efficiency of the marketing company. I gave it to them straight from the shoulder. I didn't know what they meant by efficiency. If they meant that the marketing company should sell more aggressively, the answer was that there were no unsold stocks. If they meant that people had to buy through London, there wasn't anything wrong with that, but it wasn't true anyway. Anyone willing to pay could buy in Lagos and pick it up there.

Prasad said that Canadians and others complained they had to pick up the stuff in London, why not in Lagos, saving freight commissions etc.? I said there was nothing to stop them. Someone said they couldn't. I said I frequently drove along the marina and noticed ships from all nations, including East Germans and Russians, and just what were they doing there? Sightseeing?

I was then told not to be brainwashed by the marketing company, which I in turn didn't take kindly. I said if I were to report on the efficiency of the marketing company, I wanted to know the criteria. But by any criteria I knew, Sir Eric Tansley deserved a gold medal. That stopped the discussion. Then they talked about a terminal market in Lagos, and it was plain no one had any notion what that was, that it was a futures market. Somehow they thought it had to do with picking up the stuff in Lagos. Where else could one pick it up anyway?

As you see, I was irritated. Pius Okigbo had brought a battery of his colleagues to explain their plan, with nothing in writing. So this was postponed, much to my annoyance. I had wanted to push him to produce something. After a recess the Regions were asked to give us a list of projects to discuss with the American mission, once more I was it. Neil Morrison, normally the JPC secretary, had to go, and I had to take the minutes. That wasn't too bad.

Afterwards Frank Moore came home for lunch to unburden himself. He was furious with Pius, who was staying a week in Lagos to proofread galleys of the National Accounts volume and then off to ECA/Addis instead of ER planning. Everything was shoved into Frank's lap. He found files unattended since July.

He did have a satisfactory talk with ER Premier Okpara, who blew his top when he saw £2 million apiece for farm settlements and said £500,000 was more like it. Why shouldn't farm boys work on their houses and for their subsistence while learning? He told Frank and Pius to go ahead and cut the program as they thought reasonable. That made them happy and they went ahead. But when it came to the Executive Committee Meeting, all cuts were restored and Okpara said nothing.

I tried to cheer Frank up, pointing out that I didn't care about the numbers as long as we got the priorities straight. They couldn't do everything anyway, and if we only could do first things first...

In the evening, NRMB secretary Fenn and Moore came for dinner; Lyle dropped in later. Fenn added to our woes. Even after the elections, which wiped out all but the tiniest vestiges of opposition, giving him complete control of the Northern Region, the Sardauna won't lower farm prices. I had calculated marketing board losses over the next five years if world prices fall as anticipated by the IBRD and Northern producer prices stay where they are now. They are staggering. Now Fenn says the NRMB will have trouble financing next year's crop if it is good, as expected. Jensen told me he had trouble getting past meteorological data. They are kept secret to prevent speculation on the crop outturn!

Note

1   Matthew and Thomas are the two sons of Wolfgang and Vögi Stolper.

Chapter 10

September 24–November 6, 1961
Rivkin Mission Returns, Negotiations with Regions, "Irresponsible" Eastern Region Plan, New Permanent Secretary Godfrey Lardner, JPC Discusses Plan Memo

October 2, 1961 (Lagos)

Yesterday was the first anniversary of the Federation of Nigeria, and there was both good weather and a garden party to which none of us got invited. (The American mission did, though.) Today are the official festivities, parades of schoolchildren and the military etc., but as it did a year ago, it is raining cats and dogs. The second rains, marking the end of the rainy season, have finally come after an unusually dry and not unpleasant summer, and everything is rained out...

Though the week was strenuous, there is little to tell. Part of the reason is that I am nervous and anxious to get on with drafting the central chapter of the plan on the Federal Program. And there are other problems about which I must write. I am missing Toby Lewis's skill and power. It is a real catastrophe that he went so suddenly.

September 24. We saw Toby and the Minister off. The latter was in a good mood but there was tension. Neil Morrison, who acts for Toby until Lardner comes from ECA-Addis to be acting PS, let slip that I am writing the draft plan to give the Council of Ministers by Oct. 15. Ibrahim said with icy voice: you are not to submit the draft plan to Council while I, Chief Festus and Dipcherima are absent. If you do, there will be a real catastrophe. So that is that. It means Prasad will have to go to the Prime Minister and get an order from him...

September 26. I was at the airport at 7:05 AM to meet the Rivkin mission. I got them through passport and customs in 20 minutes. For the rest of the day I worked on the draft plan. I knew the rest of the week would not be fun.

September 27. Two hours at the Dept. of Statistics. We agreed there should be a number of subindices to indicate trends in (i) import content of domestic manufacture, and (ii) prices of domestic content as well as domestic foodstuffs at wholesale. The rest of the day was spent bringing earlier calculations up to date. Some of the revisions are pretty pessimistic, and I don't know what to do about them...

September 28. First meeting with the American mission. Prasad, chairing, asked for an indication of the aid we could get. Rivkin said that depended on the plan, no project could be evaluated except in the context of the plan, and he could say no more than was in [his earlier] report until he had the plan, which he hoped to have before the Mission left.

Prasad explained our timetable, pressures and difficulties, and said all we would have by Oct. 18 was a draft by the technicians, which then would be changed any way the politicians or statesmen saw fit. And that was a slow process.

Being a democrat, Rivkin was aware of the difference between official and political decisions, and welcomed it. He hoped Nigeria would stay free and slow and deliberate in making her decisions. All he wanted was the official plan, so he could make a presentation to Congress and eventually the IBRD and an international consortium.

Pressed further, he told the Ministry of Foreign Affairs representative that America was trying to get away from making loans and grants on a political basis, hence he had to insist on a plan document, however preliminary. And he thought it was in Nigeria's interest to get away from a political decision, since political conditions were the worst strings that could be attached to aid, much worse than economic strings. Most people, including Prasad, got the point, though I am sure Neil Morrison did not, nor (I fear) did Foreign Affairs...

From my standpoint, the day's most important event was that Reg Clarke is back as PS Finance. After the meeting he asked me and Keep of the Central Bank over to his office. I hope Reg can fill the gap left by Toby's absence. He is nice and highly intelligent.

I was delighted that Clarke took my view throughout. We agreed about sterling reserves and domestic savings. I felt we should aim at maintaining four month imports' worth of sterling reserves, and should count the automatic drawing rights at the IMF as part of the reserves. This suited Clarke and we persuaded Keep to go along. Keep obviously understands nothing, but bows to Clarke's authority though not to mine, which he considers "theoretical." I tried to soothe him by pointing out that the agreed figure wasn't too different from his formula – 60% of currency in circulation – and he should humor the professor in me by getting the argument straight. Clarke and I will now be up against both the Central Bank and Prasad, hammering at us from opposite sides.

Clarke also thought we could borrow more internally than the Central Bank had thought, which pleased me too. For Keep just has no imagination, no theoretical knowledge and the most narrow technical conception of what a central bank is about.

For the rest, there was crisis after crisis. Patricia was transferred to the High Court. While we had got along fine, some friction had developed, and it was agreed with Toby that she should be transferred. But it was done in such a brutal manner that I protested, and tried to reverse the decision. It cost me a lot of energy and nerves and didn't work. I wonder who the new secretary will be, and how good. The secretaries are being pushed around quite a bit, and with Toby's protection absent, it's Patricia's turn to be kicked. I still have to see what I can do, which will be little enough.

September 29. All morning meeting with the Mission. I was asked to outline the plan's size, financing gap, priorities. I was taken back, for I had not expected it, and had brought none of my papers, but acquitted myself reasonably well. Clarke outlined our agreed position on sterling reserves and internal borrowing. Prasad registered the expected disagreement. He thought we could do with a 25% currency reserve. He noted his conception of the function of reserves differed from mine, but for purposes of bargaining he would accept the Clarke-Stolper figure.

I said that men of competence and good will could disagree on the exact amount needed, or the formula to arrive at them, but even if I accepted his figure, sterling reserves would still be pitifully below needs. I outlined our methods of evaluating programs, and explained that "payoff" was always calculated in appropriate terms: money, number of doctors trained, students graduated. I said on the whole any well-thought-out project was probably worth executing. Prasad said one couldn't always calculate payoff in terms of money, and I repeated the other pay-off criteria. He asked whether it was true that we had cut out sewerage in Lagos. I said, no, but my Minister had talked about cutting it out at NEC…

At 8:00 PM Lyle, Arnold and Wilson Schmidt came over. We showed them our program analyses, most of them Lyle's work. We were careful – though we told them everything they wanted to know – for our evaluations go only to the ministry concerned and to Finance. They are attempts to reach a reasonable position to which we, Finance and the line ministry can agree.

I also showed Arnold the papers I had written to Prasad, the Minister, and the staff, outlining the method of planning. Some responded to requests from the Minister, some were done on my initiative, eliciting answers from Prasad. By this time I am beginning to get reconciled that I have much the best in the argument, but that I don't carry people with me, and am woefully deficient at carrying my view into policy, unless I have Toby's aid, and hopefully Reg Clarke's.

Moreover, while I like Prasad and respect him – for he knows a lot of things I don't – he is not as good an economist as I am, and his arguments are frequently fuzzy and untenable. And it is clear he doesn't believe in planning, but rather in the IBRD's project approach. Still I *have* to get along with him and on a personal basis this is easy. Also he doesn't work as hard as I, and is a freewheeler. Which means that he depends on Lyle and me. When Arnold asked him whether he was working hard, he said "No, but Wolf is." That's about it. If Nigeria gets money, it will be more because of what I do. So that is one consolation for the near nervous wreck I am by now…

September 30. I dreaded today's meeting with the mission. Prasad presented the projects he wanted the US to consider, starting with the Federal ones, then going over a list of regional ones given to us at the last JPC meeting and written up by me as secretary of the meeting. Prasad talked for two hours. Rivkin answered in five minutes. He took note, said he would transmit what he was asked to do, but decisions would depend on the plan, in whose context projects had to be evaluated. Rivkin told me afterwards that he had told Prasad beforehand not to press him too hard on projects.

Prasad also complained that not enough US capital was coming to Nigeria. Most capital was British and came in to protect an existing market. Rivkin said he hoped more private capital would come in, but statements by political leaders, even if not the Government, raised doubts in the minds of investors. Prasad said this was also true in the US, and the world had learned to distinguish between official statements and statements by individual senators or congressmen. Rivkin then said he was willing to quote chapter and verse if pressed, and ended by citing "is impossible to say tactfully, the general problem of, let us say, dash," i.e. corruption. I liked Arnold's sharpness and incisiveness, even penetrating Neil Morrison, who otherwise had little clue as to what was going on.

In fact, afterwards Morrison told me: see, the meeting went well. I thought not. We needed a plan, and the pressure was on me. Morrison's idea of how things are done was "Well, you will have a plan, and if worse comes to worse, the PM will speak to Kennedy. There is just enough truth in it to be uncomfortable but not enough for consolation." I went home pretty depressed and tired...

October 1 (Sunday)....We took Arnold and Wilson to Badagri, an old slaving town on the creek west of Lagos, close to the Dahomey border. The road is paved even though the map shows it as secondary. Badagri has a quite different character from the other villages, even though the people are Yoruba. The houses are made of reed, there are fences, and it is rather pleasant to look at, not like Benin, which to this day has for me, at least, a sinister aspect...The beach was as beautiful as Lagos' Victoria beach, straight and with terrific surf. There is no natural harbor between Dakar and Lagos, and the coast must be rather frightening for shipping...

We rented a canoe for the outrageous price of £1 to take us across the creek to the strip of land leading to the open ocean...When we wanted to leave, our boat had gone after other business. The canoe that finally came was smaller...When we got back I refused to pay the £1 on the ground they had not kept their bargain. I yelled and made a scene, partly because I have learned that this is the only way to deal with WAWA.[1] The young boy who was our guide said "You have fabulous money, why don't you want to pay us?" He also wanted money for watching the car. After a while they believed I was really angry at them and started to apologize: "Don't be annoyed, sir..."

Exploitation seems to be old stuff. I am just reading Alan Moorehead's 'The White Nile,' where it is clear that none of the old explorers were permitted to proceed until the local chief had extracted what he thought he could!

This morning I drafted one chapter on the balance of payments, in the afternoon I will draft the chapter on the Federal Plan.

October 8, 1961

The letters from home are the only thing keeping up my morale. There is a tremendous amount of work, much too much for Lyle, Peter and me. Our African staff is willing in part, but we lost our best-trained and hardest-working man to the Economic Mission now traipsing around the world. The others are neither very well-trained, nor very keen; they are essentially civil servants. The Economic Planning Unit is not yet well-established; it is not seen as a means for promotion, which is what all the assistant secretaries think about most of the time. Until we get a Senior Assistant Secretary post and put one of our own men in it, we shall have this problem. Yet our influence has become substantial, entirely because we perform and because of the quality of our work.

Lyle and Peter are now working together on the Federal Ministry programs. Lyle is excellent at it. The problems are formidable. On the one hand we get good cooperation, the ministries give us facts and figures they will not give even to other Federal Government departments. On the other hand, while our job is to analyze ruthlessly and propose more sensible expenditure patterns, each PS must defend the wishes of his minister.

Moreover we have not yet succeeded in getting our planning concept across. PSs and ministers still think in terms of budgets. They see a Five-Year Plan essentially as a fixed Five-Year Budget. They want as much as possible now because they're afraid they won't get any new projects until five years hence. Our concept is the opposite. We continuously stress that we know the future as little as they do, that the plan must be flexible and continuously watched and changed in light of resource availability and emerging needs, that its main function is to give an overall picture and sense of direction...

So Lyle's task – and to a lesser extent mine – is to persuade PSs and ministers to accept cuts now while leaving the door open for later increases. We are working endless hours – I usually start at 6 AM but quit early, while Lyle starts somewhat later and works later – and it proves how much we respect each other that tempers fly only rarely, mildly and never for long. Lyle is quite indispensable now. So is Peter. I myself am supposed to be the spider in the center of the net, the central focus, but in addition I do a lot of detailed work. All hands are badly needed.

My main task is writing a first draft. The first two chapters – past performance and overall view of the future – are drafted, so is Chapter 8 on the balance of payments. Tonight I ought to finish the chapter on the Federal Government plan...It is an interesting and challenging task to get across in a paragraph or two (1) a description of the projects, (2) payoff in physical terms, and indications of (3) payoff in economic terms, (4) consistency with other programs, and (5) feasibility. I don't know how far I'll succeed, but I certainly work hard at trying.

October 3. Kingsley is back...I went over to report to him and get some moral support. The tropics do get us with their evenness day after day – it is hard to realize that in the States, they are getting cool weather just as ours begins to turn really hot.

I said that on the Federal level we were doing really well, but that in the Regions, things were not as good as we could wish. To start with, I had offended the North pretty badly with my trip to Kano, which was interpreted as snooping. Kingsley said to forget about it. Akilu, the new PS Planning, was a good man, not one to bear a grudge. Anyway, I pointed out to Don that my self confidence had suffered a small shock, that I had prided myself on tact, and now had made a worse *faux pas* in the North than Lyle had done before I came.

In the West things seemed to be going all right...But in the East, Pius had disappointed us all. In fact he had left Enugu, first for Lagos, then for Addis, leaving Frank in a position where only a miracle could bring him through.

In the North things were also not quite as dark. Jensen had performed miracles. They now have detailed projections for all major export and domestic crops, allowing for expanded acreage, getting research into farm practices, better seeds, possible fertilizer, and average weather. And on many programs they had enough data to permit analysis. I hoped they would come up with a plan which was reasonable, though perhaps a little later than we wanted.

Kingsley cheered me up. He still thought we were doing fine, that we were seven years ahead of the Pakistan group – Lyle thinks only 3–4 years – and that such disappointment was normal...

October 4 (Ibadan). I was in Wilson's office by 10:00 AM. Andrew Wilson is a tall, broad-faced Yoruba, able but new and uncertain, and as far as I can tell, straight and incorruptible. Thus far he lacks the experience and political backing of Chief Dina (who is on yet another economic mission in Europe), but he belongs to that able, honest and hardworking group of PSs of which the Western Region can boast. I am happy to be on a first name basis with him.

Andrew had asked me to come up. I was happy about that, because cooperation with the Regions must start with the Regions inviting us. That was precisely the mistake I had made in the North, inviting myself. We discussed the draft plan outline. Wilson suggested the Federal and Regional plan chapters should be appendices, while I should write a chapter on the National Plan. The idea is, of course, excellent, but whether it is feasible depends on what kind of documents I get from the Regions.

I outlined what I had been doing since I had seen him last. Then he produced the WR document, about 100 mimeographed pages, and asked me to read it critically, indicate whether it was what I wanted, etc. The executive committee was meeting that afternoon to pass on it. They gave me an office and I started studying the document. In turn I gave my draft chapters to Chukujekwe, the principal assistant secretary and second in command – an Ed Mason boy also – for his comment. On the whole I was impressed by the document and said so.

I made a lot of minor suggestions. There were also a few major ones, which nevertheless could be incorporated quickly, depending on how much and what kind of work underlay each paragraph. In our own case, about 10 pages of detailed payoff analysis underlies each program. I said we had to get across that we had many payoff calculations in economic terms, and that description of physical targets was not enough. After all the East Germans could increase their physical output and still get no richer. Could they please note repeatedly that they had made economic calculations and indicate the payoff, if ever so briefly.

Secondly, I noted they were still putting huge sums into farm settlements. Had they learned nothing from the past, were they unable to effect savings? If so, what were the sums involved? Did they get the investment per farmer down to a reasonable level etc.?

Thirdly, I noted that a very big sum earmarked for industrial expansion was a soft figure. I wanted discussion of policy towards the private sector, government participation, rolling over of capital, etc…

At 4:15 PM I went to Jerry Wells' flat to meet Chuck Brown and Ojetunji Aboyade. Brown is the ex-MIT man who married an English wife and now teaches in Ibadan where he is trying to work on a thesis for the London School. I had tried before unsuccessfully to get him access to Central Bank data, and promised to do so once more.

Aboyade is a tall Yoruba whom I met in Cambridge, England, the day he got his PhD. He is exceedingly able so I would like very much to see him teach at Michigan for a year. Him and Onitiri. He now teaches at Ibadan. He rejected a high-paid job as economic advisor to the Regional Government to stay academic.

My business with Aboyade was first to get his thesis on capital formation in Nigeria, part of the National Income Survey. We wanted his breakdown of imports by consumer goods, capital goods, etc. I also wanted his advice on some projections of construction, particularly whether it was safe to project an increasing role for cement. This is also important for assessing the steel mill. He said that outside of Lagos there was no shortage of housing, and private housing investment correlates with cocoa prices lagged two years.

For his part Aboyade wanted me to lecture at Ibadan on any topic of my choosing, and I accepted. I said they need not pay me anything, and I could stay with Jerry…

October 5.…Chukujekwe told me his executive committee had added only £$^1/_2$ million to the section on primary production, which wasn't bad, but they had not yet got around to the other parts. Until they had discussed and approved the whole, I was to keep the document secret. I obviously agreed. On my side I found the plan a responsible document, its overall size feasible, its financing possible. I was surprised and pleased at their projected budget surpluses, but wanted to be sure they were not overoptimistic.

On the other hand their projection of Marketing Board resources agreed closely with mine…Their main achievement is to hold education and general administrative expenses down, having expanded well ahead of other regions during the years of high raw material prices. I did request that they cross-reference different programs, to indicate we were dealing with an integrated plan rather than a list of projects. All this was accepted.

Chukujekwe then commented on my two draft chapters. His main objection was that I had made education the No. 1 priority. He said this was not so in the WR, where they had already achieved their aim…

I then went to see Professor Dike, an Ibo, who has taught at Northwestern, and is now Principal of UCI. He wrote the excellent book, *Trade and Politics in the Niger Delta*.[2]

He asked for Government to keep him informed about NISER's reorganization. He felt it was not doing enough in economics, too much in other social sciences, and that it did not serve sufficiently the needs of economic development. I couldn't agree more, and this is actually Government's chief criticism.

Prof. Dike felt NISER needed a better director to run it full time. There I also agreed. I couldn't tell him just what we planned to do, since that is still confidential, but I will ask Prasad to tell him. I did mention that Prasad had talked with Kingsley about supplying a top grade man. We both agreed that Barback wasn't the man for it. I was surprised, and not displeased, when Dike confidentially told me he wanted someone of more stature and maturity than Pius Okigbo. He sounded me out, but I said I was temperamentally unsuited to such a job, quite apart from the fact that, after so long an absence, I wanted to go home…

October 6.…At 10:30 AM another meeting with the Americans, this time on a special consortium for education. Prasad explained why education should be treated separately from other development. Special expenditures deserved foreign aid while the indigenous teacher corps was being built up. I backed him up as much as I could. But Rivkin wouldn't be diverted. He said he didn't want to sound like a broken record, but everything would and could be evaluated only in the context of a plan, and until they saw the plan as a whole, all he could do was bring our views to the attention of his Government. I wasn't unhappy about this, even though it means a lot of extra work for me. It is essentially what we are trying to do…

October 7.…Wilson Schmidt came for lunch to discuss a few more points of his report. I offered to read it, if Arnold and he wanted me to. I thought it would be funny if I wrote his report and he mine! Obviously it is out of the question, but it would be a new experiment in international cooperation…

At 7:00 PM we went to supper at Kingsley's. Frank Moore was there. We have to go through the Eastern Region program with a fine tooth comb. Well, a rougher one will do actually…Frank was furious at Pius, who not only had dumped everything in his lap, but had left lots of files unattended to which Frank had to clear up. In addition there is considerable administrative confusion in the East. The Eastern minister of information had published a newspaper article about the Region's achievements. A major one was expansion of social services, rescuing 20 girls from slavery. Kingsley says considerable slave trade still goes on, mostly for export to Saudi Arabia, but also some domestically. Frank told hair-raising stories about Cabinet meetings, but at least they have got the cost per farm settlement down from £2 million to a more reasonable £500,000…

October 9, 1961

Yesterday Frank Moore brought me what is humorously known as the Eastern Region Plan. It is a completely irresponsible document, much too big with no attempt at payoff calculations, feasibility and what-have-you. Frank also showed me a memo, to be introduced in the executive committee in Enugu, which lays down the law, and tries to build up a responsible and defensible program less than half the size of the present one.

Pius Okigbo had completely misled us, as I suspected. Even now, when he should have been in Enugu persuading the Premier to fight for a reasonable program, he took off for a week in Lagos and then on to Addis on a consultant job regarding a new African Development Bank, neither a matter of high priority.

We first thought the best course would be for Rivkin to talk frankly with Okpara. Yesterday Frank showed Arnold the 'plan' as he was authorized to do. Arnold was willing to take a charter plane from Kaduna to Enugu to talk with Okpara before the council meeting…Reg Clarke, PS Finance, thought it was a good idea and offered to pay for the trip…

Later, Neil Morrison refused to authorize the special trip as interference with the Regions. So Frank and I saw Prasad. Prasad took the Morrison line. It would be bad for an American to see Okpara and practically say: if you don't behave you don't get money…It was Pius' job to persuade Okpara to cut the program and raise taxes, and if necessary Prasad or I could go to Enugu to reason.

I said that Prasad's or my going would be resented just as much, not because he was Indian and I American, but because both of us were Federal boys. He didn't think so. I still feel it would be worth the risk to have Arnold go early, but I had to bow to Prasad's wishes and judgment. He may be right, but I think the risk worth it. In any case, we agreed we had to have Pius in, and pressure him to return immediately to Enugu and deal with the Premier. The trouble is that Pius' frequent absences have made him *persona non grata*. Also, Prasad's chickens are coming home to roost. He told the Easterners to think big, never mind finances, they can be found. Now they did it! It is a mess. Frank wants to resign and I don't blame him. Although on the Federal level things are all right, really.

October 11, 1961

October 9. Thirty-five pages of the Federal Plan are done. About 11:00 AM Pius came looking tired and sick. He said he wasn't feeling well…I said he had to go back to Enugu fast to talk with Premier Okpara about a sensible size of the plan, which he said he was going to do in any case. I said I was very disappointed and upset by what I got from the Eastern Region. Pius said he thought Frank could have gotten more, that he (Pius) had several times asked the Premier for a sensible plan size and composition, that Okpara had agreed and then reversed himself in Cabinet. This I know to be true and I sympathized. But I also pointed out to Pius rather sharply – for I had had little sleep – that he and not Frank was the PS; that I understood the politicians would do what they wanted with our plans, and that as a democrat I was prepared to accept that. But I was talking at a technical level. He had led me to believe that on that level the necessary studies underlying proper choices had been made, and that just wasn't so. The size of the ER plan was not only too big, considering available resources, large sections made no sense and would not be defensible even if all the money was available. Why did he tell me he had the stuff when he didn't?

He claimed there was more in the files than Frank Moore had given me, which is, of course, true. But Frank had indicated what they had and what they didn't have, and they didn't have much. I was a little outspoken and bitter about being let down by a man who is undoubtedly a competent economist and could have done the technical job.

I then insisted we see Prasad together to map out a strategy. We agreed that Pius should get home as fast as possible and try to ensure at least a sensible size for the plan. Then I insisted that, for a change, he should stay in Enugu, instead of traipsing off to Addis on low priority discussion of an all-African development bank. I said I had refused an official invitation to FAO/Rome because of the pressure of work, and I expected him to do likewise. H answered, "I could hit you for this, Wolf." I said "Go right ahead if it makes you feel better, but we've got to get the work done." I'm not sure whether we are now friends or not, but I'm sure I have done him a service by calling his bluff. If he isn't careful he will be finished with the Ford Foundation, with Rivkin and all the academics whom he likes.

Afterwards, Prasad urged me not to be too hard on Pius. The Eastern Region political situation is a madhouse, which is true. They are all crazy and volatile with the possible exception of Agriculture Minister Okeke, an ex-businessman with some sense. None of them has any concept of what they want, and personally I think they are lousy politicians. Okpara is an MD. One day he talks of nationalizing industry, the next day, that they must have private industry. One day farm settlements are to cost £2 million apiece, the next day £500,000, and only an idiot would think of more. So to escape the mad atmosphere Pius goes off to Addis or Cairo or Evanston, Illinois.

I said I understood this all too well, but why did Pius tell me one day they had studies which in fact they had not done; and why didn't he become an academic? There were perfectly honorable and lucrative alternatives to being a permanent secretary and an economic advisor to a bunch of erratic politicians.

When Pius left, Neil Morrison and Lyle Hansen came in to discuss the timetable. As far as I am concerned nothing changes, I plug along as fast as I can to draft a plan. For the November 22 meeting of the National Economic Council we agreed to prepare a ten-page paper outlining the plan as we, the Economic Planning Unit, see it, together with the original and usually higher requests by the ministries, our reasons for disagreeing, and the policy choices clearly marked – if one wants to spend more in one direction, either cut in another or raise taxes. Probably I will have to draft this, but Shaddock, the new DPS, will actually do the writing for the public. On the basis of political decisions reached in the NEC, I will redo the whole plan document in time for the budget session in March.

I went back to my office, discouraged and mad at everyone, though objectively there was no reason to be...

October 10. Happily nothing to tell today. One draft chapter got finished. And Andrew Wilson called from Ibadan that he did not yet have the revised figures. He also had the good news, that they had recalculated the growth of agricultural production and felt it would be higher than anticipated, and that they had revised their education expenditures downward. Both are good news.

October 11. Frank Moore called from Enugu: did I have a blow up with Pius? I said, yes, sort of. Well, Pius goes around telling people I had said that the reason the Eastern Region was not further along was that he, Pius, had prevented me from coming to Enugu. Also that he had offered to hit me if I were 20 years younger. I assured Frank that I had not said the first, and that Pius had not qualified his offer to hit me. What actually gets me is that he said he had stuff which he just hadn't. I expect that politicians are crazy, but on the technical level at least there ought to be decent collaboration.

Well, in the interest of the Five-Year Plan I can't afford to make more enemies. So I wrote a peace-making letter, without taking back anything substantive. The point is that these are not simply personal squabbles over minor points. If they were they would not arise, because personally Pius is charming...

October 12....Arch Callaway told me some interesting gossip. When I came, Pius was upset that we planned to stay as long as 18 months. He thought five months was enough. When Arch asked what he thought an economic advisor did, he said, "Why, you must ask them to do the plan. Then you look at it, then you say: it's no good, work some more." Well, I am afraid this is precisely why he hasn't got anything done in the East. In this place, if one wants something done, one just does it oneself.

October 13....An alarmed visit from Neil Morrison: we must have a Federal Plan for Cabinet to approve by Nov. 7. In detail and eight pages long. I said it couldn't be done. He decided it had to. One just can't use overall figures, the ministers have to know where the telephone exchanges and roads will be. I said this required technical appendices and would be 100 pages, not eight. Also I thought we had agreed on the format. So we will have another session tomorrow with Prasad on the timetable. I wish people wouldn't change dates and ideas so often. I am a nervous wreck right now...

At lunch today the staff talked about who in the Government was good, and who were the coming young men in the Civil Service, particularly in the North. They all agreed that the Sardauna liked hard advice and that Akilu, the new PS Economic Development in Kaduna, was perhaps the best man they had and would give straight advice even if it was uncomfortable. If so, this is good news.

October 17, 1961

This diary should not circulate any further for the time being. Africans are incredibly sensitive, and I am rather indiscreet as regards judgment of persons.

There have been major headlines because of the Peace Corps girl. She wrote on a postcard that people lived, ate, slept and went to the bathroom in the street – which, of course, they do. No one seems to have told her that so do people in Southern Italy or parts of France and in India. Nor does anyone complain about people reading other people's mail! Instead she had to apologize and resign, and at a mass meeting of students at Ibadan it was resolved that all Peace Corps members were American spies and should be recalled. The party-line influence is so obvious that it is hard to take it seriously. Still, my operation, which is in danger right now, could blow up over less than that!

We've had a number of pretty bad days. Lyle, who works his head off and is not only indispensable, but extremely effective with the individual ministries, is on edge. So am I. We are working from early morning till late night with no interruption. Neil Morrison, who temporarily takes Toby's place, sees everything in terms of a budget for five years, and hasn't got a clue to what we are supposed to do.

Prasad neither likes what we are doing, nor fully understands it. Moreover, he obviously doesn't read what we send him. During the meetings with the Americans he was misinformed, had to be corrected by the Americans, and talked off his hat. He does not keep me informed, and I now have evidence that he does not want to. I don't know why. Whether it is that he wants to keep a mystic aura around him, or whether he is afraid, in any case he does not play square with me, though I have with him.

October 14. Meeting in Prasad's office, Lyle, Morrison, Shadduck and myself, to decide what paper to write and when. In an earlier session with Toby it was agreed to keep the paper short and avoid details. Suddenly, Morrison decided we had to have the Federal plan by Nov. 1 with a detailed breakdown, year by year, of all individual projects with capital and recurrent costs. Which road went from where to where. Where telephone exchanges are to be located, etc. I protested it was insane. It is politically unwise to go to Cabinet with such detail, invite ministerial wrangling, and freeze a program while ministries are making up their minds.

He said, well, we have got nothing to show. I said that was nonsense. We are now on our third round with the ministries and getting them to agree to certain principles, to cut costs, cut programs, rephrase sensibly, work out details etc. I pointed out that we were to make a Five-Year Plan, not a five year capital budget to be changed every five minutes. But I lost out. Lyle must have been too weary to understand what was going on. Prasad, who with Toby had earlier agreed that such detail would come out only in February or March, suddenly switched and decided we should do it as an appendix, which could be as long as one pleased. Shadduck, who is new but looks good, and Morrison worried about typing! So I got overruled. Morrison doesn't understand anything, and Prasad not much and he's cynical about the rest.

I got to the office furious and alarmed and thoroughly upset. Lyle tried to soothe me. I pointed out to him what we had to do in a week. He said, no, we didn't. I got more excited and told him he had just agreed to it. He was hurt, and said I had misunderstood, he had not agreed to making a detailed 5-year capital budget. So we went to see Shadduck to tell Lyle what was decided. Naturally, I was right. I am all too frequently right, because I can see what is coming. But I am also politically unskilled and don't know how to prevent things I see coming. And I am emotionally handicapped, first by my conviction that one should not interfere too much and let people make their own mistakes, and secondly because I tend to personalize, even though I know it to be all wrong. In any case, Lyle apologized, and I couldn't forego pointing out to him that he did that several times to me, and that that had been the reason for any previous blowup.

So we worked all afternoon on the assignment. Again there was a difference in approach, legitimate this time. I knew pretty much what I wanted...They wanted a listing of projects, firstly, those agreed with the ministries, secondly, those not accepted, along with reasons why not. I pointed out, as I had to Prasad, that this was not workable at all. One rarely agrees or disagrees on a whole project, one agrees or disagrees on timing and size. Economics is a marginal field of scholarly endeavor. The projects we throw out entirely usually are so silly that the ministry will agree.

In the evening, Wilson took Patricia and me out to dinner. He was in as foul a mood as I was because the two non-government members of his Mission are having troubles with the two official members. So the evening was not a success. We all went home early and exhausted.

October 21, 1961

Life has been too hectic to get to writing though I tried a few times. There have been lots of fights, and I haven't recovered quite yet...

October 16. Session with Reg Clarke on Federal grants to the Regions. He had prepared a lengthy memo, essentially consisting of Lyle's and mine, to which he added a few points. We also talked over the resources picture, which is grim, and assured him we wanted to work very closely with him. In the meantime our new acting PS, Godfrey Lardner, arrived, shook hands, but waited until Tuesday to take over so he could settle his wife and $4^1/_2$ children. He happens to live a block away, which is convenient.

I then got into a fight with Neil Morrison, who kept telling me we had nothing, and I kept telling him we had a plan and he just didn't know what a plan was; all he could think of was a capital budget along traditional lines. He got red in the face, and I could feel the blood drain out of mine. He is such a stupid man, but also nasty and vicious.

Fortunately Lyle is excellent these days. Although his nerves are on edge as much as mine, and we are both fighting it, he keeps calmer and plugs away. The stuff he turns out is superb. What makes me furious is that, having foreseen that Prasad's advice is wrong, and indeed pernicious, in the interest of peace and good personal relations I have objected only gently, and he has either brushed me off or sidetracked me. Yet I saw what was coming and was unable to do something about it because I am politically not good at infighting.

The rest of the day was occupied with more or less vain attempts to rescue things. I apologized to Neil for speaking sharply with him, which seemed to please him. With Lyle and Peter I started the absurd assignment we had got on Saturday, about phasing the construction of individual roads from Banchi to Gourbe, etc., as if that were planning and had anything to do with anything. And I got more and more determined to stop that sort of thing...

At 7:30 PM our ministry gave a cocktail party for the Americans at the Federal Palace. At first I didn't want to go – and it was a lousy party – but I was more or less made to. I just couldn't get the problem out of my head of what to do in the future. At 9:00 AM ...Wilson came home with me for supper and we worked until midnight, trying various reconciliations of the plans and the aggregative model. Actually I had done most of it already and explained to him what I had done, where the difficulties lay. The really grim part was the resources picture. The regions just have too big plans and too big deficits...

October 17....At 9:10 AM I was in Clarke's office to discuss how much we could raise over the next five years *via* taxes, internal borrowing, and liquidation of foreign assets. I also wanted to know precisely what I could tell Rivkin and Schmidt. To my surprise Reg authorized me to tell them everything. As far as the Federal Government is concerned, things are grim but manageable.

...The JPC was supposed to sit as a subcommittee on conditional grants, but actually all sorts of things happened, the details of which I cannot remember. The question of the steel mill came up. We succeeded in slowing that down because both proposals before us are expensive and lose money.

In the afternoon I spent most of my time working and fighting for my ideas. Lardner, the new acting PS, looks pretty good. The young Nigerians like and respect him. He left here after a fight a few years ago to join the new Economic Commission for Africa. Neil said he was terrible and inefficient: he left 217 unattended files when he went off to Addis. Whether this is so bad remains a question. Certainly Neil sees everything in terms of files. He certainly has no notion what development or development planning is...

Lardner is a nationalist, which is or can be a good thing. He certainly doesn't particularly like the British, which is understandable, but that does not spill over to individuals. If he is interested, he will work hard and fight for it. He is an economist, and therefore understands what we are trying to do. We have since had talks with him – Lyle and I – and on the whole we see eye-to-eye: we must have more savings and some austerity. We must avoid exchange control and change the composition of imports through other means, such as tariffs graduated in favor of development goods. We must avoid inflation.

He agrees that capital budgets at this time are for the birds, and he was, or said he was, impressed by the amount of work we had done and its quality. I also told him that Prasad's project approach was impossible. Both Lyle and I pointed out to him that all of our papers, beginning with the first one in April with which we had had so much trouble, had put the choices quite clearly, and I just didn't understand why Prasad apparently neglected to inform the Prime Minister. Personally I think he just let us do the work but didn't believe in it, and paid no attention to it. Now he is shocked and tells stories about how difficult it is to get anything done in Nigeria. It is, of course. But he didn't have to wait until now.

He is an Indian. I think he has a lot more color prejudice than any of the rest of us. We don't even notice any more whether anyone is black or white or in between. By now it's just a question of who the person is. Prasad doesn't like it either that Mother Nature – at least in southern Nigeria – is so much kinder than in India. Or apparently so. So they can be lazy and still progress. They earn money by exporting cocoa which grows by itself. Actually, of course, half of the children born are dead by age 5, and workers walk or cycle two hours to work. The sassy Lagosians, who are bums like most big city delinquents in the world, are completely atypical of the country. But

Prasad doesn't go outside comfortable trips to regional capitals. No sleeping in African compounds for him. Right now I have plenty of reasons to be mad at him.

After working and thinking what to do because I couldn't find a workable answer, I saw Arnold, who was sick in bed. He was alarmed and wanted figures from me. I said I couldn't give him a figure on my own, but I told him to call Prasad and ask for a three-way meeting. Then I could say what I considered the maximum realistic program. I forgot to suggest that Lardner be called in too. I always thought that P. did not keep me informed, but I put that down to oversight and sloppiness. It was disturbing to have direct proof that there was more to it than that.

Arnold pointed out that, as things looked, they were absurd. I agreed, but pointed out that, in paper after paper, we had called attention to the problem and asked for action, only to be shunted aside by Prasad. Since Arnold had obtained the papers officially, he knew that was true. He is a good Nigerian like myself and is as upset as I am that Prasad's lack of decent economic knowledge is preventing Nigeria from getting a maximum of foreign aid.

Prasad gave a dinner in honor of the Mission. He is a charming host, and the food is excellent. For a while I was cornered by M and G, the ICA and State Department men, respectively, on the mission, both of whom are pains in the neck and rather stupid. So Arnold and Wilson had their burden to carry, and showed it. Wilson is hardly on speaking terms with them. That evening he seems to have given Neil Morrison a hard time. In any case, Neil looked grim all evening, and even his usual drunkenness didn't relax him. When Wilson told me about it next day, I pointed out that he had talked to the wrong man, that Neil was out anyway. I couldn't help feeling sorry for Neil, who is too stupid to know what is going on. Charles Thompson always said Neil got as far as he should when he was a senior assistant secretary, and shouldn't have been promoted any further.

I fled from the grimmer Americans and British to talk with Andrew Wilson, whom I like a lot. (He is PS Planning, Ibadan)…

October 18. The Northerners brought me their plan, such as it was, was more apparent than real detail, and grossly inflated beyond anything that could possibly be done or would be sensible to do…

The full JPC met for five hours. First we discussed conditional grants. After Prasad talked at length and the regional representatives had given their views, I was asked for my views. I tend to be rather blunt anyway, and my nerves were on edge. So I offered two comments. First, there was a misconception that the Federal Government was swimming in money. The fact was we were all broke. Second, I thought any conditional grants should have sanctions so the money would be used wisely in the context of the plan. Money was money. It didn't make sense to give the Eastern Region money for a perfectly good project only to have them turn around and use their own funds for absurd things like kindergartens or broiler factories which didn't pay.

Prasad did what he always does. He launched into a long speech, how we didn't want to send the army to any Region to enforce a plan, although some countries had had a civil war, how there had to be persuasion, etc. That took him 20 minutes. All of them irrelevant. The issue was simply how to ensure wise use of resources. Well, we resolved that discussion. The Regions thought there was too much Federal spending in Lagos. Look at all the building. I interjected, much to the pleasure of the

North, that the two biggest office skyscrapers were built by regional development corporations. That stopped *that* cold.

Next Prasad presented a memo on reorganization of planning, much of which made sense. Lyle presented an alternative which made more sense. Prasad tried to cut Lyle off on grounds of shortage of time. Since he always talks at length that was not a point well taken. At one point he said that in India, the PM chairs the planning commission, which meets daily – God knows whether this is really so – but that making the PM chairman in Nigeria would be unfair because as chairman he had to impose silence upon himself! This was greeted with some amusement. Then he asked for my opinion.

I said I thought there should only be one adviser. Either the planning unit should shift to the PM's office and work for the adviser there, or the head of the planning unit in the Ministry of Economic Development should be a PS and serve as advisor to the Government. I said there was enough friction as it was and if Prasad and I didn't like each other as much as we did, it would be catastrophic. (Frank Moore told me afterwards there was so much irritation in my voice that this reference to liking sounded rather hollow, even though in a left-handed way, I meant it.) Then I said the organizational scheme would depend on what was meant by planning.

Prasad interrupted and thought we all agreed *laissez faire* didn't work. I said that wasn't what I was talking about. As it happened, I had studied Russian and East German planning intensively for five years, and found it interesting that they were decentralizing their planning and trying to use the price mechanism more intensively. But this was another example of Prasad trying to twist the meaning of what I said. He knew perfectly well that I was talking of our view of comprehensive planning *vs.* his project approach.

This time the meeting ended neither in his victory nor in ours. There was confusion and the discussion was postponed. I was fuming and worried.

At 2:30 PM the Northern Region PSs of Planning and Finance, Akilu and Talib, together with Lyle, came for lunch. Akilu is Peter Gibbs' successor, Talib is John Taylor's. Both are tall Northerners, Talib from Maiduguri, Bornu Province, Akilu from Sokoto. Beforehand I apologized to Akilu for any trouble I might have caused him unintentionally, and I think the apology was accepted. In any case, I don't think Akilu is a man who nurses a grudge.

The talk was both pleasant and general. I hadn't had yet a chance to look at the NR plan, something I have regretted since, because I have plenty of questions now which the two might or might not have answered. It was apparent that both of them were being careful in what they said. It was also apparent that both of them were more careful towards each other than towards us. Northern politics is too subtle for me to understand, but it is rough.

Personally, I like both, but particularly Akilu. Like most Westerners, I have developed a liking for the North without being able to say why. There is a natural courtesy in them, at least to equals, which is disarming. They have no inferiority complexes towards palefaces, and hence treat us as equals. It makes one forget that they also used to be pretty ruthless slave raiders. In any case, it was relaxing…They left at 4:30 PM.

Wilson Schmidt arrived at 5:00 PM, and we worked over the macro model I had redone for him. Actually in some respects I was very proud. I could reconcile the independent balance of payments and investment estimates with the model; the trouble started with the financing requirements, which were just insane. All Prasad's chickens had come home to roost. The Regions had presented bargaining plans that were much too big, had no chance of execution, and in part shouldn't be executed even if the money and executive ability were there.

We left at 7:30 PM to see Arnold, who was at the cocktail party given by the Americans. I was getting more disturbed by the minute, and drank just ginger ale. I tried to tell Gray that things were actually pretty good, which incidentally is the honest truth. The economy is fine, and if they just let us we can come up with a good, realistic, feasible, defensible plan in a week. But we need cooperation of a different sort from Prasad...

At 9:00 PM I left for Lardner's house to brief him on what we were up to. Lardner was taking our view. I said I would not play to Nigerian nationalism, but give the straightest advice I knew.[3] My paper was going to put down the law, explain the hard choices and be stark and realistic. If this was not acceptable I would submit my views in a dissenting Cabinet paper, and if this was not allowed, offer my resignation. I said I could take any craziness from a politician, but a fellow technician had to play it straight and rational.

Lardner told me to calm down. Did I have ulcers? I said not at the moment, but if things went on, they would come back. Well, he said, he had had two operations because he agreed with me. Of course the paper would have to be stark and realistic. I said I couldn't get across to Neil that there was a difference between a capital budget and a plan, and that detailed phasing at this stage, when major cuts had to be made, was out and would cause nothing but confusion. Much to my surprise Lardner agreed that we had to avoid inflation and exchange control. Having an ally in this is rather important to me. So I left somewhat cheered.

By 10:00 PM I was in the hotel. First I went to see Arnold. He told me Prasad was pretty shaken by the talk they had had. He had first spoken of the difficulties of planning in Nigeria (which are real enough without his adding to them); how Nigeria should get extra marks for already doing a lot; and how the US should help its friends. Arnold said this was very well, but required a plan. He pointed out that the financing gap was bigger than the capital plans. That really shook Prasad, who was unaware of it and had not prepared Sir Abubakar for that shock. Why Prasad wasn't aware of it, I don't know, for it is in our papers submitted to JPC...

That night I did not sleep at all. All I could think of was what mistakes I had made and when. I am a good intellectual and can therefore often see what is going to happen. Yet you know I have my terrible blind spots, my erratic moments when I do something irreversible and irrevocable on the spur of the moment. Those moments are fortunately few and far between, but when I do make a mistake, it is a lulu.

In any case, all I could think of was how often I had given in to Prasad in the interest of peace, how often I took Toby's advice to let things ride, how often I may have done Lyle an injustice when he tried in his systematic, almost pedantic way to hold me back or shift me to another ground. Then there were these awful moments when everything seemed crystal clear: if I had done so and so, we would now be much further along. If I had spoken in public against Prasad's advice when we both saw Okeke, the (very good) ER Minister of Agriculture, when Prasad egged him on to make bigger and better plans, and not worry about money, instead of quickly calculating the farm settlements' payoff to influence his choice and decision.

Since then, Lardner and Lyle have calmed me down considerably. Both said this was water over the dam. Lyle told me what I had always told him: that our strength lies in our performance, which is excellent. Prasad has no staff. And *he* has to tell Sir Abubakar that the figure he had originally given him is too big.

But I am worried that we and my minister will be blamed, and I won't have it. Lardner said to let him handle this. In fact all our JPC papers since April show our record of warning. Just the same, Prasad and we always differed on such fundamental issues as inflation and exchange control. He has always taken the line that only a fiscal catastrophe will teach a country a lesson, and we have always insisted that it was worth every effort to prevent such a catastrophe. I don't think we are out of the woods yet.

October 19....At 8:30 AM we met in Prasad's office to decide on the nature of the 'Plan' to be submitted to the JPC and what would be submitted to the National Economic Council. Lardner took over, and on the whole we won the day. The paper will be essentially what I suggested, modified somewhat by giving a general description, project by project, of what we are suggesting as against what the ministries requested. No nonsense about phasing at this stage, particularly about phasing of recurrent costs, nor about excessive detail or uniformity of presentation...

At 12:30 PM we had our final meeting with the Rivkin mission. Arnold was not yet well. Prasad talked at length about the difficulties of planning in Nigeria, asked for Rivkin's impressions in the Regions, suggested (making me wild) that there wouldn't be a plan until next year, and expressed hope that we could come for help in individual projects anyway.

Rivkin said they thought the visit to the Regions was successful, though they found insufficient awareness of the need to mobilize resources. As he understood the PM, Nigeria wanted large-scale, long-term aid based on a plan, rather than piecemeal, small-scale help with individual projects. He was sorry the plan would be delayed, but saw no need for a capital budget, which wasn't worth anything anyway. This was just what I wanted him to say, though no one will ever believe I didn't put him up to it. However he left out lots of other things that I wanted him to say. Schmidt asked a few questions on the macro model and reconciliation which I answered as best I could...

October 20. Worked and talked a little in the office. Lyle was pretty good. Though on edge himself, for he too has been working like a dog, he calmed me down with a number of fatherly observations. He pointed out that obviously it wasn't my fault. It probably wasn't anybody's fault. Anyway, we were in it together. I said I couldn't have it both ways. I am the head of the planning exercise and have to take the blame, just as I get the major credit if things go well.

Lyle said Toby and Prasad also have something to do with it. Anyway, how could I be sure we would get a consortium with lots of money if I had my way? Rivkin could not promise anything definite. And nothing prevented Rivkin or anyone else from starting to organize a consortium. I agreed, of course, but said I wanted to be absolutely sure I had done everything humanly possible. And I just hadn't. On the whole the talk helped calm me down...

October 27. I have finished a draft for the JPC and must now get a draft going for the NEC, though I'm still waiting for the final Federal figures from Lyle and Peter... The regional plans are a headache, although the North is now working on reducing their ideas to something practicable. But Frank Moore, who just came yesterday, still can't convince the Easterners that profit and losses aren't the same thing...

October 31, 1961

...Had another blow-up with Lyle, because again he had not met my deadline, forcing me into unusual work. He works on the whole hard and well, but sometimes also shows a convenient capacity to deny what we had agreed on the previous day.

The major burden is on me anyway. After writing my paper for the Federal Council of Ministers, beautifully rewritten in the proper style by Ken Shaddock, who was brought in specially for this job, I had to get busy on the 'National Plan' paper for the NEC. Because I didn't get the figures from Lyle until Saturday morning, I calculated and did the necessary tables on Saturday, and then worked all day Sunday. The paper is 23 pages, plus lots of tables, and tries to lay down the law...

November 2, 1961

On Sunday I worked all day on the draft memo for NEC...It turned out to be 24 pages long, plus a few quite long tables. The picture is pretty grim, as we have known and written all along, but this time some sort of decision will have to be made. I wish Kingsley were here to discuss my strategy. I feel strongly that, if stymied again, it is no use for me to stay around any longer, and I shall ask for a transfer. We must have ministerial decisions now on the amount of taxes they are willing to raise, etc., or else there will be a catastrophe...

October 31. Shaddock on the whole did a very good job of condensation. Unfortunately he is not an economist, but a mathematician by training, and an administrator. As a result he would take two or three ideas from my paper and mix them up in one paragraph which then didn't make sense. Furthermore, he was afraid to be too blunt, and had ideas of his own which I could not accept. This time I asserted myself and insisted that I alone was responsible for the economic ideas that went into the paper. It was not altogether pleasant, but I can't afford to get a second time into a position where my normally peaceable nature puts me into a corner...

After supper I took some cigars to Lardner as a [40th] birthday present, and stayed for an hour over a glass of beer. We talked about the relative size of corruption in the US and Nigeria, how to approach planning, etc. It was pleasant and relaxing for both of us. If he is xenophobic and anti-white, as I was told, he has not shown it towards me. But then, I am rather naïve in some ways despite my 50 years of age and the many hard knocks I have got. The next four weeks will be just like that. Prasad is in a spot, and a lot better than I at political infighting.

November 5, 1961 [continued November 6]

Things have picked up a little. After I wrote on Nov. 2, we worked all day in a great confusion. The major tables wouldn't add up right, Peter had to finish one table for which he needed my decision which I couldn't make until I had finished something else. There was somewhat less of a battle against Lyle's stubbornness...

At 5:15 PM Lardner, Lyle, Frank and I discussed strategy for the next day's JPC session...We tried to think of difficulties that might arise, and how to handle them. Since Lardner has made the paper his, on that account I had no worry.

Later I raised two questions. First, suppose this paper is somehow rejected and JPC asks for a completely different paper with which I could not agree. How do I go about bringing my views to the attention of the Minister and NEC? Lardner suggested I should go to the Minister and try to persuade him to take it to Cabinet. That is fair enough.

Secondly, I asked about keeping Rivkin and the American mission informed. Here I am treading on delicate ground. For I can't be identified with anyone except the Nigerian Government. There was certainly nothing else in my mind. But as I tried to get across to Lyle – not with much success – this is a typical situation. Lyle thinks Rivkin has used his friendship with me to bully me into a position where I feel I have failed unless he gets the necessary figures to start a consortium.

It is true that I want to have done everything in my power to help Nigeria get a maximum amount of money. Lyle feels Rivkin won't be able to deliver, hence it doesn't matter, which may also be true. But what I can't get across is that, if I am wrong, we are no worse off than if he is right, while if he is wrong we are much worse off. Hence good politics supports my view. Lyle agrees when I say it, but then stubbornly does the opposite. Anyway, Lardner was quite sharp on this point. Before NEC decides on Nov. 27, nothing goes out, which is fair enough...

I had promised Lardner to take a tranquilizer before the JPC's Nov. 3 meeting and let him carry the ball...The meeting was most interesting. Prasad came in obviously subdued. He reported on his Washington mission in glowing terms, yet clearly it had been a total failure. He got nothing, as I knew he would. Except in the context of a plan, Nigeria will get only small amounts. I think everyone else at the meeting also saw the mission as a flop. In a way I regret it, but it strengthens our hand, particularly as I was told the Bank's figure for the size of the program was very close to ours.

When we took up our paper, which was basically mine, the Minister came in and sat through the whole proceedings. This cramped everyone's style, but I felt that was all to the good. After Lardner's opening statement we went sentence by sentence through the paper. It was a complete victory for me. Pius Okigbo said he didn't want a figure for the ER program, but I said we needed one, and much to my surprise, on this and many other points Prasad took my line. Pius looked as if he didn't know what had hit him. He is the heir presumptive to Prasad and tried to take his cue from him, and Prasad had reversed himself.

My own interpretation is that two things have come together. First, the failure of the Washington mission has shown the Nigerians that Prasad's line was wrong. It hasn't yet proved my line, of course. Secondly Lardner is black. That also makes it impossible for Prasad to take the anti-British, anti-white line. To be fair, he has never been anti-American, though he has always tried, usually successfully, to sidetrack me and not to discuss points of issue on which he was simply wrong.

We worked until 3:00 PM. I came home quite elated – for the first time in weeks. Some preparation was required for next day, for a subcommittee was supposed to harmonize revenue forecasts. Since I was the clearinghouse for the three Regions, and moreover had done all the projections, this was once more my baby...

Kingsley came over. I told him today's JPC meeting was the first time in months I didn't feel like a total failure. He said not to talk nonsense, I had come into a very difficult political situation and handled it on the whole successfully. I said, maybe so, but (a) if I had played things right, we should by now have had a consortium; (b) what drove me wild was my ability to foresee what would happen, combined with a complete inability to prevent it from happening; and (c) I had often mishandled the office staff. On the latter point it was clear that Lyle was trying to take over and be boss. I had just told him that, when I offered him equality, I had not offered to work under him. I didn't know how to set that right, particularly as I respected Lyle's work and thought he was indispensable.

Hence I thought my usefulness in Nigeria was limited, and once the plan was written, by March-April, I should withdraw. So was there another assignment I could have? Frank had mentioned Nepal, which sounded good.

Kingsley started lecturing me. On (a) I should have no illusions as to how much I could do. One just didn't move events, they moved one. That is true, but didn't meet my point that I had not done all in my power. Thus I couldn't be sure how different the course of events might have been. As to (b) he said again that I had done well and Lyle hadn't, which was made worse by the fact that Lyle thinks he has political skill but all he has done is read a lot of books. This I know to be true. Lyle is much better than I on certain medium- and low-level matters, but not at all on any really high-level ones.

As to (c), Kingsley said he had long known it, and was surprised it took me so long to catch on. Of course, I don't know when I caught on. It is such a nasty thing that I must have long suppressed it even after I knew it. Kingsley said he had watched me make a number of mistakes – all mistakes of the heart, not of the mind, and he could understand them. Moreover, while Lyle hadn't learned a damned thing, I obviously had. He, Kingsley, had made all these mistakes when first with the Foundation and still a professor, and I was learning fast (I wish I were!) I just had to assert myself. I said that wasn't so simple, and I had given Lyle a free hand.

Lyle has applied to prolong his contract for a year, obviously expecting to head the team after my departure. Kingsley said flatly that, whether I was here or not, Lyle would *not* head the team. He was first-rate, but not the man to head a team in a delicate situation. We agreed that Lyle was on the whole excellent, straightforward and nice. Kingsley said I obviously had licked blood by being in the midst of things in a really responsible position. Of this I am not so convinced now. Teaching is also a fine profession.

Secondly, he said I wasn't yet an expert after one tour. It took three to four years, and it would be a pity to interrupt now. I could get Nepali experience in a few years. Now there's a point – I barely begin to catch on to the nuances of local politics. That the Southern Nigerian politicians are idiots is quite obvious and doesn't take much intelligence to see. But there are more nuances and subtleties than in German or American politics, I am sure. And in another tour they would be in my blood and instinct.

But some of the politics doesn't bear thinking too much about...So I asked Kingsley why he wished this on me. He knew I was taking my job pretty seriously, and suffered by being unable to forestall developments I could see coming. But his point was that they would be a lot worse if we were not here. And it is, of course, true, that occasionally, here and there, one can do something. Anyway, at the rate I am learning, I really *would* be *the* African expert in a few years. I thought I already was. This is one point up on Don.

Then I pointed to my family. I would never again be away from them as long as this time. He replied that if a man had done a good job for the Foundation, he could write his own ticket.

November 4. JPC started with a subcommittee on taxation and resources. This was my meat, as I had done all the work on it. (Lyle's turn will come when we get to individual ministry programs.) It was rather fun to know the tax situation of all the Regions better than they, having done all the detailed calculations. It is also nice to work with the various regional PSs of finance, particularly the Northerners, Talib, etc.

At 10:00 AM the full JPC returned to our paper. I thought everything would be plain sailing. But I got a rude shock when Prasad summarized the preceding day's discussion exactly the opposite from what I remembered, and skipped the discussion of two crucial pages. I jumped in my seat, took exception, summarized what I thought had been the position and forced a discussion of the two pages. And then, in a quite unintentionally inspired moment, I asked for a glass of water and took a tranquilizer in what must have been quite a show of gamesmanship.

Lardner told me afterwards I was quite statesmanlike. The Minister was present again, and I am sure that helped. I didn't let Prasad get away with anything, always coming back to what I considered the fundamental point to be presented to Cabinet. Prasad couldn't use his usual gambit, that the ministers were wild boys and should be kept well in hand. Instead, he had to use a rational argument, which of course he didn't have. (I get to like our Minister a lot.)

Prasad made a few good points, which we agreed to incorporate in the draft. But none went to the heart of the matter. I have come to the conclusion that he is not really underhanded, just a lousy economist. Lyle always insisted Prasad was afraid to get into an economic argument with me. Maybe so. He is a smooth operator, but can't meet any lengthy argument. And I am sure he just can't visualize things. For example, he asked us to incorporate a table which he sketched. It sounded plausible, but I couldn't follow, and when I asked for more detail, he obviously didn't know what he wanted. Now that Lardner is here, I can relax and concentrate my energy, or what is left of it, to devote myself to my staff and the plan.

After what turned out to be a harder-won victory than anticipated, I tried to go home for lunch, but first Chukujekwe and Wilson of the West, and Talib of the North, wanted to discuss tax and debt burden figures, which was important for me…

November 6.…Ken Shaddock came in early, and showed me his last pages of redrafting…The revision is weaker than the original, but makes the points we have to make. I then announced in the office that from now on I was taking over. I must have learned enough from Shaddock and Kingsley for it went without a hitch and quite effectively.

At 1:00 PM the Minister came in and wanted to see the plans. He kept me until 3:00 PM. I was glad for the chance to talk with him alone and freely. He wants hard advice. I think he trusts us, and he can. We will tell him what we think. He scares me at times. For example he wants the Federal Government to go into agricultural projects with the Regions, which is quite unconstitutional. So he just wants to change the constitution. This sort of thing worries me, perhaps unduly. He wanted to know about Soapy Williams, and why he was called so. On the whole his ideas are sound, and I expect to have fun briefing him. Obviously he knows more politics than I do. Still, as ministers go he is young and inexperienced, and it is important that he be briefed correctly. What he does with this in Cabinet is then his baby...

For the rest of the day I am relaxing, listening to the gramophone, and at 9:00 PM I am going to the Dolgins for a game of Scrabble. The last thing in the world I want is to hurt Nigeria and Nigerians, whom I like in a sort of exasperated way...

Notes

1   'West Africa Wins Again'.
2   Dike, Kenneth Onwuka, *Trade and Politics in the Niger Delta, 1830–1885: An Introduction to the Economic and Political History of Nigeria*. Oxford Studies in African Affairs, Clarendon Press, 1956.
3   I remember coming stinking mad from my defeat in the meeting with Prasad about inflation, etc., staring at Lardner and telling him, "If you think I will cater to your nationalism, you can think twice." His answer was, "I have the reputation of being anti-white, but I make my distinctions," and he offered me his hand. We were friends from that moment on.

Chapter 11

November 7–December 13, 1961
Efforts to Trim Investment Programs, Possible Stretch to Six Years, JPC Discusses Plan Outline

November 13, 1961

I must by now have written at least one book, mostly in the form of JPC papers and memoranda on various subjects.

I won't have to see the Prime Minister, which would not have done much good. In any case, Prasad has come around completely, and now takes our line. So the fight was not all in vain, though it is questionable whether it was my effort that won it. Lardner deserves a lot of credit, along with the IBRD and Arnold Rivkin. Apparently, Bank President [Eugene] Black saw Prasad at length, which seems to account for some reversal. Then Skillings of the IBRD and Arnold have given us quite a boost. Arnold wrote on his own to the Ford Foundation and testified in Congress about us. All of which seems to have contributed. In any case, things are on the upgrade. Kingsley has also contributed.

In the office I have asserted my leadership *à la* Kingsley. I now order a morning staff meeting to see what everyone is doing, and get an accounting of the previous day. I am still the only one meeting deadlines. And the work is after all useful and interesting. I am quite amused at Shaddock, who now tells me he can't work under our conditions, and I tell him I have done so for nine months. As a result I am getting a separate room with airconditioner – finally. I hate working in an office while conferences and telephone calls are going on. Also, performance still counts, and the fact that I am unfortunately the only reliable man seems to have paid off. But at what cost to my nerves!…

November 7. We finally got the NEC paper out, minus an appendix on the limits to foreign borrowing due to balance of payments effects of debt service. Lardner has some objections to my formulation…

November 8.…I had Reg Clarke (PS Finance) and his wife, Lyle and Ann and Count Posadowsky-Wehner, the German ambassador, for dinner. Reg is half German, but won't talk German since the Nazis. He has the DFC and was a wing commander. He is also very nice and extremely able, and probably the most powerful civil servant.

Reg came early to talk about the discussions with the Bank in Washington. They did not go too badly. I am now reading the second IBRD report, which takes our line completely, and quotes some of my paper without actually mentioning it. Reg then told me about Prasad's meeting with Black. He also said the IBRD wants him to join the staff after he retires here…

Later Posadowsky and the Hansens came. At first the talk turned around the Eastern Region. We gave the ambassador a hard time, complaining about all the factories the ER buys in Germany that it can't afford and which won't pay off. Reg argued that the German government should be concerned about all their factories becoming state-owned. The ambassador not unreasonably pointed out that his government gave no credits and could not interfere. He also said he had investigated Frank Moore's complaint and had found the German group was competent and serious and has done good work elsewhere.

Later the talk focused on corruption…Apparently, attempted bribery by expatriate firms, including Americans, is pervasive and varies from the subtle to the not-so-subtle. Posadowsky said he was tracking a case where the bill for a party he had given had been paid by someone and his own check not cashed. For whoever pays will present a bill sooner or later. Reg Clarke thought that a lot of Nigerians who are basically honest may fall for this kind of sophistication, if you can call it so...

November 9.…At 9:00 AM I had to give a lecture on the "Need for Prudent Planning" at the Federal Training Institute, an in-service training scheme for beginning civil servants. They asked some good questions. I was flattered that two of the fellows wanted to know about the old article Paul Samuelson and I wrote together. I run into this quite often, people are pleased that a well-known theorist is doing their planning…

At 8:00 PM Kingsley and Lardner came for supper. Kingsley wanted to broach the continuance of the Ford project. Lardner was quite cheerful, expecting the birth of his fifth child. (It was born the next morning.) Hardly any business was talked. We spoke about long-run problems; how everyone had to make his own mistakes, including underdeveloped countries. I didn't doubt it, but felt it was my job to prevent as many as I could. And I just could not feel 'historical' about present suffering.

November 10. I worked like mad to finish the Council paper,…then took off for Ibadan to give my lecture on planning in East Germany. I was flattered that the audience of 16–18 people included Chief Adebo, Western Region Secretary, i.e. chief of the civil service, in my book the greatest Nigerian. (He looks absurdly like William Bendix, the TV actor in the Life of Riley.) I think the talk went well. The discussion brought out several prejudices as well as good questions and comments. Some people were not at all pleased that I thought East Germany less efficient than West Germany…

November 11. I spent a fascinating hour with Adebo, who had asked me to drop in. He wanted to know more about East German planning and also about our work in the EPU. He agreed with our planning concepts, described some of his troubles with the WR's semi-autonomous agencies, and asked me to let him know in advance the next time so he could invite me home…

November 12. I spent the morning with Arch Callaway, who has excellent stuff on capital formation, having interviewed about 3,500 businessmen, just about all there are. He has a sample of 1,000 unemployed school leavers and 1,000 apprentices.

Arch wanted me to come to Sam Aluko for lunch…I don't trust Aluko, whom I consider a confused, if honest, bad economist. Arch said one of his Nigerian friends told him Sam didn't really believe all the newspaper stuff he writes, but does it for political reasons. Which I find hard to forgive in an intellectual.

I was finally persuaded to go along. I'm afraid I misbehaved and was rather provocative. I said I had been shocked at my lecture when a Nigerian talked the nonsense of there being two German states. I said one was just a colony, with literally a brick wall around to hold it, and I thought an ex-colonial should have more sympathy for another colonial enslavement. That wasn't so bad, but then Sam talked about capitalism being dead. I said, maybe so, but dead capitalism had to keep Poles and Yugoslavs alive, literally, by shipping wheat and helping their development. At this point I was told the Russians had single-handedly won the war, and when I said this wasn't quite so, I was called a dishonest Western intellectual. So I said goodbye, having been excessively provocative. I felt rather elated...

November 13. ...At noon I went to Reg Clarke at his request...He wants help with a fascinating problem: how to rewrite Central Bank loans to Government to increase the scope for monetary policy. Also, how much long-term bonds could the Bank absorb? How much could we raise taxes without bad effects on private saving or a popular revolt *à la* Ghana? I have tonight and tomorrow to find some answers! Then, on Wednesday Reg, Prasad, Governor Fenton and I will sit down. This is real influence, and again one of the things that make this assignment so fascinating.

Back in the office at 1:00 PM I was interrupted by the Westinghouse consortium that wants to sell us a steel mill...

November 18, 1961

November 14. ...Reg Clarke shows me all his papers and asks for advice at times. He is smart and nice, and my improved morale has a lot to do with his presence.

An evening cocktail party for a World Bank loan mission...I got into a discussion about Miss Michelmore with ambassador Palmer, who thought she was a first-class girl but had been indiscrete, while I thought she had done nothing specially wrong, and the Nigerians' reaction to her postcard had been absurd. I didn't dare tell them about my diary! That would really send shivers down Palmer's spine. It does mine once in a while. Zik's[1] boy for instance is at Harvard. The Palmers are very nice people, and obviously enjoyed a purely personal party. It must be very rare for an ambassador to be able just to relax and to enjoy himself...

November 15. I spent quite a bit of yesterday and today reading the statutes and rules and regulations of the Nigerian and Indian Central Banks. At 11:00 AM met with Prasad, Fenton, Tibbets (the General Manager) and Henry Omanai (DPS Finance) to discuss how many long-term loans the Central Bank could take up during the Plan period. The Central Bank was of course conservative, and we all ganged up on them, saying it was safe to take more than they wanted.

But the real concern was not the immediate issue of the loans, but the whole question of monetary policy in a developing country. The CBN was worried about any inflationary finance spilling over quickly through the balance of payments and causing a drain on foreign reserves, a very legitimate point. Prasad pointed out correctly that one needs a balance of payments policy, and he had always promoted the CBN's role as chief guardian of the reserves. I agreed, but said the CBN had to develop a domestic capital and money market. This they are, of course, trying to do, if unimaginatively. It touches directly on how to mobilize domestic resources for growth.

At this point we got back to possible changes in the law. The commercial banks here are subject to liquidity rules, but the banking ordinance is essentially British, with central bank control based on persuasion, and the fact that banks are few in number. The situation is more as in America, with a few big expatriate banks easily controlled *à la* UK but also enjoying tremendous freedom of action because they are simply branches of British banks. Then one has a few big African banks and lots of very small African ones.

The liquidity rules do not discriminate, but in fact African banks don't maintain the required liquidity and no one has a taste for suing them or otherwise using anything less gentlemanly than persuasion. As a result the CBN has no real control over the banking system, although this is or ought to be one of its chief functions. The American approach of reserve requirements in the form of deposits with the CB would clearly be preferable.

One could have an American-style distribution between country and city banks, done by size rather than location, since Nigeria has nation-wide branch banking. And the banking system could hold secondary reserves in the form of relatively high-interest, long-term Government bonds. Reg Clarke actually suggested reserve requirements. And for once Prasad and I were on the same side of the fence.

I hadn't thought about this problem for a long time, and was glad to be brought into the discussion. It will be fun to help write or rewrite a country's banking legislation!...

November 17. JPC started at 9:30 AM, ending at 1:30 PM. It was an unusually quiet meeting. Only Pius Okigbo had come from the East, and three palefaces from the North. None of the powers – Talib, Akilu and Lawan – attended, and it was clear they wanted nothing to happen. The papers were accepted, and the issues were mainly how to approach the NEC meeting, who would brief the Premiers and Ministers, and how.

Prasad got religion and took more or less the line I had been advocating. The size of the program and the projected amount of foreign aid are just about what we thought they would be in April. In fact the outcome of all the fighting and maneuvering is that we are back where we were in April. Everyone says it's a big victory because everyone has finally accepted our ideas as their own. This is true enough but we could have had the plan practically written by now, and there would be that much less pressure on me...

7:00 PM – cocktails at the Sudanese embassy...My minister was there, enjoying himself being impish. First he made the Saudi ambassador shake hands with the Israeli ambassador, which didn't go over too well. Then he insisted that I debate free enterprise *versus* Communism with the First Secretary of the Soviet embassy. The Nigerians wanted to know what Khrushchev and Kennedy would say if they saw an American and Russian talking together. I said I didn't know about Khrushchev, but Kennedy couldn't care less. After all we had Russians in the US, and disagreements were political, not personal. Then the Nigerians wanted to know when the Russians would stop testing. Malakhov got heated and said they had. I couldn't help grinning. We then talked about Malishev and other Russian economists, but it got boring, so I left...

November 21, 1961

...The next few weeks will be pretty full, but I have a chance to write what I want to before everyone else puts their fingers in. Perhaps things are normal, but I am not used to the political infighting and never will be. Also while I am confident that I know what makes the Nigerian economy tick, I still don't understand its politics – or that of India for that matter. I need another talk with Kingsley, who has a feel for such things.

November 18....I worked mostly on Reg Clarke's memo. I was pleased to see it took a lot of my ideas and copied stuff from my JPC papers and other drafts. Reg's paper will go to the Federal Council of Ministers through the Minister of Finance. I also read the latest attack by Chief Awolowo, leader of the opposition. He doesn't know my name and always refers to "Dr. Prasad and another gentleman from America." I had the pleasure of seeing that Festus interrupted to say, "Isn't he a good gentleman?" I am told that for a minister to defend an expatriate, even obliquely, is quite unusual.

Had Saunders, NR DPS Finance, to lunch. He told me the size of the Northern Plan, £52 million, just about what I thought they could execute. He also told me no public decision would be made until after the NEC meeting, if then. Things are just as I thought. We would have had no trouble but for Prasad going and telling everyone to think big. Now he has the Regions putting up absurdly big programs that no one wants to cut. Everyone wants to do not only more than they can – which would be easy to handle – but also a lot of nonsense that they shouldn't do even if they had enough manpower and cash.

It is also by no means clear that economic development is very high on the list of NR priorities. Those boys want power, and know how to get and keep it. The Southerners, with all their development and relative riches, just kid themselves if they think it is going to get them power. I keep telling them Machiavelli was no capitalist but knew his politics...

Supper at 7:00 PM with Ann, Lyle, Bernie Jensen and his wife and goddaughter. Bernie talked about the attitude in the North, which is grimly political and power-conscious. After all, the emirs have been juggling power for centuries. The attitude towards the British is ambivalent. Some are liked, no one is secure. Some are thrown out on 24 hours' notice. Bruce Greatbatch, the Sardauna's Private Secretary and once *the* power behind the throne, tries to hang on to his job as long as possible by becoming a yes man.

Lyle always talks about the time bomb that increased education builds under the system, and I rejoin that the newly educated generation can be captured by the system, and can and is likely to become part of the Establishment. Certainly, Akilu or Talib, who are completely westernized when one sees them alone, but on their toes when one has just two of them together, are completely the Sardauna's men, and think it quite normal that politics and power come first. It is a cruel system, but I believe quite capable of adaptation. Another matter to discuss with Kingsley.

November 19 (Sunday)....George Dolgin tipped me off that Prasad had discussed the size of the plan with the PM, who suggested extending it from five years to six to avoid the unpleasantness of cutting. Even though Dolgin in the line of duty always puts pressure on me, I was glad to have some advance notice. It is difficult to do one's job if one isn't kept up to date. Ambassador Palmer has been called home because the Nigeria program is the first to come up in Congress. Well, it left me a little upset but not too much...

A little later Andrew Wilson called from Ibadan. His minister wanted him to redo the Marketing Board forecasts. So I went back to the office, got my stuff and telephoned him with the figures. Always glad to be of service, especially to Wilson...

Reg Clarke came with another memo. He related some talks with Prasad. I was pleased to see some of my ideas getting across. Reg offered to see that any memo I wrote would go to the PM if I wanted...I said I was going to write the plan the way I saw it and if some people didn't like it they could lump it. I had had enough of giving in and then having to undo what others had written. He seemed to agree.

November 20. The day started with the usual staff meeting. Even if I have no orders to give, it's good to see everyone together. At 9:00 AM Stephen Mbamara, one of our assistant secretaries, and I met with the Ministry of Education on their program. I pointed out that we had to save money, particularly on recurrent costs. Our main proposal was to share specialist teachers – math, physics, etc. – among schools. Very small schools, say with 150 students, don't use qualified staff efficiently. So now we are trying to build bigger ones and make teachers teach in more than one at a time. We'll get a memo next week on how much money this will save. More important, it means saving qualified people, which in turn means improving the quality of teaching...

At 6:30 PM Lardner and I went to Prasad, who told us the PM had taken calmly the news that the program as submitted would have to be cut. But he had said he anticipated trouble at the next NEC meeting. Everyone would want to cut other people's programs in lieu of their own. So why not make it a six-year plan? There was nothing sacred about five years. He wanted our advice.

I agreed no number was sacred. Hence we might just as well make it a six-year plan. But that wouldn't meet the basic problem, which was to shift priorities towards productive sectors and cut out lots of nonsense. Prasad agreed we should insist on shifting priorities. I said I wanted to be quite sure. The size of the program was not the only thing that mattered. In fact, investments represented cost and we wanted to minimize cost for any given rate of growth, not maximize it. Prasad agreed.

Then he asked if we were agreed on a £650 million program over six years. I said that was too big. Prasad thought we could cut it. I said we would just have to go through the damn procedure again. I had worked 14 hours a day so that by November we were right back where we had been in April. I had been right about size and resources, and for the right reasons, too. I was not going through this again – £600 million was the maximum we could do, and even this was too big for six years. For the only time I have known him, Prasad showed irritation at me. He raised his voice and said he didn't believe in these statistics, but in deference to me he would stay with £600 million. I left it at that. But later he said again he wanted a six-year program of £600–650 million, but closer to 600.

He turned to me and said – as I already knew from Reg – that our own [Federal] resources were up to £40 million. I said I knew, but we couldn't use up everything. The point was still that we had to cut now, had to prevent the purchase of jets and ships, had to shift more into agriculture. Lardner was with me. I said if the program remained too big, we would run into the same trouble later. I was *not* going to be the man to right it. Prasad then mentioned his worry that the Ministry of Works was losing too many expatriates. I was sorely tempted to remind him how he had put me on the spot when I mentioned executive capacity; I resisted the temptation. He also complained that Toby had left him in the lurch (it was for perfectly good reasons).

I finally asked Prasad to arrange for me to be present when he talked with the PM. He agreed to ask the PM. I have no desire to fight Prasad, but would like to meet the PM and get a chance to say my piece when asked. But I want Prasad to be present.

Prasad noted that he enjoyed working with the PM and found him reasonable and responsive. Also that the quality of ministers was on the whole good. I always thought so. Things certainly have changed.

I came away a little depressed. To be sure, Lardner backs me. We see eye-to-eye on most things. We both want to avoid waste. He probably wants more austerity than I. I feel one must give some luxury goods even to the poorest as an incentive, some imported textiles, etc. But it is clear that I am just not good at political infighting. I am definitely put in my place, and Prasad is top dog.

This wouldn't worry me much if I saw eye-to-eye with him. But I dislike not being informed of what is going on, and then suddenly having problems sprung on me. Clearly I have lost in the political power struggle. If it doesn't affect work I don't mind. If it does, I get upset. Of course, I am new to this sort of thing, and am learning fast. I have made up my mind to get on my hind legs and struggle. After Christmas vacation I will be in a position to take things easier.

Despite my exasperation, which is genuine enough, I continue to find the job fascinating. I only wish I could take it easier and personalize less. I still like Prasad. I also admire his political *savoir faire*. But as an economist I am becoming quite conceited. My predictions were correct and he still cannot visualize the effects of his suggestions. By now I am not impressed when he pulls his experience on me. One of these days I will point out that I have had as much experience in Nigeria as he, and I question the relevance of Indian experience. Anyway things have their own logic…

November 21.…Minister just called from Parliament – he wants me to organize and head an investigation of Nigerian wholesale and retail trade. I asked when. Soon. I pointed out that I had to write a draft plan, that I was no expert on marketing, that the study was a long-term job and probably required an application to the Ford Foundation. He said that was OK, but he still wanted me to organize and direct it. I am flattered, but I don't know when and how to do this…

November 22.…The Minister sent a letter reminding me of the trade survey, only he had added transportation to it. It seems he made a long speech in Parliament about it…At noon Shaddock and I saw Prasad about the Plan document format. Prasad was reasonable this time. Shaddock wanted a uniform approach for each of the regional chapters. I didn't see the point. After all, their problems and plans are different. So why impose uniformity on inhomogeneous material.

A man from the Ministry of Information Film Unit came to talk about making a film on the plan. I told him to see Lardner. Lardner sent him back. So I told him to come back next year…

November 26, 1961

Peter Gibbs and Dick Latham dropped in, Lardner and Shaddock came along, Peter Clark was working with Cheido and the place was suddenly transformed again into a Marx brothers movie. Peter afterwards said, "It's quite clear the whole ministry would collapse without you. Why not tell them where to get off?" (He used stronger language.) My comment was that I am beginning to. Next week I will finally have my own office – if the air conditioner arrives.

Another crisis at 1:30 PM. Pius Okibgo telephoned from Enugu: his half-Congolese wife, who has an American passport, had returned from Paris and was stuck in Kano without a visa. Could I go over to Immigration and fix it up. So off I went, and got the necessary cable sent to Kano. All in a day's work – and it ought to help planning.

Pius had previously related the ER executive committee's latest decisions on the plan. Now that the elections are over and Okpara has won a landslide victory – every one does in Nigeria – some sense is prevailing, and things are improving.

Peter Gibbs is going north, but doesn't know into what job. Certainly not his old one, which has been elevated to PS status and Nigerianized (Talib). He would like to help set up the Niger Dam Authority, but neither of us knows its status. He was rather unhappy about the uncertainty. Certainly the old powers have fallen, and the powers that are in, delight in knifing the outs and twisting the knife in the wound. It is, as Bernie Jensen remarked, a cruel society.

Peter also gave me some insight into Northern personalities, most of it unpleasant, but unfortunately all of it with the ring of truth. That most of my troubles – and everybody else's troubles up north – stem from Ken Baldwin I knew already. But to find one's way through the jungle of who is and who isn't the Sardauna's boy, is too complicated, and naïveté may be a better safeguard against abuse than shrewdness. But Peter confirmed that I could trust Talib and Akilu, and probably Lawan…

November 24. I went over the draft Plan outline once more, and for a change tried to think. Leisure is such an important part of both thought and peace of mind…

At the staff luncheon I invited comment on the intent of the Minister's speech. Just what did he want me to do as director of a study of trade and transport? Cheido thought he really wanted two things: to document expatriates' role in trade, and to ensure that the investigation, though under my direction, was undertaken by Nigerians. We discussed what might be included in such a study. It was a useful luncheon…

November 25.…The Minister asked to see me. We agreed to start the study around March or April, after the budget. Obineche had interpreted him correctly: he wanted Nigerians to do the job under my direction. I said I had talked with Kingsley and Ford would underwrite such a study. A study of domestic trade would hold interest from both an academic and a policy viewpoint, because the economy was moving rapidly towards monetization and we needed to know more.

I said I thought I understood the Nigerian economy pretty well, but trade still stumped me. The minister replied it was very simple. The expatriate firms were the importers and wholesalers. They sold to Nigerian retailers on credit, which was fine. But then they also sold to their own retail outlets at lower cost, driving the Nigerians out of business, which he felt to be wrong. I already knew that, and said what puzzled me was the petty trading system…

Later I wrote part of what I hope will be a technical appendix to the Plan. What I am doing is constructing our model backwards, as it were, putting in the independently calculated figures for government consumption, import surplus, etc., to see whether they are consistent. We have finally gotten the figures and estimated the plan so that the exercise comes out all right. It is also intellectually satisfying, and I am even reasonably sure I invented the technique. It would be a miracle, however, if someone else hadn't thought of it too.

December 3, 1961

I went to make peace with Prasad, apologizing for any rudeness. He in turn said he never minded since I was obviously sincere. Also, since visiting Washington he has completely turned around and for the first time we are all pulling in the same direction. Obviously new problems arise every day. Someone is always trying to push, to dominate. I have to get on my hind legs and dig in against Shaddock, our new DPS. I like him but have to make clear from time to time that I am the economist and head of the planning unit, not he, and that I take orders only from the Minister and perhaps Lardner, but no one else. Cooperation yes, but not taking of orders. I have learned one must do that from the beginning.

...It has been arranged that I go to London on Jan. 1–3 to help Barbara Ward with a newspaper supplement on the Development Plan. It has Lardner's and Prasad's enthusiastic OK. Prasad said such a supplement was worth £1 million in free advertising...

November 27. Some relaxation. With the NEC paper finished, not much to do but wait. I worked on the draft Plan. I had hoped to attend the NEC, but the PM vetoed it, saying he wanted to keep me out of politics. In a way I was sorry, yet it was probably the right decision...

The three top Northerners, Akilu, Talib and Lawan, came by. They wanted to know where I had gotten some figures. Fortunately I was able to produce a document which they had given me, showing that any error was theirs.

They were also touchy on two other issues. Firstly, I had put in an arbitrary figure for the resource mobilization I thought they could do. Apparently I came so close to the real figures that they felt there must have been a leak. There wasn't, I just know the economy by now.

Finally, we had a table showing the regional distribution of capital works. The Department of Statistics had done this for years, and we anticipated no trouble. But it caused more trouble in NEC than anything else. Because the Niger Dam is in the North, the Northern figure was of course rather big. I couldn't get across that we were assuming that *all* Federal expenditures in the North were national rather than regional in scope. Only in the case of Lagos did we make a distinction, because only in the Federal Territory is the government both national and regional. This trouble illustrates the general sensitivity, and also my lack of political understanding. I just didn't understand why they were so upset, and why they wouldn't comprehend that we were not talking of benefits but only of location.

November 28. The NEC met. I spent my time dictating a chapter of the draft plan, hoping for the best, trying to get a good outline going. At 5:30 PM I went to see Prasad. He responded magnificently to my peace making.

First, he accepted all my pet ideas in the draft outline. Secondly, some recent developments worried him. The attacks on him and me in Parliament suggested radicalization. People are taking the attitude that, if planning was left to Nigerians, it would be further along. Also, Nigerians took for granted they would get large-scale foreign aid. When one thinks how India has had to struggle to get it! Of course, every new country understandably has an exaggerated sense of its importance.

He also was unhappy about Lardner, whom I defended. Lardner had written a strong briefing memo to the Minister, who enclosed it as a covering memo for the Federal Council paper we had written, for which use it was not intended. Prasad called it a poisonous document. I hadn't seen it before the Minister, else I would have objected to some of its ideas. But I didn't see it as poisonous, and felt Lardner made a number of points worth making. In any case, Council accepted the paper but the PM asked for the covering memo to be withdrawn.

Prasad does have a point. I think Lardner has been as straight with me as I with him. That he is a strong nationalist with a small *n* is clear and to the good. I don't understand local politics and want to stay out of it if I can, but would also like to understand it better. I can't really measure the effect of Lardner's memo. It is my feeling that he and most nationalists push too hard, too fast, to strengthen the central government, whereas the PM's slower pace is sounder and will get to the desired goal faster.

The trouble with Lagos is that everything gets personalized. People come back from leave fresh and peaceful, seeing things objectively, but after a few months on the island everything degenerates into a personality struggle. If I continue the work here I will insist on going home or to Europe every three months, and once a month into the bush just to restore equilibrium.

November 29. Another NEC meeting. The real decisions, taken the day before, were roughly what we wanted as to size, duration of the plan period, and priorities. We are now instructed to go ahead and shift the plan priorities our way. The Minister will back us to the hilt.

During the morning Barbara Ward called, and I invited her for lunch, which lasted until 5:30 PM. She and her husband, Commander Jackson, are leaving Ghana for good...She is still emotionally involved there, but agreed that Nkrumah might be too much interested in Pan Africanism and too little in Ghana. I thought that Pan African leadership was slipping out of his hands into the Nigerians' – I still think our PM's quiet way is superior to Nkrumah's loudness and will bring results. Nkrumah had to slip his troops quietly back into the Congo after withdrawing them loudly. He doesn't develop properly. He has wasted tremendous amounts of sterling assets. She agreed with all of it, but was not as certain as I – if I was – that our PM would succeed.

I also mentioned a talk I had had with Sudhir Sen, whom she knows[2]...Sudhir asked whether I would come to Ghana as adviser to Nkrumah. He is looking desperately for someone he can trust, and whose advice is sound. The wastefulness of past expenditure has become apparent. According to Sudhir they have neither a plan, nor any well thought-out projects.

Lady Jackson agreed to most of this. In addition she was full of stories about Russian and East bloc aid. First, the Ghanaians are about to withdraw all Ilyushin planes. They cost four times the maintenance of a DC8 or Boeing 707, and no one wants to fly in them. They must be completely overhauled after 5,000 flying hours, compared to 20,000 for American planes. Moreover it takes about five to ten times as many Russian technicians to run things. The Russians also bring their wives and families, and in places like Guinea where housing is exceedingly scarce, the Russian invasion is a major catastrophe. Moreover the Russians always stick together in their voluntary ghetto. Hordes of them are setting up factories, and they are a great deal less polite with the locals than Westerners. They are so sure they know all the answers that they tell everyone off in no uncertain terms.

In Guinea, the Russian ambassador has tried to see Sékou Touré for four months. The Guineans are fed up. A western spraying operation took two Piper Cubs plus four people. A corresponding eastern one takes three planes plus ten people. Both the Guineans and the Ghanaians badly want contact with the West. I hope they don't get advice like Tommy Balogh's, who may be responsible for Ghana being so hostile to the Common Market, or Kaldor, who is responsible for the recent riots and repressions with his withholding tax.

So Lady Jackson thinks the best thing for the West is to get the Russians in. The disillusionment is apparently quick.

November 30. JPC meeting at 10:00 AM. The main topic was how to translate the NEC decisions into practice. I pleaded for data on taxes and other resources, overall size of plan and major sectors by Dec. 7, so I could finish the macro chapters before leaving for Switzerland. I got the promise, but as usual one has to wait and see.

I also asked for regional representatives to come to Lagos not later than Dec. 7 to write the chapter on the regional plans and help in writing the National Plan, so we could work out a reasonably uniform pattern for presentation. This too was agreed.

Going through the draft Plan outline, some changes were suggested. I prevented some, accepted others and for the most part succeeded in getting the outline I wanted. On the whole the meeting was pacific. The Western Region boys unfortunately were ignorant of what was going on, because Wilson and Chukujekwe didn't come. From the North, Akilu, Talib and Lawan were all there. Very impressive.

I had Lardner and Lady Jackson for lunch. The purpose was to clear the lines for a supplement in the Economist, and clarify what I could and couldn't say. The instructions were rather general. Say anything that a smart reporter might find out. Avoid anything suggesting leakage from the planning unit. Fair enough…

December 1.…From 11:00 AM to noon we worked in Shaddock's office with Waterston, the director of Agricultural Research, on some possible large-scale projects. The Minister wants £10 million for this. It makes sense but is unconstitutional since agriculture is a regional prerogative. I suggested working out projects that combine research, large scale-experimentation putting it into practice, seed multiplication, and training of master farmers and extension workers. This way it becomes constitutional and gets away from pure research, which our ministers don't much like. Actually research has done well, but transmission from experiment to farmer has not worked. The Minister wants it, as is his prerogative, and is willing to fight for it in Cabinet. Moreover, constitutional or not, the regions seem to like it and it makes sense…

Dinner at the Dolgins' in honor of a team from the Ex-Im Bank. One, Bush, a brother of the senator from Connecticut, was quite impressive.[3] I sat with ambassador Palmer, with whom I am now on first-name terms…

December 2....I worked until almost 1:00 PM on a rewrite of the Federal Council paper in the light of the direction given by NEC and the Council. It was mainly a question of new figures, so Shaddock could do the actual formulations.

The whole Ex-Im Bank team spent $1^1/_2$ hours in the office. They are here on a general information mission, customary when the Bank first enters a new country. They didn't want to know confidential information. I explained what we were trying to do and what we hoped to accomplish. By now I can give this speech with the greatest of ease.

At 7:00 PM a cocktail party at Bill Kontos', deputy AID (former ICA) director, also in honor of the Ex-Im Bank team. Somewhat to my embarrassment, the Minister spoke of how much he trusted Americans – but not English – and specifically me. It was all very flattering and rather frightening. He virtually said: I trust you completely, but watch out if I don't. "I told the PM I couldn't work with Lewis. I don't trust Englishmen." I replied that I was flattered, thought I deserved the trust, Lewis was my friend and the Minister should know it, and if I thought the Minister didn't trust me I would resign on the spot. I must have been somewhat more agitated than I wanted to be, because Joe Palmer immediately intervened as if to calm me down, and suggested there was no need to resign.

The Minister then insisted we had no secrets from the Americans. After all, he had told Awolowo, "Why do you attack Stolper and Hansen? We want aid from the Americans, so they have a right to know. As for Rivkin, the Americans also sent teams to England after the war."

All of which was eminently sensible and fair. Except there are some things that must remain internal to the Nigerian Government, and which the Minister must believe I won't tell the USG. Palmer said the USG had nothing to do with the Ford Foundation and that was the difference with the Soviets. He also said he didn't get information from me without the Nigerian Government's permission. I felt a little uncomfortable throughout the talk about trusting me, because I believe it means that in fact they will *not* tell me anything they don't want the USG to know. Which is fair enough. But why not say so.

The Minister then reminisced about his days as manager with UAC,[4] and promised to show me his final accounts. He was happy to have been invited, and while he doesn't accept invitations from British, he does from Germans and Americans.

I left both flattered and uneasy, and went to the Dolgins'. The uneasiness was over the flattery and subtleties of the Northern mind. What I wanted to know from Dolgin was what message the ambassador had given the PM from President Kennedy about US aid for the Plan. I didn't get it, since Abubakar won't even tell the Cabinet. But I was given to understand that it is good news. I had had a letter from Arnold Rivkin accompanying his (excellent) testimony, strongly pro-Nigerian and complimentary to the Economic Planning Unit. The letter ended by saying I had undoubtedly heard the repercussions. Well, I hadn't. Before Prasad left for India he told me it was good. That's all I found out...

December 7, 1961

...During the past few days I have succeeded in drafting a good bit of the Plan for which I am primarily responsible. Still, one of the crucial chapters can't be finished until the Regions have made up their minds and let me know. Even this doesn't help always. Peter Gibbs phoned yesterday from Kaduna to give the NR's revised plan and resource picture – pretty alarming.

December 3 (Sunday)....Too tired to work, instead I played the piano. My neighbors across the street, Clive and Ethné Gray of ICA, or AID as it is called now, came to listen, which was a welcome change. He is a young fellow from Harvard working on foreign aid.

Almost had an international incident. My neighbor to the right is the High Commissioner of Sierra Leone, who had a severe car accident in the Congo. I had given his son a lift two days earlier. The son dropped in to tell me his father was all right. I didn't immediately recognize him. That was bad. But he also complained that Felix hadn't let him in without inquiring his business. I told Felix to let the neighbors come. Felix afterwards told me "It is not wise to have them too much. They are dirty. And the house will be a mess..." [See Photo No. 24 for photo of Felix and family at WS' house.]

December 5. We worked on a new paper for the Federal Council, cutting the program....The only interruption was Sadler, the UK trade commissioner, who wanted to know more details of our new six-year plan, which I either didn't know or was not allowed to tell him. In fact I had thought that even the fact that it was now six years instead of five was secret, but my Minister talked about it in the Senate. So I guess I can talk about it too. The more I think about it the less I like it, however. It causes a lot of trouble all around, and simply postpones hard decisions that must be made sooner or later.

The advantage of meeting Sadler is that he gives me copies of otherwise expensive reports on cocoa production...Recently the cocoa price has risen rather spectacularly because of expected small crops everywhere, particularly in Ghana. Nigeria and especially Brazil are less affected.

December 6....A call from Peter Gibbs. It is alarming that a lot of the North's decisions amount to a thinly veiled attempt at blackmail to get more resources out of the Federal Government at the expense of the other Regions and perhaps the Federal Government itself.

December 7....Peter Clark returned from his trip north refreshed. He said he got a different slant on our work. That when people talked about getting standards improved they talked essentially of Lagos. Elsewhere there were no standards. In short the trip was a success.

A Mr. Thomas appeared in alarm, sent by the German Ambassador. We had spoken critically of his firm's equipment sales to the Eastern Region. We don't believe the brewery and certainly not the glass and bottle factories will pay. He denied it hotly, and said their calculations indicated both would be profitable. I was skeptical and suggested he talk with Frank Moore when Frank came on Saturday.

Thomas said they had big plans in Nigeria, and a reputation to maintain, and had refused to sell a brewery to the WR because it was too big. I wasn't really prepared for the visit, which fortunately lasted only half an hour, because I didn't have all the figures, but I believe Frank Moore's critique. I pointed out we were trying to build up a strong private sector, and could not look without alarm at the fact that supposedly free-enterprise Germany was selling factories to governments with abandon.

At 2:00 PM Nicolescu appeared from Ibadan, where he interviewed as a candidate to head the Economics Department at the new University of Ife. The interview was apparently only partly satisfactory. He had the impression they wanted him to keep the seat warm for a Nigerian, probably Ogunsheye, at present working on his PhD at Harvard. Ogunsheye is a good man. Nicolescu was naturally not interested in a short-term appointment, but he was impressed by the seriousness of intent and quality of the people behind the new university, particularly Chief Adebo, who is indeed a first-rate man by any conceivable standard...

Chukujekwe just called from Ibadan to give me the latest WR figures. But I still need more before I can make the calculations necessary to draft Chapter 5, which is important.

December 8. Interrupted for about an hour by Gould of AID.[5] He wanted a session with Lardner on technical aid. The problem was really very simple. The question was: did we consider any technical assistance we might get to be part of the foreign exchange gap? The question was so simple that I didn't quite understand it. The answer was that on principle we tried not to worry where and in what form the foreign aid was coming, but simply calculated first the total program, then our resources and finally the resource gap, which would exceed the balance of payments gap. Whether we would succeed in getting all the required financing was another question that I couldn't answer...

December 10 (Sunday). A hectic day. Frank Moore had come from the East, Chuke from the West and Bernie Jensen from the North to write their chapters for the Plan document and to coordinate with me. Peter was also there, to be prepared to brief Lyle on Lyle's return. The Regions wanted briefing from me, and I outlined what I thought should go into the chapters. The regional plans enter into the federal document to make it a national plan, but the Regions will submit detailed plans separately to their parliaments. I said they should aim at short chapters, bringing out targets, justified priorities, the overall picture and some payoff calculations...

Each Regional representative had given me financial details, and I wanted to know what was publishable *versus* for internal use only. Also what had already passed the Executive Committee.

At 3:30 PM Jensen handed me the North's documents. The details were frightening – they were glibly assuming they could get about £50 million more from the Federation. On the other hand, Jensen had permission for the first time not only to show me everything, but also to relax the bargaining atmosphere and outline what the North really expected to do...

At 7:00 PM I went to see Reg Clarke in secret and alarm to tell him the Northern story. He agreed that what the North wanted was nonsense, and will figure out a way to handle it...

December 11. First priority was to call Kaduna to discuss revenue and expenditure with Talib, PS Finance, and Leyton, who did the projections. I needed a firm fiscal picture in order to finish my central Chapter 5. I must have been on the phone for an hour, pleading with them to be reasonable. Not much success. I had projected revenue last May when I was up but have since revised the figures downward twice and given them the revisions. Nevertheless they insisted on using the higher figure. We agreed that Leyton had used some double counting. For the rest, Talib would not budge. Finally he said the Sardauna was confident he could get the money from the Federal Government and had given orders to leave the figures in. They had no choice in the matter. Neither did I. So I put in both our Federal and the Northern figures, and deducted £49 million for double counting with a footnote. This business was somewhat upsetting.

Over lunch I briefed Peter on Chapter 5 and Appendix 1. The tables are carefully laid out, but the figures will have to be changed when our own Council of Ministers has given final approval. I showed Peter exactly how to do the recalculations...

In the evening ambassador Posadowski and Frank came for supper – Frank wanted to discuss the role of German businessmen which we think is in the interest neither of Nigeria nor Germany nor the West. The trouble is that much revolves around questions of fact. The Germans sold the ER a glass factory. Frank objected that no one knew what it would cost; all we know is what the machinery cost. The Germans say there is ample sand for glass making. Frank says there is not. The firm is reputable. Still it is an uncomfortable situation.

December 12. At 9:30 AM saw a representative of English General Electric, who asked me indiscrete questions about contractor finance. I was diplomatic and pointed out that the Federal Ministry of Finance had to give permission for all foreign loans, that we welcomed private capital, and that we were watching the balance of payments...

In the evening a cocktail party given by the Ford Foundation. Ambassador Palmer took me aside to ask whether I had heard the announcement. I hadn't. Well, the US has promised $225 million over 5 years. I made some calculations: we need $300 million. I must have sounded sour, because Palmer patted me on the shoulder and said "Now, Wolf, this is just an order of magnitude. It can get bigger." Actually I thought it was pretty good as a start.

On the whole, a good party. Everyone was elated and felt that for a change things were going right. Reg Clarke took me aside to tell me my troubles with Prasad were over. [World Bank President] Black had talked to him. "And Prasad doesn't know it, but Fenton and I had something to do with it. And you did a brilliant job." The 'you' referred obviously also to Lyle.

In general, I have won my fight. Lardner took me aside to congratulate me on the Plan document, and while changes would have to be made, he would see to it that it would in essence go through. Reg Clarke offered to have me meet his minister, but since his minister hates mine, this is probably not wise. Still, Festus is powerful. Clarke then told me he had asked Festus to leave the Economic Planning Unit out when quarreling with my Minister and Festus had promised to do so – and kept his word. "You have good relations there, eh?" he asked Clarke and Reg said he had indeed...

December 13....At 5:00 PM to the airport, where we saw off Kingsley for London and New York and I had two hours with Lyle about what needed to be done, and when...

Notes

1 President Nnamdi Azikiwe.
2 Sudhir Sen was a fellow member of the Schumpeter Seminar in Bonn – unusual for an Indian, since most of those studying abroad in the 1930s went to Britain. He was attracted

by Schumpeter, with whom he eventually took his PhD. Before joining the UN he was part of the inner circle of Mahatma Gandhi, whom he tried to convince of the advantages of modernizing agriculture and industry. He also served as head of an Indian agency modelled on the US Tennessee Valley Authority.

3 The senator was Prescott Bush, father and grandfather, respectively, of two subsequent US presidents.
4 United Africa Company, the largest expatriate trading company in Nigeria.
5 Burton Gould, USAID/Nigeria program economist.

Chapter 12

January 21–March 3, 1962
Cabinet Debates Program Cuts, Tensions in Ford Team, Corruption, Integrated Plan *versus* Four Separate Plans, Stolper Attends NEC Meeting in Ibadan

January 27, 1962

I'll try to bring the diary up to date. Neither Cairo nor Addis are places where you want to write indiscreet things. They are both obviously full of fear and hatred, and there is undoubtedly censorship, mitigated by inefficiency…

Rossen, the ECA research director, cabled from Addis Ababa to Lardner asking whether I could stay an extra week. The answer was a long telegram: I must decide myself, there was enormous pressure on everyone, Lyle couldn't work my method, which alarmed me and which turned out to have a good reason. So I decided I would go home as scheduled on the 21st.

January 21.…Lyle and Peter kept me until 11:30 AM …In short, a white paper had to be written, all my chapters and the regional chapters had to be rewritten. Finance had lent us a Senior Assistant Secretary to rework the Federal chapter and make capital estimates for the 1962-63 budget. Lyle had to work on the Federal Plan. Editorial meetings were held every afternoon at 4:00 PM in Prasad's office.

I spent Monday getting back into the routine. The chapters were distributed for rewriting and we met every afternoon, working until 9:30 PM. Prasad suddenly got it into his head that he wanted more poetic language and was politely asked to supply it himself. He didn't quite succeed, but he spotted a number of words likely to act like red flags to a bull.

On the whole not much happened to my draft. It is more watered down than I wanted it to be, less terse, but I got most of my points in. I can completely count on Reg Clarke's backing. The atmosphere has been good, since Prasad and I joke at each other. But he still tries to sneak in things by the back door; and when I catch them, he accuses me as the American who sees communists in every bit of planning, although his remarks, as is typical, come out of the blue sky and seem rather irrelevant. He even accused me, of all people, that as an American I couldn't see that resources were scarce. I gasped. Reg afterwards said: "I hope you pardon me if I derive a certain amount of sardonic amusement from all this." Well, all this is almost finished, two more days perhaps. Then I have to help Lyle with his chapter, and pay attention to the Federal chapter proper and the lengthy annex…

Toby and Jean Lewis returned yesterday morning. I was the only one at the airport. Patricia, who meant to go, didn't get permission from her current PS. And the Ministry of Communications, to which Toby has been posted as PS (and which is in the same building as we are), had not sent a car. So it was good that at least I was there. I told Lardner I was going, and to tell it to the minister, so he wouldn't think I do anything behind his back...

The weather is surprisingly decent. There is wind, it is foggy all morning with wet air mixed with desert dust. Until the sun burns it off it isn't bad. Two days ago we had a heavy downpour.

January 25, 1962[1]

Since I got back, things have been not so much hectic as a steady grind. The drafting committee meets, and Prasad, Reg Clarke, Lyle, Shaddock, Lardner and I are rewriting chapters on the basis of instructions from JPC. We meet every afternoon at 4:00 PM to discuss the rewrite and have the chapters stenciled. We so far have stopped at 8:00 PM or later...

Still, the interruption has done me a lot of good. Among other things I am uncertain what I want to do in the future. I have serious doubts whether I want to continue here if asked. The only thing I know is that I can't stand the tempo and nerve-wracking squabbles of the past, and am determined not to let anything faze me. This is important, because not all things are going as I had hoped, but on the whole they are all right. Decisions on the size of the program, etc., have fallen, and there is no use fighting now that Cabinet has decided. So I do what I am required to do, but won't knock myself out, as I did before – which still means a 10–12 hour day.

I still think the program is too big, and a smaller program would lead to a higher growth rate. But in reality the program as carried out will be smaller anyway, so I need not worry. And I think the country will achieve faster growth than projected in the figures and the Plan.

Personal relations with Prasad are now good, partly, no doubt, because I have come refreshed from the meeting with my family. But probably also because Prasad has his problems, too, and as I say, I am determined not to fight now, since it can't conceivably do any good.

My crucial chapter – one of two in the document – must be finished today. (Lyle is responsible for the other one.)

February 2, 1962

January 28 (Sunday).....I was in a grim mood all week until today. Things did not seem to go right, and even Godfrey Lardner was discouraged.

January 29. Back in the office at 8:00 AM. I'm not yet back to the 6 AM routine, except occasionally, when absolutely necessary. I am determined not to let anything get me any more. The week before with its constant editorial meetings and fights to keep things on the straight and narrow path had got me down somewhat, but I was and am determined not to care too much. I worked on two appendices – or annexures as they are now called – to my crucial Chapter 5, interrupted several times.

Reg Clarke brought me suggested changes in the Central Bank and Banking Ordinances, and I tried to study them to give him my opinion. I had never done this before, and it was a curious mixture of dull work and interesting problems. Most changes deal with clearer formulations of the law, mainly due to Nigeria's being no longer a colony. However some changes dealt with aspects of monetary policy and in particular with regulations to make it more effective…

By evening I was fairly blue. And Reg Clarke was also worried. He told me Festus was, too. A Sunday Cabinet meeting had left things open. Earlier there was a vicious attack on us in Cabinet, accusing us of falsifying figures. Festus and our own minister had beaten it back with the aid of two excellent memos by Lyle, pointing out that (a) the Economic Committee of Cabinet had suggested hiring an independent firm of accountants to get the right figures, something the complaining minister didn't mention; and (b) no alternative figures on the crucial question of payoff had been adduced.

Then everyone jumped in, demanding restoration of cuts we had made without giving ministries an adequate hearing. This particularly hurt because we had been at great pains to discuss details with the ministries concerned. In one case we knew the PS was a son of a bitch and hadn't briefed his minister, simply withholding from him our comments and queries. In another case, the PS is honorable, but inefficient and ineffective. Both are Englishmen.

In any case, the PM decided to call another meeting today, where everyone could talk to their hearts' content and fight it out among themselves. Festus was worried, so was my Minister, and so was I. I pointed out to Reg, I don't know for the how many-th time, that the program was too big, that somewhere along the line I was doublecrossed on this by you know whom, that somehow the absolute maximum size had become a minimum. I was worried about the economic consequences, and even more about the political ones. Reg said I should write a memo on my fears that he could use for briefing Festus, and he assured me it would go to the PM. I did. No one must know, though, particularly not Prasad.

January 30. I started dictating the memo. I wrote: if the program is too big, we get inflation and exchange control. Inflation causes political trouble in towns with semiliterate unemployed and alienated intellectuals. Moreover, in Nigeria, where people react to incentives, too much austerity backfires. A new country can't afford to start independence with no increase in living standards. And pampering an army would do no good. It went on in this vein. As Reg advised me, I didn't worry whether it was political or theoretical.

Reg came back about noon "from the source of all my troubles," but saying it went well. I gave him the memo on the sly – the fewer people know, the better. Reg said I should give him my points and he would rewrite them. I also said I had no comments on the proposed banking amendments, they seemed OK to me, but I had too little experience to see offhand what was omitted. He said Prasad had said more or less the same, asking for a month to study the details – I have no doubt he will get ahold of the Indian law and suggest inserting all sorts of provisions from it. Some may even be applicable to Nigeria…

January 31. …Lyle is carrying the brunt of the writing the Appendix on the Federal program. I have the main task of rewriting and editing which will be plenty of work.

We debated strategy. Lyle has developed the strategy of saying: "You have a fine idea. Unfortunately we haven't got the resources as far as we can see now, but if we have, you can have it in the program." That avoids an outright row, and leaves everyone happy. For a long time I thought this was a great idea, but I don't like it any more. Lyle says I needn't worry too much about overall size, because there will be substantial shortfalls anyway. My answer is: I hope so. But first I want a realistic program.

More important, shortfalls will come. not in relatively low-priority sectors and margins, but in the most productive sectors where it is hardest to spend. This will slow growth unless it leads the private sector to grow faster via incentives and higher consumption. If, rather than lowering taxes, the money 'saved' through shortfalls in productive sectors raises spending in lower-priority schemes, we will get an unbalanced program and slower growth and an inflationary situation. Thus we must devise a different way of formulating what we are after in the Plan, namely flexibility while preserving priorities.

I then went to see Godfrey, who added to my gloom. I wanted to talk with him under four eyes about the future of the planning unit, the Ford Foundation project, myself. I wanted to know, over wine or tea, whether we were trusted or wanted. In general I have the uneasy feeling that we have been a little pushed to one side since Toby left the Ministry. I suspect it is part of the general deterioration of administrative efficiency. Files just don't come to our desks as they used to in Toby's day. But I wanted to talk freely at home. I also wanted to find out from a Nigerian – not from Kingsley, Rivkin or the World Bank – whether they view our operation as worthwhile and in their interest. And I wanted to know whether we were used or abused.

Anyway, Godfrey came for tea but otherwise only added to my gloom. He was as tired as I and even more pessimistic. No minister except ours was really interested in economic development, just in contracts and kickbacks. To be sure, Festus and our Minister are on the same side, but why shouldn't Festus be: he holds the purse strings. The PM is weak, that's why the British put him in. He, Lardner, would show me documents he had written years ago urging staff expansion and training so that now, five years later, people would be ready. The British civil servants had told the PM that Lardner wanted to Southernize the civil service, and Peter Stallard just didn't show him the memoranda on training Northerners which Lardner had written. The PM just doesn't like him and vice versa.

Then he said, "Just don't work your head off. I've had two ulcer operations and can't afford any more. They had to order me back from Addis, at a cut in salary, and I've had enough and am ready to resign and apply to the UN, although it is against regulations for a civil servant to do so without government permission." He also said, "I told the Minister, Stolper has a good professorship to go back to. He doesn't want to stay and create a position where he is indispensable. His advice is unbiased and can be relied on. If you don't like it, he'll go back." Good to know that we are trusted after all.

So all this – which is, of course, between us – didn't help much, except that there is some sort of catharsis in the process of talking it out. Godfrey is a little like me, elated and depressed alternately, because both of us work hard and with our nerves. I sometimes envy Lyle for his steadiness, which, I believe, is the result of a combination of lack of sensitivity and a very big ego which, despite my occasional big talk, I really lack.

Frank Moore's arrival in the evening added more trouble. Our Minister had egged on the Regional ministers of agriculture to demand large-scale subsidies from the Federal government, and had promised they would get them, or at least that he would fight for them. The figure Frank reported is appalling: £50 million. Frank reported he was impressed with Lardner's standing up to the Minister in a debate that was occasionally acrimonious.

February 1, 1962

At 9:00 AM I went with Peter see Col. Tom Bull, whom I met when I first came. I wanted to say hello and it was just as well. He had sold out his business to the Otto Wolff concern, a big German firm. Since they were trying to sell us a monorail, I had avoided contact with him. He told me he was leaving the firm. He couldn't take their politicizing, their combining racial superiority towards the Africans with corrupting them. They weren't straight in this respect...11:00 AM to 2:30 PM we spent in Reg Clarke's office writing briefs for Festus and our minister explaining why all the requests for funds should not be granted. We discussed each point with Reg, who then dictated the briefs, in excellent form which Lyle and I couldn't have approached, to two secretaries whom he kept busy. Lyle delivered copies to our minister and to Godfrey, who felt he had talked all he could to the minister, who, if he didn't know what the points were, would never learn them.

Actually both Festus and Ibrahim studied the briefs and our papers until they knew them virtually by heart. Reg also showed me the general policy paper he had done for Festus, incorporating most of my points in a vastly improved and more effective form. Now there is nothing to do but hope for the best.

The Minister didn't mention the £50 million for agriculture he had talked about in Ibadan. Frank was upset, because he (Ibrahim) had been so strong there. He and Godfrey talked about just what went on in that meeting, Frank insisting that a decision had been reached to ask for the money, Godfrey insisting it was only a recommendation. In any case, he made two comments. "Do you think the Minister is a fool? He had his hands full with one thing, and didn't want to raise the other issue which could have opened up the whole discussion again." The other was: "The Minister is the Economic Planning Unit's best friend." I hope so.

February 4, 1962

February 2. Got a call from Mordecai Kreinin[2] who has a research project on Israeli technical aid to Africa. Kreinin said the Israelis were all down on Frank Moore, and despite his (Kreinin's) efforts he could not find out what Moore's criticisms were. Apparently anyone who is critical of Israeli aid is suspected of anti-semitism or at least political motives.

In fact, Frank is of Jewish origin. As he once pointed out to the Israeli ambassador, they were born within 50 miles of each other, and it just happened that the parents of one went to the States and of the other to Palestine. Instead of giving the Nigerians hard advice, the Israelis tell them what they want to hear; worse, they play both sides of the street. They establish joint companies, with Israel taking 49% of the capital in order to prove they are not 'imperialist,' then sell them a bill of goods and, when questioned, turn around and say that as minority shareholders they had no choice!

Our criticism of farm settlements was reported in Israel as being anti modern agriculture and *pro* gradual development of native methods! We pointed out that we wanted just as much to break out of the traditional methods, but not at a cost of £4–6,000 per settler! No one had made decent cost-benefit calculations. It is all very well to talk about noneconomic aims, but one must also take into account such noneconomic factors as the fact that, at age 18, Nigerians have at least one wife who for several years produces a child a year that may not survive but which prevents her from working full time – i.e. providing 300 days of labor a year. The story that it was the price of land that inflated total cost was simply not true, and Frank gave detailed figures. We left Kreinin shaken. He will see Frank in Enugu.

Back to the office. Godfrey came in to report victory all along the line. The Minister had just come from Cabinet. All we had to yield was £5 million; Cabinet had ordered the Minister and Festus to cut 5 million somewhere from the program. Apparently it was a confused meeting, how confused we only found out today. Only Ibrahim and Festus had done their homework. Every time another minister would say something, our Minister or Festus would go through the papers and say, "and the Economic Planning Unit says ... the figures are right here..."

The Minister backed us to the hilt against the assembled Cabinet and carried the day with one minor exception. We even cut out the Parliament building. And our *very* substantial cut in military spending stuck – something I was really afraid would be reversed. Lyle and I immediately went to congratulate the Minister and thank him for his confidence, Lardner joined in, and all was sweetness and light. Cabinet had to take major unpleasant decisions and faced them in a really impressive manner. The program is still too big and they're not ready to implement it – which means it will get underway slowly. But the first and in many respects biggest hurdle has been cleared, and we have every right to be proud of the work. The labor has been worthwhile, and it's good to know we are trusted after all...

February 3. There was a reaction today. We tried to find out just what happened in Cabinet, and where to cut out £5 million. As to the first, the Cabinet meeting seemed to be confused. Festus and Ibrahim couldn't agree on what was decided. Festus thought the additions were so small that the PM had said they just should be added and one should let things go at that. Ibrahim thought he had orders from Cabinet to cut out £5 million at his discretion. So they called up the two secretaries, who also could not agree what was decided...

Lyle had spent some time working out possible cuts. Then I dictated a memo to the Minister, and took it to him with our suggested cuts and the reasons therefor. Another minor shock. First the Minister said he wanted to wait for the PM's decision. He was always accused of being arbitrary and this time wanted to avoid the accusation. Secondly he wasn't really interested in our suggested cuts: Cabinet had said they should come out of education and health. This was news to us. We still have to find out when the minutes come our way.

I then asked about comments on our White Paper. He let the chapters pass except the one on the Federal program. He was really upset that we, i.e. Lyle, had cut 10 million from one of his pet projects, and said he wanted it back in or else he wouldn't support the paper. I promised to raise this and the other minor points with Lyle and Godfrey. But I felt my head was in the lion's mouth. It can really throw a monkey wrench into the machinery. I hope Godfrey will take care of it.

At lunch I had Peter and Professor Letiche from Berkeley, long familiar by name and writing. He's working at ECA/Addis for a year on the important problem of unifying the French and British monetary systems. It is immediately relevant to the Cameroons, but also elsewhere. In general he shares my feeling that (a) the French territories are independent only in form; (b) French subsidies have not led to real development, but to monuments such as post offices and government buildings and indirectly to subsidies of French firms selling equipment; and (c) the villain in the piece is the French Marketing Arrangements, which are restrictive in nature and cause stagnation.[3] His feeling was that Nigeria is vastly advanced and lively. I thought a change in policy could do the same for other countries of Africa...

February 7, 1962

Work is very hectic again. Lyle was supposed to have written the Federal Plan Appendix. He did produce 100 pages, but not only was the English atrocious, he had not really given any thought to what he wanted to do. He was somewhat miffed at my criticism. He does not like criticism, though he takes it from me on the very few occasions when I offer it. But it wasn't all his fault. The original idea was to omit most detail and payoff calculations and write the paper in the usual white paper style, which I loathe. But he made it worse by simply cutting up earlier papers, including my original, and pasting them together. In the process of cutting and rearranging, all continuity got lost. So I have been alternately rewriting and dictating. And the whole staff has to sit next door to produce data for me as I require them.

February 4 (Sunday)....We had to correct the final chapter in light of the latest Council decision, which it turned out was to keep the program within the original limits...The Minister made the first of five phone calls, and I couldn't give him an answer because Lyle had taken the relevant document home: the secret Council minutes...The Minister was obviously preparing himself very carefully to present the document to Cabinet and NEC...

At 5:30 PM I had a personal talk with Lardner. I am somewhat mixed up what I really want to do. I know Kingsley, Rivkin and the World Bank think we have done a good job, but what I have to know is how we look to the Nigerians. They are after all the consumer of our services and the test is whether they think they got what they wanted. Godfrey said we had done a very good job. And when the present emergency job was over he wanted me to do two things: think about monitoring Plan implementation, and provide a list of necessary studies. Still, I have a bet with Lyle that when the Plan is submitted we will be attacked in Parliament. Or there may be a deal of some sort.

I have established very good personal relations with Godfrey, which is important both personally and professionally. But my feeling is that we are no longer at the center of things. This goes even more for Prasad...

February 12, 1962

February 7. My main task was to rewrite Lyle's draft – to which he didn't take kindly. He worked as hard as everyone else to supply me with the additional data I needed – much of which it now turned out couldn't be used because of confidentiality...

Reg Clarke called with a message for Lardner. There had been a dispute over exactly what Cabinet had decided – the Minister thought it decided to keep the size of the plan constant, and authorized him to make cuts offsetting increases. Reg said the minutes he had just received showed the Minister to be wrong. So Lardner decided to raise the figures, and we made those changes. This led to some trouble (see below).

I went to dinner with Col. Bull, whom I had met on the plane when I first arrived in Lagos...Other guests were Lt. Col. Fullbrook, the Nigerian Army's Quarter Master General, and Chief Justice Sir Adetokimbo, a very pleasant man of considerable power...Most of the talk was small though pleasant. In fact, for Nigeria there was a remarkable absence of gossip. Col. Fullbrook complained we had cut £10 million from his budget, but admitted they probably could save that much by proper scheduling of work. Anyway I pointed out that we cut mostly clubs and barracks, and not firepower. His point was mainly that it was impossible to build up discipline with the soldiers living in mud huts, and the police being treated more nicely...

February 8. Lyle and I argued. He had given me a table that made no sense; interrelations of the figures were all wrong. He wouldn't see it, and started to talk about time lags. Then he told me I didn't understand because I hadn't worked through the tables. I couldn't get him to see the rather simple mistake. When he finally saw it he shifted the argument. All this I found exasperating, childish and fruitless.

As I was leaving, the Minister stormed in. Shaddock and Lardner were out so I was the first one he could hit. What is the idea of raising the figures and restoring the cuts he had made? Who is the Minister, he or I? Who runs the ministry – the Minister, the Planning Unit, Festus, or Clarke? If the document comes up in this form he will not present but fight it. I was taken aback, and pointed out we had got the information, had passed it on to Godfrey, and had tried to get ahold of him (Ibrahim). Then he went into Lyle's office to start all over again. Lyle made matters worse by patronizing him. Then the Minister went into a tirade against Reg Clarke, for whom he had no use, who should never have been brought back, etc. Lyle kept arguing and I went home leaving Lyle to cook his own goose, since my attempts to stop him were not effective...

February 9....Lyle blamed me for putting Reg in a false position – a typical Hansen performance. I asked him how I could have given Reg's message to Lardner and not mentioned where it came from. That stopped Lyle just long enough to put the blame on Godfrey. The fact Lyle doesn't appreciate is that we are innocent bystanders in the middle of a power struggle between our Minister and Festus. One just has to expect that sort of thing in politics. Lyle tends to talk down to them as if they were undergraduates. It's no longer amusing. People don't like to be patronized, and one can't do it to a minister. I just had time to call Reg Clarke to tell him my Minister was after his scalp and how it had come about. There will be fireworks in the Cabinet and NEC meetings...

All this may sound rather childish, and to a point it is. But this is an important country. If you live with this sort of thing, it gets you down. And the point is that Lyle is trying to take over. I will, of course, continue to work with him since I tend to give in. But he has not always kept me informed – his explanation is that he wanted to protect me from detail. And he is not as good, and certainly not as fast a theorist. Well, never mind. The trouble is, the Nigerians want me to stay as long as I can, but not Lyle. Yet he wants to stay, and I don't...

February 10. The editorial committee went over my draft. The only interruption was a call from the Minister asking for the latest commodity report. Then he apologized and asked me to forget everything. Obviously Godfrey, whom I had told things, had spoken to the Minister. I was rather pleased, because as far as I know I am the only white man to whom he has tried to be pleasant.

Then he wanted to know why you [WS' wife] weren't here, and whether I had your picture. When I explained as far as I felt necessary, he wanted to know whether you too were of German stock. I said you were Swiss. Wasn't that the same? Obviously being German or Austrian is OK. He just dislikes British and Indians.

He also asked how I liked the work, and I said, on the whole very much, despite some frustrations and issues where I wanted to throw up everything and go home. Then to my surprise he wanted to know on what conditions I would come back for another tour. I replied, it depended on the family and myself, the University and Ford. What was my relation to Ford?

I was pleased because it is the customer who has to be satisfied. The unfortunate thing is that Lyle will never believe I did my best to save his position. I may yet succeed, though I doubt it – and I have given up teaching him anything. You remember when I wrote the things he said. At the time I didn't take it too seriously. But now it comes from the Nigerians.

The Minister then looked at me and said: of course, you are naïve about trying to cut building costs. Building costs are high due to corruption. Contractors quote a price to make a profit. Then the minister wants some money. So they add the bribe to the price. One never can get the cost of building down. I told him I was aware of the problem though not of its extent, and that we had it too in the States. He then asked about Sherman Adams, etc., the practice of Senate investigating committees, etc. So things were pleasant again for a change...

After lunch, the Minister called. He was worried that we had cut £5 million from the ministry's recurrent budget. He wanted it back in. I tried to argue, but without much success. He wanted £20 million, not £15. I promised to talk with Lardner. He didn't like what I had written on his pet scheme. "You hate research and experiments." I pointed out that the section had been rewritten. I read the passage back to him over the phone and he passed it. Then he said, "You said, I couldn't do these things, but you will see, Cabinet will vote for it." Lardner called and argued, with me briefing him. We got our point across.

I dropped by the Dolgins' for supper...George had just come back from Jos where Chase Bank was looking at a tin smelter. His account was not too complimentary to the British. For years the biggest British tin smelters said one couldn't smelt tin in Nigeria. Then a Portuguese came and told the Northerners that he could, and he did. Whereupon the British started a big smelter, and persuaded the one private power company to withhold power from the Portuguese. He complained and got the ministry to write a nasty letter. The company replied it had been unaware of his needs and he would now get the power! This sort of thing makes Britishers distrusted, though I dare say other nationalities are not immune to these shenanigans.

George then told me some other bits. AID rents a staff apartment building from Festus. They had a long-term contract. Festus wanted a substantial rent increase. The Americans declined. Now Festus has served an eviction notice! How greedy can they get! And how stupid, when they are seeking major loans and grants from the Americans. Festus and Benson, the Minister of Information, split a substantial cut from the TV contract. What do they care about the development program as long as they can control the contracts?

I told George what the Minister had said about ministerial corruption. He had told the same thing to ambassador Palmer. He had also wanted to transfer the granting of all contracts to the PM's office, but the PM had demurred. I wonder whether the Minister is as weak as I am constantly told he is. The game could very well be to influence us not to put much trust in him, since he won't last, etc. Right now I think he is likely to last quite a long time…

February 12. This morning I stood over Lardner literally until he had dictated the final changes. He had lost the last page, so I had to think up another final paragraph, which he changed completely – for the worse, I think. I still have to do the proofreading. I was friendly with Lyle in the interest of working harmony. But I don't want to write a book with him and I told him so. Our temperaments and speed of working are too different. And I told him to take a few days off to recuperate. I will do the same now that the editing is done…

February 14, 1962

February 13.…Dinner with the Dolgins' *et al.* The Dolgins are somewhat fed up with Nigeria, too much corruption. We are all worried about that. It isn't the stealing itself so much as the effect it has on priorities, on costs, and on the morale of the people who know. It is not just 'intellectuals' who talk about and know it. It goes much deeper. This makes the problem of enforcing the Plan priorities so important, fascinating, and probably impossible…

February 15, 1962

We learned the PM did not want the Plan as a whole presented to the Federal Parliament, only the Federal Plan, and each parliament should debate only its own plan. This was upsetting, because we were hired after all to produce a national plan, not four separate ones. We had done a lot of integration and coordination. Prasad had tried to see the PM but was told he was fasting.

We both agreed that no Plan means little or no foreign aid. Of course, ultimately aid is given on political grounds, but preparation and acceptance of a Plan and its implications play a big part in the political decision to give or not to give aid. Prasad said he was writing the PM on this. He also said he had written to request my presence at NEC. Apparently at the last meeting in Enugu, he was asked questions he couldn't answer about the Plan, and noted I was the only one who knew all the calculations behind it.

I asked again why I hadn't been invited last time. He said I was white. The Nigerians want as few expatriates as possible in their inner councils. They feel they have to put up with Reg Clarke and a few others who are still indispensable. They accept Prasad as an Indian (questionable), but don't want new faces. This sounds plausible and makes sense. Prasad then said he would seek a compromise by having the PM accept the general policy chapters of the White Paper but include only the Federal Plan. This would be acceptable to me...

February 17 (Ibadan). Starting at the university, I called on Aboyade, who wanted to see the Plan and ask questions about it. We also discussed whether he would consider teaching at Michigan. He is a tall, well-built Yoruba,[4] extremely intelligent, outspoken and straightforward, politically in the opposition, like most people in the Western Region, without however being wedded to Party politics.

Next I went to see "the Prof" (as the Nigerians always refer to him), Barback, unfortunately not an impressive man, and disliked by the Nigerians. He is not a good director of NISER and from what I can gather not a good Prof either. Barback wanted to know the future of NISER. I said all I knew was that it was going to be expanded. He said he was never consulted, and after all it was only reasonable that the people who had built NISER up should be asked since they knew most about it.

I said I had been on a JPC committee which wrote an NEC paper on what to do with NISER, and since then I had had nothing to do with it. (Decision, it turned out, was again postponed at NEC.) But I was brutal enough to tell him that in my opinion the days of all palefaces in policy making were numbered, and I made it as clear as I could, without actually saying so, that in my opinion he would *not* be the head of the expanded NISER. I was glad to get away, because Barback has all the British snobbism without the offsetting intelligence that one often finds in the expatriates – actually I believe he is Australian.

At 11:00 AM I saw Chief Adebo, the WR's top civil servant, a truly impressive and honorable man, in my opinion the greatest Nigerian I have met. He is of course in the center of things. What I told him about the PM's sudden decision did not make sense to him. Then he asked how the White Paper had been written. There were some good chapters and one chapter that neither he nor any of his colleagues liked. While I waited for Adebo a call came from Prasad, telling me the PM had decided I was to go to NEC in Ibadan, but wait outside the meeting room on call in case questions arose that only I could answer...

Febraury 19. Worked all morning to brief myself for the NEC meeting, then Shaddock and I drove to Ibadan...We reported to the Minister on his arrival. At first he was disagreeable. All Moslems are during Ramadan. They are not allowed to eat, drink, smoke from sunup to sundown, which means from 4 AM to 7:15 PM Moreover, some figures were wrong. I told the Minister we had sent out Chapter 6 before the changes were made, and the figures in the Federal Plan were exactly as he had instructed us. We thought he had been briefed on this. He said, well, it wasn't your fault, and took it quite well.

Then he said I had to restore the cuts he had made in health. The Minister of Health is a friend of Abubakar, one just can't touch him. Anything he wants, the PM gives him. Chuke called: were Shaddock and I not coming to the cocktail party given in NEC's honor by the Oba Aderau, the WR Minister of Planning, and a traditional Yoruba king – from Badagry, I believe. We went briefly…

February 20. We had breakfast with Daramola, and I met Stanley Wey, the PM's private secretary, whom I liked immensely. We then saw the Minister, who was disturbed because the program listed him after the Minister of Mines and Power, whom he outranked in protocol. Shaddock said the WR people had printed the program. The mistake was promptly corrected. Having nothing else on his mind, Ibrahim left for the meeting. Stanley Wey decided it was silly for me to wait outside, and I should sit in the chamber. So I was present at the second-highest political assembly; the highest are Cabinet meetings, where no outsider is ever permitted.

The meeting was opened by the WR Governor, the Oni of Ife, who spoke very well for ten minutes. There was a long table. On one side sat the Federal and WR delegations, on the other the NR and ER. In the center sat the PM with Akintola, WR Premier, opposite him the Sardauna and ER Premier Dr. Okpara. Behind them sat the advisers. Once the Governor had left, all press and photographers were excluded, the PM took the chair, and they got down to business.

Now the whole thing is supposed to be secret, and I have no intention of breaking confidences. But I will describe the atmosphere and perhaps give an idea how top political decisions are arrived at.

First, the previous evening the four premiers met alone, then dined with their finance ministers. Secondly, outside the official meetings there are plenty of meetings among ministers, and nothing penetrates below. No advisers are present. Third, the PM is a magnificent chairman. When he doesn't want to make a decision, he claims he has no vote, he just is the chairman. When he wants something, he makes the decision no matter who says what. A qualification: the Sardauna hardly said anything, so I have no evidence that the PM ever goes against the Sardauna, as indeed he went against *all* his ministers and the ER Premier, who theoretically is his ally.

The PM let everyone talk except the Federal ministers. The discussion was supposedly on our documents. We were warmly congratulated on our magnificent job, and then just as vehemently attacked. All Prasad's pet sentences were spotted. The first sentence, "Nigeria is a rich country in which poor people live," was lambasted. Toby told me afterwards – I couldn't understand it – that the Ibos don't think of themselves as poor. They are proud. Anyone could spot this as an Indian sentence. Frankly, despite Toby's explanation I am still somewhat in the dark just why this sentence was offensive. We have orders to change it.

Next, everyone wanted to know who had written Chapter 3, which came in for serious criticism. Prasad answered that different people had drafted different chapters, etc. This was about the only moment I enjoyed, when they all said they liked everything except Chapter 3 and the first five paragraphs of Chapter 1 – all Prasad's! I am a little ashamed, but I still feel some satisfaction akin to Schadenfreude.[5]

Then it got a little grim. My minister was clearly double-crossed by his own Northerners and the Westerners. Only the Easterners supported him. I don't want to describe the issue – it had to do with the Federal Government's role in agricultural development – but the Northerners attacked violently, and the Westerners, when they saw which way the wind was blowing, switched to their support.

The Northerners sat opposite my minister and stared at him with what seemed to me incredibly malevolent expressions. Whenever my minister wanted to speak the PM slapped him down ruthlessly. The Sardauna, an enormous man, 6'6" or 6'8", with a lively, impressive face, just stared. Beside him sat his finance minister, a wizened man, obviously intelligent and kindly if stern. I am told he has cancer. He stared, but more paternalistically.

But the others! They were younger men – I should guess in their late thirties or early forties – with cruel faces and expressions. Some had voluptuous faces, one of them rather good-looking, the others not that either. I should hate to meet any of them alone in the desert, particularly if he has a knife and I don't. They were soft faces, unlike the Sardauna and his finance minister, whose faces show a lot of character. The agriculture minister in particular looked as if he enjoyed pulling wings off flies. There was a fantastic contrast between these fellows on the one hand, and on the other hand, the Sardauna and his finance minister, as well as my Minister, who has a good face and is erratic but absolutely honorable and intelligent, and also the three PSs – Lawan (Agriculture), Talib (Finance), and Akilu (Economic Planning).

Okpara made quite a different impression. A fighting cock, eloquent, ruthless, a demagogue, intelligent. Still, as far as I can tell, not the best politician. These Northerners can dance rings around anyone when it comes to political skill. Sometimes when the argument got heated, he wouldn't stop, interrupted the PM, kept on talking. The PM let him, while keeping his own ministers in check. The other Easterners backed their Premier, were in part attractive. I like particularly P.N. Okeke, Minister of Agriculture. The planning minister is also called Okeke, which in the East seems to be a name like Smith – he is an intelligent and honorable man.

The meeting's Western hosts were dignified. There was some deep politics I couldn't quite fathom. WR Premier Akintola is an attractive and I believe responsible politician, apparently a favorite of the PM. Rumors fly that a national government will be formed with all three parties, or that the Action Group (the Yoruba WR party) will replace the NCNC (the Ibo ER party) in the existing coalition. I don't pretend to understand what goes on politically, but there is something. One felt the West was trying to befriend the North, and the East didn't like it. But by now the North is within striking distance of an absolute parliamentary majority and will no longer need the NCNC. Well, all this is guesswork, and may be all wet. I only want to suggest the political cross-currents that were very much in evidence, even if I can't plot them.

Prasad was called to speak briefly, I think three times. He was ignored, it seemed to me with contempt. Okpara wanted to know why the Central Bank kept such high reserves. Festus was called to answer and did, I thought, an impressive job. But Okpara kept pressing about India. It seems in India reserves are only 40% of annual imports. Prasad was called upon. He said the Bank of India had a reserve of 10% gold and 30% government paper (which doesn't make sense). The PM said 40%.

Prasad tried to repeat: only 10% gold, but the PM just shut him up. Festus pointed out that the legal requirement was only 40%. Why were reserves higher than required? Prasad tried to talk about getting reserves down to 40% by shifting the rest to the Banking Department, which again makes no sense, as it is purely bookkeeping. Anyway I am sick and tired of hearing how things are done in India, with no one asking whether what they do works. And it doesn't. For the next plan they have forsworn deficit financing! So why must we repeat their mistakes? Anyway the point is that Prasad was ignored.

Then came the real drama, as far as I was concerned: the fate of the Plan White Paper. The PM decided each parliament would debate *only* its own plan, and the White Paper would not be taken to any parliament. He did not want Regional matters debated in the Federal Parliament, and vice versa. Elias, the Attorney General, gave the unanimous opinion of the four attorneys general that every parliament could discuss what it wanted. The PM did not budge.

Prasad offered a compromise: the first five chapters of the White Paper, plus Chapter 10, concerning general policy issues, plus the Federal Plan, would be submitted to Parliament, with the regional plans omitted. The PM said no. Okpara said the ER was prepared to print those chapters as the introduction to their plan. All Federal ministers wanted it. Festus threw up his hands and said "But Sir, how can I defend my policy without it?" The PM said no. The Northerners said nothing. Akintola backed the PM against Dina's and Adebo's advice. And so it was decided.

Then the PM said the White Paper and the four government plans would be printed in one volume as the national Plan, but as an NEC document, *not* being submitted to Parliament.

With this the meeting adjourned. Dina came up to me and shook his head, saying he didn't get it. My minister had asked me whether I wanted to speak. I declined, feeling that a new man should keep quiet in the first meeting. I explained to him that my views were already expressed by Festus.

Minus the Northerners, who were fasting, we attended a luncheon given by the WR governor – chicken, no speeches. I asked Okpara if he wanted more for agriculture, and where he wanted me to cut. He said: housing. I said we had hardly any housing in the plan, and that was self-financing. He looked upset, I am sure not for long…

After lunch I spoke with Stanley Wey. He was upset that I had written most of the document and that Nigerians had so little to do with it. Also, I raised a question that seemed to disturb him. I said I had thought I was responsible to JPC, but being in the Ministry, I had to take orders from the Minister and PS. He said he would like to talk more with me, but I doubt anything will come of it. He is the busiest man next to the PM. I would like to get to know him more. He also plays the piano, and he is a gentlemanly sort of chap…

At 7:30 PM Akintola gave an excellent steak dinner. The PM made a short appearance, no other Northerner took part except the Sardauna.

Chief Awolowo was there. I went up to him to introduce myself and protest his attacks on me. He said, "So you are the Ford Foundation man." I said I was and didn't like his attacks on me. He said, you know budget time is coming up again. I said, I knew, but, by God, I had got malaria and a fungus infection in the service of his country, had left my family and job for an unconsciously long time, didn't like his attacks and wished he would stop. Then he said, I didn't attack you, but the Federal Government. I said I understood that, since my father had been a politician. He interrupted and said, maybe your father's sins are visited upon you. So I wagged my finger and said, oh no, my father was a *good* politician, at which he laughed and went away.

After the dinner Shaddock and I accosted our minister. At first he was surly. "There is nothing to discuss, you saw how things went." We commiserated. I said I felt badly about the decision. When he saw we meant it, he thawed and we walked up and down for two hours while he talked freely about politics and his fights with the PM and fellow ministers.

He confirmed my impression that he was double-crossed, but attributed it to Northerners' fear of letting Southerners in the door: "They know I would never discriminate against Southerners, and they want only Northerners in the North – and in the South, too, I might add. Until 1959, when I was elected and appointed minister, I was NEPU (the Northern opposition party, which hardly exists) and wouldn't talk to any of these fellows. See, there goes Leventis.[6] He's always around when anything is going on. He has corrupted Nigeria." There is a lot of truth in this. I am not in a position to write more. He *was* frank. "How many ministers have talked to you like this?" he asked. I said I would keep it to myself, and have done so...

February 21. Breakfast at 7:30 AM with Daramola. Later Reg Clarke joined us, and then Stanley Wey. Meeting started promptly at 9:00 AM. Our ministers had their say, finally, but the PM made the decisions. When the agenda was dealt with they talked about salary cuts. No notes were taken. The talk was very frank and the PM made quite a few cutting remarks against his fellow politicians, all well taken. Meeting adjourned at 1:30 PM...

(Back in Lagos) I had a chance to talk with Toby alone. He is allowed to know everything since he will get the minutes anyway. I explained my disappointment that the PM had vetoed the national Plan, while I was pleased, of course, that the Federal Plan had been accepted without trouble.

Toby immediately congratulated me. He said the PM had in effect saved the national Plan. His concern was to hold the Federation together, and he had to prevent discussion of Regional matters in the Federal Parliament, which would disrupt the national effort. He thought the PM had acted wisely, in statesmanlike fashion.

What Toby said has just been borne out. I was worried about the effect of the PM's decision on our chances for sizable foreign aid. Shaddock and I talked with the Minister about it and Reg Clarke with Festus. The PM has decided that all the Plans and the draft White Paper will go to the IBRD, the Americans, and all governments that might join the international aid consortium. So that will work out all right, too. I think Toby is right in his analysis, at least I hope so. He convinced me my pessimism was wrong.

February 22....The Minister wanted to see Shaddock and me before he left. We talked over the results of NEC and its implications for our work. I got the Minister's OK to expand the introduction to the Federal program, which we had written as an appendix to the White Paper. He was pleasant, though obviously tired and under strain from fasting.

At 2:15 PM, Cheido Obineche came for lunch. We are trying to send him to Harvard. It is true that manpower is scarce, but unless they train their better people, they will never properly Nigerianize. I offered to tutor him to improve his chances...

February 23....At 9:00 AM I went to see Elberton, DPS Commerce and Industry, to collect material for the book Ed Mason wants me to write. I explained that I came as a scholar, privately, not as the head of planning, but, of course, the contacts help...

Back to the office. Tanner had called, he is a young man from the NY Times who is stationed in Leopoldville and did the dispatches on the Lagos Summit. He had been given my name by Kreinin…He is doing a long article on Nigeria, and I was glad to help as much as I could without breaking confidences. He knew quite a bit already. A colleague who had got it from "an advisory source" had told him quite a few facts. Since we hadn't told him, that source was, of course, Prasad…

In the evening a lively party with Posadowski *et al*… I tried in vain to get the Ambassador to agree to plug for aid unconnected with particular projects. I might say he is a very effective man, more so, I feel, than most.

February 24.…A good talk with Reg Clarke, who also has his troubles with Prasad. Apparently Prasad now wants government to take over retail distribution of gasoline. Earlier I opposed the partial nationalization of the refinery, which we owe to Prasad, but taking over retail distribution is sheer nonsense. It was the first I knew about it. It is typical of him to do these things, and not tell those of us who ought to be informed. Reg told me a few similar things, and also said Prasad has lost all prestige.

Part of it is that he sits on his pride, and refuses to go see ministers on his own. As a result he is on bad terms with Festus, who despite his greed and corruption is a darn good finance minister. Incidentally, Lardner hates Prasad's guts.

Reg mentioned as an aside that Ghana, which tried the Indian system that Prasad wanted to introduce here, abandoned it last week. I read the Indian Central Bank law some time ago, and must say I was shocked at the Bank's complete subservience to government.

Because of Reg the evening was not entirely lost. Daramola was also there and I am fond of him too.

February 26, 1962

Most of the week was spent getting a new introduction ready. We sent it to Prasad for the Prime Minister's approval. I just learned Stanley Wey and the PM feel the introduction needs approval of the Council of Ministers, which meets next Monday. I don't know how we will get it to the printers in time…

February 26. I had Obineche for lunch and a tutorial session to ready him for Harvard. I was shocked at how little he knew. He stayed until after 4:00 PM. We are going through Samuelson[7] and I try to get him to work on the relevance of what he reads to African conditions…

February 27. Professor [John] Due of the Universiy of Illinois appeared to talk about a research project he has on fiscal systems in Africa. We told him as much as we could. Besides, we can't be indiscreet even if we wanted to because I approve of the British tradition of budget secrecy, and try *not* to know fiscal details…

February 28.…Toby wanted to see me on a few things…Strange that he now has to deal with all the problems he created when he was our PS, but from the receiving end. And of course, he is in sympathy with our problems as well as his new ones.

For lunch I had Lyle, Frank and a Dr. von Keiser, the German Foreign Office expert on capital aid to underdeveloped countries…We are getting more aid from the Germans. He wanted to know about consortia, who was selling the Plan, etc…

March 3. We had a call from Stanley Wey that the PM had approved our draft and felt it did not have to go to Council. We had already mobilized Festus in support…

Notes

1 This date appears to be mistaken; the entry is situated between letters dated Jan. 27 and Feb. 2.

2 Kreinin, a native-born Israeli, was Professor of Economics at Michigan State. I served on his doctoral committee.

3 In my ECA paper on Comprehensive Development Planning, I gave my reasons for viewing the French territories as less than fully independent. The French controlled the national budgets completely, deciding the amount of spending and how much they were willing to finance. I felt they were quite generous in their aid, but it was they, not the locals, who made all the important decisions. The West African Central Bank was located in Paris. The one country that balked at this was Guinea, with consequences we all know. I was told that the French ripped out the telephone lines and other capital equipment. I do not know whether this is true, and President Sékou Touré was not much to brag about.

4 Aboyade had tribal marks cut into his cheeks as a child. As he jokingly remarked to me, "so that if I get lost, the marks say, 'Return to Oyo, please'."

5 'Pleasure at someone else's misfortune,' according to Langenscheid's German-English dictionary.

6 A prominent local trader of Greek origin.

7 Paul Samuelson's *Principles of Economics*.

Chapter 13

March 5–April 26, 1962
Visit to Eastern Region, Trip to Cameroon, Ford Team's Future, AID Queries about Plan Assumptions, Parliamentary Debate and Vote on the Plan

March 18, 1962[1]

I finally get to bring my diary up-to-date…I am now sleeping again regularly. There is also a let-down, since the creative work is done. Still, I must write memos on monitoring the Plan.

March 5.…[In Enugu] Met with Coatswith, the extremely able and nice PS Agriculture. He gave me a nearly two-hour lecture on how not to get depressed about not getting one's way. I said I understood the vagaries of politics, but got depressed when fellow expatriates could not be relied on to carry out their part of the bargain, and about politicians when their policies were obviously self-defeating.

Of course, I agree with him: our function is to advise honestly and fight for what is right, but then, when the ministerial decision is reached, to carry it out loyally. Unlike myself, as an adviser, a civil servant can put on record that a decision was taken against his advice, and in the worst case, ask for a transfer. I, of course, can resign. In my case I have won most of my points, except the overall size of the plan.

My main reason for seeing Coatswith, however, was to get his cooperation in collecting material for my book, and he was most helpful.

In Enugu they work until 2:30 PM, starting at 8:00 AM. The climate is better, they don't need airconditioners. They are more informal, Philip Barton works in shorts, and most of them don't take their coats to the office as we have to. I also saw Frank Moore, and Kathy Reynolds and her husband, both working with the Ford Foundation on what nowadays is called organization and management. Nice people and obviously competent. And Dave Fogg, an MIT fellow, about 25. These MIT fellows are worth their weight in gold.

March 6.…The Plan document has gone to the printer more or less unchanged. Still, they have more TV than we wanted. Despite all the talk of austerity, the Premier insisted, and over Pius' protest got money allocated, for a new lodge, scheduled on paper to cost £150,000, which means it will actually cost £200,000.

The farm settlements have again gotten out of hand. Now there are to be seven of them. Someone discovered none was planned for Calabar province, so the Premier ordered one to be included. The planned costs are again too high. Of course no one knows what will happen. The Israelis now admit their plans are not feasible. Still, Okpara has ordered Okeke to go ahead, though Okeke himself, being a sensible minister, would prefer to do one experimental settlement!

Moreover, some remarkably foolish political decisions have been made. Okpara wants a settlement in his constituency, but the constituents don't want it. They're having trouble getting the land. Because the constituency is thickly settled, the settlements will take fewer people than the land supports now – although they will be too big for individual family farms, so they'll have to employ hired labor. Government establishes a Kulak class in the name of socialism!

So far they have only 3,000 acres, so Okpara has ordered them to take the required additional 9,000 acres by force if necessary. A good beginning! There is going to be real rioting. On the other hand, the people in Bende division not only made the land available, but by community effort have cleared 18 miles of border and have started to clear the land. Yet Okpara has ordered Okeke to withdraw all extension and other supervisory workers from Bende and concentrate them in his division! Pretty depressing.

The ENDC (Eastern Nigeria Development Corporation) continues its foolish ways on a large scale. The chipboard factory is going up, so is the glass factory. Chipboard is a fancy, expensive material. UAC runs the world's biggest plywood factory in Sapele, with plenty of waste material. Yet they didn't find it profitable to make chipboard.

The glass boys, German crooks about whom I wrote before, finally brought out a geologist to look for sand, which they earlier claimed they had already found. The ENDC manages to lose money on Pepsi Cola, which must be unique in the world. Its cashew nut processing plant doesn't work. In fact, after more than a year the machinery still hasn't been unpacked. It may have rusted by now. And so it goes. Fortunately the other regions aren't quite as erratic, and the Federal Government is in fact pretty good…

Philip Barton took me around to the new Liberty set-up with elegant ministerial homes, not as nice as the old ones, but bigger. When the hotel opens the Catering Rest House will close to the public so as not to compete with it, but operate free of charge for legislators. One gets the worst of every world that way. Operating costs without revenue. The ER really is topsy-turvy…

March 7. Frank and I left for Calabar at 7:15 AM. At Reg Clarke's suggestion we didn't take the paved road, but went via Okposi to Arochuku. From there to the Cross River, which we crossed to Ikot Okporo. [See Photo No. 25.] Interesting, though the dustiest trip I have ever taken. I was literally red, shirt, hair, everything, from the laterite dust. The landscape was first mildly hilly, then more so, and somewhat more picturesque than is common. The villages were mud with painted walls, though nothing spectacular. Further south there were numerous funeral markers of a kind I had never seen, cement statues, people sitting on chairs on top of columns. They seem to be typical Ibibio, where the masks also come from, and where there is a good bit of rattan work.

When we got to the river – one of the oil rivers, rather picturesque – we had to wait in infernal heat until the ferrymen on the other side had finished their chat. We were late, and I guess they have a right to take two hours for lunch.

Once across the river the landscape changed somewhat. They are different people, Efik, more thinly populated. We passed rubber plantations of Dunlop and

ENDC. The difference in looks as well as productivity is startling. It also showed how much investment is needed – smokehouses for the rubber, storage places, housing for expatriate staff...

Calabar is a romantic spot, but dying. It used to be a slave trading center in its great days, and an oil exporting center. One gets the feeling that people are waiting for slavery to return, bringing back the intermediate trade! At least this gives the atmosphere of the place. I never saw so many grown people sitting outside their homes playing games, a version of draughts (Dame) with I believe a 12 inch-square board. The market was interesting, not for what was sold – dried or fresh fish or gari had no interest for me – but it was a beautiful spot and evening. It had rained – the rainy season seems to be early this year – so the streets were washed clean...

March 8....Back in Enugu, to a dinner in honor of the AID mission. Guests included four ministers, permanent secretaries, etc. I had a chance to talk again with Okeke, whom I like a lot. (Another Okeke, Minister of Planning, is no great shakes.) Also to watch Okpara close up. I didn't change my opinion. A lively, interesting man – an MD – but erratic, and I don't share the common view that he is a good politician. Too shortsighted. He just won an election, and has five years until the next one. Yet he talks as if it were only two months away.

There were, of course, speeches. Okpara gave a glowing account of the Plan, the priorities, but then, to show how much he wanted money to do things, he railed against research and experimentation. "I am a doctor; when a man has an accident and bleeds, one has to do something. One may kill him, but one must do something. One can't wait for research!" I wonder how the dead man feels, whether he might rather have nothing done on the chance that will save him. The hurry in which people are supposed to be is dubious. I suspect it is more the politicians. In any case, their kind is bound to be self-defeating. Okpara stressed the hurry, the need to do something, anything, to promise people a better life and show action. Fascinating, but I didn't really like it.

Hutchins, the American mission boss, answered very well. He ended by saying: "Mr. Premier, we had a presidential candidate who promised two chickens in every pot. There were then 48 States in the Union. He carried two of them." He may have mixed up his historic personages – I don't think it was Alf Landon – but he made his point amply clear...

March 9. We left Enugu at 9:15 AM with water for two days and some food, going east via Abakaliki and Ikom to Mamfe in Southern Cameroons. An interesting if less than beautiful trip. Abakaliki is a very backward area. Some rice is grown, Frank said it's no great shakes. The trouble is that the local people lease the land to outsiders who have no real incentive to improve the situation. East of Abakaliki the area quickly becomes savanna. Even Abakaliki is noticeably dryer than Enugu. We saw a few cows. Irrigation might help...After Ikom the landscape grew more hilly as we approached the Cameroons.

Crossing the border at Ekok took some time; it is certainly more complicated to cross an African than a European or American border. On the Cameroon side the Nigerian pound is still legal tender until March 31, when the exchange against CFA francs takes place. This made the visit easier than it will be in a month. The border guards still wore Nigerian police uniforms. The new French African military was not particularly in evidence, except that in Nigeria one never sees any army. We met three police checks on the way, probably because there is still some terrorism. It was peaceful enough.

The Mamfe rest house was like all rest houses. Comfortable, lousy English food – beef and kidney pie – and a bathroom without running water…A pipe had burst. So the man brought water in buckets. Somehow this sort of thing isn't as irritating in Africa as it would be at home. One sits in 3 inches of cold water in the bath tub and washes happily, glad to get rid of the dust.

The area is noticeably poorer and less active than Nigeria. The people seem to be smaller and less well fed, certainly poorer. Their tribe is different from the Eastern Nigerian Ibos and Ibibios, hence they voted to join Cameroon rather than stay Nigerian. The landscape also changed at Ekok, becoming suddenly lush tropical rain forest. The soil also looked better, less laterite, more what we are used to. The huts became poorer and the grave masks cruder.

March 10. We left Mamfe early for Bamenda. The unpaved mountain road is so steep and narrow that for 60 miles it is one way: Tuesday, Thursday, Saturday one way to Bamenda, Monday, Wednesday, Friday one way to Mamfe, traffic banned on Sundays. It is two ways until Akagbe where the road to Buea and Victoria goes south. This time the police check was friendly. The policeman said our passport photos were handsome…

The landscape differed from the Alps due to dense tropical vegetation, thinning out only at Bali, fairly high up. Our water hose sprung a leak – fortunately there is plenty of water, and brooks are clear like in the Alps, not muddy like in Nigeria (but still not necessarily safe to drink)…

Got to Bamenda at 1:00 PM. The rest house was full, mainly with Frenchmen come to prepare the exchange of currency. So we went to the African-run Bamenda Highland Hotel. It was spotlessly clean. The proprietor and his wife tried hard to please…

March 11. The ring road from Bamenda takes at least two days. Hence we only went as far as Wum. The one-way road – in the morning up, in the afternoon down – was not too bad…One fascinating aspect of the Wum market: so many tribes can't understand each other, even in a relatively small radius, that they communicate in pidgin English. [See Photo No. 26.]

The map showed a road from Wum to We and then south to Njinikom back to Bamenda. We were assured in pidgin that it was good but steep. Until We the road was no worse than before. In We they had widened it to use as an airstrip. But the road to Njinikom was the worst I have been on, not counting Chad, where there was no road at all. It was narrow like the Kleinschmidt grade,[2] much steeper, always steeply up or down, over I don't know how many mountain chains…Villages were poor but clean. Houses are mud over a bamboo frame. The roof and walls are prefabricated, then lifted into place and covered with straw and mud. It is high enough to be mainly pasture land, but the vegetation was bamboo and bananas. It was wonderfully cool. In places we must have been over 6,000 ft.

About 25 miles from Bamenda we stopped at a Baptist Mission leper colony. Young Dr. Fluth was pleased to see compatriots. They were amazed we had driven that road with a Ford Taunus…

The colony has 450 people. Infectious cases are separated from the others. Each has a small plot to grow his food. They work two days a week for the mission, which is trying to grow coffee and also has cattle. Leprosy can be arrested and cured, but the damage once done can't be reversed. It is not very infectious, takes prolonged contact to contract.

Dr. Fluth wanted to show us examples of infectious cases. We were a little squeamish when he unbandaged case after case. Actually they have no really bad cases. One can control it now. They treat several thousand cases. Tribal attitudes vary from not worrying about lepers living in their midst to casting them out. On the whole people come early for treatment. Leprosy first destroys nerves so that one doesn't feel pain, hence there is no physical defense mechanism. People cut their feet dangerously without noticing it. The children's section has a school. Men and women live separately. Amazingly, petty trading went on within the colony…

March 12. The border crossing went fast. The border guards recognized us. They wanted to know why the Ford Foundation didn't work in the Cameroons, and if it did come in, could they get a job!…

In Enugu we went to DPS Finance Padgett for a drink. He was upset, had requested a transfer to the bush, anywhere. Even offered to resign. His letter said he could not conscientiously continue to serve. The reason: ENDC had illegally got an overdraft of £250,000 for some foolish thing. Padgett wanted a criminal prosecution, for the thing is in effect theft, but the finance minister vetoed it. The ER attorney general, a fine and honest man, would have loved to prosecute.

Happily, the ER is only a small part of the Plan, although they will surely get into serious trouble. I asked whether a Region can legally go bankrupt and lose its independence, as did New Brunswick (or Nova Scotia?), which lost Dominion Status over a similar case. No one knows, but it seems the Constitution does not permit a Federal receivership…

March 13. The Ford Foundation had brought in Arthur Gaitskell, founder of the successful Gezira scheme in the Sudan and a brother or cousin of UK Labor Party leader Hugh Gaitskell, to investigate farm settlements and make suggestions for a sensible farm policy. Pius, Frank, Hugh Elliot – an Englishman assigned to farm settlements – and I met him in the morning.

Pius explained he was trying to limit the cost per worker to that of a plantation. But it had come out higher. Elliot had been investigating the Western Region settlements. One trouble the Westerners ran into was that the settlers develop a civil service mentality: they don't want to work, but can't wait until they become supervisors, showing others how to work! As if this were surprising. The East wants to pay them less than the West, and require more work from them. Given the Ibos' self-help tradition and community spirit, this should work.

Frank wanted Gaitskell to investigate their various schemes: extension, plantations, farm settlements. Staff, capital and seedlings were all scarce. For example, assigning palm seedlings to farm settlements would endanger the success of palm grove rehabilitation.

I said that plunging into farm settlements on a large scale posed two big dangers. First there was the enormous cost. This not only wasted resources, but led to a negative selection of people, would cause unemployment and could not be replicated. Thus the policy's social aims, to transform and modernize agriculture, could not be achieved.

Secondly, I pointed out we didn't know enough about the soil, crop rotations, etc. There was tsetse, which could be controlled, but the question was how? What would be the effects on erosion, etc.? I asked Gaitskell to talk sense about research to Okpara and my own minister. These people simply assume we know all the answers and research is a waste of money and effort, a scheme by colonialists to prevent development. Gaitskell described successes in raising East African smallholders' standard of living *via* mixed farming and land consolidation...

Back in Lagos, Prasad had got a complaint from the Ministry of Transportation that we had refused to make the requested 'stylistic' changes in the White Paper. We had done so because they ran counter to a Council decision and in effect tried to reverse it under the guise of 'improving' the English. Prasad had written the right answer.

Reg showed me the budget speech's policy sections. I was pleased with them, and made only minor suggestions which Reg may or may not accept. He had incorporated what I wrote for him earlier, though changing the style completely. Anyway, it got lost in the 65 pages I read...

March 14. Spent all morning dictating a draft of my minister's speech for Shaddock to work on, adding the flourishes, etc. It was a *tour de force*, and I like it better than Shaddock's revision. After lunch I worked with Reg, Farrant, Lyle and Peter, putting the final touches on the 62–63 Capital estimates. The Ministry of Health had simply ignored the Council decision allocating them £10.4 million over six years, and produced a plan costing £17 million, of which £7 million in Year One. All plainly idiotic. They even submitted the capital estimates in a form unsuitable for the budget. I had the task of calling them.

In the evening the electricity was off. Something 'never previously experienced' went wrong with the boilers installed only two years ago. Except for the fact that the pipes were corroding, I can't find out whose fault it is. The papers of course blame British imperialists and colonialists for buying lousy UK machinery instead of cheaper German, American or Czech equipment. Willi of UTC thinks they should have installed extra filters. Others say the equipment works satisfactorily all over the world, and the fault lies with Nigerian technicians who are supposed to test the water's acid content daily. Whatever it is, it is WAWA all over again. Another reason to build the Niger dam. A hydro installation is less trouble and requires less skilled labor...

March 15. Stewart called about the Ministry of Health capital budget. It was idiotic. They wanted £750,000 for 11 health centers in the first year. They hadn't even got the land yet! The minister wanted them fast, and open full-time. That would require four doctors and 15 nurses for each one. There just aren't that many in Nigeria. No planning had gone into anything. Instead of doing their bread and butter work, they just lobbied for funds as if that were development...

8:15 PM – dinner *chez* Willi, UTC General Manager...He complained Basel would not let him go into manufacturing and training of Nigerians. He felt, correctly, that the future for an expatriate distribution firm was limited. I asked why UTC didn't imitate Sears in Brazil, or Migros in Switzerland, by building up their own suppliers. He said that was what he wanted to do, but every time he proposed it, Basel refused, saying they were importers and exporters.

Willi thought they could make more money and help Nigeria by gradually shifting. "Why, I would just need a telex system, and run the show from my desk." I agreed to write him a memo to take to Basel. He also wanted to know whether I would do a paid consulting assignment. I said I would, after my return to the States. He said he would arrange it in Basel.

March 16.…A talk with Lyle, trying to make peace. He complained there was not enough contact. But I had asked dozens of times for regular meetings. I didn't feel particularly guilty. He complained I didn't let him know what I was up to. Which of course isn't so. I said nothing. He still doesn't see he has to report to me, not *vice versa*. I finally gave up and did my work. I hope our agreement will be stuck to this time…[See Photo No. 27.]

Later met Hobson from Cooper Brothers. They are investigating the costing of the Niger Dam. We had gone on the assumption that, except for a spur to be built from Jebba to the dam site, the railway would be ready to move cement. In fact, they will need extra equipment, and the Jebba bridge isn't strong enough. We had assumed most cement would move by rail from the Western Region. If roads have to be used, £14 mil. will be needed to strengthen roads and bridges…

Our planning keeps running into this sort of thing. E.g. with the phone system. RCA people misled the government into thinking they were official US. They not only tried to sell equipment at twice the competitive price, but the documentation isn't enough for an application to the Development Loan Fund.[3] So after we thought all that remained was to sign on the dotted line, we find the technical submission still has to be done. We in the planning unit can't be expected to do the technical work. That's what ministries are for.

Peter thinks I'm pessimistic. I think I'm realistic. I intend to present an optimistic front to the public, but I see no point in kidding myself within the unit. Lyle and I still have serious differences about how much will be executed at the Federal level. I think we'll be lucky to do £300 million in six years, Lyle thinks at least £350 million. He got a little shock when he found out the degree of underspending last year, but it just hasn't registered. If we can prevent the money 'saved' by underspending from being wasted on jets or navies, etc., it will be all to the good.

March 17. The early staff meeting I had scheduled came to naught because as usual I was the only one in the office at 8:00 AM. Apparently I'm expected to think excuses suffice…

March 23, 1962

March 19.…Went to the doctor, who changed my malaria pills and started a series of vitamin B_{12} injections to pep me up. All this is fine and necessary, but the trouble is that much of it is psychological. "You look unhappy," he said. I responded, "Well, I am…"

March 20.…Lyle gave a lunch for Robert Brooks of Williams College to meet Nigerians, both our counterparts and other economists in Finance and the Central Bank. The talk was quite amusing. Ayida (pronounced Aida) of Finance argued that Nigerians had to work harder than they were doing, while Igwuagwu, our Wisconsin PhD, opposed it. We also discussed austerity, which received only lukewarm support.

March 21. Went to the House of Representatives opening. The Governor General's Speech was all about the Development Program. It was stately and rather colorful, with the Northerners in flowing robes and turbans – mainly white with gold embroidery – and the Southerners in colorful robes...

In the evening I had Elkeston and wife. He is DPS Commerce and Industry, and is helping me to get together material for my forthcoming Nigeria book...

March 22. Went to the House, where the main excitement was the PM's introduction of a bill to create the Mid West State, to be carved out of the present Western Region. The Westerners had mishandled it badly and were proposing an amendment (opposed by the PM) to create nine more states. There was a fascinating duel between the PM and Awolowo, leader of the opposition...Later it turned out the government had mismanaged its forces and lacked the necessary two-thirds majority to pass the bill! So the Minister of Communications, who was on his way to London, had to get off the plane and rush back...

March 23....I don't get much done in the office these days, at least not by my standards of past performance. Was just about to leave at 1:45 PM when the Minister called. He was in a very good mood, wanted to know what had happened to his idea for an investigation of the retail trade. I told him Kingsley had tried in vain to get in touch with him. So he made me call Don right away and we will meet tomorrow.

Then he asked about my plans, making it plain he wanted me to stay. I told him I was sure Ford would stay in Nigeria if he asked them, but the initiative would have to come from him. As for myself, I didn't want to stay away from my family again for so long, but wanted to stay in touch and would be delighted to come as a consultant for two months or so at a time. He was apparently not aware – and rather appalled – that my contract ran out in June. I'm glad this is moving...

March 24....Kingsley and I saw the Minister about the study on retail and wholesale trade, which he still wants me to do. I told him I was no expert on this. He said one didn't have to be an expert in selling pots and pans. I tried to explain that, if he wanted me to do the study, I had to give thought to it, just what was wanted, what one wanted to know, how many people and how much time was involved, and my not being an expert meant I was apt to forget some ramifications, or underestimate the time and manpower the study would take.

The Minister answered that in his own business he didn't need to worry. The market was there, he just had to pick up the stuff from Kaduna Textiles, bring it to Maiduguri, and people would queue up right at the lorry. He had to ration them so the hinterland would get textiles. If UAC said they had a wonderful distribution system and the expertise to deliver the stuff everywhere, this was just a lie. Anyone could do it. He then turned to Kingsley and said he didn't want any British in the study. He liked Americans and trusted them because if they were generous enough to give millions of dollars, they wouldn't begrudge an ordinary Nigerian trader a profit of 1/6. He liked Germans, Swiss and Swedes, but not British.

Kingsley then explained that the proper procedure was for the Government to approach the Ford Foundation. The Minister's comments were interesting. He stressed that economic research and intelligence was his responsibility, and he therefore could make any decision he wanted. Nonetheless there were jealousies in Cabinet. Dipcherima of Commerce and Industry regarded trade as his prerogative and Cabinet had never accepted his ministerial statement on trade. He therefore would clear it with Cabinet, especially the PM and Dipcherima.

Then I reminded the Minister that he had wanted to raise the planning unit's future with Kingsley, and excused myself...Later Kingsley told me he had left the Minister only two minutes after me. The Minister wanted to give the matter more thought and let Kingsley know by May 2nd. Lyle, when he found out about it, was amazed, though I don't know why he should have been. I had tried to tell him for weeks and months what was happening, but he won't believe me. He has remarkable little sensitivity, and so has Peter.

March 25. Godfrey came at 10:30 AM. We went in detail through Barbara Ward's proposed Economist article..., discussing what could and couldn't be said without making it apparent that she had inside information. Some of the difficulties arose from the fact that the version going to Parliament is much bigger than what I had shown her in London, and the Policy White Paper won't be published for quite a while. Also I was a little disturbed by her tone – she ended on more of a note of doubt than I thought justified.

Then I told him about the talk with the Minister, and asked him to see Kingsley soon. It was unfair to Lyle to let him dangle. Godfrey said he would see Kingsley but depended on me to remind him of it. "You know how I forget things." Next, he said he hated this life in which he had no time to think. "I know the civil service tradition is to make decisions first and then to think, but I don't like it." Then he said he wanted to think more about it and sound out the Minister and Stanley Wey. He continued: "I might as well tell you there won't be a white man in the Ministry by June, I mean in an administrative and decision-making position." This did not come as a shock, though I was surprised and somewhat flattered that he would say it to me.

He reminded me he had already said he wanted me but not Lyle. His comments on Lyle were perceptive and true, even though I thought he could and should use Lyle. He told me how Lyle had behaved when I was away – I won't repeat it because he was rather unfair to me – and how he, Godfrey, had dealt with it (which struck me as politically admirable).

I told Godfrey I had made a bad mistake by offering Lyle equality. Lyle is an organization man who must know who gives him orders and to whom he can give orders. I just don't work this way, and neither does Godfrey, though he can. I knew Lyle would welcome a Nigerian head of the planning unit, and given clear channels of command, there would be no trouble. Lardner disagreed – he was convinced Lyle could not work with a Nigerian superior and would have to be boss.

I then said Lyle is an excellent technician, which is certainly true. He has been invaluable on this level while causing me a lot of trouble on the political, personal and purely economic levels. [Lyle does not know how much I have protected him and how much trouble I have avoided for him. He would never believe if I told him, because he thinks of himself as politically wise and sensitive.] That gave Godfrey the idea of using Lyle on a special project, such as the steel mill, on which he was good and could be his own boss. I told Godfrey I would be personally grateful, because Lyle wanted to stay and would never believe I hadn't prevented him from succeeding me...

March 28. My first task was to write comments on Sayre Schatz' paper for the NISER conference. As regards policy, it was lousy, conceited, illogical and pernicious. He accused the Keynesians of being one-dimensional, whatever that means, and then proceeded with a remedy for underdevelopment lacking even this dimension. He obviously didn't understand classical theory, yet proceeded to criticize it in a snooty manner. Here I was in Lagos, only to be told by this incompetent that all we needed was to print money. I was rather strong and direct.

At 10:00 AM we all marched to Parliament for the Minister's big day. We sat in the officials' box. As in Britain, only MPs are allowed on the floor, but there is a box accessible from the floor where PSs and others sit to advise if necessary. The speech introducing the program went very well. Ibrahim spoke for an hour and was listened to in comparative silence. There was big applause – the thick end, namely the tax increase, would come only the day after.

The Minister was pleased that I was there. Sule, the Minister of Mines and Power, told him that if it was his speech, he would have bragged more. Sule shook my hand, remembered me from the NEC meetings in Ibadan, congratulated me on our work and thanked me in the name of Nigeria and the Government. There was considerable sincerity mixed in with obvious theatrics, but Lyle, the other EPU staff and I were pleased to finally see our output in print.

Since then the Minister has had nothing but congratulations from his colleagues, even the opposition, as well as the press, and that has affected his mood in the ministry. When the Plan debate starts April 2nd, somebody will have to be in the box at all times to take note of what is said, the attacks and questions. I want to be present when Awolowo lets go at me. He recognized me in the box, grinned and waved. I expect my presence will inspire him to extra efforts of vituperation. We all stood around as if following a first performance, with the Minister as the star and the rest of us as the supporting cast.

At 2:15 PM three AID people – Haven North, Burton Gould and Clive Gray[4] – came with questions about the Plan. They were concerned about foreign exchange needs, and we had made one mistake that exaggerated them. It is an error which intellectually I should not have made, although from the policy standpoint it is all to the good. Briefly, we forgot to deduct the liquidation of sterling assets from the calculated balance of payments gap. We then talked about the need for detailed foreign aid applications. Gould was worried about getting project documentation acceptable for US aid. They needed to obligate funds by May 31st, otherwise the current fiscal year's appropriations would go elsewhere.[5] I have always felt executive capacity is decreasing, as British and other expatriates leave, and for that reason insisted from the beginning on proper policies to implement the plan.

In any case I tended to agree with Gould that the projects had on the whole not been worked out. We, the economists, have done an excellent job, but the ministries have not. We're not technicians, we can't be expected to draw up blue prints and feasibility studies. Ministries have spent more time jockeying for funds than doing their daily bread and butter work – another consequence of too big a program. Moreover the PM has said there will be no more consultants, all construction has to be done through the Public Works Department, but they can't handle it all. They have just three quantity surveyors! I said Parliament might change this, but it was a handicap.

Lyle disagreed. He admitted the telephone boys had given us a jolt. We thought a £25 million program was technically ready, and they had certainly led us to believe it. It turned out not to be so, and a team of experts is coming in to work on it. But Lyle thought the plans for the Lagos Teaching Hospital were ready for execution. He claimed to know that the Americans were being held at arms length until a government committee was ready with the precise priorities. I was in no position to contradict him though I don't believe it. It is certainly not true for the Regions, which are not ready.

Afterwards Lyle told me I was being negative – he used the term with Kingsley – and that towards foreigners we had to be positive. I thought I was just being realistic. He felt that AID was trying to put pressure on us, which may be true, but I am not sure it is relevant.

The talk turned to the Regions. We agreed that the East and North were in poor shape, but not the West. Nevertheless, I felt that the relations of individual programs to the aggregate was insufficiently understood in the Western Region and certainly not worked out to the same extent as in the Federation. Lyle disagreed here too, but was on weaker ground...

I have always taken the line that our best bet is to be honest throughout. Lyle has agreed, and it is one of our basic disagreements with Prasad, who wanted and to some extent got a bargaining plan. Lyle believes we have a realistic plan. I expect more underspending than he, and believe this poses serious dangers for distorting priorities, although details are still unclear in my mind, which causes some unrest. Later I learned that Lyle's irritation was aggravated by news that his mother is dying of cancer...

The party broke up at 5:30 PM, friendly but irritated. I could see Lyle didn't like me much and Peter took his side. He is so proud of our plan and our work. So am I, but I have never been able to kid myself about anything, and you know I have never suffered from overconfidence.

I went over to Kingsley at 6:00 PM. He thought it was wise to leave my future open. He was sure Ford would use me any time I was free. My name was very high with them. "And that won't hurt you with universities either..."

March 29. ...Festus presented the budget in the House. I heard only the policy part, with which I was familiar, and not the tax increases, which he announced only after stores were closed, to forestall a run to beat the excises.

I left for Ibadan at 3:30 PM...Bill Bevan, the Vice-principal, welcomed me heartily since UCI got most of what he wanted in the budget...I showed my critique of Schatz' paper to Barback of NISER because I felt uncomfortable about the fierceness. My original opening sentence had been one of disgust at the futility of discussion after reading Schatz. Barback suggested I start off a little more gently.

March 30. The NISER meeting started at 8:45 AM with Schatz's paper. I had warned him of my attack. Schatz was little more careful in what he said than in what he had written. In the meantime I read his article in the QJE, and don't understand how that ever passed the editors. In the debate the Nigerians to a man supported me, so did an Israeli and so did Polly Hill, who knows more than anyone about cocoa marketing and native economies...

Back in Lagos I learned the Minister wanted a weekly meeting with us on general economic policy questions. For a start, he wanted a memo on the effects of the new budget on the cost of living and transport costs. Although this adds substantially to our work load, I am glad. We are turning into a sort of economic intelligence unit. The Minister needs such briefs to be ready in Parliament.

April 1. ...Igwagwu thinks the budget might wipe out the middle classes, which seems rather unlikely. But expatriates will be hurt badly, and there will have to be adjustments throughout the economy. Some of the changes are walloping but I can't get too excited if the duty on big cars such as Chevies and Mercedes is doubled...

Polly Hill-Humphries arrived with her five-year-old daughter Susanne...Mrs. Hill is a niece of Keynes and daughter of the Nobel-prize physiologist Hill, who was on the Tizzard-Lindeman Committee discussed in the booklet by C.P. Snow. After ten years in the civil service, Mrs. Hill went to Ghana to do field work as the only way to escape the oppressive weight of having Keynes as an uncle. Her daughter's middle name is Maynard, and that is how she talks of Keynes.

She just had 14 months' leave in Cambridge to write a book on migration of Southern Ghanaian cocoa farmers. Her knowledge of the indigenous economy is extraordinary. All too many foreigners and locals simply ignore the extent of these economies, assume the locals don't know anything, don't own anything, don't get credit. In fact they buy land in large tracts; it is they, not the city people, who own the trucks; and they give extensive credit. While I read a paper she gave me, she read mine. She said I was the first economist in my position to express any interest in what she was doing. I think it is important. So is the work of Arch Callaway, otherwise one of the world's biggest bores. Mrs. Hill is rather shy, well educated, neither a bluestocking nor an obvious intellectual. But I am impressed by her, both intellectually and in human terms.[6]

April 8, 1962

April 2. I took Mrs. Hill to the House to hear the Plan debate...I was sure I would be attacked as an imperialist, but couldn't have been more wrong. Chief Awolowo was absent. I assumed the debate would be opened by the government's supporters. Wrong again. The Speaker gave the first word to Chief Rossiji of the opposition Action Group, who proceeded at length and with great intelligence to commend the government and the Minister on the bold, dynamic, imaginative Plan, made a number of constructive suggestions – which however would have to be implemented by the Regions rather than the Federal Government, because they related to agriculture – and then said he would support the motion. This means the Action Group accepts the Plan, and chances are it will pass unanimously.

I still have to ask Godfrey what happened. I know, though no one else here does, that part of the price of harmony is jettisoning the Ford operation *in its present form.* Also, the last Action Group party conference saw an unholy row between Awolowo and WR Premier Akintola, in which Rossiji, the party secretary, was involved. It looks as though Awolowo lost thoroughly, but he may yet have his day when the budget debate starts day after tomorrow.

The next speaker was a Dr. Kaly Ezera of the ER's NCNC party, who has Oxford and Harvard training. He lauded the "brilliant Godfrey Lardner," Dr. Prasad, and said, "and at the least I must pay tribute to the Chief of the Ford Foundation Economic Advisers, who, I understand, also took part in formulating this program." This was quite unexpected. Godfrey and I, sitting in the officials' box, shook hands.

Ezera spoke intelligently, attacked Shell-BP, wanted the Italian AGIP in – and supported the program wholeheartedly. Other speakers, representing all parties, supported the program even when they had detailed criticisms. One, an Action Grouper, pleased me particularly when he presented some ideas almost literally in the form in which I had written them to Chief Adebo. There was a row in the Western Region about government ownership, and this particular MP advocated selling government's shares to the public at a profit and reinvesting.

Japan was mentioned several times as a model. I felt of course pretty good: I had written much of the Federal program, Reg Clarke had taken a lot from my JPC papers for the Budget speech, and now I found my ideas coming back from the opposition. What more can one ask? All the work wasn't in vain after all, and there was some reward for the work and the fights.

Mrs. Hill was impressed by the debate, and said, "It makes me cry for Ghana." She said no one of any caliber or education is left in Ghana's Parliament. Everything is chaotic. Nkrumah's effort to control every detail means there is no control at all. She is quite fed up with Nicky Kaldor, Joan Robinson and other people who know nothing but go around saying how democracy can't work in underdeveloped countries, and development requires central control or even dictatorship. I admire Kaldor as a theorist, but he has the dubious distinction of being responsible for two bloody revolutions in a year – in Ghana and in British Guyana. To raise taxes without saying anything about spending is irresponsible and incidentally poor economics. I am also fed up with pseudo-liberals who think democracy and individualism are only for the rich.

April 3. At 8:15 AM Professor Sven Helander, a Swede, came for a chat. He had given lectures at UCI and seemed to think six weeks made him an expert on Africa…Some of his questions were all right, others showed he had been taken in by other pseudo-experts. He was amazed at the uncertainties we face. I tried to explain that was how things worked in underdeveloped countries with little executive capacity. This is why I insist that the only control methods that really work are indirect ones using incentives and the market.

Then I had to start a memo for the Minister on the effect of the tax and import duty hikes. The effect has been rather absurd – I wouldn't have predicted it. It shows again how little we understand the working of the indigenous economy. Taxes went up on whisky, etc., air conditioners, cars (but not trucks) and gasoline – the latter about 10%. The increases hit mainly expatriates and a few rich Nigerians who drive Mercedes, Cadillacs and Rolls Royces. Spare parts and tires went up just a little, yet prices in the local markets rose by 20–30%. People talk of price control, which couldn't be administered anyway, and profiteering expatriates are upset, which is understandable though all one has to do is drink a little less. The whole process of price formation on local markets escapes me.

I met with the two top Nigerians from Finance on what information to request from ministries for preparing foreign aid applications. Alison Ayida, the SAS responsible for foreign aid, is first class, and the new DPS, Garba – a Christian Hausa from Zaria – makes a good impression. My main concern was to use the application process to monitor Plan execution and respect priorities, while Lyle is mainly responsible for formulating the submissions and actually getting the foreign aid. We agreed to ask first which projects were ready to go ahead.

Then my suggestion was accepted that we immediately push the ministries into working on the high-priority projects. Otherwise they will assign all their manpower to the easiest things, leaving the difficult but more important projects to the last. If we don't get started on high payoff projects, we will have a cumulative decline...

April 4. Parliamentary debates on the Plan went well. Had lunch with Macintosh, a political scientist from Edinburgh temporarily at UCI. He wanted to know about Federal-Regional relationships. I told him what I knew and what I was permitted to say. I am after all not a political expert, and have been immersed in the Plan and economic issues. Moreover, it would be catastrophic if our unit got involved in politics.

Then back to the House. At 5:00 PM the Minister made his concluding statement. The PM was not present, but is connected to the House by loudspeaker. While we had prepared the speech tabling the Plan in the House, and he read it with very few spontaneous changes, the final plea was entirely his own and he spoke freely from copious notes he had made during the debate. A demagogic speaker, he had the House eating out of his hand. He started with a violent attack on the British, who were assailed in the debate for having exploited Nigeria and held back its development. He wanted expatriate firms to go into industry, which would be the rational thing to do. He spoke favorably of America, implying that one could trust Americans because the profits to be made by exploiting Nigerians were not big enough to interest them.

The feeling of this session was very different from the NEC meeting in Ibadan. This minister is erratic and makes enemies. But he is also powerful. And he is apparently the Sardauna's hatchet man in Lagos. Which would explain the NEC-Ibadan situation adequately.

There were more speeches. An MP asked why a certain police station in his district hadn't got a Land Rover promised two years ago. The Parliamentary Secretary promised it within a month.

At 6:00 PM the Speaker interrupted proceedings, and the Plan was voted *unanimously*.

I decided a long time ago not to believe what I hear unless it fits into my picture. It's not that I believe I know better. It is simply a precaution against becoming a tool for others for ends opposed to mine. I am conscious that I have not always succeeded; certainly not at the beginning, before I realized what was going on. And even then it took a while before I believed in my head what my heart knew what was happening. It took much the longest *vis-à-vis* Lyle.

April 5....I started putting down ideas for an article on economics and politics in development. The point I am trying to make is that economists yield too readily to other disciplines. I wrote a letter to Schatz, making amends for my sharpness. It turned out to make matters worse, but I sent it anyway.

April 6....Went with Lyle and Peter to the Ministry of Finance, where we met with the individual ministries on their capital programs. The object was to identify the projects that were likely to be attractive to foreign aid agencies and were ready to submit to them. I was anxious to be present although it is mainly Lyle's baby. First, Lyle may have to leave suddenly for the States because of his mother's health, and I may have to jump in. Secondly, I am continuously worried about distortion of priorities and want to use the exercise to push them in the right direction.

April 7....Kingsley finally spoke with Godfrey. He said it was frank and pleasant but inconclusive. Godfrey is working on reorganization of the ministry and also waiting for my brief. Kingsley said that it looked as if Ford would be asked to stay forever, and agreed that I had reported correctly. I had expected to be torn to pieces, and was wrong on that. But not on anything else. I'm sure there was some deal with the opposition: they lay off me and I get jettisoned in due course. Fair enough, particularly as I did not want to stay on full-time, though I want to continue to be involved part time. I left my draft with Kingsley for comment.

At 8:30 PM Peter and Clive Gray came. Clive is a Harvard man with AID. We talked until after midnight. We probably need another session after I have read an article by Polak.[7]

April 11, 1962

April 9. We are trying to get the Nigerians to do most of the writing now. At Finance Lyle and I continued the ministry budget and foreign aid discussions. I left early for a German luncheon at the Federal Palace. Among the PSs present was Ajumogebia, the extremely nice and able PS Education. At Finance he showed he had done his homework…

Also present was a representative of Cuttino Caro, a German firm that Frank and I don't like because they sell ENDC lots of machinery and factories that can't possibly make money. They said their geologist had found the sand needed for the bottle factory. Frank and I asked where? Well, not in one place, but in many places. After all, the Eastern Region government wanted to create jobs, and bringing the sand to the factory would do that. Now, I am no industrial expert, but even I know you can't supply a modern bottle factory by crews of workers delivering sand in head pans! There is no question too stupid to ask! I knew that one Swiss factory supplied all of Switzerland. I said it was my duty to protect Nigerian industries, and the Germans' irresponsible behavior was hurting the West and the good name of private enterprise.

Dinour, the Israeli economist from Ghana, came for supper. We talked about our Plan, and the contrast to Ghana. Planning in Ghana has one man, Mensah, whom I met in Addis, but who is under orders. He hasn't even got a secretary. To show the nonsense, he projects resources on the basis of a £250 per ton cocoa price. The present price fluctuates around £170 and it is likely to fall to below £150. It is an old story: centralization and 'strong man rule' are just plain inefficient as well as unpleasant.

Dinour asked penetrating questions on our Plan. I promised to show him the basic model and consistency calculations which haven't yet been published…I introduced Dinour to Godfrey. He was impressed. Nigeria seems like an oasis of rationality in a sea of unreason. He also said, "I used to be like Schatz and the others, thinking that old fashioned economics was no good, hindering development. There were a lot of us like that in Israel. It just doesn't work like that in Africa, I am with you now" (referring to my second Addis paper)[8]…

April 17. A call from Finance about the Ministry of Information. They had told us their transmitter cost £300,000. The figure is now £1.1 million. I told them they couldn't have it. If they wanted it, they should go to Cabinet. I told them their allocation included any foreign aid we could get for them. The Nigerian Broadcasting Corporation's new director, a New Zealander named McKay, said he had tried to get together with the Regions. They had four services, whereas a single one would do better. Why not first develop a good domestic service before trying external broadcasting? I said he should just keep trying.

Then the PS Information came to talk about government starting a TV receiver assembly plant so people could receive their TV broadcasts. I told him the best thing would be to scrap the whole TV program. Finance was all the way with me, so this idiotic scheme will get nowhere...

They are now negotiating with Aboyade of UCI to head the planning unit. He is very good, will learn and do a good job. Pius was vetoed by the PM as lazy, which he is. Prasad tried to get Chief Adebo as Economic Adviser, which would have been marvelous. But Adebo doesn't want it. The UN is after him, and Harvard wants him next year.

The Nigeria aid consortium met, everyone was there except the Dutch and French. The Dutch will come in when their Guyana trouble is settled, the French probably will wisely stay away. The Japanese are anxious to help. We will undoubtedly get more foreign aid than can be spent wisely. I repeated how I thought the Plan was too big, making control that much harder.

Lardner also is in trouble. The PM feels he is too volatile to be confirmed as a PS. Which is true. But he is personally nice, and I hope trustworthy and good.

April 19. At 9:15 AM saw a Dutch economist named Jansen.[9] He is setting up a planning operation in Liberia under UN auspices. Since Tinbergen had sent him he was welcome...What he told about Liberia was pretty grim. No facts. Population estimates vary between 0.8 and 2 million. In practice forced labor, paid 36 cents a day. No wonder it must be forced because the subsistence economy pays better than that. AID people swarming over the place to do planning, but no professionals among them. There are all of three Liberian economists.

They started collecting statistics in 1959 but stopped after half a year to organize a census that still hasn't taken place. Jansen spoke warmly of a Northwestern University survey team. AID and the UN are much too rigid. They have rules that must be obeyed whether or not they fit a particular country. Our AID people in Lagos may be dull, but they are pretty competent...

At a cocktail party in honor of the new general of the Nigerian army I talked with CB Governor Fenton. He said he wanted a chat with me about problems of monetary policy in an underdeveloped country with private banks having huge proportions of bad loans, etc. My reading knowledge on this is somewhat out of date, but I'm looking forward to it.

April 23. ...Clive Gray came with questions on the Plan, which he is reviewing for AID. We had quite a good discussion and then listened to a Beethoven Quartet.

April 24. ...IBRD Vice-president Knapp dropped in briefly. He asked general questions. Prasad was also present. In the evening a large reception in Festus' garden...The only interesting thing was Knapp's answering speech to Festus: Now that we had a good plan, it was important to come up with well worked-out projects. Several Action Group MPs came up to congratulate me on the Plan. Since they are opposition party, this is gratifying.

Later, dinner at Prasad's...Reg told me he had had three blow-ups with my minister in the past two days, and the PM had told him to be patient. At the moment the Minister doesn't like me. At the cocktail party we shook hands, but otherwise he avoided me. Well, I'll survive. There may be no real reason for this behavior...

April 26. Toby and Jean came for supper. We discussed political developments. The Northerners have played their cards skillfully and are taking over the whole country. I always thought the notion that, because the North is economically backward, the Southerners would take over, was fallacious. More and more Northerners are coming south into the Federal Government. Some are excellent, but this leaves the NR administration rather depleted. Others are no good, but promoted simply in order to pre-empt expatriates or Southerners. The NCNC feels trapped. Being in the opposition, the Action Group can at least squawk. The NCNC being a coalition partner can't do even that. I always thought both AG and NCNC played their cards wrong. Zik is effectively isolated. If Nigeria becomes a Republic, which is likely within two years, the Northerners will be the ones to wield power.

Notes

1 An original letter describing WS' upcoming trip to the Eastern Region and Cameroons has been lost.
2 A steep dirt road down to the Snake River at the Idaho-Oregon border, where I once took my family.
3 The then US agency making project loans on concessional terms to developing countries.
4 Program Office Head, Program Economist and Assistant Program Economist, respectively.
5 The US fiscal year then ran until June 30, but federal agencies were required to obligate 90% of their budgets by May 31st in order to forestall a last minute rush at the year's end.
6 Polly Hill described herself as an economic anthropologist. Later, when I was directing the Center for Research on Economic Development at Michigan, she joined the Center at my invitation. I financed her research in Batagarawa in Northern Nigeria.
7 WS is referring to two articles by J.J. Polak in the IMF *Staff Papers*, 'Monetary Analysis of Income Formation and Payments Problems' (November 1957) and (with Lorette Boissoneault) 'Monetary Analysis of Income and Imports and Its Statistical Applications' (April 1960).
8 'Social Factors in Economic Planning, with Special Reference to Nigeria,' published in the *East African Economic Review* in 1964. This paper was commissioned by, I believe, UNESCO, but when they got it they were unhappy because it was so strongly economic and not enough 'social,' as they understood it. They asked me to change it. I refused, and told them they did not have to pay me or send me to Addis. That apparently was not possible – I guess they would have been without a presence in Addis, so I went. When I presented the apper, the unexpected happened. After the other economists had expressed their unhappiness with my insensitivity to social issues, the representative of the World Health Organization spoke up and said there was finally an economist who talked sense about health and social problems!...I was happy to see somebody recognize that talking beautifully and sensitively was not going to solve anything, while careful resource allocation had a chance of doing so.
9 Cornelis L. Jansen, a Jesuit priest, student of Jan Tinbergen and later a highly regarded Professor of Economics in the Netherlands.

Chapter 14

April 27–June 3, 1962
Nigerian Economic Society Meeting, Israelis Promote Farm Settlements, Visit to Jos Tin Mines and Other Eastern Region Sites, Stolper Offered a Job in Malta, Visit to Ghana, Clash with Prasad Peaks, Stolper Insists on Coherent Macroeconomic Framework, Disputes about Projected Underspending, Plan Completed

April 27. Off to Ibadan at 8:15 AM. My minister opened the Forest Products Research Laboratory. Some Eastern Region businessmen were present. All agreed the chipboard factory was a cockeyed idea. One said he had been asked to come in as a partner and refused. There was no market in Nigeria, and the European market was saturated. I asked about prefabs, which they now expect to make. The director of research, a Pole of German origin, said the houses would melt away in one rainy season. There might be a market in the Northern Region, but it would have to be built. The project was twenty years too soon.

One businessman said it was crazy to locate the chipboard factory in Calabar and a furniture factory in Enugu where there wasn't any material. In short, the usual combination of German crookedness and Nigerian stupidity. Yet Posadowski says the German firm is well known and honorable. They are just damn crooks in Nigeria, however honorable they may be in Germany. So are the Nigerians and the American dealing with this stuff here...

Oje Aboyade is chairing the Nigerian Economic Society (NES) meeting, and is also supposed to criticize us. He was slightly unhappy that I accepted most of his criticisms and, in fact, was making them myself, personally though not officially. He thought it was optimistic to assume 50% foreign aid for capital. I said I couldn't agree more, but this figure constituted a victory as initially they had wanted more. He thought that 5% underspending for the Federal Government and 10% for the Regions was too low. I agreed and told him Lyle now accepts 25% underspending. In my opinion it will be even more, and a good thing too. The only thing we disagree on is government participation in industry, which I want to minimize, and exchange control, which I want to avoid, almost at all cost. We agree that inflation is no good...

April 28. Andrew Wilson, PS Economic Planning, had arranged a meeting in the Treasury with about 15 people from various ministries. My task was to find out what problems they were encountering in preparing foreign aid applications, what help they needed. It was a heated, very open meeting, efficiently chaired by Isaac Dinah. There was agreement that at the lowest level in the ministries, the Western Region had sufficient manpower to prepare the basic engineering and other data – they might not be up-to-date, but they could do it. The trouble was that the technicians had too many administrative tasks. This could be fixed by internal reorganization.

On the next level, however, they wanted to set up a high-powered evaluation team to screen projects and work with the ministries to improve them. For that they needed technical assistance. They were prepared to take expatriates. Afterwards Andrew mentioned some of his doubts regarding expatriates. He was worried that I might be upset. I knew he would never have expressed doubts in front of me if he didn't trust me.

They have an Israeli economist seconded to prepare projects for submission. The Israelis are not trusted as much as they used to be; and for good reason. They invented the farm settlements, which are idiotic, almost criminally expensive. And now, Andrew said, they have stopped defending them as a vehicle for transforming traditional into modern agriculture. They obviously can't, costing as much as they do. He said the Israelis had had the contract to construct the farm buildings, which had turned out much too expensive. The same was true for lots of their water supplies. He felt that another Israeli adviser would simply push contracts in the direction of Israeli firms. One irony is that some of these firms are run by the Israeli trade unions. Still, he didn't want this bandied about. He just wanted to explain his stand in the meeting. Incidentally, they *are* cutting down on farm settlements.

...Following the afternoon NES session, I had dinner with Chukujekwe. First we went over my write-up of the morning meetings. Then he talked about the future of the WR planning unit and his own future. He had wanted to come to Lagos and join the Federal Service, but he isn't sure now. He might like to go abroad again. I told him I had no influence with the UN or other international bodies, but I had some in the academic world, and if he wanted to teach and write, I could try to get him to Michigan. He would be very good, not as good perhaps as Aboyade or Onitiri, both of whom are outstanding, but he is very good and very pleasant...

April 29, 1962 (Kontagora)

Aboyade gave an excellent talk, making a thorough critical analysis of the Plan. Since he had had quite a bit of the unpublished stuff he knew a lot more what was behind it, and made the most of it. I spoke next as a kind of rejoinder. I had jotted down 17 points he had made, all of which but one I agreed with: the role private business was to play. This is, of course, essentially a political issue and not a purely economic one. Lyle talked next. He did a good job...

Kontagora is a typical northern village, with round mud huts and compounds, quite unlike the typical Yoruba square mud buildings, or the Ibos' fortress-like mud compounds, and the poverty shows in that most roofs are thatched...

May 1, 1962 (Kaduna)

April 29....My main concern in Kaduna was to set up a meeting with either PSs or their deputies similar to the Ibadan one. No one was in. Akilu, Talib and Greswell were in London. So we organized a meeting with Saunders, the Undersecretary in Planning, and Leyton in Finance. I talked first with Peter Gibbs about my Harvard book, trying to collect material. There is no such thing as Government and business in the Northern Region. Latham in Finance gave me the tax ordinances, and I got hold of the budget, that was all.

Jensen wanted to see me. He is frustrated. Nothing happens, he is not informed. He wants to stay out his contract, get some research going and then get another Ford contract in Asia. He does not want to work any more in Africa, partly because in Kaduna he has no social contact with Africans – with Moslems this is next to impossible, and the Fulanis feel racially superior towards whites. He is isolated in Kaduna, and can't get along with Kingsley, which I understand but regret. He also couldn't get along with Lyle – but then he doesn't have to.

Bernie and I see eye-to-eye on what is really needed: a lot of field work on agricultural production and trade, the extent of the money economy, etc. We cheerfully agreed that the 'subsistence sector' hardly exists. It may have twenty years ago, but now the penetration of the money economy is amazing. Bernie paid me a compliment which, I confess, I really liked. He said he had never met anyone before who could immediately see the whole context. I was pleased, because this is the result of many years of theoretical training. He wanted to know my plans. I told him about Harvard, that I wanted a year to think and write and sort myself out, and rest. He said he didn't see how I stood it so long and got the work done, and that I must have nerves of iron! This was pretty ironical, but I didn't disabuse him about the state of my nerves...

May 1....The meeting I had requested about project preparation was pretty grim: nothing is ready. The NR needs technical aid badly. No project will be ready before at least 6 months. After the meeting I saw Peter Joes, the Industrial Officer, on NR 'industrial policy,' which doesn't exist. I got the little material there is.

May 2. Got up at 6:00 AM, had breakfast, packed the car and was off with Felix for Jos by 7:45. First the road was paved while going north to Zaria, then it was good laterite when it branched off to Jos. Shortly after the turnoff a huge baboon crossed the road. Having seen a monkey in its natural habitat almost made the trip worthwhile by itself.

The road rose first gradually and it nowhere got really mountainous. It is a high plateau – the Province is called Plateau – with mining and vegetables of the European type. Potatoes, for example, still grow here. It is cool by Lagos standards. There are lovely open vistas, strange not only because of the villages, but also because of granite rock outcroppings all over, somewhat reminiscent of the Craters of the Moon in Idaho, except that it is less black.

Jos itself is a pleasant town, particularly the European section. I checked in at the Hill Station, a luxury hotel with reasonable prices – £ 3:10/-, all meals included, but rather old-fashioned. There are chalets, but I am in the main building. Though all rooms have private bathrooms, for some mysterious reason the private baths are all across the public corridor from the rooms. The food is quite good and tie and coats are required in the evening.

Peter Gaskill, the Chief Mining Engineer arrived half an hour after me and told me that the party would meet next morning at 8:00 AM. I had a quiet lunch and went off to Vom, where the ministry has its veterinary Research Station. I didn't see the director, since it was after working hours but a nice African student, a prospective laboratory technician, showed me around and explained what went on there. Most of the station is devoted to training and the production of vaccines for animals. I could not see the stock multiplication unit because of an outbreak of rinderpest.

Back in Jos – it is about 19 miles away – I went to the museum, where I looked up Mr. Fagg, the Director of Antiquities. They were just mounting the Nok find I had seen in Lagos, and it looked good. Fagg showed me his building and plans. He had built a lovely mud building with a pond like an atrium in the middle and a plastic glass roof like Armeria in Sicily, to house the collection of pottery. The museum itself is small and has only samples of the many kinds of artifacts found in Nigeria. With it is a zoo of local animals, such as leopards, warthogs and mandrils.

Before I left I asked Fagg to lend me a Nigerian to go and see some of the pagan villages. This will happen tomorrow. I also asked him for an opinion of the Yoruba carving I had bought in Oyo. I was flattered to be told it was so good I might have trouble getting an export permit. It would have to be checked against what the museum had, and the Antiquities Commission would have to be asked. But he thought I could probably take it out. He wanted to photograph it. Anyway, I have learned something about African art since coming here.

Dinner with Gaskill, who is a pleasant man, 48, a bachelor, with 25 years Nigerian experience. One of the few Englishmen they asked to stay on...

May 3. I was ready at 8:00 AM, but the PS Mines and Power Mallam Musa Dagash didn't appear until 8:30 AM. I sent Felix with a message to the Museum and gave him the day off. His uncle, he told me, worked at the Amalgamated Tin Mining Company of Nigeria (ATMN), the world's second biggest tin mine.

We got first to a company called Jan Tar, which had been about 45 years in Nigeria, was rather small – employing about 700 people – and had been brought out of the red by its present manager, White. We first talked about their Nigerianization, and Musa Dagash was rather aggressive, because they had only four Africans in senior positions and only one man trained as a mining engineer, who was from Ghana. We were then shown the old housing – round huts made of mud, costing £6 to build and given rent free – and the latest attempt to build a model village. The first block was going up. It was built of mud block with cement admixture, had iron window frames, electricity and water, and cost about £100–£150 a room.

For me, the mining operation was the most interesting. it is placer mining. The overburden is removed, the rock which contains the cassiterite – the tin oxide – and columbite is blasted and high pressure water hoses are applied to wash the mineral out. It is then pumped up to a separating plant where the first attempts at screening and washing are made, before the cassiterite is shipped to the beneficiating plant.

We saw such a plant at the second company we visited, the Bisichi (?) Company which employs about 2,000 people. The process of beneficiating essentially repeats the first process of cleaning and washing, but then uses [word illegible] and magnetic separators for the columbite. The ores are then packed for the smelter. The manager, Hannon, went on the attack with Musa Dagash, declaring that the Minister had been unfair in his speech. But not much came out of the altercation.

The next stop was ATMN. This company produces more than half of Nigeria's tin ore and employs between 8,000 and 9,000 people. The atmosphere was quite different. The general manager, Farmington, received us, talked Hausa (which I do not understand, of course). The offices, everything, were rather baronial. Musa Dagash did not attack, nor did Farmington, It was pleasant. I found out later why. Farmington is the only white special member of the Northern House of Representatives and a power. There are five such special appointed members. The company is evidently run extremely efficiently. There was a gentle complaint about the increase of the duty on Diesel oil. It raised the cost of operating the big Euclid Earth moving equipment by 8.5%, and I was shown the detailed figures.

We were shown two operations. First, in the office, the prospecting. The maps of the concession were 1:500. They drill holes at regular intervals until they hit rock bottom and analyze the content of the test borings, hundreds of such test borings. From that they make a content map of the deposits and decide where to start mining. All very scientific and very thorough.

After lunch we were first shown the housing and then Farmington took us in his air-conditioned Olds to a new site about to be developed, about 10 miles of road they had just finished. 22 of the huge American Euclid dump trucks were being filled by scrapers and bulldozers to remove the overburden while a huge dragline was being assembled for the eventual removal of the tin ore. As a heavy thunderstorm was coming up, the whole operation was even more picturesque, with the heavy equipment throwing up dust, heavy equipment lying around waiting to be assembled against the background of African villages, rock outcroppings and black sky rent by lightning. [See Photo No. 28.]

Lunch itself was at the Farmingtons' for Gaskill and myself. Steak, pleasant talk, magnificent house.

By the time we left ATMN it was 4:00 PM. We stopped at both his smelters. The English one first, brand new with a diesel heated smelter, big, noisy, capable of smelting the whole of Nigeria's cassiterite output. The Portuguese next much smaller, much quieter, using an electrolytic process, and probably more efficient. I told before about the smaller one which has trouble getting power. Farmington was not displeased to have two smelters: the price he got for ore had gone up as the result of competition.

It was 6:00 PM when I got back to the hotel. I called up Fagg to see whether he had got my message. He had, and asked me for a drink. I had a bath, changed and drove over. We sat on the terrace of his lovely house he built of mud, overlooking the hills. He is giving me a boy tomorrow to go and see a pre-historic stone bridge and a pagan village in an all-day expedition. He might go to Nok on Saturday, in which case I would come along. instead of going to Makurdi directly. I should like to see an archaeological site with an archaeologist. No one knows the age of the 'prehistoric' bridges, anything more than 100 years, but the Nok culture dates about 2 000 years back. He promised me an interesting day tomorrow, possibly a wild one. In any case, be prepared to pay 1/- a photo in the village, and that after a palaver.

Back for supper at 8:15 PM, washing shirts since Felix isn't back yet, and this letter. Off to bed now at 10:30 PM.

May 4. I got up as usual and was at the Museum at 8:00 AM to pick up my guide, a Fulani youth of 21 years who was pleased to know that I had a son of 21 years myself. I drove about 150 miles today, 40 miles paved, but none bad.

The first stop was the prehistoric bridge, really a causeway across a fast river, a beautiful example of experimental engineering, as Fagg put it. It was just stone, granite, laid on top of each other, without cement or mortar, wide enough for one person to walk across, with the water going underneath through three sluices. It was nicely curved to take the pressure of he water.

Most of the landscape was plateau, grassland without trees, with volcanic outcroppings. The route (which is on the Shell Independence map) went from Jos south to Bukum (where the ATMN Co. is), Ropp, Bokos, Mbar, to Richa, which was the pagan village. [See Photo No. 29.] Actually, before the pagan village there was a Hausa village. The landscape was wild, prairie-like until Richa, when it suddenly got lush and tropical again, yet rather pleasant because of the many rock outcroppings.

A fully dressed – shirt and shorts – pagan boy with a smattering of English was our guide. The big chief had gone to town, to Panyam. I had been warned that photographing was expensive, and it was all that. I hope the pictures will turn out, because it rained continuously.

The village, if you can call it that, was picturesque. The site was hilly, with rock outcroppings all over, and on back of each rock a man or a family had built their compounds: high, sort of split-level, and all inward. You just saw walls outside. You went in through a small door into a courtyard, which itself was narrow and into which individual mud huts opened. I saw no artifacts, but there are, of course, spears, etc. which had been locked away.

Most of the people were away in the fields. Still, there were some about, most of them naked: i.e., the women had beads and jewelry and a sort of loincloth. and the men similar adornment including rather extraordinary penis shields of horn, held up by leather straps. By paying 1/- a picture, I was allowed to take a few. Except for money discussion through my Fulani interpreter – all speak Hausa – they were friendly enough, but I was warned by Fagg beforehand that anything might happen.

Something almost did. The Pagan guide wanted me to take him to Jos. I said I would. Fortunately the Fulani guide asked him whether he knew anyone in Jos. He didn't. He just thought I might take care of him for the rest of my days! I gave him a lift to the next Fulani village, though on the way a naked old man came along who turned out to be his father. I took a picture of both of them. The old man wanted to get his shilling, the young one didn't.

I got back to Jos at 6:00 PM. Fagg came for a drink. Tomorrow, after going with Gaskill to see native African mining, I will have lunch with Fagg and we are off to Nok. I am keeping my fingers crossed, because I am told I have the worst road in Nigeria ahead of me…

May 7, 1962 (Enugu)

May 4 (continued).…I met Chief Mining Engineer Peter Gaskill, Antiquities Director Bernard Fagg and his wife, and the newly arrived Nigerian Inspector of Mines with a pretty Welsh wife, for a drink at the hotel. The Nigerian had worked five years for the English Coal Board in Swansea and just returned home after ten years' absence. Both he and his wife were obviously dazed by Nigeria. They had driven north and found the roads terrible – it is bad, but pretty good for an underdeveloped country at that, better than Yugoslavia. The inefficiencies had got them. He had been in Jos for ten days and still hadn't got down to work. He's meeting the problem that Nigerians, though they complain about colonialism and how the British never did anything for them, really had everything done for them, and now have to face real competition…

May 5 (Jos). I went with Gaskill and Mines and Power PS Mallam Musa Dagash to see African tin mining. We saw two operations, one completely unmechanized, the other with a pump. The basic principle is the same everywhere: you dig test holes until you hit rock, then wash the paydirt, calculate what you get and whether it is worth mining. The holes tell you where the deposit is. Then you remove the overburden, start lifting the paydirt and wash it. I am sure I could learn the technical competence of an African miner in less than 3 hours.

The interesting thing was the complete lack of economic sense. The pump was going, using precious water that went to waste and diesel fuel that cost cash. Yet no washing was done until Gaskill asked why. He wanted to know where the second operation was. Well, a few hundred yards away, where the stuff was carried by head pan. Why wasn't the washing done right now? Well, it was easier that way. How much tin did the paydirt contain? The respondent wasn't sure. Every time Gaskill made a suggestion it was listened to respectfully but disbelieving. I overheard the borer tell Musa Dagash, "This is all theory. We know the practice."

Afterwards we met with the African Tin Miners Association. Gaskill explained the Minister's desire to help, what he could and couldn't do. The miners' spokesman tore into him. Why can't we get loans like anybody else? Why do we have to combine? We know the Minister does what you tell him. Gaskill asked how they knew. Musa Dagash intervened. "I am the Permanent Secretary. I advise the Minister. I am a Nigerian. So complain to me." He completely covered Gaskill.

The miners want help in the form of loans. The issue was that the Federal Loans Board (FLB) lends only with an independent check on the availability of ore and the technical competence of the miners. The Ministry does the check, hence they consider Gaskill their enemy. The Minister has told them he will back their loan applications if they form a cooperative or combine into a bigger company. Also, the FLB won't just give them money, rather it will buy the machinery for them. They were upset about the whole thing. They wanted money, no check, no cooperative, no combination, and it was all Gaskill's fault. After all, they had competence.

Dagash and Gaskill kept hammering that the FLB was a *Loans*, not Gift Board, whom they would have to repay with interest. I pointed out that, no matter who wanted a loan, the claims would always be subject to an independent technical check, technical competence for a large-scale operation was different from that for a small one, and a loan had to bear some relation to equity, hence if they wanted larger loans, they just had to combine. I was ready to say that, with their general inefficiency, they were not likely to get machinery that would ruin them and that the difference between them and the Europeans was not capital but 'theory' which they despised. But I forbore. They wouldn't believe me anyway. Everybody regards machinery as some sort of juju. They just don't see the problem of know-how, of 'theory'…

I then went on to Nok with Fagg. Nok is a stone age culture, with perfectly lovely figurines – about 25 have been found – and lots of implements…The place is part of the tin mining area, and that is how the first figurines were discovered. The English miner didn't know what he'd found and didn't care, but when it came to Bernard's attention, he went down and got it. Geological tests, confirmed by carbon 14 tests at Yale, placed it at about 2,000 years old. The relics were found widely apart in the bottom layer of alluvial soil, about 40–50 feet down.

With minor exceptions, there is no systematic archaeological exploration. The archaeologist has nothing to guide him, no documents, no aerial photographs. Mud huts leave no trace, with one exception: laterite brick with wattle bark on the outside shows mild firing and the bark impression. They have discovered traces of house foundations. This method of hut building is still used in East Africa.

On the whole they depend on finds made by mining labor. Everyone is now alerted and pays some attention. Fagg comes down at least once a month to inspect and buys things from them, making sure they collect the stuff and pay attention to it. He takes more than he wants, because if he takes too little they won't find it worth while collecting. Also he has to keep them guessing what he is interested in, otherwise they just bring one type of find…

May 6 (Sunday).…In the early morning we looked at where they had found the various things. By 8:00 AM we were back at camp. About a dozen people had come with head pans full of stuff for Bernard to pick. To their amusement I took a picture of him sorting out. They obviously thought only black men were of interest. Most of the stuff was broken shards beyond any use…Among many stone-age tools he gave me a lovely bluish adze. (An adze has a rounded cutting edge, as distinct from an axe which has a straight one.) It is about 2 inches long and 1 inch high. There were a few fragments of figurines, all of which he kept though he felt reassembly was hopeless. Actually, a lot of the shards will be used in the training school for museum technicians to be set up in Jos under UNESCO auspices…

May 7 (Enugu). Met with outgoing agriculture PS Coatswith…His post is being Nigerianized, which means he will come back on Special Duty rather than in the regular PS position. We talked about our various plans. People like him have a difficult time. He is taking the home [UK] civil service exam, but even if they pass, they get a relatively subordinate position. A major attraction of working in a place like Nigeria is that you are *not* an organization man, and it still matters what you as an individual do. This is after all the reason I like to work uncharted fields in economics. Some of us like to get our hands dirty, both actually and figuratively…

May 12, 1962

May 7 (continued). The evening was most comfortable. Both Padgetts are extremely nice people. I think I wrote before how he is a truly self-made man without much formal education, rising to a very high position in the colonial and post-colonial administration. In fact, he and Coatswith in the Eastern Region, Clarke and Toby in Lagos, Taylor (now in Sierra Leone) and Gibbs are about the only really able and nice Englishmen I have met. I should perhaps add Roy Fenton, the Central Bank governor, whom I have incidentally underestimated in the past…

Padgett told me his woes, chiefly the lack of understanding how serious the financial situation is. The new premier's lodge cost £185,000, which must be about what the White House cost, and about £35,000 more than planned. (Even what was planned was too much.) He had just received a letter about the overrun from the English architects, saying not to worry since the premier (Okpara) himself had OK'd it! Tony thought he would have to resign after all.

May 8. Felix and I left at 7:00 AM for his home town. A detour of 175 miles to spend two hours with his people. It was worth it.

Felix' name is Oguala, also the name of the village. It is large, decentralized in typical Ibo fashion into family compounds. On the way Felix pointed out his wife's village. I asked how he'd met her. He said his father and mother had selected her, as per the local custom. The bride price in Owerri is the highest in Nigeria: £75, paid in installments. Felix's and his wife's villages are only a few miles apart. Land is getting scarce. Felix told me they had let strangers in, but the strangers refused to give back the land, so now they refuse land to anyone not of the family. It costs about £160 to get enough land for a family. Three fourths is fallow at all times. Felix still knows how to farm.

As we approached his village, people waved at him, their faces lighting up as they recognized him. The village chief on his bicycle stopped and greeted us, but then excused himself because of court duty. Felix's mother and wife came out, overjoyed to see us. I was greeted like a king. Of course, no one had expected us. I was led first to his mother's house, where his wife and two daughters are visiting, a mud house with a thatched roof, two rooms, one a living room, the other a sort of kitchen. Two beds of Ibo structure, no mosquito netting, palm fruit on the floor waiting to be boiled, disorderly but homey. Hordes of people came to see me, most of them not speaking English. I never saw so many children in my life in one spot outside a kindergarten. Felix's father has nine wives!

The family compound is more like a village…Father's nine wives notwithstanding, he is a Protestant, while all the children are Catholic. The reason: when the Catholics came they built a large school in the bush and announced they would take only Catholic children. I suppose this is as good a reason as any for becoming Catholic.

Everyone smiled at me. It appears I was the first white man ever to visit except for the priest, which at first they assumed I must also be. Felix let me take any pictures I liked. I shot them making palm oil. One of the women insisted on putting on a blouse. Not that she was ashamed of working with bare bosoms. It was vanity, not shame. The working hut was a friendly place…

Felix' father arrived, a bearded man perhaps in his fifties, sturdy, with the dane gun he always takes to the field in case he comes across some bush fowl. For several years he has applied for permission to have a rifle, but it is rarely granted. He shook hands to indicate my special welcome: they place the hand so the thumb is specially rubbed The women use both hands for the same purpose.

He then retired to wash and change. They have piped water about 300 yards away. When he was ready, he, Felix, one of Felix's brothers and an older man adjourned to the father's house, a bigger, recently completed, cement block structure. There I was offered an easy chair which I refused so the old man could sit in it, while I chose an ordinary chair besides him, evidently the right thing to do. The conversation was obviously handicapped by the need for translation and mostly confined to pleasantries. But Felix said it was a day his people would never forget. Nor will I.

I had a little trouble getting away because they were gathering presents: the car was full of oranges for me, oranges and yams for Felix. Also I found a carving in the car. Felix had told them, Master likes carvings, so they gave me the only one they had. I was very touched. It turned out to be Indian, quite good but definitely not African. There was no way of giving it back. I will send Felix's father my candy-striped suit as a counter present.

I was intrigued what an Indian carving was doing in an Ibo village. Felix said they had had it for a long time. He remembered that as a child he had to dust and polish it. His father had worked as a road laborer in Port Harcourt when he was young. Perhaps he had brought it from there. When I asked whether I couldn't give it back, since it obviously was an Ibo family heirloom, Felix said no. Besides, our people do not value carvings highly. So I guess, valuable or more likely not, I have it and treasure it as a present from some very nice people.

I excused myself at 11:45 AM and went on to WAIFOR (the West African Institute for Oil Palm Research). The oil palm breeder, a Dutchman named Spanaj (?), explained the statistical and biological problems of crossing the palms to get a variety that grew slowly so it would not be too difficult to climb – this itself lengthens the trees' useful life – also to get a higher oil content, breed thinner shells, etc. He showed me the laboratories where they produce seeds for palmgrove rehabilitation in the Regions, Ghana and Sierra Leone, and their experimental plots. They still don't know much about the effect of fertilizers: some make the plants grow faster, which is opposite of what is desired, others change the proportion of male and female flowers in favor of the male flowers, which means less fruit on the palms, etc. Other experiments deal with intercropping, keeping cattle, pesticides, spacing, etc.

In the afternoon Frank Moore arrived and we went to see the Chief Oil Palm Research engineer, Nwanze, a very gifted man who has done a lot for his country. He took us first to the Stork oil mill. Stork is an Amsterdam firm. It was a lovely piece of machinery but too big except for a plantation. Nwanze explained the process and the improvements he had made. I went to see their Pioneer Oil Mill, an older type which cost £18,000, had less capacity, but had once been a good kind of a mill for the country. Here, too, he had made improvements which eased the work and increased oil extraction…

We then continued to Benin to look at figures to buy…During a stop enroute back to WAIFOR, two beauties came to ogle at me and suggest that perhaps they could come along. My answer, that I already had a wife, evoked peals of laughter. People laugh easily and even in Benin, which is sinister, they are friendly. Frank and I agreed that after the ER government had gone broke, such was the people's resilience that Nigeria would still make progress.

We had dinner at WAIFOR director Hartley's. They knew Frank well and were pleased to have company. Morale problems are serious: staff is constantly leaving, the Ministry does not make decisions, the governing body is inter-territorial – it is a West African, not Nigerian institute – and, of course, the place is isolated though pretty. It is amazing what a little love can do for a place: lawns and flowers instead of bush. One major difficulty is, of course, that people simply do not understand what research is. They mix up agricultural research with extension services. It was a pleasant evening and we evidently did the Hartleys a lot of good.

May 10. Frank and I talked over breakfast. He wants us to go together to Bhutan, where they have asked Ford for an economic advisor. Frank is convinced that nothing can stop the ER government from going broke, that it is coming apart at the seams fast. He takes the line Prasad took from the beginning: every country has to learn the hard way that resources are scarce. I still try to do something about it. I always feel it is immoral to take a historic view of current events. Frank told me the African Continental Bank was broke again, that the ENDC had increased its unauthorized and illegal uncovered overdraft with the Bank to £250,000, which was horrifying. He only hoped he could put the skids under Daniels, the American Negro who heads ENDC's industrial division, is lord of it all and really dangerous. God knows what hold he has on Okpara.

In any case, Daniels may have overstepped his bounds. He signed a contract with the German firm for chipboard manufacture, stating it was with Okpara's express approval. While possibly true, this was not what Okpara wanted. Also, he just built an unauthorized £5,000 addition to his house, already a fabulous mansion. This is the sort of thing that trips people up…

At 9:00 AM we went back to WAIFOR to see a demonstration of the hydraulic hand presses designed by Nwanze and built by Stork. It was impressive. Nwanze not only had the basic idea, he had refined it and designed the necessary auxiliary equipment. Extracting oil from palmfruit consists first of cutting up the bunches, boiling them to loosen the fruit and sterilize it, preliminary crushing to loosen the pulp from the kernel – they call this digesting – then pressing and finally cleaning the oil of impurities. The amazing thing was that the auxiliary equipment was designed to be made of empty oil drums.

One hand press could handle 4 tons of fruit a day. To be efficient it needed about 100–150 acres of palms. Fifty farmers could produce enough to supply it and eight people could do the work. Initially all eight quash the bunches as they are delivered to the press, then two go off to boil, two more go off to press and finally two do the filtering once the whole operation has become a continuous process. The press has only two moving parts. Several ER agricultural assistants were being trained in its use so they could teach farmers to operate the presses. I noticed they tended to use a rotary motion on a straight pump handle. Nwanze said this was one of their problems; they had to break the operators of this habit or else the shaft would break.

The whole thing including auxiliary equipment costs less than £400 and two of the mills do the work of an £18,000 Pioneer Oil Mill. Purchase of 1,000 such presses figures prominently in the ER plan and is indeed the best piece of the plan.

A postscript: you would think that, with only two moving parts, nothing could go wrong with such a simple machine. You would be mistaken. Back in the shop Nwanze showed us a rusty press, originally sent to the WR government. They complained it didn't work. The Department of Agriculture had left it standing in the rain instead of protecting it under a thatch. They had injected oil where water should have been and *vice versa*. They must have had a hard time thinking up all the wrong things to do. But there it was: a beautiful, simple piece of machinery ruined. So there will to be problems. People always talk glibly how the underdeveloped countries can jump over stages of development and how they are in a hurry. It just doesn't work that way…

May 11 (Lagos).…Lardner was really glad to see me back. I like him enormously, and he obviously reciprocates. He really should be in academic life, and I must help him get to the States. He isn't too efficient. This is due in part to his lively intellect, in part to the fact that he is as excitable as I am and dislikes dishonesty. He does not delegate much, although he delegated a really important piece of work to me today. (See below.) The problem is that, because of the Minister's xenophobia, he can't as a rule delegate important work to expatriates and the Nigerians he has aren't much good. I don't know what he will do without Lyle, Peter and me. Shaddock is good, but basically an intelligent administrator. It is our little group that keeps pressing for the substantive decisions with long-run effects. He was so pressed that he again forgot the most important decisions...

I first wrote up my report and took it to Lardner, adding orally a few pieces of information I did not want written up officially, such as Wilson's misgivings about Israeli aid. Andrew Wilson had written and phoned about my visit, and was enthusiastic. As I wrote before, in Ibadan, and only there, I was really useful. I came at a strategic moment, and pushed matters along substantially. Besides, like Lardner, Andrew Wilson and Isaac Dinah like and trust me. This is not a statement of vanity, though it pleases me, of course – one likes to be of service, and loves to be loved. The point is that someone like me can only be useful if he is completely trusted. And just as an engineer usually builds in a safety factor of 7–10 to make sure his bridge works, so an advisor must be told ten times as much as he needs to know to be useful, and a scholar must collect ten times the material he will use in order do his work efficiently.

When Arnold comes tomorrow I have to talk with him about Israeli aid. He had a glowing article about it in *Foreign Affairs* about 18 months ago. I think the roof is about to fall on them. What looked like a friendly relationship has been highly exploitative. They go into partnership with the Western Region (or Ghana, etc.), taking 49% of ownership and leaving majority control with the Africans. This pleases the Africans, who unfortunately are rather simple-minded about what constitutes control. After a while the Israelis are happy to sell their share, which has meanwhile appreciated. Doesn't that show they have African interests and national ambitions at heart, and don't want to exploit?

Unfortunately, anyone who knows a modicum of American corporation history knows all the gimmicks: how a minority directorate milks the corporation dry by controlling a supplier firm and buying from it at exaggerated prices. This is exactly what has happened here and in Ghana. The houses in the WR farm settlements were Israeli built and cost twice what they should have. Nigersol, a joint Israeli-WR venture for water development, is very expensive. The hotels, everything, cost too much. And when they have milked the country dry, they generously sell out – after all we must be nationalizing, mustn't we – and repeat the trick elsewhere. Godfrey Lardner told me the Ghanaians are mad at Israel now.

The thing is so immoral. Of all people the Israelis, most of whom have suffered, shouldn't do it. And what makes it worse, much of the aid is given by a trade union. I wrote before that Frank's and my names are not well-liked in Israel and we are suspected of anti-semitism! It is so stupid. The purpose of much of the aid to Africa was to neutralize Arab nationalism. The black African countries couldn't care less about Arab-Israeli feuds. Even Nkrumah, who is intimately associated with the Casablanca group and Nasser, and who has an Egyptian wife, never gave in to Nasser's pressure against his relations with Israel. But what Nasser couldn't achieve, the Israelis will achieve by themselves.

Of course, the Germans and British do the same. The Germans are worse because they are more efficient. But they are carpetbaggers just the same. It sounds very well that they supply not only the whole factory 'turnkey,' but also the management. So what? They have no risk. They cheerfully sell glass and chipboard factories, together with management, when there is no sand for glass and no market for chipboard. Why should they care? They promise management, not profits or markets. They are an irresponsible bunch. I have to get after Posadowski again. Americans *are* slightly better, though not much. The whole thing is immoral – exploit the ignorance of a new nation which, in its understandable nationalism, is asking to be exploited – it will backfire politically very badly...

Posadowski gave a lunch for Dr. Engler, head of the German Bank for Reconstruction,[1] which originally handled Marshall Plan aid and now deals with all capital aid to underdeveloped countries; and Koch-Weser, who heads technical assistance to West Africa...K-W is as skeptical of German business as I because, with all due admiration for their achievement, they are the most ruthless bunch. I sat beside Engler and described my skepticism about the aid by Cuttino-Caro, the German firm selling the glass factory. Also present was J.B. Daramola, another of the few magnificent Nigerians. You will meet him and his wife. They are really fine people. If there were just two dozen more of their kind, what a difference it would make!...

Lardner goes to London today for a week in connection with the Niger dam. Peter had the task of evaluating the economics of the dam locks. It turns out there *won't* be enough water, even with the regulated flow over the dam, to provide a steady minimum draft of 5 feet everywhere below the dam. Not, that is, without additional dredging and training of the river. So the water engineers were wrong. But how are we economists to know this? Peter was stuck on the facts and the theoretical approach. I could help with the latter, not the former. He also wanted me to read his application for Ford money to make a more thorough study of the Niger. I was a little upset because he didn't go about it the best way, and Lyle in his insensitivity to Nigerian xenophobia had neglected to tell Peter first to clear matters with Lardner, whose OK is indispensable...

At 5:30 PM I received a Maltese visitor named Pardo. The new PM, who just won election over Mintoff, urgently wants an economic advisor, who will also prepare a plan...The Nationalists have four years to show what they can do. They want a liberal economy, with more self-government and more control, particularly over their commercial relations. Their big problem is unemployment...

Would the Ford Foundation be willing to supply a planning and advisory operation? To whom should they write? They don't want a socialist, Fabian or otherwise. In fact, they want me. The Prime Minister knows about me. I am just the ideal man for the job. It is important for Malta. What happens in the next two years will shape its history. Also, it might in a negative way be important internationally. If a democratic-liberal policy fails and Mintoff comes back to power – and according to Pardo, he is intelligent – things could go wrong. The word Cuba did not fall, but a Cuba in the middle of the Mediterranean would not be pleasant. So an ounce of prevention...

I said I was flattered, but how did they even know I existed? I had tried to remain anonymous and operate within the civil service in order to be politically discreet and not jeopardize the Plan. Pardo said, "Oh we know all about you, what you have done here. I told the PM all about you. You are the ideal man. They want a Westerner, not an Englishman. They would accept a West German, but they want you. You will get a letter from the PM before the end of the month."

I repeated that I was flattered, even tempted; I wasn't an organization man, but liked small, human-sized operations where the individual counted. I certainly would count. They would entirely depend on me, he said. I said I had been away from my family for 18 months and hadn't liked it. Also, I was tired. I had worked 12–16 hours a day for many months and needed a rest. And I was committed to write a book on Nigeria at Harvard. Oh, he said, no need to work in Malta like that. You would like it. They are friendly people with overdeveloped medical and legal services, but no economists. You would have time to write a book.

...I said I like to look things over first. Now if I could come three months at a time, then go back to the University for a semester, then come again, that might be possible. Well, he thought, if Ford would pay the trips and bring you frequently to Malta, why not. Except by 1964 there had to be a Plan, *my* kind of Plan, depending more on policies than on projects.

I wasn't encouraging, but I didn't say no...I am curious what the Maltese government and Ford will do. And what a letter from the PM will look like...

May 12....I saw Godfrey about answering an important letter from Reg Clarke. We and Finance had met with the individual ministries on project priorities, foreign aid needs, etc. The first round was over, not too satisfactory but still OK. Now Finance had to issue the general expenditure warrants. The ministries wanted warrants totaling £60 million which, as Reg correctly wrote, was nonsense. They couldn't have more than £25 million. The problem is to scale down – my old problem. You see how right I was on the size of the Plan. (I wish that, like Frank, I could enjoy political infighting. I don't really like it, in fact I rather despise it. It is both laboriously complicated – I couldn't match the average emir – and at the same time rather childish. I had a letter from Lincoln Gordon[2] in which he challenged me on the relative degree of complicatedness of politics in Nigeria and Brazil. He wrote that Brazil has the most overdeveloped politics he ever encountered. But then he is an expert on it, I just have very good economic insights.)

Godfrey was apologetic that he hadn't written the letter to Reg. Perhaps it was just as well, as it would have been blistering. In my absence they scheduled a meeting that was suddenly canceled by Finance. Now the pressure is on again. It is, of course, all part of the war between Finance, which has the purse strings, and our Minister, who wants a say, and should have it. After all, this is what a planning unit is for.

So now Godfrey asked me to call a meeting of the relevant PSs and get the project evaluation exercise going in a hurry. This is really a top-level job that he should do but which now falls on me and Peter! When JPC meets on the 18th, Godfrey will still be in London, which is also absurd. To make matters worse, Reg is apparently going abroad with Festus. Garba, his DPS, is good but not yet familiar with the situation. With Reg it would have been relatively simple. Well, it will take the next three days to prepare all this...

For the first time in a long while I know some peace of mind. I hope it will last. Tomorrow, Sunday, is my 50th. I will start off with the communion service, then work leisurely until it is time to fetch Arnold from the airport in the evening.[3] I always wanted to spend my fiftieth birthday alone, no party, just playing Tom's gift record...[4]

May 17, 1962

I am in great hurry now. I'll write soon in detail. It has been hectic here with Rivkin visiting, and it is hellishly hot. To make matters worse, the airconditioner in the office is off. No electricity anywhere.

May 20, 1962

May 14....I took Arnold to supper at the Dolgins'. The Ambassador came to ask Arnold about a recent trip to Japan, when he persuaded the Japanese to join the Nigeria Consultative Group. It is the biggest such group ever assembled. Even the Swiss are members. We'll get all the money and won't be able to spend it!

Also present was Massaglia, the embassy political officer. He was lively, but like so many political scientists, tended to take words more seriously than facts. We were talking about the 'dynamism' of Nkrumah vs. Nigerian lack of 'projection.' I had a similar discussion with Barbara Ward. I am not impressed by Nkrumah's dynamism.

Similarly I am not impressed by Pan-Africanism. Africa is a geographical concept and nothing else. West Africa makes some sort of sense, so does North or East Africa. But Pan Africa is paper-thin, and a purely negative reaction to colonialism. With the last colony out – Arnold gives Angola at most three years[5] – it will fall to pieces. The Commies try their best to invent neo-colonialism, which is any contact with the West, but while this may do harm in the short run, I don't see it as important in the long run. Arnold backed me on most of this, while Massaglia thought the trouble with us economists was that we looked at facts and were too logical, and didn't see the impact of illogical concepts. I thought the criticism rather a compliment, and still think concepts without facts or logic behind them will vanish sooner or later, probably sooner...

May 16. Worked on one really important file, dealing with the so-called General Warrants, that Godfrey had dumped into my lap. Briefly, Finance has to authorize the Accountant General to issue warrants so that individual ministries can spend money. This is about the most important control mechanism. The ministries had requested warrants totaling £75 million, which as Reg pointed out, was nonsense. They should be not more than £15–20 million.

I disagreed, however, with another of Reg's views, that projects in the old program should get money automatically. Many of them haven't started yet, are of very low priority, and shouldn't be executed. My problem was to devise a form to elicit the necessary information, while preventing ministries from lying, as they are apt to do, when they want cash. I think I succeeded, but I wanted to talk it over with Peter, who had last worked on these things.

I also had a Ministry of Health request to get extra money in the first year. What they wanted was to start every damn project they had, and in fact it amounted to a request to do what they liked, regardless of priorities. I wrote an impolite 3-page memo. When my secretary saw it, she censored the sentence, "The Ministry of Health is lying through its teeth," but otherwise let things stand. The morning was a madhouse. The telephone rang all the time, and it took all my energy just to keep going...

May 17. Aboyade appeared and I asked him for lunch. He is going to Addis for two years. I had hoped he would be my successor, but he wants an academic career: "And you know if one wants an academic career one has to work ten years at it."...Later I talked general warrants with Garba, who made some suggestions on his own agreeing with my views, which had been vetoed by Frank Tarrant, an SAS from Finance seconded to our Ministry. I was rather happy about it...

At 5:00 PM I went to the Federal Palace for tea with Arnold. Andrew Wilson was driving down from Ibadan to see Arnold and to bring me a message from Chief Adebo. Before he came I had another chance to talk with Arnold about his future. I think he would be a marvelous Director of the Center for Development Research at Michigan...I don't want to write what Adebo is going to do, but it is wonderful.

Posadowski called. He practically accused me of torpedoing German projects! Yet all I had said was that contracting management services when buying machinery was fine, but didn't solve the basic problem of making profits. He also said the Northern Region had signed up for a cement mill in Sokoto with Ferrostahl. He was happy, I less so. At least Ferrostahl is bearing 30% of the cost – I figure this is their profit. Also the Northern Region Government guarantees purchase of the cement for four years, I don't know at what price. I bet Ferrostahl doesn't lose. Sokoto is a hell of a place to locate a cement mill. That is the sort of thing a planning unit should analyze. I don't think the NR planning unit ever did. The Sardauna wanted it and got it...

Arnold told me the IBRD knows what Lyle and I have done, and are unhappy about some things Prasad has done, such as the exchange control legislation. They are also somewhat embarrassed, because they don't know what to do with him when he comes back. Arnold also told me he would probably join the Bank, although it wasn't yet certain. Anyway he thought it was flattering the way Burke Knapp went around saying he had already joined. A flattering way of putting pressure on a man...

May 19. Got stuff ready for Lardner, who returns today...I was supposed to bring Lyle up-to-date. I told him what I had done in his absence and tried to give some fatherly advice. Perhaps I made an impression on him after all about is what academic quality, and what theory, good theory, is about. Not the stuff that graduate students are supposed to turn out as part of their training. I mean creative stuff.

At 10:30 PM Peter Kyle of AID/Enugu brought a message from Frank and we chewed the fat. Kyle is a bright young man at the end of his tour of duty, anxious to go home. He said *some* projects in the East that Frank had opposed were good, while he missed others that were bad. Which is likely to be true. If you are the only person with sense, this sort of thing is bound to happen. Kyle also told me the Arthur D. Little Group had been kicked out of the Eastern Region. It doesn't surprise me. They came like the proverbial elephant into the china shop. They refused to work in the small industries center in Owerri. One of their people was unstable, another drunk.

After all that, Kyle made his own assessment: Nigeria is a society without discipline, corrupt through and through, with no executive capacity and no shame. The University at Nsukka, the Railway, the Electricity Corporation, all are being milked dry by Zik, Ikejiami and smaller fry. Unfortunately there's a lot in this. Yet if only the government program can be reduced in size and market discipline can be introduced, and if God can be induced to look after Nigerians as well as after drunks and the United States, things need not go so badly.

May 25, 1962

This will be a short letter because I have to leave for Ghana in half an hour.

May 24. I wish there was some quiet. Yesterday I worked from 6:00 AM to 1:00 AM, with one hour each for lunch and supper, to clear up the mess that Prasad, Lyle and Peter caused in my absence. I'll explain later what it is all about, but it is serious. I wrote Lardner a memo on what I propose to do and asked him to show it to Prasad and Stanley Wey, the PM's extremely nice and able Secretary (who in this capacity is also the head of the civil service). If my changes are not adopted there will be serious trouble at the next Consortium meeting. I told Lardner that if Prasad objected I would walk out and suggest he do the chapters himself. Godfrey agreed to that.

May 25, 1962

I had hoped to be able to take it easy. Nothing of the kind. The matter with Prasad is coming to a head, and this time I am fighting and going on record. But back to the diary.

May 21....A pre-pre-JPC meeting on what to do with the Plan. I had worked out what I wanted and Godfrey accepted it and backed me. The original idea was to consolidate the Regional and Federal Plans by economic sector, and substitute the new sectoral chapters for the Regional Plan summaries, which were now obsolete. The idea was sound. Unfortunately the junior staff wasn't quite up to it. I can't blame them, for one really has to go to the Regions and probe. One just can't do these jobs at headquarters. So I suggested re-writing Chapters 1–5 and 10, substituting the plans for the summary chapters and publishing this as Volume 1. Volume 2 could then be the consolidation by sectors with as many payoff studies as possible, omitting, of course, those that were too sketchy. We agreed on this as the only feasible alternative.

I had Pius Okigbo for lunch, and asked him point-blank about his plans. Particularly, whether he would succeed Prasad as economic adviser. He was amazingly frank. He said he probably would, but was still negotiating with the Federal Government, which hadn't met all his conditions. He was tired – I don't know from what – and first taking a vacation...

The budget contains a line item creating the post of Deputy Advisor to the PM. Pius is to understudy Prasad, which is absurd. I have finally begun not only to distrust Prasad, but to dislike him personally. Anyway it is absurd to think such a position could be understudied. Every man has his own style, and though Pius is as lazy as Prasad, he thinks straighter. On the other hand, he is more afraid to make decisions, so he probably would not be too bad...

May 22. We met at Prasad's office. My suggestion was accepted; since I have to do the work there was little else to discuss. Mention was made of the London meetings of the Niger dam committee, which were inconclusive, except that the accountants had raised the cost by including all sorts of contingencies. Some could undoubtedly go wrong, but it is unlikely that all would do so at the same time. Still, it is best to be in a situation where things can go only up.

At 9:30 AM we went to JPC. Prasad talked for $1^1/_2$ hours about nothing. The Consortium was being called a Consultative Group because the plan might be underfulfilled by 40%. I almost jumped out of my seat when he said that. Another preparation for an alibi. I put forward my own proposal in about as many sentences as it took me to write here; after a brief discussion I excused myself to get to work. Lyle and Lardner stayed. Lardner let drop (so I was told, since I had left already) that a memo on control mechanisms had been prepared – by me, actually. Prasad insisted it should go around the regions. The Regions didn't think so. And apparently Andrew Wilson with his usual forthrightness asked Prasad what he wanted, whether he had to be consulted on everything. Prasad said he had no personal interest, but felt that the Economic Advisor to the PM should have been consulted.

He is just interested in personal power. The damn thing is too silly; the Africans are getting rid of all the good things about colonialism, but not the bad things, and centralized decision making is a bad thing now. Everything bogs down because no one wants to make decisions. Much too much has to be decided by Godfrey, and Prasad is a bottleneck.

I started rewriting Chapter 5, my pride and joy and a sophisticated piece of reasoning. It is crucial for the next meeting of the Consortium. I had got a critique from Clive Gray, the young Harvard boy[6] at AID, which had been damn good and with his permission I gave it to Lardner to show what we were up against in Washington: not Prasad, but really good economists. Because of that valuable criticism I went back to the worksheets. (Sorry, all this really happened on the 23rd.) I started rewriting the technical appendices. I wanted to make my procedures and reasoning crystal clear. Also to put in the new figures from the Regional plans. I made considerable headway and am now proud of it.

Back home, Fogg brought disturbing news from the Eastern Region. It is rumored that an Indian economic advisor is to be brought in. Frank must do what he thinks best, but he should write to Kingsley immediately to bow out. For the first time in my life I am getting racial prejudices – against Indians.

Clive Gray came in to bring me his criticisms, apologetic because they were so detailed, but I was grateful. After I read them I thanked him profusely…

May 23. Worked all morning like a madman. Going over changes made while I was in Italy over the holidays, I hit the ceiling. I had given strict instructions not to change anything except the figures coming in from the Regions. Yet substantial changes had been made. Reworking this whole nonsense really hit me. Clive Gray had spotted something fishy without quite knowing what.

The Chapter's whole point is to summarize the Plan in macro terms and provide a consistency test through the National Income framework. I had always insisted the Plan was too big, and that underspending would be substantial. When the new figures came in, they showed that recurrent expenditure would have to be cut if consumption per head was to be increased. Peter took this alarming result to Prasad, who arbitrarily assumed different and bigger underspending for the macro accounts than for the financial resource picture. The whole point of a consistency test is to see whether consistent assumptions yield consistent results – which they did not! Prasad just cooked the figures to come out right. Lyle, who is a superb project analyst but doesn't know these things well, gave in and in his own words, goofed. I recall vaguely that Peter told me about it, but it didn't register in the general mess.

I decided this time to fight in the open. So I told Lardner what had happened, that Prasad had altered assumptions without authority of JPC or NEC, which neither he nor I were empowered to do. I wrote a memo asking to be put on record, to protect myself. A copy went to Prasad and another to Stanley Wey. So I am going to the PM after all.

All morning I worked like mad so the plan could go to the printers on June 1. I felt badly that I had to fight but I had to protect the man who will present Nigeria at the World Bank meeting, particularly as it is to be a man whom I like very much and admire greatly…

Toby had called off our squash game because his minister, who is the leader of the opposition in the Western Region, wanted him. All hell has broken loose in Ibadan…In the fight between Awolowo and Akintola, the latter lost, apparently (and to my surprise) in something like a coup d'etat. The Governor dismissed Akintola on the ground that he had lost the confidence of Parliament, though no vote of confidence was taken. The Governor is apparently within his right to do this, though it is bad business. In the intra-party struggle Awolowo was both accuser and judge, which I don't like. But it was an Akintola man who later apparently started the fighting in the House. They were so proud of their political stability. Still, if the Federal Government can handle it well – and I think the PM will – we will have proved that Nigeria can handle a major crisis by constitutional and democratic means.

May 24. I worked from 6:00 AM to 1:00 AM. Chapter 5 got rewritten. It was one of my most strenuous days…I had to finish the chapter to be able to go to Accra.

May 30, 1962

It is 4:00 AM. I have been awake since 2:00 AM and might just as well get up and work. Things have come to a head with Prasad. Lardner and Reg Clarke back me. I am stinking mad and told Prasad yesterday that he has double-crossed me for the last time. I am still upset. Fighting is strenuous, and the energy could be used for more interesting purposes. I have to put things in writing and force Prasad to do the same. He is a charming host, a smooth operator, a poor economist, a catastrophic adviser, and an untrustworthy colleague. Fortunately the PM doesn't take his advice most of the time.

May 25 (Accra).…At 4:30 PM I lectured at the university on Planning in Nigeria. About 40–50 people were present. Both government and university plus a few stray students and wives. There were questions and comments. Despite considerable effort I had evidently failed to make clear that profitability referred to economic, not financial profitability. But at the end Jan Drewnowski, from Poland, thought I had become a socialist, while I told him, on the contrary the Poles have finally become capitalist. Actually the Poles back me completely in the notion of economic calculation and decentralization. Jan is wrong: the ideas are all western, and have been introduced in the Iron Curtain countries only since Stalin's death.

Afterwards we were outdoors at the Lawsons. She teaches economics and he is a botanist…There was agreement that the arbitrariness of Nkrumah's regime was holding back the country. Austin, who teaches politics at LSE and the Royal Institute of International Affairs, told of his researches into the early history of Ghana's CPP, the ruling party. He obtained documents on early CPP proceedings from Danquah, the grand old man of Ghana, who invented the country's name and was once a presidential candidate. He now languishes in prison under the preventive detention act. Since his arrest the atmosphere has changed; I could confirm this from Nigeria. Ever since, Nigerian nationalists have been cool to Nkrumah.

I also asked the tactless question whether, when Leventis sold out to the government for about £3–4^1/$_2$ million, an independent accountant had gone over the books to value the properties. People looked at me as if I was crazy: "Shall we say, a government accountant did." I had my answer.

May 26. Polly Hill took me first to the statistics office to see the Government Statistician, Omaboe...The office was impressive in its efficiency: the only government office in Africa I have so far seen where people evidently worked. There were lots of advisers from iron curtain countries, but also others, and most important, there were many highly competent Ghanaians. I was there until 11:30 AM, collected lots of material and many excellent impressions.

The next stop was Mensah, chief of the planning unit. Harvard trained. Also lost. They have no plan. I asked who advised Nkrumah. No one knows. I asked where the crazy party program came from. (The chapter on 'socialism' discusses price control and monogamy among other 'socialist' features of the economy!)...I asked what he would do. He said he had to wait until talk of the party program died down. "Then we start from scratch." An excellent man, very badly used...

8:30 PM – dinner with among others Sudhir Sen and Phillips, an almost white Ghanaian who is Permanent Secretary of Finance and very influential. We talked frankly. I told him the difficulties I anticipated due to the exaggerated size of our Plan. He seemed to feel our problems were nothing compared to theirs. Everything was arbitrary. Reserves were running down at the rate of £20 million a year, and things would come to a halt when they ran out in a year. He agreed that African societies were corrupt, and exchange controls in these circumstances were catastrophic... Phillips broached the idea of a West African airline. I said we in the Planning Unit had urged that, as well as a West African shipping line. He expressed pleasure and surprise. The impression in Ghana had been that Nigeria didn't want to cooperate. Nigeria had the same impression about Ghana.

May 27 (Sunday)....Back in Lagos, the Ministry car was waiting. There was a letter from Prasad, official as I had wanted it, but nasty and beside the point. I was upset.

Clive Gray and wife expected me for supper. Clive wanted to know whether it was true that I expected only 5% underspending. It turned out that Prasad had said at a cocktail party that he expected 35% underspending, as against Stolper's 5% and Hansen's 10%, and he wished the Economic Planning Unit would make up its mind. This is so exactly the opposite of the truth that it made me more determined than ever to pin Prasad down in writing.

I left the Grays as soon as I decently could and searched out Godfrey. Obviously, compared to what the nation faced, my problems were relatively unimportant. Parliament had been summoned to deal with the situation in the West, where there was no working government. Still, I told Godfrey about Ghana, and Prasad's latest switch.

"What is the use of a Plan when you underspend 35%?" Godfrey wanted to know. I pointed out that, from the beginning, I wanted a realistic plan and Prasad wanted a bargaining plan. Actually, Clive had said that when he asked where the 35% figure came from, Prasad said that was the underspending in India's first Five-

Year Plan. As if this were relevant! Godfrey said: go ahead, write a memo, and I'll transmit it to Stanley Wey.

May 28....At 7:00 PM I attended a cocktail party given by Stanley Wey. Wey expressed surprise that I was leaving so soon, and wouldn't be back. I pointed out that Lyle was staying. He said pointedly he preferred me to stay. While I was flattered at the sentiment, I pointed out that what was needed in the future was Lyle's talents, not mine. Still he wanted to see me, and I have an appointment today at 8:15 PM at the Cabinet offices.

May 29....Another editorial meeting at 4:00 PM. Godfrey was late, but Reg was there. I sat as far away from Prasad as was physically possible.

It takes me a long time to get mad, but as Reg said "My God, it takes a long time to convince you." Prasad said he had got my letter and would answer it, and then would put both to the PM. I said this was fine. He then asked, "What do you do about hoarding in your theory?" I was taken aback, for the question is about as logical as, "What is the relevance of the Prime Minister's hair color?" I said that hoarding would change the volume of production, etc. In other words, I tried to be logical on *his* terms.

Finally I said, and this was my second mistake, "This concept doesn't belong in the Keynesian context." I immediately knew I had made a boner. I should have said "National Income framework". He replied that not everyone accepted the Keynesian framework. I said that was fine with me. I was willing to tear up the whole chapter and let him rewrite it, but would refuse to do anything else. He accused me of not tolerating differences of opinion, as if the question whether $2+2=4$ or 5 was a matter of opinion. I finally accused him of double-crossing me and not sticking to our agreement on the Plan's size. His comeback was weak: "You mean to say that £7 million a year can make all the difference?" But a man who is 6 feet tall and can't swim drowns in 7 feet of water as easily as in 7,000 feet. The issue is one of resource availability, which Prasad just doesn't understand.

Reg was evidently amused, though he told me later I had burst out much too early. His tactic was to hold the discussion to Chapter 10 as long as possible. By 9:30 PM we must reach an agreed formulation. Lardner said, "We'll cram it down his throat." But the trouble is, as Reg put it, "Wolf is the only bugger who really understands the figures. We really just have to believe him." Which is true enough.

Godfrey said the issue was simple: we couldn't monkey with the underspending figures agreed with the Regions without getting into political troubles of the first magnitude, and we couldn't swindle the Bank.

May 31, 1962

...At 8:15 AM I had an appointment with Stanley Wey, Secretary to the PM, who is also the highest civil servant in the country. I wrote before that I like Wey immensely. A smallish men compared to my bulk, pleasant, self-effacing, of transparent honesty and a quick mind. He started by saying he was sorry he had not had an occasion to talk with me before. He had been new at his job and had to learn it. Had I ever met his predecessor? I hadn't. He was sorry I couldn't stay, but understood I had been absent from my family for a long time, etc.

I said I felt guilty bothering him with my troubles at this time when he had more important troubles to talk about – I was referring to the troubles in the Western Region. He pointed to the pile of files on his desk, and said he was sorry, but didn't know what I was referring to. So I told him he had received or would receive letters I had written Godfrey for transmission to Prasad, which at Godfrey's suggestion had been copied to him (Wey).

I then showed him the correspondence, adding that I could cite further instances of double dealing, and in confidence told him how Prasad had double-crossed me with Rivkin. I pointed out that Rivkin would never have told me if I hadn't been present when he telephoned Prasad at my request to set up an appointment for both of us with Prasad, and Prasad replied he did not want me present. I had said nothing at the time because I didn't wish to embarrass Rivkin.[7]

I told Wey I had blown up and said, before Reg Clarke and Shaddock that he, Prasad, had double-crossed me for the last time. I added that the Plan was very good, and could have been superb, had we been able to devote the time we lost fighting for sense and going over the same ground over and over again, to constructive work that would eventually have to be done anyway. I would, of course, abide by Government's decision, but would not let Prasad make it for the government, and against the express decisions of JPC and NEC. [Incidentally I am now sure there won't be a letter from Prasad, nor will he take it to the PM.] I told Wey I had ceased to trust Prasad as a person, had refused to meet him, and to safeguard my integrity as well as the Ford Foundation's, I preferred to be on record.

Wey was disturbed. He said Nigeria had got Prasad as advisor, but had no idea that he would run everything. I said one of the worst aspects taken over from the colonial regime was that only the top man could take decisions. I repeated what I had told Wey at the NEC meeting in Ibadan – you (Wey) never answered my question whether you got my letter. It is important for me to know whether it was lost. I was put in a very difficult position by being simultaneously in a Ministry and thus responsible to my minister, and responsible to JPC where Prasad is chairman, talks and talks and tries to pull everything into his hands. I also said that, at the peace meeting Toby arranged in April, after the first blowup, I had told Prasad I would cooperate to the limit but would not take orders from him or anyone except my Minister and my PS.

Wey said it was too bad that, because the British had deliberately excluded Africans when real decisions were being made – which is undoubtedly true – they had not really learned their job and needed assistance. Moreover, they felt, or had felt, that they wanted it from an Indian, and you have to be careful with Indians. I laughed and said I never had any racial prejudices before but was developing some, which made him smile.

He then repeated he wished it was I who was staying. I said I had contracted with Harvard for nine rather than twelve months so as to be able to come out at any time up to three months if I was needed; the length of stay could be extended with Harvard's consent; and I was sure Ford would pay for it. I was also ready to assist at any time whomever would be Nigerian Ambassador in Washington responsible for negotiations over the Plan. He then told me it was not yet announced but no secret that Chief Adebo would be the ambassador. I said I was delighted and that Chief Adebo was the greatest Nigerian I had met, and a great man by any standard. Then I said: but first I need a rest badly. And under no circumstances would I work in the future under Prasad. I added that I got along with everybody and left many good friends in the country – I mentioned Godfrey, Daramola and a few others – but couldn't work with Prasad anymore.

The fact is that I have never thought much of Prasad as an economist, and now have lost all respect for him as a person. I did not say this, although God knows I might have. The fact is that Prasad isn't as good an operator as I feared, and rather foolish. He could have had the best economist on his staff, self-effacing and loyally supporting him. *My* status is determined by the profession and the University, not in Nigeria and as an adviser. Besides, I loathe the exercise of power. At the same time I am extremely jealous of my integrity and personal freedom. I think this combination of a wish for personal freedom rather than power was outside Prasad's previous experience, as I know now (but not earlier) that it also puzzled Lyle and caused some of our difficulties. I just don't like to be taken over, though I am willing to submerge myself voluntarily.

Finally, I raised the issue of publishing the – still secret – first planning paper which I did in April 1962. [I am in fact rather proud of it since we had tapped most of the major problems by then. Although written by me, it is signed by both Lyle and myself. Lyle did some editing, most of which made rather clumsy reading. At the time I wasn't as sure of myself as I am now, and believed with Lyle that we had to spell things out in great detail for officials. I know now that this is wrong in Nigeria – it may be true elsewhere – and that Lyle's troubles, all of them, stem from his terribly pedestrian and detailed approach. But I shall leave it as it is, although I think my original version, still somewhere in the files, was better.]

I told Wey Godfrey would have to decide whether the paper contained anything Government wished to keep secret. I added that originally I wanted it published because I thought it interesting for the profession and the training of planners to see both the first planning paper and the final plan. Now I had a second interest: I wanted to publish it as a means of safeguarding my professional integrity. He promised to read it.

Wey's last words characterize the man: "When your wife and son come, my wife and I would like to have you for dinner in our house. It is a small house, but my own. I do *not* live in a government house." I don't think you can quite appreciate what this implies. Few government people could say they live in their own house. All too frequently, officials get a low-interest loan from government, build a house, lease it at an outrageous price, and then live in a subsidized government house, paying 8% of income as rent.

At 9:30 AM I was at Reg Clarke's. We worked until 1:00 PM going over the draft of my chapter with a fine tooth comb, word for word, cross-checking figures. I explained the details and procedures to Reg and the reasons. Though he disclaimed understanding, he got it quickly enough. It was invaluable for me. We removed any words or formulations that might be a red flag to Prasad and substituted new ones that made the point clear without giving offense to the Indian soul. We made sure that no formulation could be attacked because it wasn't strictly true. We rewrote four of the 40–odd paragraphs completely, but my manuscript came through unscathed, and I had now the complete backing of Reg – which I really already had.

Back at the office, Lyle told me the Minister had heard of the ruckus with Prasad – from Godfrey – and wanted more explanations. So I got ahold of Godfrey and we went together. The minister was in shirt and white trousers minus robe or hat, and remained informal...He started off by saying he had only one complaint: Rivkin had been in town. Why hadn't I brought him in, an important American visitor? Who ran the Ministry anyway, he or we! I pleaded guilty, said I had worked so hard it had slipped my mind, but when I remembered it, he had left town.

After a while, he turned on Godfrey: Why hadn't he got certain papers to sign? Why were things kept from him? Godfrey replied that he himself had known only the evening before, had been in meetings, and didn't want to interfere with Sam Akande, the SAS in charge of technical assistance. Next: why was he not brought into my disagreement with Prasad? Why were letters sent to Stanley Wey, but not to him, the Minister?

Godfrey explained that I wanted to be on record. I said I felt I had to defend the position taken by JPC, NEC and the Ministry, and was fighting for it. I knew I could count on the Minister's support but if I could win using machine guns, I didn't want to use the really big gun and my last resort, i.e. himself. He read from the constitution – not for the first time – what he was responsible for, including the Plan. "Prasad has nothing to do with it. How does he come in?" Godfrey replied, "As chairman of JPC." The Minister: "Only the PM can change my decision, no one else." I said that was one point at issue between Prasad and me, and one reason why Godfrey backed me to the hilt.

The Minister then asked, "Who is Prasad anyway? We thought we needed advice from an underdeveloped country. But no one wanted him to try to run everything." I said nothing; the sentiment echoed some things Stanley Wey had said.

At 2:15 PM I went home for lunch with Bronislaw and Olukampo, an able young Nigerian teaching at UCI, who had been a tutor at the LSE for two years. Their company kept my mind off the forthcoming fight at the afternoon editorial meeting.

I took a tranquilizer, made good resolutions and went to Prasad's office at 4:00 PM. Again I sat at the other end of the table. Prasad said he had some suggestions: Chapter 5 – the central piece of the Plan *at this stage* – would go into the Plan document with only such minor alterations as we (the EPU) would make and without references to the technical annexes. Annex I, on GDP projection methodology and the consistency test, would be printed under my name and not advertised but automatically distributed to all CG members.[8] It would not be restricted and could be given to universities, UN agencies, anyone who wanted it or to whom I wanted to send it.

Annex II, giving detailed import and export projections, would be mimeographed under my name, but restricted. In this way, Government would not be associated with my methodology, and assumptions on future prices and oil production would remain secret. I quickly agreed to all this. It was much more than I had asked for. I certainly never dreamt anything would come out under my name. Actually the 'disassociation' is rather funny. It takes Indian 'logic' to accept results but not the assumptions and methods used to arrive at them.

We then went through Chapter 5. I let Reg lead. With minor amendments – a word here and there, omission of references to the technical annexes – everything was passed as formulated by Reg and me. It all took just over an hour. It was a complete victory, indeed a complete rout of Prasad. He was pleasant and so was I, although I resisted all overtures to become friendly again. I am sure he will never forgive me, but now there is nothing he can do to the Plan.

As is inevitable over 18 months, I have opened myself to attacks through indiscretions, etc. (which is why I want this diary restricted), but I have never lied, nor been underhanded or double-crossing. I am a little troubled by one thing, though. I think that at times Prasad was unaware of what he had done. He knows, of course, that he wanted absolute power to run the show by himself. That he is slightly afraid of my superior training and intellect is also clear, but I don't think he understands why, after taking it so long, I exploded just now.

I left quickly. I told Godfrey that from now on I would talk with Prasad only in front of a senior African official. I don't want to be left alone with him. I thanked Reg and went to Godfrey to do the same. Godfrey said Wey had called Prasad, but he did not know what was said. Wey had then called Godfrey and told him to prevent an open clash with me. I was elated at the success, left Godfrey and briefed Lyle and Peter, who were anxious to learn the outcome. Then celebration over dinner with Bronislaw Oyzanowski, who had invited me. For the first time in a long while I slept more than 4 hours, though not much more. It was quite a day.

May 31. First I dropped by George Dolgin, who was still at breakfast, to tell him the news. He thought the whole thing was fantastic. When I told him Prasad was staying another year, he thought it was catastrophic, as do I. And it won't help the Bank either.

Later I ran into Joel Bernstein, AID/Lagos director, and Ambassador Joe Palmer. I described the victory, and told them to give a gold medal to Clive Gray. I also told them I had broken with Prasad, but nothing else about it. Only George Dolgin knows. (I also told the general news to Clive Gray the evening before. He deserved to know.)

Then the Minister came. I told him I wouldn't need his help. He asked me into his office with Joel and Joe. Press and photographers were there. It turned out to be the signing of a $6^1/_2$ million technical assistance agreement. Joe read a statement, so did the Minister, interpolating comments about why people distrusted foreigners, but why he and the Federal Government felt they could trust the Americans. It was nice of the Minister to ask us in, but I was on pins and needles to get back to work…

Now I have to get the annexes ready, start proofreading the first galleys, draft an introduction to be signed by the PM, write a memo for Reg on control of recurrent expenditures, and write a long essay on likely future problems – how I would either try to prevent them or, if they arose, how I would deal with them. The latter – which is really Prasad's job if he knew it – was requested by Godfrey, Reg and Wey. It seems I have a lot more influence beyond the EPU than I realized. I don't know when I am going to do all this.

June 4, 1962

…Dead with work and lack of sleep. Am now reading the galley proofs of the Plan – I must be the highest paid proof reader in the world. Even this can't be done locally…

June 3 (Sunday). In the evening Reg Clarke and Roy Fenton came for a bottle of wine. We discussed how to make monetary policy in a country like Nigeria, and I got some very original ideas from Fenton. I believe I wrote once before that he was probably the man I underestimated most…

Notes

1 Kreditanstalt für Wiederaufbau.
2 Professor at the Harvard School of Business, former US ambassador to Brazil and a personal friend. I had written him because I had heard that Sears Roebuck was trying to develop local suppliers in Brazil and wanted to find out whether this might be applicable in Nigeria.
3 According to WS' next letter, Rivkin was stopping over in Nigeria on a mission for the Ford Foundation, to evaluate interest in establishing a civil service training institute in francophone Africa.
4 WS' 50th birthday was May 13, 1962.
5 Angola remained a Portugese colony for another dozen years, until after Portugal's 1974 revolution.
6 Gray [the present editor] was going on 29 at the time.
7 Addition 1998: I had told Rivkin I was not authorized to give him the information he wanted and needed, but Prasad was. I also told him Prasad knew nothing of the Plan because he didn't understand it.
8 It was eventually printed and distributed under the title *Prospects for the Nigerian Economy*.

Postscript (1999)

In June 1962 I flew to Dakar at the invitation of the USAID mission to Senegal and the Senegalese planners, to talk about the Nigerian Plan and the methods of analysis I had developed. Black, the USAID mission director, was married to my former tutee, Martha Mooney, from the days I taught at Radcliffe. It was possible to time the invitation so that I could join my wife and older son, who flew in from the United States. It was a joyful reunion.

It happened that Hans Wolfgang Singer was on the same plane. "Hawosi", now Sir Hans, was then a United Nations staff member. He is the last surviving friend from Schumpeter's seminar in Bonn. He disembarked in Monrovia on some assignment.

On our return to Nigeria, Reg Clarke noticed with amazement my changed personality, looking happy for the first time since we met. I invited my African friends to meet my family, but have only a hazy memory for whom I cooked. But there were two very nice and unexpected events. When saying good bye to Waziri Ibrahim, we had to wait for almost an hour after he had made the appointment. He had asked Joe Palmer to come, and then made a moving speech how, because of me, all Americans would be trusted. OK.

The other and much nicer event was my farewell party. The usual party for a retiring civil servant was a dinner at the Federal Palace to which not everyone invited actually came, a speech was made, a present was given. And then good-bye.

In my case, Godfrey gave a high-life party at his house, to which the only white people invited were my family, Lyle and Ann Hansen, and (probably) Peter and Gretel Clark. A good time was had by all. I was very happy, because I was now certain that I had been trusted as well as liked. (I had the same feeling on a later occasion, when I stopped in Lagos on the way home from leading a World Bank mission to Dahomey (now Benin), and found three cars at the airport, from USAID, my old Ministry and the University of Ibadan.) At the American party given for me I was told that all the invited Nigerians, who on other occasions had shunned such invitations, came to the party. You will forgive me, if I feel proud as well as touched by this.

We traveled for about three weeks in Hans Willi's air-conditioned Olds, getting as far north as Ilorin. Chief Inneh received us in his compound. He presented me with a wonderful copy of a ceremonial drinking vessel, in the form of a leopard, which is displayed in the Benin Museum. The copy now has an honorable place in my living room. He also gave me the statue of a servant, mentioned in the text, and a traditional Benin head. He allowed us to photograph in his house and gave my wife and son a small present. And we also visited the Oba. [Photo No. 30 shows WS and son Tom on their farewell visit to Benin.]

I had not wanted to say good-bye to Prasad, but my English friends insisted. So I did. He told me he admired me for the way in which I defended my position. OK. But he obviously had no idea of the harm he had done by exposing my dear friend Chief Adebo to extreme danger as the Nigerian Representative in Washington.

(Chief Adebo wrote the foreword to my *Planning without Facts* (Harvard University Press, 1966)).

Nor did Prasad seem to realize that we had agreed in writing what our respective roles would be before we came to Nigeria. I have either originals or copies of all these documents.

For the rest, we traveled more or less leisurely around the world, where I visited planning commissions the way one visited cathedrals during the Grand Tour of Europe. In Addis, Bronislaw met us. And there were several instances of particular interest. In every other stopover, the Ford Foundation met the plane, saw us through the controls (which were difficult in Teheran), and took care of housing etc. In Teheran, the planners told me in desperation that Mosadegh had been their last chance, which turned out to be prophetic, pathetic as it was.

In India, I had a particularly interesting discussion with Pitambar Pant who, to my pleasure, completely agreed with what I had been doing. When I mentioned Prasad, his comments were not very polite. So Prasad either knew nothing about his native country, or had lied. In any case I found that the people who did all the dirty work, physically and metaphorically speaking, thought alike, whether they were Indian or Polish, 'capitalist' or 'socialist'. Ideology simply became irrelevant for them.

Ken (John Kenneth) Galbraith, at the time our Ambassador, whom I had known at Harvard and later as a member of the US Strategic Bombing Survey, gave a small luncheon with some Indians. (My personal relations with Galbraith are now closer than they were then.) In India I also saw Chrakravarty, whose book I had reviewed in a long article, and he invited me to give a lecture.

One of the most fascinating stops was Pnomh Penh, where we visited Angkor Wat and Angkor Tom. And then the only mishap of the trip happened. When we were ready to fly from Cambodia to Hong-Kong, it turned out that the airline on which we were booked did not exist. In retrospect I believe that it probably was one of the CIA airlines, whose usefulness had expired. That forced us to fly to Vietnam, the only country we could fly to without a visa. We arrived just after president Diem was assassinated. One could not leave the narrow confines of the city for security reasons. The signs of Vietcong bombings were still fresh.

As a result we were a day late in Hong-Kong. I had an introduction to the Financial Secretary of the Colony, and gave his name as contact for my younger son [Matthew], who was to meet us there. As a result, the Police Chief met my son at the airport instead of me. From an economic policy standpoint, the week in Hong-Kong was absolutely fascinating for me, as the Financial Secretary himself showed me around and explained in detail what they were doing.

Our next stop was Japan. The plane had stopped in Taiwan, and because of that, there was a medical alarm when we reached Tokyo. So Shigeto Tsuru, who was to meet us there, had to wait several hours until the medical matters were cleared up. He had arranged for us to stay at a University guesthouse. I was also invited to give a lecture in Kyoto. And we toured Japan for about three weeks, all arranged by Shigeto.

Japan also provided the one pleasant mishap. Japan Air called up and asked sheepishly whether we would mind staying another day, as they had overbooked. We did not. As a result, they flew us first class to Honolulu, where we stayed for a week. By that time, we were rather tired and anxious to get home.

Michigan gave me another year's leave, which I spent at Ed Mason's invitation at Harvard's Center for International Studies, where I wrote my *Planning without Facts*. I might say that I showed Ed a half-a-page outline of what I wanted to do. I would be lost if I had to write these long proposals which our graduate students are now expected to produce. How the hell can you really know what you are going to do until you actually do it? As a mythical English lady is reported to have said: "How do I know what I think until I see what I write?"

I accepted the assignment in Malta, but the only similarity to Nigeria was, that there too, Tommy Balogh appeared. He had been advisor to Mintoff, the socialist predecessor of Borg-Olivier, the conservative premier. In fact, Tommy's advising added spice to my acceptance, and his advice had been excellent. The British High Commissioner told me that when he had heard that the Maltese had specifically asked for me, he made inquiries "and what we found made it unnecessary to deflect the Government." In fact I did not enjoy Malta as much as I had hoped. As a Protestant I found the pre-reformation Spanish atmosphere somewhat stifling, and the Government's inability to make any decisions, good, bad or indifferent, was frustrating.

My commitment to Africa remained through most of my remaining career. Returning to Michigan, I became director of the Center for Research on Economic Development, CRED, for which the Ford Foundation gave me a grant of $400,000 on the basis of a half-page letter. The only restriction was that the Center was limited to research on Africa.

I worked in this context in ten LDCs, about one year in three four-month installments in Tunisia, but also in Turkey (on an IBRD Team), Syria, and once in Malawi. I declined an invitation to advise the Minister of Finance in Morocco when, after a three-week tour and discussions it became obvious that the civil servants did not want me and would refuse to cooperate. Moreover, the civil servants were highly sophisticated people and my French simply was not good enough to deal with that. And the Minister really wanted an American to hit de Gaulle over the head with.

The visit nevertheless had an unexpected benefit: I was able to open the door for Andriamananjara, a Malagasy student of mine, to do research for his thesis. A Malagasy was especially welcome in Morocco, because King Mohamed V had been in exile in Madagascar. It is these kinds of events that make one a success or failure!

After my return to Michigan, UM invited Aboyade as visiting assistant professor, and I believe he was the only African in the United States teaching the course on Economic Development. He was a big success.

I continued to have contact with Nigeria. Aboyade, Onitiri and I figured out modes of collaboration that bypassed bureaucratic hurdles. I saw no point in creating another expensive bureaucratic layer to do what could be done without one. We simply would take care of each others' students. This led to a brilliant doctoral thesis on cocoa by Sara Berry, published by Oxford University Press, based on previously unexploited court documents, etc. As far as I (but not Sara) was concerned, the idea for this had come from a casual remark by Polly Hill.

I served as an advisor to Edmond Hutchinson, assistant USAID Administrator for Africa, but excluded work on Nigeria because of possible conflicts of interest. However, after the Biafran civil war I was asked to join an official American team to assess the situation and see what might be done. I accepted only after my Nigerian friends told me they would welcome it. As the result of that welcome, Mr.

Cleveland, from Washington Polytechnic, asked me to consider teaching at his all-black Washington DC institution, which I declined.

One feature of the visit was viewing the Niger Dam from the air. Unfortunately I was not allowed to photograph the war devastation and how people had coped with it. I saw people digging up cars which they had buried, and recovering other possessions.

Aboyade invited me back to Ibadan as guest professor under Rockefeller auspices. When I got there, he asked me not to teach, because they were overstaffed and did not know what to do with all the people they had. It was one of the things I had feared and tried to prevent. I had urged the appointment of expatriates until good Nigerians came along. You could get rid of expatriates, but not of incompetent Nigerians. Of course, I do not know what pressures forced Aboyade to appoint the Africans.

In the event, the visit was quite uncomfortable for me. Most of the junior staff were quite hostile, and openly accused me of being a spy who reported what he saw to Rockefeller. And Aboyade refused to defend me, which I did not understand. On the other hand, I could understand his not wanting me to accompany him on a trip to the north, given the volatile political situation. I did see my old steward Felix again, which made both of us happy.

The trip by car to the airport was memorable. There were several uncomfortable checks by the military, but ironically, belonging to a white tribe seemed to be an advantage! The airport departure was very uncomfortable, as my heart was giving me trouble and I stood there helpless trying to get through all the exchange controls, until somebody noticed my weakness and finally pushed me through. At least nobody wanted to extort money, as had happened in Kinshasa, despite having a passport that identified me as a US Government official. I was glad finally to settle in my first class seat on Swissair.

After seven years of directing CRED I resigned, having run out of ideas, and Elliot Berg took over as director.

Addendum (June 2001)

Do I have any advice to give to members of a future generation who might find themselves in a situation which is not too dissimilar from the one in which I found myself? This is a difficult question to answer in general terms, for two reasons. The first is unique. No white man ever had or ever will have the role I was destined to play in Nigeria where I was de facto an Associate Permanent Secretary in the Ministry of Economic Development, in charge of developing economic policy for the Federal Government and of coordinating the Federal Regional plans, with full access to and backing of my Minister, and daily intimate contact with my African Permanent Secretary who in the course of our work became also a close friend.

The second is not unique but sufficiently rare so that it, too, is not easily duplicated: my reputation within the profession as the result of my collaboration with Paul A. Samuelson is secure. In fact, three Nobelists, two in economics and one in physics, are (or have been) close friends. I can think of only a few living (or recently deceased) economists, who would be able to enjoy the same name recognition. Nicholas Kaldor, for one, until a short while ago the late Harry Johnson, the late Gottfried Haberler, possibly Thomas Balogh. Or Hans Wolfgang Singer (now Sir Hans), with me the last survivor of Schumpeter's Bonn Seminar. With this kind of name recognition, people whose opinion you seek will be ready to spend some time with you, even if, as was certainly my case, you are totally ignorant of the situation about which you are seeking advice. I do not know, of course, whether any of those economists ever felt that they had to learn the specifics of the situation on which they were asked to give their advice. I do know that when Thomas Balogh visited me in Nigeria, he gave unsought advice to my Minister, not to permit industrial investments slip by, not realizing in fact that I couldn't keep unscrupulous equipment salesmen off my neck. Which I pointed out to him after I came back from my game of squash. (But this was really a minor matter. In Malta, where we met again, he had in fact given excellent advice.)

There are two matters about which I am quite certain, both not quite easy. I believe that is advantageous (as well as fascinating) to steep oneself as much as possible in the culture of the country. The reason is really obvious: advice which is merely rational – and it must be rational – is useless if the cultural environment does not permit its execution. It must be pointed out to the political leadership that there is a problem, which only political leadership can resolve. It would be a rare advisor who is sufficiently well informed to understand all the constraints under which the political leadership has to operate. And it would be an equally rare political leader with sufficient charisma to wrench a country into a totally different direction, while explaining to them that he does not have to the power to undo the past.

And in this context it might be wise to remember, that possibly one's experience in one situation does not necessarily help in a different one. Experience may, in fact, get in the way of understanding a situation. Related to this is an important Schumpeterian point: The same advice given at a particular moment may be excellent advice at that moment but becomes completely wrong later. And one has to be sensitive to what Brian Arthur has shown to be path dependency. In a dynamic economy, time moves only in one direction. You cannot, as a rule, say, "Sorry, I made a mistake, let's start all over again."

There is a second point which, I believe, I learned. Sensitivity to the realities of a political situation which the advisor practically never fully understands, requires a total openness and honesty on the side of the advisor. I myself had had an excellent political training, my Father having been a member of the Reichstag, and I myself having been active in anti-Nazi student politics. The idea that the advisor somehow can get to the political level to behave in specific ways may be rather dangerous. For one thing, the advisor practically never knows the native language sufficiently well. For all he knows, the locals conspire with a smile on their faces to have him assassinated on his way home. Survival depends on gaining the trust of the advisees, and that precludes playing games with them. They must be convinced that your advice is based on what you believe, for better or for worse, in their best interest.

An advisor can not expect that all his advice will be taken. He can not consider this a failure or a reason to resign. But there are some matters when he must refuse to go along. In my own case, I made up my mind that under no circumstances would I be party to a decision to impose exchange controls, or even a standby legislation in case the need for it should arise. And that I would be very careful before agreeing to any subsidies. As to the former, there was no question in my mind that exchange controls were a very profitable method of helping the rich and powerful to organize their capital flight. As to the latter, I had to disagree with Kaldor, who thought all subsidies were from the poor to the poor. All the cases I came across in Nigeria – it may, of course, be different elsewhere – were from the poor to the rich.

My final advice is to be ruthlessly honest. It is all right to be wrong. Nobody knows everything. It is okay to refuse to give any advice in particular situations. I tried to stay clear of sensitive questions of defense policy, and I was careful in my advice in dealings with the Soviet Union or soviet-bloc countries. By all means trade with them, but insist on legally ironclad contracts and on Western conditions. No barter deals in situations when you could sell against hard currency. (Ghana found itself in a situation where cocoa they had sold to the USSR competed with cocoa sold directly by Ghana.) But the advisees must be convinced that you mean what you say.

Index of Names

Index of Subjects

Note: site references are followed by regional location, viz. [ER], [Lagos], [NR], and [WR]. "WS" denotes Wolfgang Stolper. Government agencies are grouped under the relevant jurisdiction, viz. federal and Eastern, Northern and Western Regional governments.